Significant
FOOD

Significant
FOOD

CRITICAL
READINGS
to NOURISH
AMERICAN
LITERATURE

Edited by Jeff Birkenstein
and Robert C. Hauhart

The University of Georgia Press
Athens

© 2024 by the University of Georgia Press
Athens, Georgia 30602
www.ugapress.org
All rights reserved
Designed by Kaelin Chappell Broaddus
Set in 10.5/13.5 Miller Text Roman by Kaelin Chappell Broaddus

Most University of Georgia Press titles are
available from popular e-book vendors.

Printed digitally

Library of Congress Cataloging-in-Publication Data

Names: Birkenstein, Jeff, editor. | Hauhart, Robert C., 1950– editor.
Title: Significant food : critical readings to nourish American literature /
    edited by Jeff Birkenstein and Robert C. Hauhart.
Description: Athens : University of Georgia Press, [2024]. | Includes
    bibliographical references and index.
Identifiers: LCCN 2023053690 (print) | LCCN 2023053691 (ebook) |
    ISBN 9780820366722 (hardback) | ISBN 9780820366715 (paperback) |
    ISBN 9780820366739 (epub) | ISBN 9780820366746 (pdf)
Subjects: LCSH: Food in literature. | American literature—History and
    criticism.
Classification: LCC PS374.F63 S54 2024 (print) | LCC PS374.F63 (ebook) | DDC
    810—dc23/eng/20240220
LC record available at https://lccn.loc.gov/2023053690
LC ebook record available at https://lccn.loc.gov/2023053691

Contents

Acknowledgments

I am so grateful to so many both far and near who have sustained me, even if over a Zoom call, during our collective global pandemic experience, a tragedy from which this current book project sprang forth. But most of all, I am grateful to my wife (and article co-writer), Ericka Birkenstein, for all her love and support during this latest project and, of course, beyond. And to little Madeline, now not so little and four years old. Born just before the pandemic, she has known nothing else, and yet thrives anyway.

I have long understood the best of academia as a site of collaboration, and I have been lucky to work with some of the finest, including my co-editor, friend, and colleague Robert C. Hauhart. On this project, he took the organizational reins and, fortunately for both of us, never let go. How I yearn to return to New Mexico with him for another ski trip.

Additionally, I am grateful to Saint Martin's University for a strong and enduring history of supporting sabbaticals and, now, family leave for any parent or caregiver in need. I believe I had the second *paternity* leave on campus, but others have followed since. Also, I would like to thank friends and colleagues at Saint Martin's University and beyond, including Olivia Archibald, Irina Gendelman, Igor Krasnov (of Petrozavodsk State University, Russia), Jamie Olson, David H. Price, and too many others to name, all of whom have helped me immeasurably on my journey. And my mother, Diana Michaels, who never fails to support and edit my writing.

Thank you, also, to the editors at the University of Georgia Press who saw the merit of our project, and, in true collaborative spirit, thank you to all the essayists in this collection, without whom there would be no book.

Jeff Birkenstein
Olympia, Washington

It is a challenging, but pleasant, task to reflect on all those who have supported my intellectual efforts of one sort or another over many years, given my two careers—in law and academia—and my somewhat peripatetic transit between institutional homes. As a consequence, the number of colleagues who deserve recognition always offers a daunting prospect and a rather impossible duty to fully execute.

In Slovenia, I am indebted to Professor Oto Luthar, director of the Research Centre of the Slovenian Academy of Sciences and Arts for his willingness to have the centre act as my Fulbright host in 2019. Although the present volume did not arise from my Fulbright project, Dr. Luthar found time to be a genial host and personally facilitated many details related to my stay. For this, and many other gestures of support, I am very grateful. I would also like to thank Mitja Sardoč, Educational Research Institute, Ljubljana, who was instrumental in inspiring my Fulbright award and has become a valued colleague.

In the United States, I would like to thank the Saint Martin's University administration for actively supporting a regular program of sabbatical leaves as well as unscheduled leaves for recipients of grants like the Fulbright Scholar Award. I would like to especially thank my friend, colleague, and co-editor, Jeff Birkenstein; our contributors to this volume; and my personal supporters: Diane Wiegand, Rossitsa Terzieva-Artemis (Rossie), Julia McCord Chavez, and many, many others too numerous to name.

Finally, I am grateful to the editors and staff at the University of Georgia Press for expressing interest in publishing our collection and creating an attractive book.

Robert Hauhart
Petit Manan Point, Maine
Placitas, New Mexico
Lacey, Washington

Preface

In the introduction to *Significant Food*, we place special emphasis on those instances in which literary commentators address the role, and prominence, of food within American writing. We find that literary criticism has focused on the role food plays in literary production to a greater extent than recognized at first glance; it is also true that discussions about the place of food within American literature have become increasingly common only in the last two decades. Still, while there is analysis and critical commentary regarding authors' use of food across the expanse of American literature, there are gaps, one of which is the lack of a unifying critical theory to guide critical commentaries about food moments in writing. In response, we propose the theory of "significant food"—a method that asks literary critics to evaluate and assess the extent, nature, and role that food plays in literary production and analysis. When food, and "food moments," are used intensively and significantly within the drama, memoir, poem, novel, short story, or other writing, then one can say that food has achieved a status that makes it indispensable to the work at hand.

Significant Food in Mid-Twentieth-Century American Realism

Literary realism has been a popular genre within American literature since the late nineteenth century. Many classic American short stories and novels have been written in this style. It is easy to find instances within American realism in which authors have introduced, and relied upon, food passages and references to support important plotlines, themes, and characterizations within their work. Three examples, all from post-World War II narratives, are Philip Roth's *Goodbye, Columbus;* Sylvia Plath's *The Bell Jar;* and John Updike's *Rabbit, Run.* Each is now regarded as a classic piece of American writing, perhaps due in no small part to the effective use of food within the respective stories. Robert C. Hauhart argues that each author uses food "significantly" to advance each story's plot; to support each work's major and minor themes; to build characterization and explore identity; and to create a dense, deep background that is immediately recognizable so that realism's underlying premise—that the story you are reading is true to life, indeed, that it might even be true—is convincingly achieved.

Modernism, the Grotesque Body, and Food in Anderson, Kafka, and Hemingway

Considering first the exploration of the grotesque in two modernist works—Sherwood Anderson's *Winesburg, Ohio* (1919) and Franz Kafka's "A Hunger Artist" (1922)—Jeff and Ericka Birkenstein then explore how food plays a role in the grotesquerie that is Jake Barnes and his world in Ernest Hemingway's novel *The Sun Also Rises* (1926). In the book, the divide between gluttony and abstemiousness, between the physical acts of eating and (not) having sex, is an important narrative use of food and food spaces, ideas also intimately connected to the supposedly modern world that came to the fore with World War I. Again and again in the novel, Jake and those around him weave in and out of significant scenes that both confirm and challenge these important cultural signifiers of eating and not eating. In turn, these food scenes are almost always connected to the grotesque specter of Jake's inability to move on, both physically and psychically, from the trauma of his war wounds. The alienation in Jake is the creation of an irresoluble divide: he identifies within himself, and cannot reconcile, that which is intolerable about society as well as his place in it, and he must either opt for, or be forced into, exile by his inability to conform and/or perform. Ultimately, Jake remains in stasis throughout the novel, and while he valiantly, if futilely, uses food and drink as tools to conquer, or at least dull, the pain of his injuries, he, like many in the so-called Lost Generation, is simply unable to make any significant forward progress.

Southern Comfort in the Age of Jim Crow: Representing Soul Food in Ralph Ellison's *Juneteenth* and Beyond

Defining the relationships among food, spirituality, representation, and identity has been a formidable but necessary undertaking in African American literature. Exploring such connections involves reconfiguring traditional boundaries, specifically those related to America's reductive notions about the consumption patterns and religious beliefs of African Americans. Arguably, soul food—which derives from the historical circumstances African Americans experienced during slavery—involves more than the pleasure of eating and feeding.

In two sermons from Ralph Ellison's second novel, *Juneteenth* (1999), preachers embrace soul food to salve their congregations by inspiring them to remember the fevers and deaths of the Middle Passage, to recall the subsequent destruction of African languages and cultures, yet also to celebrate the acquisition of a new identity that would incorporate these elements of their shared history. In doing so, Anton Smith argues that Ellison represents soul food as a form of southern comfort and cultural resistance that was effective in inspiring solidarity among African Americans as they initially faced the shared experience of slavery and, later, as they grappled with a newfound freedom, endured Reconstruction, lived invisible lives in the North, and fought for equal civil rights.

Wild or Wilder Food:
Subsistence Eating in American Children's Literature

In this chapter, Gregory Hartley analyzes the first novels of Velma Wallis and Laura Ingalls Wilder to examine subsistence eating within Indigenous and pioneer settings. As he notes, both writers portray characters who live or die wholly by collecting and consuming natural food sources, producing nearly constant examples of each subsistence type. By juxtaposing such values as independence vs. dependence, surviving vs. thriving, and attention vs. distraction represented by each author's vision, Hartley's study shows that Wallis's land-based subsistence offers distinct advantages over the heavily mythologized settler subsistence portrayed by Wilder. The values related to food practices of Alaska's Gwich'in Athabascans lend an authoritative context to Hartley's close readings of both texts.

Kogi, Tía Perla, and KoBra:
Food Trucks and Identity in Texts for Young Readers

American texts for young audiences depicting cultural diversity often use food to approach this topic. Like texts for their adult contemporaries, texts for young audiences discuss how identity and food are connected, which mirrors how food influences the ways in which we see different communities and how they see themselves. Indeed, countless children's and young adult (YA) texts draw connections between food and identity. Katy Lewis's essay focuses on these ideas about food in literature for young audiences, examining three contemporary texts. She argues that food trucks, as places and spaces that are seldom permanent or stationary, signify the liminality, movement, and dynamism the characters experience as they come to understand their identities. These texts suggest how we can understand our own and others' identities in correspondingly complex, rather than reductive, ways.

Bad Children and Hungry Women:
Food and "Hansel and Gretel" in the Later Work of Shirley Jackson

Shelley Ingram's essay begins with a review of Jackson's play *The Bad Children* (1957), a retelling of "Hansel and Gretel" she wrote to be performed by the students in her daughter's school. *The Bad Children* clearly shows that "Hansel and Gretel" was of keen interest to Jackson, as it explicitly links food, witchcraft, uncanny children, and ambivalent mothering. It then looks at her later novels *The Sundial* (1958), *The Haunting of Hill House* (1959), and *We Have Always Lived in the Castle* (1962) to argue that "Hansel and Gretel" is an avenue by which Jackson interrogates domestic and familial feeding and consumption, as she uses the shape of the tale to construct counternarratives to the decade's formulations of womanly domesticity. "Hansel and Gretel" provides a template for Jackson's negotiation of feeding mothers and eating children who live together in unsettled and sequestered homes.

The Ingredients of an Emblematic Personal Self:
Autobiographical Memory and Autonoetic Consciousness
in Diana Abu-Jaber's *The Language of Baklava*

In this chapter, Sanghamitra Dalal reads American author Diana Abu-Jaber's memoir, *The Language of Baklava* (2005), in order to examine how the concepts of autobiographical memory and autonoetic consciousness reinscribe an emblematic personal self by a process of fusing disparate ingredients into a sense of transcultural belongingness. Born in Syracuse, New York, to an American mother and a Jordanian father, Abu-Jaber had to learn to meld her two identifies. Forced to move homes between Jordan and America a number of times throughout her childhood, she was compelled to learn how to be an Arab at home and an American in the street when she was growing up. Cooking, one of the most significant identifiers of Arab cultural legacy, became one means of achieving this biculturalism. Abu-Jaber eventually realizes that consciously recalling and reliving the taste of food, memory, emotions, and sensibilities can help unravel the intertwined layers of competing, dual selves. Rather than experiencing the loneliness of a series of new homes, idly drifting forever through similarities and differences, she finds cooking and cuisine to be a way to anchor a self within a self.

Kitchen Secrets:
Food Stories and the Politics of Silence and Voice in
Ana Castillo's *Black Dove: Mamá, Mi'jo, and Me*

This chapter focuses on the political dimension of storytelling and on food as a facilitator of storytelling in Ana Castillo's memoir, *Black Dove: Mamá, Mi'jo, and Me* (2016), reading the memoir as a hybrid between the traditions of *testimonio* and culinary memoir. In the text, which explores her trajectory as a daughter of immigrants from Mexico growing up in Chicago, Méliné Kasparian-Le Fèvre argues that Castillo uses food strategically to share women's stories and to explore the silencing of women's voices in patriarchal society. Food appears as a realm that can be reappropriated by women, from a space of oppression to a space of expression: both for female cooks exchanging recipes and stories in the communal space of the kitchen, and for the writer herself who uses food metaphors to evoke painful and taboo memories of her own gendered experience of victimization, breaking the silence that was imposed on her.

Food and the Public/Private Body in Nella Larsen's *Passing*

Food is the most frequent disruptor of the boundaries of self. It is a constant reminder to us that the categories of self and other, public and private, are easily transgressed and, therefore, destabilized. In this chapter, Molly Mann Lotz reads moments of eating and drinking in Nella Larsen's *Passing* (1929) as scenes of heightened racial and sexual anxiety, where categories of public and private are interrogated and subverted. Building upon Kyla Wazana Tompkins's work on the orality of racialization, Mann shows how Larsen uses food-related scenes in *Passing* to reveal categories of identity and their imagined boundaries as both unstable and unsustainable. "Passing"—both Clare Kendry's act of presenting herself as white, and the passing of food and drink through the body—disrupts discrete categories socially constructed as real and fixed, including racial, gendered, and sexual binaries. As Mann argues, Larsen's emphasis on eating and drinking in *Passing* contributes to the novel's interrogation of race as a social and historical construct, not unlike those other artificial boundaries of the self we often cling to for safety.

Queer Hunger, Eating, and Feeding
in Toni Morrison's *Song of Solomon*

Throughout Toni Morrison's oeuvre, her characters experience intense hunger and cravings; they feed each other poisons and potions and eat the inedible. Carrie Helms Tippen argues in this essay that Morrison presents characters with queer hunger, feeding, and eating practices—with a particular focus on Ruth from *Song of Solomon* (1977)—as an entry point into discussions of nonnormative sexuality and gender identity. Ruth, notably among Morrison's characters, engages in many taboo food practices, which other characters interpret as deviant and sexually charged. Other characters in Morrison's novel interpret these as deviant and sexually charged. While Ruth is following a familiar script that suggests food can communicate love and build relationships, her queer performance of that script highlights its artifice. The problem with Ruth's feeding behavior is that it insists on reciprocity. Unfortunately for Ruth, these relationships, overdetermined by patriarchy and heteronormativity, do not permit the display of mutuality. When Ruth's attempts to satisfy her desires in normative ways fail, she turns to queer sexual and food practices as the only alternative offered to her.

Appetites and Identity:
Mixed-Race Identity Construction through
Food and Sex in Carmit Delman's "Footnote"

This chapter takes up questions about food, sex, and mixed-race identity in Carmit Delman's short story "Footnote." Can one construct an identity through food? And can one connect to one's heritage by becoming closer to the bodies of people who also belong to a particular racial group? Rachel Fernandes reads "Footnote" through the lenses of food studies and critical mixed-race studies to argue that the cultivation of a nuanced mixed-race identity may include the practices of eating and sexual activity, but these activities ultimately leave the story's multiracial protagonist unfulfilled. Fernandes argues that multiracial identity is complex and ever-evolving: food or sexual contact can be an important aspect of connecting to one's multiple heritages, but the engagement with either, or both, must extend beyond the superficial.

Recasting the Culinary Arts: Cooking, Ethnicity, and Family in the Queer Novels of Bryan Washington and Bill Konigsberg

During the past decade, a growing number of artists have broken new ground in the storytelling of cooks and cookery in the literary arts. Instead of revisiting the lives of so-called happy homemakers and stoic male chefs, this chapter examines the stories of cooks who are seldom profiled by employing the framework of "recasting" to elucidate the queer narratives written by the Black American author Bryan Washington and the white American novelist Bill Konigsberg. Edward A. Chamberlain examines how a set of queer and culturally diverse cooks become the preparers of food in Washington's familial novel *Memorial* (2020) and Konigsberg's young adult novel *The Music of What Happens* (2019). These texts portray a rearrangement of family life, which causes the queer protagonists to take on the role of cook and push the boundaries of gastronomy, thereby extending what the Black and gay historian Michael Twitty envisions as "culinary justice."

Cultural Dichotomy Crafted through Food in Willa Cather's *My Ántonia*

The simple act of baking bread demonstrates othering through food in Willa Cather's *My Ántonia* (1918). The dichotomy between the Bohemian immigrants and the more established Nebraska settlers is depicted through the preparation and eating of food. Food, Mary-Lynn Chambers argues, is used as a literary device to demarcate the economic status of varied families in the 1870s fictional Nebraskan town and, further, to craft the immigrant story of transitions that is part of the assimilation process experienced by Cather's protagonist, Ántonia. Cather crafts the novel by utilizing familiar food that tugs on the readers' senses, allowing the comfort of the fare offered to affirm the assimilation process. Thus, the cultural dichotomy seen at the beginning of the novel is dissolved as the gap between the have and have-nots diminishes, as evidenced by the food that is eaten.

Katherine Anne Porter's "Flowering Judas": Mexican Politics, Appetitive Language, and Alimentary Religious Symbolism

Heidi Oberholtzer Lee offers a reading of the appetitive language, gustatory imagery, and alimentary religious symbolism of Katherine Anne Porter's "Flowering Judas" (1930), situating the short story within its modernist literary context, Porter's socialist milieu, her understanding of the Catholic eucharist, and early 1920s Mexican politics. Oberholtzer Lee argues that through the appetitive lens and language of eating, "Flowering Judas" points to the limits of abstract ideology. Porter's story underscores the importance of a corporeal, personal connectedness to neighbors and local community as the healthy focal point of ideology. She recommends secularized and moderate appetites for the realization of revolutionary change that will rely not on the idealism and practices of fallible leaders, who inevitably disappoint, but rather on the ability of both leaders and followers alike to amend error through accepting the forgiving love of others as expressed in concrete, embodied forms of ideology that promote true individual and communal flourishing.

Dial "Saucisse Minuit" for Murder: Nero Wolfe and the Art of Detecting Well

Among popular fiction genres, detective fiction is still one of the most widely enjoyed. In his famous essay "The Simple Art of Murder" (1944), Raymond Chandler defines what he calls the "classic detective story" in a rather unflattering way: following abundant examples of the English tradition, he concludes that this model is outdated and the characters are "puppets and cardboard lovers and papier-mâché villains and detectives of exquisite and impossible gentility" (230, 232). This chapter offers a close reading of the early novels of Rex Stout, one of the grand masters of the classic detective story in American literature and creator of his emblematic private eye, Nero Wolfe. By exploring these early books in the Wolfe series, Rossitsa Terzieva-Artemis discusses how food—an idiosyncratic "character" in Stout's impressive oeuvre—manages to gain a central place in this canonical genre. In both hard-boiled and classic detective stories, the mystery tends to outshine what is considered a trivial description of food. The puzzle, in other words, "beats" evocative realism in the descriptions of meals. However, in the Wolfe series, food is difficult to dismiss. Stout blends elements of the classic detective story with qualities of the "hard-boiled" (food pun intended) story by creating a street-smart Archie Goodwin to assist Nero, literally a larger-than-life protagonist. Terzieva-Artemis gently and lovingly profiles the detective who looms in each of these works as a gigantic man of both appetite and intellect, often seated at the opulent table of a brownstone on West 35th Street in New York, enjoying absurd amounts of delicacies and gourmet dishes.

"I can't work up an appetite just because you want me to": (Not) Eating One's Identity in J. D. Salinger's Short Stories

In his short story "Franny" (1955), J. D. Salinger exploits food choices made by the main characters to shape their contrasting identities. Touching upon issues of gender and culture through a close reading of the text, Serena Demichelis's analysis offers a new perspective on Salinger's story, one that highlights the centrality of identity-making in the author's oeuvre in general and in the Glass stories in particular. In addition, Demichelis addresses a rather neglected aspect in the realm of Salinger criticism—namely, the author's relation to the tradition of Jewish-American writing. In this sense, food choices displayed in "Franny," and elsewhere in the Salinger corpus, offer significant hints about the writer's stance concerning Judaism and how it productively interacts with identity and art.

Significant
FOOD

Introduction

ROBERT C. HAUHART AND
JEFF BIRKENSTEIN

"Is the English and litritcher that does beat me."
In Elias's mouth litritcher was the most beautiful word I heard.
It sounded like something to eat, something rich like chocolate.
–V. S. Naipaul, *Miguel Street* (34)

This book is a collaborative work of literary analysis and criticism. Our subject, generally, addresses important examples of food used strategically in American literature. Although we titled the volume *Significant Food: Critical Readings to Nourish American Literature*, the collection just as easily could have been simply called "Food in American Literature," since many uses of food in writing are to some degree both intentional and important. Still, questions of importance typically demand some evaluation as to the matter of the degree, or extent, of importance. In this sense, the qualifier "significant" announces that evaluative criteria will be invoked to measure the level of importance to which the various uses of food are put within the texts under examination. Also, and not coincidentally, co-editor Jeff Birkenstein first used the term "significant food" in a published essay in 2011 and has continued to expand upon his work since then.[1] As such, this volume stands at the intersection of three disciplines: literary studies, food studies, and the study of American literature, specifically.

Food, as a source of sustenance and sometimes of pleasure and sometimes of pain, is of constant interest in human affairs. Outside of literary studies, there are many people from a wide range of disciplines arguing for the study of food and food cultures. After all, "[e]ating is," as Gordon Shepherd observes in *Neurogastronomy,* "our most common behavior" (ix). Warren Belasco tells us, in *Food: The Key Concepts*, that "[f]ood is the first of the essentials of life, the world's largest industry, our most frequently indulged pleasure, the core of our most intimate social relationships" (1). M. F. K. Fisher begins her book *The Gastronomical Me* as follows:

> People ask me: Why do you write about food, and eating and drinking? Why don't you write about the struggle for power and security, and about love, the way others do?
>
> They ask it accusingly, as if I were somehow gross, unfaithful to the honor of my craft.
>
> The easiest answer is to say that, like most other humans, I am hungry. But there is more than that. It seems to me that our three basic needs, for food and security and love, are so mixed and mingled and entwined that we cannot straightly think of one without the others. So it happens that when I write of hunger, I am really writing about love and the hunger for it . . . and then the warmth and richness and fine reality of hunger satisfied . . . and it is all one. (353, ellipses in original)

Or as Ernest Hemingway's first wife, Elizabeth Hadley Richardson, explains to the writer in *A Moveable Feast:* "There are so many kinds of hunger. . . . Memory is hunger" (48). Just as food is produced, acquired, prepared, consumed, digested, incorporated into, and expelled by the body, food in literature, and its study, exists in many forms and is commensurate with myriad layers of understanding.

As such, it is not surprising that food has been a matter of interest in literature since time immemorial. Food is prominent in Book 1 of Homer's *Odyssey,* for example. Zeus, having decided to intervene on Ulysses' behalf and help him return home, sends Minerva (Athena) to Ithaca disguised as a visitor, Mentes, chief of the Taphians. Telemachus, Ulysses' son, anxious for news of his father, welcomes her and escorts her to the hall where she is seated on a richly decorated, comfortable chair festooned with damask and a footstool for her feet, whereby:

> A maid brought water soon in a graceful golden pitcher
> and over a silver basin tipped it out
> so they might rinse their hands,
> then pulled a gleaming table to their side.
> A staid housekeeper brought on bread to serve them,
> appetizers aplenty too, lavish with her bounty.
> A carver lifted platters of meat toward them,

> meats of every sort, and set beside them golden cups
> and time and again a page came round and poured them wine. (82)

Before politics and intrigue can begin, food must be served. Or as food, then, becomes part of the story—part of the narrative, part of the plot— perhaps food *is* part of the intrigue, and thus does not exist merely for its own sake. Literature since Homer's time, regardless of cultural origin or historical period, has likewise incorporated references and scenes replete with food, drink, eating, and cooking or, conversely, the notable absence of such things. Famously, Virgil's *Aeneid* has several scenes where the men eat "flat-bread scored in quarters," a precursor to pizza (217), and Chaucer's *The Canterbury Tales* is so well stocked with food references that contemporary international literary conferences on the work commonly hold sessions dedicated to issues of food, drink, cooking, and eating in the durable work. Shakespeare, too, is attracting an ever-increasing amount of food-focused criticism, for, as Joan Fitzpatrick argues in *Food in Shakespeare*, "early modern dietaries make clear the view that food and drink are not mere necessities but also indices of one's position in relation to complex ideas about rank, nationality, and spiritual well-being; careful consumption might correct moral as well as physical shortcomings" (3). We understand explicitly today that this is also true for every other period and place of human development.

A quick look at the history of literary criticism suggests that this volume follows in the footsteps of a long line of commentators. M. A. R. Habib begins his magisterial *A History of Literary Criticism* by arguing that in the wake of the attacks on the United States on September 11, 2001, "it has become more important than ever that we learn to read critically" (1). Habib's rather lofty ambition for literary criticism—that it will somehow reduce "the dangers of misunderstanding and inadequate education" generally, along with critical reading in other disciplines, while hopeful and welcome, seems rather more of a justification than is needed for reading literature—and certainly more than we can offer. A pair of earlier critics, William K. Wimsatt Jr. and Cleanth Brooks, observed in their *Literary Criticism: A Short History* that the first goal of such criticism (and their own contribution to it) was simply to argue for "continuity and intelligibility in the history of literary argument" (vii). This rather more modest justification seems closer to what we have in mind, although not quite where we begin, either.

Even as modern American writers continue to write about food, students and critics of this literature, too, have begun to more systematically and completely identify and analyze food scenes and references to food and drink for their import. Indeed, in recent years there has been a growing stream of critical commentary centered on food within the works of American authors and across a broad spectrum of genres. Thus, the works of well-known American writers like John Updike, Flannery O'Connor, and William Faulkner have been mined for the meaning and symbolism within their food passages (Farmer; Miles). Literary critics have extended similar analyses of food references in the works of major American poets (Viswanathan; Reder) and the authors of American short stories (Lo; Magistrate). The interest in the use of food in American literature has even expanded to include less well-known novelists (Carey; Eads), American dramatists (Wang, "The Image of Food"; Wang, "The Smell of Food"), the writers of American children's literature (Keeling and Pollard), writers of fairy tales and modern women's bestsellers (Andrievskikh), and representative authors of America's multicultural palette (Claramonte et al.; Baker; Naranjo-Huebl; Zubiaurre; Dagbovie; Moreau; Graves). In sum, a veritable food movement has begun among some literary critics, especially over the last decade or so. Critical commentary regarding food in literature now spans centuries, continents, cultures, and categories, even as gaps in coverage remain to be explored. Indeed, two of those gaps are arguably (1) the scarcity of collections of critical commentary focused exclusively on the strategic use of food in American literature and (2) the still-developing/evolving need for a theory or theories of literary analysis specifically designed for probing the relative importance of food events in a work of literature. What we have in mind in offering the present volume, then, is an effort to take an early stab at addressing these two issues.

Our survey of American literature suggests to us that there are many examples of food used significantly in works written by American authors that have not yet received their due critical engagement in this regard. This is not to say that these works have not received any critical attention. Rather, with respect to any number of American works discussed in the following essays, some are already identified as "American classics" and have thus been subjected to extensive criticism from one perspective or another. Rather, we are suggesting that critical examination of the role of food in literature generally, and American literature in particular, is, curiously, a rather recent undertaking, given the long history of commenting on many other elements and features within literature. And, in the somewhat arbitrary and haphazard way many disciplines progress, the particular analyses and arguments made in the following essays have not seen the light of day in the way our contributors make them here. Moreover, even when criticism has included commentary on the role food plays in a particular literary work, that criticism has not been embedded in a broader theory of how and why we should consider the use of food to provide a substantial and integral element that informs the literary value of the poem, play, short story, memoir, novella, or novel under study. A brief review of those critical literary studies that have addressed food in literature, and food in American literature particularly, will perhaps illustrate our point.

There is some disagreement about when literary criticism in general began to seriously take note of food as not only an important element in literature but one that must be studied in depth in order to more completely understand the texts in question, but the differences in view may prove minor. This is particularly true, perhaps, if one treats food studies in literature as just a subset of studies of food through a range of disciplines, such as anthropology, sociology, history, cultural studies, and so forth. Michelle Coghlan, writing in the introduction to her recent edited collection, *The Cambridge Companion to Literature and Food,* concedes that "there are a number of possible origin stories for the field of food studies" (2). Brushing aside other possibilities, however, Coghlan suggests that many who have considered the matter share the view that the field may have been nurtured in its infancy by the "pioneering work" of Claude Lévi-Strauss, Mary Douglass, and Pierre Bourdieu in the 1960s and '70s. An alternate pathway suggests that food studies, and especially literary food studies, emanates from the work of French literary theorist Roland Barthes, beginning with his 1957 volume, *Mythologies,* and specifically his essay, "Wine and Milk" (3). As Coghlan recounts, Barthes's reflections on wine, in particular, received a lukewarm, even an unsympathetic, response from an early reviewer, yet decades later his observations strike many as indispensable, forming another entryway into our intellectual examination of the role of food in social and literary terms. Gitanjali Shahani, writing in her collection *Food and Literature,* begins her discussion of food writing by quoting Francis Bacon's essay "Of Studies," written in 1597, and proceeds in short order to reference Terry Eagleton, Barthes, Lévi-Strauss, Ben Jonson, Brillat-Savarin, Hemingway, and Sandra Gilbert, thereby destroying any suggestion of chronological linearity and, indeed, perhaps destroying the idea that it even matters.

Regardless of which historical account one credits with primary influence, or none at all, it is apparent from the number and range of publications—not to mention the university curricula that favor studies of food in one discipline or another—that food studies, with literary studies of food increasingly prominent among them, have prospered over the last three decades. Arguing that "food is not a new discovery," Lorna Piatti-Farnell acknowledges that "an [academic] interest in food has become increasingly evident" (1). She follows by itemizing, as do Coghlan and many others, her preferred lineage of seminal texts, beginning with Stephen Mennell's *The Sociology of Food and Eating*, then winding through the 1990s and into the early millennia. But while Piatti-Farnell finds that interdisciplinary food studies generally grew during this period, she contends "food/literary scholarship grows more scarce" in recent years (3). Thus, she finds Sceats's *Food, Consumption, and the Body in Contemporary Women's Fiction* (2004) to be that "rare example of a major theoretically informed study of food in mid- to late twentieth-century literature." Looking over the present-day landscape a decade after Piatti-Farnell, it is difficult to fully credit her lament unless one parses the field of literature with a very fine-toothed comb, as she does, by restricting one's view narrowly to mid- to late twentieth-century literature. Despite this, there is reason to look further.

As Coghlan observes (3), even before Piatti-Farnell published her book, one can find a number of critical books about literature, taste, and food in the new century, including as a somewhat random sample: Doris Witt's *Black Hunger: Soul Food and America* (2004); Andrea Adolph's *Food and Femininity in Twentieth-Century British Women's Fiction* (2009); and Kara K. Keeling and Scott T. Pollard's *Critical Approaches to Food in Children's Literature* (2009). Though over the past decade there has been a cornucopia of offerings, there are increasing indications that the field of literary food studies has not been exhausted but, rather, only now has opened up to the possibility of what is to come. Indeed, a review of the contemporary food and literature landscape reveals perhaps as many empty, or unfulfilled, pockets as it does comprehensively examined genres, eras, and national literatures. This is understandable since even a single national literature offers an almost unlimited number of opportunities to investigate the role of food in the letters, memoirs, novels, short stories, poetry, and other extant writings that constitute a literature. American literature's vast expanse is no exception in this regard.

In developing this volume, we start with the proposition that Coghlan, quoting Molly Wizenberg (who, perhaps, borrowed the general idea from Sigmund Freud or Brillat-Savarin, by analogy), asserts: "Food . . . is never just food. It's also about a way of getting at something else: who we are, who we have been, and who we want to be" (1). Immersed as we are from birth in a world of symbols—symbols over which we have only modest control—how, exactly, could food, or anything else, be otherwise? It is foundational that we are all deeply submerged in a collective, communicative, symbol-filled "yellow submarine," one element of which is the material reality of food, but one so freighted with meanings that we seldom, if ever, stop talking about food, food acts, food spaces, and food culture. We talk about food while we are consuming food, while we are purchasing food, while we are preparing food, while we are serving food, after we have eaten food, in anticipation of the next time we will eat food, but also while we are facing any sort of difficulty with food . . . well, we could go on, but for now we will swallow our words and soon close our mouths. Our point in this regard is this: just how much more justification do we need to read about, think about, and write about two things that are essential to humanity—food and literature? We don't believe we need much more justification than what many others, like Coghlan, have said. We agree with the proposition that food is elemental. It is integral to many literatures, and it is worth carefully considering and analyzing when it appears in American literature.

Of course, this recognition does not end our reflection, as we must consider *how* we will go forward writing about food in American literature. As we started out, we looked for intellectual standards and analytical guidelines that would help us identify and collect a selection of papers that—each in its own way—grapples with what a particular American author or authors who wrote a very specific text or texts was getting at, whether consciously or unconsciously, with their discussion of, reference to, extended scene about, or pages of dialogue regarding *food*.

A principal criterion we applied in developing our collection is announced in our volume's title: we looked for critical analyses where the contributor was making the argument—even if not explicitly labeled as such—that the particular work, or works, under consideration used food intentionally in *significant* ways to achieve a desired literary effect. This standard, to us, supplies a unifying concept that heretofore has been missing in literary food criticism. Rather than isolated, solitary, perhaps arcane perusal of a text or two, readings that search for the use of food within literary works that contribute significantly to the production of a text's literary effects distinguish those works whose intellectual heft and gravitas (even when the work's central modality is comic) from the use of food in ways that are less literary, and less essential to the work in question, in nature and degree. Thus, we believe—and argue based on the readings we offer here—that the concept of *significant food* brings to the table a unique tool for slicing and dicing, so to speak, and separating and evaluating the relative importance attributed to any writer's use of food in their work. By invoking this standard, it is apparent one can discriminate between the occasional, adventitious, or purely elementary appearance of food references in literature as compared to those uses of food by an author that contribute meaningfully and intentionally to achieving the author's aesthetic, thematic, and/or technical goals for the work.

Although concentrating on selecting those essays that we believed would be instrumental in further developing the concept of significant food, there were other considerations, too. Admittedly, we have shown a preference for analyses of American works predominantly, but not exclusively, from the twentieth and twenty-first centuries. This is in part due to our own interests but, perhaps more importantly, due to the range of proposals we received, which was dominated by literary selections from the long twentieth century. This has had the effect, we believe, of making a valuable contribution since there seems to be such interest in "filling in" what might be characterized as "missing" literary food studies from these eras. Moreover, it should be apparent to any reader that when making selections for this collection, we consciously included contributions that focus on a broad range of writing forms: novels, short stories, memoirs, fairy tales, young adult fiction, detective stories, and even narratives that build upon the influence of advertising testimonials. In approaching the collection in this way, we reflected on—but did not necessarily adopt in every instance—some of the more traditional principles of literary analysis, although, admittedly, some are considered today rather passé. (We need not subscribe to everything ever written in the past to comment that in some ways we think this is too bad.) In sum, our selection process was intended to emphasize quality, contemporaneity to a degree, variety in genre, and inclusiveness within the limits of our ability to do so in a standard-length volume.

Geoffrey Hartman, trying to come to terms with, justify, and explain literary criticism in the 1970s and '80s, noted: "[The art of literature] is as much a staple as bread, even if it comes after bread and can't substitute for it" (2), thereby tying together our two principal concerns—food and thinking critically about the art of literature. Hartman, trying to reconcile the many schisms that appeared in the critical literary firmament of his day, hoped to examine the field to "understand how these critical traditions grew apart" (5). Still, he anticipated, indeed predicted, that literary studies would never conform to some stable and static conception of the endeavor but would "remain in flux: disconcerting, disputatious, disorderly." It is enough to give one trepidation about entering such a domain, as though one were about to enter the realm of the cyclops! And we *know* what they eat. Hartman, though, does not seem to have been dissuaded from continuing to practice literary analysis and criticism, and neither are we.

Among the substantive observations that Hartman offers, with which we are in accord, is his acknowledgment that he has been unable to find an independent, historical, distinctively "American" perspective on criticism (9). Rather, he wishes to talk about a broader "Anglo-American" tradition. He also wishes to talk about the New Criticism, the English Romantics, the Arnoldian tradition, critical style, and many another quality and feature of one era of literary criticism or another that he believed worthy of his time, effort, and thought, as was his function as a theorist and investigator of criticism. Nevertheless, so much of his discussion—not unlike the discussions of Northrop Frye (originally published in 1957) and many other commentators before and after—seems to elide, if not obscure, the central issue: Just what is it that the critic is supposed to do? Although Hartman buries himself in parsing Heidegger, Wittgenstein, Derrida, and others, he returns—as almost every literary critic must do in the end—to *the text* and reading the text closely. As Hartman concedes, while the critical essay has perhaps been successful in "recouping its freedom to theorize, [it] continues to bind itself to close reading" (175). In the end, Hartman finds no substitute for the patience, and work, required for "critical reading" (188). Summing up criticism's continued reliance on close readings, he notes that reading, like writing, is *more* than a technique; it is, rather, a variable, complex, and independently creative act that takes a cultural object and subjects it to the sensibility of the individual critical reader.

Hartman's reflections are thus informed by the long tradition of critical literary analysts whose work he examined. To take but one example, the former Canadian critical superstar, Northrop Frye, who some will argue has died a welcome death among contemporary critics, also tethered the entire business to close and informed readings of texts. As he observed, the idea of criticism necessarily rejects the notion that the poet "is or could be the definitive interpreter of himself" (6). Literature, as Frye recognizes, is really the study of "an order of words," and since there is no limit to which the order of words may be regulated, or constrained, there is clearly "an inexhaustible source of new critical discoveries, and would be even if new works of literature ceased to be written" (17). This understanding permits Frye to make a point that few who think about his literary criticism—and criticize it—bring to the surface: "All efforts of critics to discover rules or laws in the sense of moral mandates telling the artist what he ought to do, or have done, to be an authentic artist, have failed" (26). This is because, as our earlier quotation from Frye's introduction suggests, there is no limitation on literary analysis other than the quality of argument that can be gleaned from the text of a work itself. In short, regardless of the critic, there seems to be no alternative anyone can suggest other than beginning with, and perhaps ending with, the reading of the text. Hartman makes this point obliquely by quoting John Crowe Ransom's well-known justification for criticism:

> A thing of beauty is a joy forever. But it is not improved because the student has had to tie his tongue before it. It is an artistic object, with a heroic human labor behind it, and on these terms it calls for public discussion. The dialectical possibilities are limitless, and when we begin to realize them we are engaged in criticism. (qtd. in *Criticism* 17)

Like many others, we could not say it better. So it is on this basis that we offer the selections that follow, close readings of many well-known, and some less well-known, examples of American literature, funneled through the informed food and food culture sensibilities of our contributors, all readers, critics, and eaters who dare to offer their analyses for public discussion. We hope you are edified by their reflections, but—perhaps more importantly—we also hope you are satisfied by the full plate of ideas before you!

Bon appétit.

NOTE

1. Birkenstein argues that "Significant Food in fiction is food used as a significant plot or other substantial narrative device, where the important concomitant cultural signifiers related to nourishment and the table—or the absence thereof—assume a crucial narratological role" ("Teaching Significant Food" 78). Or, as Birkenstein puts it another way: "The significance of food—which is a foundation for what we might casually call 'culture'—is inextricable to a story or narrative when this story's meaning cannot exist without it in its current form" ("How Significant Food" 198).

WORKS CITED

Adolph, Andrea. *Food and Femininity in Twentieth-Century British Women's Fiction.* Ashgate, 2009.
Andrievskikh, Natalia. "Food Symbolism, Sexuality, and Gender Identity in Fairy Tales and Modern Women's Bestsellers." *Studies in Popular Culture*, vol. 37, no. 1, 2014, pp. 137–53.

Baker, Christopher. "You Are What You Eat: Connecting Food with Identity in Paul Beatty's *The Sellout*." *The Explicator*, vol. 77, nos. 3–4, 2017, pp. 128–31.

Barthes, Roland. *Mythologies*. Translated by Annette Lavers, Hill & Wang, 1957.

Belasco, Warren. *Food: The Key Concepts*. Berg, 2008.

Birkenstein, Jeff. "How Significant Food Can Make a Short Story into a Meal: The Hyphenated Immigrant Experience in Contemporary American Short Fiction." *Liminality and the Short Story: Boundary Crossings in American, Canadian, and British Writing*, edited by Jochen Achilles and Ina Bergmann, Routledge, 2015, pp. 198–209.

——. "Teaching Significant Food in Carver's Fiction." *Carver across the Curriculum*, edited by Paul Benedict Grant and Katherine Ashley, Cambridge Scholars, 2011, pp. 79–92.

Carey, Allison E. "Food in *Finding H. F.* and *Secret City* by Julia Watts: The Food of Home and the Food of the Big City." *Journal of Appalachian Studies*, vol. 20, no. 2, 2014, pp. 170–80.

Claramonte, MaCarmen, África Vidal, and Pamela Faber. "Translation and Food: The Case of Mestizo Writers." *Journal of Multicultural Discourses*, vol. 12, no. 3, 2017, pp. 189–204.

Coghlan, J. Michelle, ed. *The Cambridge Companion to Literature and Food*. Cambridge University Press, 2020.

Dagbovie, Sika Alaine. "From Living to Eat to Writing to Live: Metaphors of Consumption and Production in Sapphire's *Push*." *African American Review*, vol. 44, no. 3. 2011, pp. 435–52.

Eads, Martha Greene. "Sex, Money, and Food as Spiritual Signposts in Doris Betts's *Sharp Teeth of Love*." *Christianity and Literature*, vol. 54, no. 1, 2004, pp. 31–49.

Farmer, Michial. "'Never the Right Food': The Physical and Material Worlds in John Updike's *Rabbit, Run* and Flannery O'Connor's *Wise Blood*." *Religion and the Arts*, vol. 19, nos. 1–2, 2004, pp. 84–106.

Fisher, M. F. K. *The Art of Eating*. Wiley, 2004.

Fitzpatrick, Joan. *Food in Shakespeare: Early Modern Dietaries and the Plays*. Ashgate, 2007.

Frye, Northrop. *Anatomy of Criticism: Four Essays*. Princeton University Press, 1957.

Graves, Brian. "You Are What You Beat: Food Metaphors and Southern Black Identity in Twentieth-Century African American Literature and Goodie Mob's 'Soul Food.'" *Studies in Popular Culture*, vol. 38, no. 1, 2015, pp. 123–37.

Habib, M. A. R. *A History of Literary Criticism*. Blackwell, 2005.

Hartman, Geoffrey H. *Criticism in the Wilderness: The Study of Literature Today*. Yale University Press, 1980.

Hemingway, Ernest. *A Moveable Feast: The Restored Edition*. Scribner, 2009.

Homer. *The Odyssey*. Translated by Robert Fagles, Penguin Classics, 1999.

Keeling, Kara, and Scott Pollard. "Power, Food, and Eating in Maurice Sendak and Henrik Drescher: *Where the Wild Things Are*, *In the Night Kitchen*, and *The Boy Who Ate Around*." *Children's Literature in Education*, vol. 30, no. 2, 1999, pp. 127–43.

Keeling, Kara K., and Scott T. Pollard. *Critical Approaches to Food in Children's Literature*. Routledge, 2009.

Lo, Yi-Jou. "From What We Eat to How We Are: Food and the Father-Daughter Relationship in Yiyun Li's 'A Thousand Years of Good Prayers.'" *Explicator*, vol. 73, no. 1, 2015, pp. 65–68.

Magistrale, Tony. "O'Connor's 'The Lame Shall Enter First.'" *Explicator*, vol. 47, no. 3, 1989, pp. 58–61.

Mennell, Stephen, et al. *The Sociology of Food: Eating, Diet, and Culture*. 2nd ed., Sage, 1992.

Miles, Caroline. "The Right to Eat: Money, Labor, and Commodification in Faulkner's *If I Forget Thee, Jerusalem.*" *Faulkner Journal*, vol. 30, no. 2, 2016, pp. 69–82.

Moreau, Nichole E. "Erdrich's *Love Medicine.*" *Explicator*, vol. 61, no. 4, 2003, pp. 248–50.

Naipaul, V. S. *Miguel Street*. Penguin, 1971.

Naranjo-Huebl, Linda. "'Take, Eat': Food Imagery, the Nurturing Ethic, and Christian Identity in *The Wide, Wide World*, *Uncle Tom's Cabin*, and *Incidents in the Life of a Slave Girl.*" *Christianity and Literature*, vol. 56, no. 4, 2007, pp. 597–631.

Piatti-Farnell, Lorna. *Food and Culture in Contemporary American Fiction*. Routledge, 2011.

Reder, Kimo. "The Word Made Flesh Writ Edible: Emily Dickinson's Micro-Eucharist of Crumb and Berry." *Christianity and Literature*, vol. 66, no. 3, 2017, pp. 520–33.

Sceats, Sarah. *Food, Consumption, and the Body in Contemporary Women's Fiction*. Cambridge University Press, 2004.

Shahani, Gitanjali G., ed. *Food and Literature*. Cambridge University Press, 2018.

Shepherd, Gordon M. *Neurogastronomy: How the Brain Creates Flavor and Why It Matters*. Columbia University Press, 2012.

Virgil. *The Aeneid*. Translated by Robert Fagles, Penguin Classics, 2008.

Viswanathan, R. "Stevens's 'The Emperor of Ice-Cream.'" *Explicator*, vol. 50, no. 2, 1992, pp. 84–85.

Wang, Quan. "The Image of Food in Julia Cho's *The Language Archive.*" *Explicator*, vol. 75, no. 2, 2017, pp. 129–32.

Wang, Quan. "The Smell of Food in *The Language Archive.*" *Explicator*, vol. 73, no. 3, 2017, pp. 153–56.

Wimsatt, William K., Jr., and Cleanth Brooks. *Literary Criticism: A Short History*. Routledge, 2021.

Witt, Doris. *Black Hunger: Soul Food and America*. University of Minnesota Press, 2004.

Zubiaurre, Maite. "Culinary Eros in Contemporary Hispanic Female Fiction: From Kitchen Tales to Table Narratives." *College Literature*, vol. 33, no. 3, 2006, pp. 29–51.

PART I

The Influence of Food in Twentieth-Century American Literature

Significant Food in Mid-Twentieth-Century American Realism

ROBERT C. HAUHART

The question of whether the use of food in literature serves some aesthetic goals or genres better than others has not been adequately addressed. The question is of interest because a number of major works within the ambit of twentieth-century American realism incorporate and commonly rely upon food references and food scenes to advance the narrative and achieve the aesthetic goals of their authors. Food, although common in this literature, is too often neglected in scholarly criticism. As Renée Dowbnia argues, an analysis of the function of food in literature can be a key component to understanding a text. "Such an analysis [of the role food plays]," she observes, "not only reveals the role of food in character development but also how characters' relationships to food—what they do or do not eat, their feelings about food, and their motivations for these urges—reflect larger cultural ideas about appetite, consumption, and the body" (567). Yet, although Dowbnia touts the merits of food-focused literary criticism, she finds that it has been largely neglected. Thus, literary criticism that focuses on the contribution that food and food-related passages make to narrative goals and aesthetics is perhaps overdue.

Realism itself, while not the completely dominant genre it once was in the fin de siècle nineteenth century, remains an influential and popular style of narrative exposition. Moreover, many of the authors widely considered to be among the United States' (and the world's) foremost practitioners of fiction—Nobel Prize and Pulitzer Prize recipients among them—wrote principally, even exclusively, in this vein. Philip Roth, John Updike, Sylvia Plath, Amy Tan, Richard Yates, and others wrote well-known realist stories and novels that also make extensive, and effective, use of food in their critically and commercially successful narratives. This chapter, then, will analyze three examples of American realist novels with respect to the authors' use of food.

Realism, of course, is a genre that depends on accurate observation and portrayal of details that envision for the reader a perception or sense that the narrative one is reading actually occurred or could have. As William Dean Howells, an early and ardent advocate and practitioner of realistic fiction, held, fiction—like journalistic "sketches"—must be filled with representations of living, breathing life so that realistic fiction can be read as though it was directly witnessed or experienced by its author/narrator/protagonist (Lannum 36). In essence, Howells evolved his fictional realism by learning to imaginatively substitute constructed depictions of common, everyday life arising from a particular culture and locale rather than just transcribing what he saw and heard in his experience as a travel writer-cum-journalist (Lannum).

While to date there is a general paucity of literary theory regarding the use of food in literature, a tool that offers a helpful starting point for analysis is Jeff Birkenstein's concept of "significant food." Birkenstein defines significant food in fiction as "[the use of] food . . . as a significant plot or other substantial narrative device, where the concomitant culture signifiers to nourishment and the table—or the absence thereof—assume a crucial narratological role" (Birkenstein 79). In essence, the concept of significant food is a means to distinguish between incidental references to food, eating, and so forth from uses that are in one way or another deeply embedded in the structure of a narrative, so indispensable to the author's narrative purpose that the food elements could not be other than they are without diminishing the literary effect of the work as a whole. Like other critically important analytical tools, the concept of significant food provides us with a means for distinguishing between food uses within literary works that are absolutely necessary to support the narrative, themes, or other authorial purpose and move the narrative forward in deliberate fashion from those uses that are mere decoration, illustration, or otherwise relatively unimportant. In short, the concept forces us to focus on a particular use of food in a text, or among a cluster of uses, in order to excavate, and thereby reveal, its relation to the work as a whole. By giving food references and food scenes due credit, doing so permits us to recognize and fully acknowledge the significant contribution the food references make to a work.

Significant Food in Philip Roth's *Goodbye, Columbus*

Roth's early novella, *Goodbye, Columbus* (1959), offers an example of mid-twentieth-century American realism in which food, and things related to food, arguably play an essential part in advancing the plot, displaying character, and developing themes crucial to the work. In the case of *Goodbye, Columbus,* Roth is particularly adept at constructing elaborate set pieces that individually and cumulatively work to effectively tell his story, reveal and define character, and establish the core themes that permeate the narrative.

Goodbye, Columbus famously begins with Neil Klugman envisioning future erotic possibilities with Brenda Patimkin, who has asked him to hold her glasses at the country club pool:

> I watched her move off. Her hands suddenly appeared behind her. She caught the bottom of her suit between thumb and index finger and flicked what flesh had been showing back where it belonged. My blood jumped. (3)

In this manner, Roth quickly establishes the novella's central plotline: Neil pursuing Brenda, landing Brenda, and—until we learn the outcome—either losing or winning Brenda's love and commitment. He tells this story within the context of the tensions arising from issues of class, economic inequality, Jewish identity, and social status in post-World War II Jewish life in the urban, northeastern United States. Neil is from a lower-middle-class/working-class family while Brenda is from upper-middle-class strivers who have moved out of Newark to suburban Short Hills, and "[n]early everything in the novella follows directly from this difference in achieved social status" (France 83).

Quickly though, Roth begins to use food in significant ways to complicate and embellish this basic structure, thus allowing Roth to better explore his concern with class differences and class tensions among American Jews, and, less directly, to examine the question of ethnic identity. In less than a page, the narrative segues to the Newark home of Aunt Gladys and Uncle Max, where Neil is living while his parents are in Arizona. Gladys is fixing dinner, and Neil, in his role as narrator, informs us:

> None of us ate together; my Aunt Gladys ate at five o'clock, my cousin Susan
> at five-thirty, me at six, and my uncle at six-thirty. There is nothing to explain
> this beyond the fact that my aunt is crazy. (4)

As we later discover, though, the ensuing scene is part of Roth's strategy
to subtly develop the world of Gladys, Max, Neil, and the Klugman clan
generally so that he can contrast it with the upwardly striving Patimkins.
The food and drink scenes in the novella, of which there are many, are
one crucial means of achieving this effect.

In Gladys's home, Aunt Gladys prepares all the meals herself. Moreover, consistent with a plausible portrait of a 1950s Jewish American
wife, mother, and woman from the working class, Gladys is the absolute
ruler of her domain—the kitchen and all things food related. When Neil
suggests that the family all eat together, urging that "It's hot, it'll be easier for you" (4), Gladys brushes his suggestion aside, saying:

> Sure, I should serve four different meals at once. You eat pot roast, Susan
> with the cottage cheese, Max has steak. Friday night is his steak night. I
> wouldn't deny him. And I'm having a little cold chicken. I should jump up
> and down twenty different times? What am I, a workhorse? (4–5)

When Neil raises the obvious objection ("Why don't we all have steak,
or cold chicken"), Gladys asserts the authority that resides in her traditional gender and class roles: "Twenty years I'm running a house. Go call
your girlfriend" (5).

Although the principal authorial purpose seems to be Roth's desire
to use dinner to point out the class-based differences between the Klugmans and the Patimkins, the picture he paints is more complex than that
simple equation. The two dinner scenes, one at each home, also reveal
similarities, albeit ones that also bear differences. Thus, at each meal
Neil is treated as someone who is not really known, and whose preferences do not matter, even where he lives with family at Gladys's and
Max's house. Asked if he wants soda with dinner, Neil declines. Gladys,
intent on fulfilling her gendered food-provider role, says, "You want water?" whereupon Neil is forced to protest, "I don't drink with my meals,
Aunt Gladys, I've told you that every day for a year already" (5). Roth
uses food here to shape each character's identity as well as to inject co-
medic relief into his story: Gladys is made to appear as the stereotypical Jewish mother, hovering over her charge, shoveling food and drink
toward Neil, complaining about her martyred plight but refusing to
have it any other way. Neil, correspondingly, is the grown-up but smoth-

ered little Jewish boy, thereby creating a portrait that is nearly cliché, but one that sets in motion opportunities for humorous asides, a technique that Roth can then put to use in Neil's interactions with Brenda, Brenda's family, and Neil's co-workers at the library. The food scene between Aunt Gladys and Neil is the catalyst for each of these narrative trajectories.

Food and eating are also the settings for competition and conflict at both households. As Gladys serves Neil his plate of food, she cuts two pieces of rye bread and places them next to him on the table. Aunt Gladys then seats herself across from him and "watche[s]" (6), monitoring his every bite. The effect is to turn what should be pleasurable eating into a battle for autonomy, on one side, and control on the other. At the same time, it may be a subtle reminder that Gladys and Max are not well off (Kutlu 58). Gladys's concern that the bread will go stale or that she will be forced to discard leftover meat are not sources of anxiety in the Patimkin household:

> "You don't want bread," she said, "I wouldn't cut it it should go stale."
> "I want bread," I said.
> "You don't like it with seeds, do you?"
> I tore a piece of bread in half and ate it.
> "How's the meat?" she said.
> "Okay. Good."
> "You'll fill yourself up with potatoes and bread, the meat you'll leave over and I'll have to throw it out." (6)

Neil's grudging and even hostile response to his aunt's oppressive surveillance reaches a crescendo when she realizes that she has not put salt on the table. Noting that Gladys did not serve pepper because she had heard it was not absorbed by the body, Neil explicitly remarks about the relative importance of the pleasure of eating in Gladys's house: "it was disturbing to Aunt Gladys to think that anything she served might pass through a gullet, stomach, and bowel just for the pleasure of the trip."

The scene is capped by Neil's decision to forgo dessert because "I wanted this hot night, to avoid the conversation that revolved around my choosing fresh fruit over canned fruit; or canned fruit over fresh fruit; whichever I preferred, Aunt Gladys always had an abundance of the other jamming her refrigerator like stolen diamonds." Here, too, Neil is forced to recognize that his preferences do not matter; if Gladys has a refrigerator full of grapes that she needs to get rid of, well, then . . .

Woven into the midst of this dinner narrative, Roth works to develop his portrait of a working-class post-World War II Jewish home counterpoised against the relative affluence of the Patimkins' lifestyle. Neil, looking to call Brenda, asks his aunt for the suburban phone book so he can find the number in Short Hills, a swank neighborhood outside of Newark, then and now. Gladys crisply informs him, "That skinny book? . . . I never use it," confirming Neil's earlier assessment, "as if she knew anybody who belonged to the Green Lane Country Club" (4). Gladys's solution is to use the book she does not need "[u]nder the dresser where the leg came off," a practical formula that one cannot imagine the striving, class-conscious Mrs. Patimkin adopting. Later, as Gladys prepares to serve Neil dinner, she turns a black fan up to high; its mild breeze "managed to stir the cord that hung from the kitchen light" (5). As Neil's first trip to Short Hills emphasizes, the lawns there seemed to twirl water on themselves and "no one sat on stoops . . . for those inside . . . regulated with a dial the amounts of moisture that were allowed access to their skin" (8–9). During his drive to see Brenda, Neil's thoughts turn to another simple culinary delight Aunt Gladys and Uncle Max share— eating a Mounds bar "in the cindery darkness of their alley, on beach chairs, each cool breeze sweet to them as the promise of afterlife" (9). In short, the places where the Klugmans consume, the manner in which the Klugmans live and eat, and what the Klugmans eat and drink all contribute to Roth's depiction of a working-class family. Dinner at the Patimkins' home will be used to offer a different picture.

The day after meeting Brenda, Neil is invited for dinner with her family. When Neil telephones his aunt to say he will not be home to eat, Aunt Gladys responds "Fancy-shmancy" (20), a figure of speech that reinforces Gladys's class origin. As Neil explains, the Patimkins do not eat in the kitchen one at a time; rather, Brenda, Ron, Julie, Mr. and Mrs. Patimkin, and Neil share the meal at a dining room table while Carlota, the "Negro" maid, serves the meal (21). Yet the class-based experience of eating the meal in a room designated exclusively for dining and being waited upon by a servant is belied, in part, by Mr. and Mrs. Patimkins' origins, who—like Aunt Gladys—hail from inner-city Newark (and whose forebears, like hers, perhaps hail from the same, or similar, East European shtetl). Thus, Mr. Patimkin is described as "ungrammatical" and a "ferocious eater" (21). Everything about the setting, though, sets the Patimkins apart from Aunt Gladys and Uncle Max. Inside, the family eats in "the steady coolness of air by Westinghouse" (22), not by the faint hot breeze stirred by a small, black fan turned up to high. Acknowledging the comparative opulence of his surroundings, Neil notes, "It was a pleasure."

Conversation at dinner, too, although minimal, is different than a solitary meal with Aunt Gladys. Although eating was pursued as "heavy and methodical and serious," the talk is constant and often requires jousting for attention. Eating itself seems to be something of a competitive sport, with Neil/Roth tabulating the results: Mr. Patimkin ate three servings of salad; Ron had four; Brenda and Julie had two servings each; and only Mrs. Patimkin and Neil limit themselves to one (21). Indeed, Neil's lack of competitiveness is the factor most clearly separating him from the family of strivers. When offered further servings, he declines, permitting Mr. Patimkin to label him as "not one of us: 'He eats like a bird'" (23). When Mr. Patimkin asks about Mickey Mantle, it is but another open invitation to compete. The fact that the dinner table is considered a suitable site for this competition should not be glossed over:

> (Ten-year-old) JULIE: "'Three twenty-eight.'"
> RON: "'Three twenty-five.'"
> JULIE: "'Eight!'"
> RON: "'Five jerk! He got three for four in the second game.'"
> JULIE: "'Four for four.'"
> RON: "'That was an error, Minoso should have had it.'"
> JULIE: "'I didn't think so.'" (23–24)

Questioned by his wife about whether he is eating too much to play golf later, Mr. Patimkin pulls his shirt up and slaps his black, curved belly: "What are you talking about? Look at that!" Ron, not to be outdone in the ways of macho, competitive display, yanks his own T-shirt up and says, "Look at *this*" (23, emphasis in original). Brenda, acutely aware of the competitive dynamic at work in the Patimkin household, says to Neil, "Would you care to bare your middle?" Neil responds with a curt "No" (23).

The contrast between mealtimes at Neil's home with Aunt Gladys and Uncle Max and the dining culture of the Patimkins becomes significant because, as Roth portrays them, the gulf between the two is emblematic of the class gap that exists between the post-World War II lower-middle-class/working-class Jews and the nouveau riche Jews. These two scenes, and several others, are reflections of literarily significant food because of their direct bearing in furthering the novella's plot, major themes, and social identities. Neil, characterized from the start as the outsider because he "eats like a bird" (23), is continuously tested—and found wanting—according to the Patimkins' competitive, class-conscious standards. As Alan W. France recognizes, Neil's "lack of alimentary gusto suggests his larger inability to join the great banquet of American commodity culture" (84). This reading is reinforced by Roth's later use of food resistance, symbolizing Merry's disaffection for American food abundance and American ambition in *American Pastoral:* for post-World War II Jews, who endured the Holocaust, the Depression, wartime deprivation, and second-class status in a Christian nation, nothing is more reflective of success than to submerge oneself enthusiastically in the American cornucopia (Bylund 14, 18). As Mr. Patimkin points out when asked to help select silver patterns for Ron and Harriett's wedding, "When I got married we had forks and knives from the five and ten. This kid needs gold to eat off. But there was no anger, far from it" (Roth 95). Neil, highly conscious of his plebian status compared to the upwardly mobile Patimkins, is defensive and peevish when confronted with reminders, including how one eats, of the class difference between him and Brenda.

The contrasting dinners are integrally embedded in Roth's story and work at nearly every level to contribute to the whole, including through the use of a food-related observation that Roth injects relating to his examination of the central question of identity: "Who is a Jew?" As dinner at the Patimkins' house breaks up, Mrs. Patimkin directs "Carlota not to mix the milk silverware and the meat silverware again" (Roth 24). Later, Mrs. Patimkin interrogates Neil about his Jewish identity, trying to get him to tell her whether he is Orthodox, Conservative, or Reformed, to which he answers evasively. Yet when Neil is invited to spend a week (and then, two weeks) at the Patimkins' house, he and Brenda go out for "corned beef sandwiches, pizza, beer and shrimp, ice cream sodas, and hamburgers" (54). Shrimp, of course, are shellfish and thus not kosher. In short, food references in the text intersect with economic mobility but also with religion, which raises the issue of religious status, which itself intersects with status generally, which intersects with Americanness, which, almost by definition, involves a degree of competitiveness, which leads back to abundance and the dinner table. As Neil muses while under the withering gaze of Mrs. Patimkin: Is one's religious identity only dependent on whether Martin Buber's wife has only a single set of dishes in her kitchen? (88).

An after-dinner basketball game of "five and two" between Mr. Patimkin and Julie unites these strands further, moving the narrative from competitive eating and table talk to competitive sports to tense, bitter rivalry. Thus, when Mr. Patimkin swishes his third straight set shot through the basket, Julie—disgruntled—"[stomps] so hard on the ground that she raised a little dust storm around her perfect young legs" (26). Later, when Mr. Patimkin tires, Neil is recruited to finish against Julie. Neil, knowing that he hasn't held a basketball since high school, daydreams a nightmarish experience with demanding, competitive, ten-year-old Julie:

> . . . the sun had sunk, crickets had come and gone, the leaves had blackened, and still Julie and I stood alone on the lawn, tossing the ball at the basket; "Five hundred wins," she called, and then when she beat me to five hundred she called, "Now you have to reach it." And I did, and the night lengthened, and she called, "*Eight* hundred wins," and we played on and then it was eleven hundred that won and we played on and it was never morning. (27–28)

When Julie misses a set shot, Neil admits to a "slight gay flutter of heart." Julie asks to take it again, and Neil, under the gaze of Brenda and Mr. Patimkin, agrees. Moments later Neil misses his set shot and, laughingly, asks Julie whether he can take it again. Her resounding "No!" tells Neil "how the game was played" (29).

> Over the years Mr. Patimkin had taught his daughters that free throws were theirs for the asking; he could afford to. (29)

Neil, all too aware of who he is and where he is from, feels he perhaps doesn't deserve any free throws.

Neil, having braved his first evening with the Patimkin family, has quickly become the boyfriend, but when he pulls up to the Patimkin house the following night, he meets with an unexpected request in the form of a *fait accompli* demand: Ron must go to the airport to fly to Milwaukee to see his fiancée, Harriet, so Neil must look after Julie until the family returns. Neil, standing in the Patimkins' front hall, tasting his bitter resentment, wonders why he doesn't "[get] into my car, and [go] back to Newark where I might even sit in the alley and break candy"— that is, food—"with my own" (40). Comparing his servant status to Carlota, Neil reflects that he is "not even as comfortable" as she is; rather, while he is nominally the boyfriend, Brenda and her family think nothing of peremptorily using him as a nanny. In short, even in this brief paragraph, Roth uses eating food to symbolize Neil's recognition of his reduced standing in relation to the Patimkins' world.

Left alone with Julie, Neil wanders through the otherwise empty house and goes down to the basement where he finds a "mirrored bar that was stocked with every kind and size of glass, ice bucket, decanter, mixer, swizzle stick, shot glass, pretzel bowl" (41). It is, as Neil recognizes, "plentiful, orderly and untouched, as it can be only in the bar of a wealthy man who never entertains drinking people, who himself does not drink" (41–42). To the extent this display of drinking accoutrements needed punctuation, there is a "picture of Brenda on a horse, and next to that, a velvet mounting board with ribbons and medals clipped to it" hung above the liquor shelf, which itself held "twenty-three [bottles] to be exact—of Jack Daniels, each with a little booklet tied to its collared neck informing patrons of how patrician of them it was to drink the stuff" (42). In short, consumption and status mobility, in all their forms, are tethered tightly to competitive achievement and conspicuous display.

As Neil discovers, the basement also holds a "freezer big enough to house a family of Eskimos" and next to it "a tall old refrigerator" whose "ancient presence was a reminder . . . of the Patimkin roots in Newark" (42–43), and, thereby, its own reminder of the Patimkins' various status achievements. As Baumgarten and Gottfried point out, it is "a fridge that holds the promise of America for the Jews" (35). Opening the refrigerator door, Neil finds it is

> heaped with fruit, shelves swelled with it, every color, every texture, and hidden within, every kind of pit. There were greengage plums, black plums, red plums, apricots, nectarines, peaches, long horns of grapes, black, yellow, red, and cherries, cherries flowing out of boxes and staining everything scarlet. And there were melons—cantaloupes and honeydews—and on the top shelf, half of a huge watermelon . . . (43)

Aunt Gladys, of course, still lives in Newark. As Neil knows, her refrigerator is for the everyday, rather than a repository for a cornucopia of delight. Aunt Gladys doesn't take joy in accumulating food that may well go to waste: "her greatest joys were taking out the garbage, emptying her pantry, and making threadbare bundles for what she still referred to as the Poor Jews in Palestine" (7). In the Patimkins' case, their energetic striving has earned them a refrigerator that has "literally borne fruit" (France 84). As Neil muses on this overabundance, he thinks to himself, "Oh Patimkin! Fruit grew in their refrigerator and sporting goods dropped from their trees!" (43). Here, too, food is used to suggest the harvest of plenty the Patimkins can afford to possess, not unlike the array of sporting goods that seemingly, like apocryphal dollars, "grow on trees."

Neither Neil nor Roth are quite done with the generously stocked bar, enormous freezer, and fruit-bearing refrigerator, though. As Neil grabs a handful of cherries from the old Frigidaire and bites into a nectarine, Julie warns him: "You better wash that or you'll get diarrhea" (43). Dressed like Brenda in her own little Bermuda shorts and white polo shirt, Julie's reminder that the fruit has not been washed was said "in such a way that it seemed to place the refrigerator itself out-of-bounds, if only for me" (44). Neil's perception evokes a biting sting since Carlota routinely ate the Patimkins' fruit while working as their maid (24, 77). As if to confirm his feeling, when Neil disposes of the cherries in his pocket with his keys and change, Julie "peek[s] to see if [his hand] were empty," confronting Neil seemingly with "a threat in her face." It seems that even a ten-year-old striver knows that while sporting goods may grow on trees, fruit does not, and the family's hard-won fruit—like the parents' hard-won social status—must be preserved and protected, lest it be indiscriminately consumed by just anyone.

While one might think that Roth has made his points during Neil's food and drink tour of the Patimkins' underground stores, he follows with what can only be called a *coup de grâce*—a game of ping-pong between Julie and Neil that connects greedily safeguarded fruit with the competitive American desire to win. As Neil tells us, "I have no excuses for what happened next. I began to win and I liked it," so when Julie asks to take her serve over ("I hurt my finger yesterday"), Neil naturally says, "No" (44). As luck would have it, Neil continues to win, playing "ferociously" (45). Rejecting Julie's every objection ("That wasn't fair, Neil. My shoelace came untied"; "Neil, you leaned over the table. That's illegal"), he "smash[es] [the] return past her," so that Julie is reduced to screaming, "You cheat" and "I hate you" (45). Running away as Brenda and her family return, Julie sums up her emotional response to losing under the new rules, saying, "You cheat! And you were stealing fruit!" (45). The scene is a final testament (although not the final food-related scene in *Goodbye, Columbus*) to the important role food and food-related culture plays in Roth's saga of post-World War II, upwardly mobile American Jewishness.

Sylvia Plath's *The Bell Jar*

A second, well-known novelistic example of twentieth-century American realism is Sylvia Plath's *The Bell Jar* (1963). Like Roth in *Goodbye, Columbus*, Plath uses food scenes and food mentions in significant ways, although in a manner distinctively different than Roth. While it is beyond the scope of this chapter to fully explore why that may be so, it is worth noting the gender difference between the two authors (Dowbnia 567; Sceats 2). Plath's emerging feminism at the time she wrote *The Bell Jar* is reflected in Esther Greenwood's dilemma, confronted as she is by the problems Betty Friedan identified in *The Feminine Mystique*, published the same year (Leach 35). The fact that Plath was a lifelong gastronome likewise should not be disregarded (Bundtzen 79–80, 82–83). Individually or collectively, these are factors that may well have contributed to the manner in which Plath's use of food-related mentions played a part in her writing, as they are integral to her narrative. A careful review of her use of food scenes and references reveals how deeply embedded the mentions are with respect to the novel's plot, themes, and character development.

The Bell Jar is a bildungsroman that tells the story of nineteen-year-old Esther Greenwood, an achievement-oriented, aspiring poet at an elite women's college in the northeastern United States in the 1950s. Esther has won a summer internship contest at a women's magazine located in New York City. The selection of an internship at a women's magazine is both autobiographical (Plath won just such a prize in a writing contest) but also canny, as Mariana Valverde explains: a women's magazine presents a particular ideology entailing "Upward mobility, consumerism, competitiveness, keeping up with the Joneses . . . [all] values . . . presented as universally valid" (78). Esther, though, has developed qualms about her gender role in 1950s America, her academic and career aspirations, her virginity, her relation to other women (and particularly to older women), and to the prevailing political climate in the early 1950s United States. Unhappy with the direction of her life and with the prevailing social and political climate of the nation, Esther's state of mind spirals downward from its frayed beginning at the start of the book through deep clinical depression and suicidal ideation to a tentative, fragile recovery by the novel's end. In the novel's semitragic narrative, Esther has many opportunities to entertain dark thoughts, experience disappointing situations, and reflect on the sources of her despair.

In *Goodbye, Columbus*, Roth uses food primarily to highlight the social class gap between Neil, son of working-class/lower-middle-class Jews whose roots remain closely tied to urban Newark, and the upwardly mobile family of his achievement- and status-oriented girlfriend, Brenda. While issues relating to achievement and upward mobility are also central to Plath's Esther Greenwood, Esther's narrative has a downward trajectory from the beginning, and Plath's use of food is tightly connected to the gloomy prospects that Esther envisions for herself as a woman. Thus, while Esther envisions various futures that include accomplishment and upward mobility, she almost uniformly envisions failure or disenchantment with them, or realizes that as a young woman in the 1950s an accomplished career may not be her fate. These negative visions of an unfulfilled future are often associated with mentions of food, Esther's bad experiences with food or drink, and her recognition that access to food is a class-based resource allocated by economic strata within 1950s capitalist America. Indeed, virtually every food scene or food reference is a precursor or consequence of something negative Esther experiences or visualizes. As Caroline Smith states, "Consistently, in *The Bell Jar*, Plath expresses Esther's anxiety through food moments" (4). Given the number and frequency of food scenes and images, Plath's incorporation of food in this way makes her adoption of them highly significant within the overall creative strategy she employs.

Plath's use of food, drink, eating, and culinary preparation images in *The Bell Jar* begins almost immediately. Lamenting the convictions and pending executions of the Rosenbergs, Esther associates that summer with her own disquiet and dismay. Describing Esther's experience of New York City—when she "was supposed to be having the time of [her] life" (2)—Plath focuses on the "fusty, peanut-smelling mouth of every subway" (1); her recollection of the first time she saw a cadaver, the cadaver's head "float[ing] up behind [her] eggs and bacon" (1–2); the "uncomfortable, expensive clothes, hanging limp as fish" in Esther's closet (2); and the hollow emptiness of "drinking martinis in a skimpy imitation silver-lame bodice stuck on a big, fat cloud of white tulle, on some Starlight Roof, in the company of several anonymous young men with all-American bone structures hired or loaned for the occasion" (2). For Esther, these are all negative experiences, and Plath's use of food-related imagery here is significant.

These opening images are emblematic of the novel's tone. Esther, accustomed to winning academic prizes, is despairing and disheartened; negative thoughts accompany almost every experience and litter the book's pages. Although outwardly successful, Esther harbors doubts about herself, and she is particularly bothered by her inability to settle upon a direction for her life. As she reflects on her situation, she sees herself as a young woman who "wins a prize here and a prize there and ends up steering New York like her own private car" (2). Yet she also knows this is not the reality, saying, "Only I wasn't steering anything, not even myself" (2). Esther's loss of the ability to steer her life—that is, a loss of agency due to perceived and actual powerlessness as a woman— is the novel's central narrative. More specifically, Marjorie Perloff and other critics often describe Esther's dilemma as experiencing a divided self because she is "a woman in a society whose guidelines for women she can neither accept nor reject" (511).

Early on, Esther is drafted by Doreen, another magazine award winner, to accompany her when she allows a man, Lenny Shepherd, a well-known disc jockey, to pick them both up. They go to a bar with Lenny's friend Frankie in tow. When offered a drink, Doreen readily orders an old-fashioned. Esther admits that "Ordering drinks always floored me. I didn't know whiskey from gin and never managed to get anything I really liked" (10). Still, she asks for a vodka "plain," explaining untruthfully, "I always have it plain." Later, they accompany Lenny to his apartment where he "began to mix drinks from several different bottles" (15). Esther, who has become a reluctant chaperone as Frankie soon departs their company, records her experience: "My drink was wet and depressing. Each time I took another sip it tasted more and more like dead water." Watching Lenny and Doreen dance, Esther observes, "I felt myself shrinking to a small black dot. . . . I felt like a hole in the ground" (16). Drunk, bored, lonely, and depressed by the scene, Esther lets herself out of Lenny's apartment "and managed to get downstairs by leaning with both hands on the banister" (17). Discovering that she is forty-three blocks by five blocks away from her hotel, she walks until, upon entering the lobby, she is "perfectly sober" but sees "a big smudgy-eyed Chinese woman staring idiotically" into her face (18). It is her own reflection, of course, looking back at her from a mirrored elevator door. Esther is "appalled [at] how wrinkled and used up" she looks. Here, drinking— meant to accompany a good time—is like other food images to come, a subtle messenger of the disarray, unhappiness, and spiritless lack of purpose that Esther's life has become.

Done with the easy warm-up, Plath recounts Esther's attendance at a banquet where the table is covered with "yellow-green avocado pear halves stuffed with crabmeat and mayonnaise and platters of rare roast beef and cold chicken, and every so often a cut-glass bowl heaped with black caviar" (24). Claiming that she had "never eaten out in a proper restaurant" before coming to New York (even though she "love(s) food more than just about anything else," especially dishes "full of butter and cheese and sour cream"), Esther proceeds to satiate herself with the luxurious offerings. She covers her plate with chicken slices and spreads caviar thickly over them. As she consumes the feast, she thinks of her grandmother, who "always cooked economy joints and economy meat loafs," commenting as everyone lifted a forkful, "I hope you enjoy that. It cost forty-one cents a pound" (26). Food, it seems, is a reminder of her middle-class status as a scholarship girl at college, unable to afford the expensive, rich food she craves but is withheld by American society based on class and socioeconomic status.

The consequence is that while she inhales avocado halves stuffed with crabmeat in indulgent ecstasy, Esther entertains the thought that "all the uncomfortable suspicions I had about myself were coming true.... I was letting up, slowing down, dropping clean out of the race" (29); tears "plopped down into my dessert dish of meringue and brandy ice cream" (31). "Unmasked" by her boss at the magazine that day, when Jay Cee queries her about her future, Esther can only stammer the words, "I don't really know" (32). True to form, upon leaving the luncheon she goes along with three other interns to a movie—and begins to feel "peculiar" (42). Filled with an "enormous desire to puke," Esther vomits twice in a cab on the way back to the hotel. As Dowbnia argues, episodes of binging on food and then purging it in the novel are representative of Esther's heretofore eager consumption of the 1950s American way of life followed by her increasingly fraught rejection of it (577–79). The beautiful gourmet food, eaten while she is consumed with thoughts of failure and loss, has made Esther ill (43–49). Food, the ostensible source of gustatory pleasure and physical health, is rather a purveyor of illness and pain.

As the banquet scene makes evident, consuming food is symbolically equated with the predominant consumption culture of 1950s American life. Esther, a girl "so poor she can't afford a magazine" (2), initially exults in enjoying the "prizes" she is accorded by winning the summer internship—"a month, expenses paid, and pile and pile of free bonuses, like ballet tickets and passes to fashion shows and hair stylings at a famous expensive salon" (3). Later, though, she dispenses symbolically with her identity as the perfect American female consumer by throwing the expensive clothes she purchased, which hung as "limp as fish in [her] closet," off the roof of the Barbizon Hotel (2, 111; Leonard, "'The Woman Is Perfected'").

As most critics agree, the predominant motif that typifies Esther's plight in *The Bell Jar* is symbolized by the story of the fig tree and Plath's appropriation of the image to illustrate Esther's struggle (Smith; Séllei). Esther, given a copy of *The Thirty Best Short Stories of the Year* for suffering ptomaine poisoning at the banquet, flips through it to read a story about a fig tree that grows between the house of a Jewish man and a convent. The man and a beautiful nun meet at the tree to pick ripe figs. One day the two watch a bird egg hatch in a nest in the fig tree and touch the back of their hands together. Thereafter, the nun doesn't come to pick figs anymore; rather, a mean-faced kitchen maid comes to pick them and counts the number of figs the man picks. The Jewish man is angry—but the nature of his anger is not clearly stated (Plath 55). Esther likes the story and imagines herself crawling between the printed lines and falling asleep "under that beautiful big green fig tree," associating food with a comforting thought.

Later, anxiously enumerating all the things she cannot do (cooking, shorthand, dancing, singing, walk graciously, ride a horse, speak German, read Hebrew, write Chinese), Esther envisions her life "branching out before me like the green fig tree in the story" (76–77). From the end of every branch, "a wonderful future" dangles before her eyes like a "fat purple fig" (77). She images one fig as "a husband and a happy home and children"; another fig as a famous poet; still another as a brilliant professor; still another as "Ee Gee, the amazing editor" (77). Yet faced with these alluring opportunities, Esther sees herself "sitting in the crotch" of the tree "starving to death, just because I couldn't make up my mind. . . . I wanted each and every one of them." Unable to decide, Esther imagines the figs "wrinkle and go black," and one by one they fall off the tree and lay inert at her feet (77). In essence, a tasty, attractive, healthy fruit within her reach turns to dross, just as Esther believes will happen to the many wonderful life choices she imagines for herself drying up and desiccating. This dilemma of the girl who wants everything and the female conundrum that cautions one cannot have it all, symbolized by a food metaphor, is a precursor to the central plotline of the second half of the book—Esther's descent into mental illness occasioned by her inability to reconcile herself between the conformist ideals of 1950s womanhood, the disempowering actuality for women during the era, and her own desires.

The significance of food references in *The Bell Jar* is hardly limited to these few passages. Although often overlooked, Plath's use of food peppers Esther's every moment as she wends her way through her internship summer. Even minor disappointments and offhand assessments are often bathed in negative food images. Leaving the magazine offices, Esther rues the fact that her hope she can spend the day in Central Park "died in the glass eggbeater of *Ladies' Day* revolving doors" (41). Recovering from ptomaine poisoning, Esther looks down at her bathrobe sleeve and sees a hand extending from it "pale as a cod" (45). Recollecting her blind dates at college, Esther remembers how she "hated coming downstairs . . . and finding some pale, mushroomy fellow with protruding ears or buck teeth or a bad leg" (58). Recounting bitterly her boyfriend's summer affair, Esther sums up the woman as a "tarty waitress." The effect of each of these food mentions is to charge each experience with a negative aura that relates to a type of food or food-related item. Food, ideally a universally enjoyed human experience, becomes for Esther simply a symbol for one more source of disappointment, ennui, and unpleasantness.

Plath's use of food moments is characterized most often, however, by her deft melding of Esther's anxiety over becoming a woman in the 1950s through food associations, thereby tying food to the primary tension over her identity. Invited out on a blind date set up by her boyfriend's mother, Esther starts enjoying the fact that the restaurant "smelt of herbs and spices and sour cream" (77). They drink pine-bark wine and Esther acknowledges, "I felt so fine by the time we came to the yogurt and strawberry jam that I decided I would let Constantin seduce me" (78). This thought inspires Esther to ruminate over all the anxieties that such an act can give rise to for a young woman. Esther reflects, "I might have a baby," but the thought seems too distant and abstract to be real (80). This unfairness in being a woman gives rise to thoughts about the double standard; Esther, feeling burdened by her virginity, notes resentfully that purity was "the great issue" for women in the 1950s. Women, it seemed to her, had to preserve themselves for marriage so they could exchange their purity for "infinite security," but as Esther bitterly reflects, "I wanted change and excitement and to shoot off in all directions myself, like the colored arrows from a Fourth of July rocket" (83). Imagining what it would be like "if Constantin were [her] husband" (84), Esther summons up an immediate food image:

> it would mean getting up at seven and cooking him eggs and bacon and toast and coffee and dawdling about in my nightgown and curlers after he'd left for work . . . to wash up the dirty dishes and make the bed and then when he came home after a lively, fascinating day he'd expect a big dinner and I'd spend the evening washing up even more dirty plates till I fell into bed utterly exhausted. (84)

Esther concludes: "This seemed a dreary and wasted life for a girl with fifteen years of straight A's" (84). Esther knows this to be what marriage means because she once found her boyfriend's mother, Mrs. Willard, braiding a rug out of strips of wool from her husband's old suits. Noting that even though Mrs. Willard "spent weeks on that rug," she didn't hang the beautiful result of her work, as Esther believes she would have wanted to do. Rather, "she put it down in place of her kitchen mat" (85), nicely tying a woman's fate to a food space. The consequence, of course, was that "in a few days it was soiled and dull," a harbinger of what men secretly wanted: for women to "flatten out underneath [men's] feet like Mrs. Willard's kitchen mat." Reaching what for Esther is the obvious conclusion, once "you were married and had children it was like being brainwashed and afterward you went about numb as a slave in some private, totalitarian state." Food, used as a pleasurable lure on blind dates, would then be used to tie women to food and food spaces in perpetuity.

Esther's vision of marriage as slavery, closely identified with kitchen duty, of course, might seem bad enough. It turns out, though, that another humiliation for Esther, again associated with food and drink, was forthcoming, because "apart from holding my hand Constantin showed no desire to seduce me whatever" (82). Esther, feeling a "powerful drowsiness drifting through [her] body from all the pine-bark wine," decides to lie down. Taking her shoes off, she rests on Constantin's bed. Rather than the exciting seduction she fantasized, Constantin lies down next to her. When she awakes, it is to the sound of rain punctuated by the "sound of somebody breathing" (84). Constantin, too, has fallen asleep.

Although Esther is explicit in her rejection of marriage as a possible future, her attitude does not help her choose the best, fat, purple fig on the tree. Given a single rose to hold and asked by the *Ladies' Day* photographer to "Show us how happy it makes you to write a poem" (101), Esther dissolves into tears, burying her face in the "pink velvet façade" of her boss's love seat (102). Unable to resolve her anxiety about her identity and career, and equally unable to give up her chastity with Constantin, Esther is set up with another blind date by her internship friend, Doreen. Meeting a tall, dark man dressed in an "immaculate white suit, a pale blue shirt and a yellow satin tie with a bright [diamond] stickpin" (105), Esther is ferried off to a country club dance. It is unsurprising in a realistic narrative that alcohol will be served, but Plath's purpose, of course, is to use drinking as she has earlier—to associate what could be pleasurable with an experience that turns out to be awful.

Noting that "I'd never had a daiquiri before" (106), Esther accepts one from her date, Marco, and drinks "one daiquiri after another." Holding her fourth drink, Esther refuses to dance with Marco, who angrily pulls her onto the dance floor and, when the music stops, into the garden. Feeling "the whole desolate unfamiliarity of the scene" (108), the muddy ground soars toward her and strikes her "with a soft shock." Having struck her, Marco throws himself down "as if he would grind his body through [me] and into the mud" (109). Fighting him off, Esther smashes her fist into his nose, crying and sucking at her "salty knuckles" as Marco dabbed at the inky, dark blood spreading from his nose. In short, the earliest, most ubiquitous, and most essential food preservative, a seasoning that adds "the spice of life" to food, is inserted into the narrative not as a complement to a pleasant meal but as a minor, but telling, detail in the scene of Esther's sexual assault. Having failed to answer her questions about identity and her future, having failed to steer her own sexual desire into a chosen liaison, Esther's stay in New York ends with a sour, salty tang in her mouth, not unlike drowning in seawater.

Returning home after her dispiriting summer in New York, Esther is stranded in suburbia, her problems intact. Denied admission to a Harvard summer seminar (114), confronted with living again in the same house with her mother (118), spurned by her boyfriend in a "Dear Esther" letter (119), desultorily starting a novel on "virgin sheet[s]" of paper (120), persuaded against her better judgment to let her mother teach her shorthand in the evenings (121–22), Esther decides she will put off the novel she thought of writing. Instead, she thinks she will spend the summer reading *Finnegans Wake* and writing her honors thesis (122). Mentally thrashing about, Esther admits her fate may be limited to becoming a typist or a waitress, one a depressing food-related career option that equals, in her mind, a paid Mrs. Willard. It is a portrait of her future that she returns to repeatedly in her dejection (122, 125, 130). Consistent with my reading of Plath's use of food in the novel, Esther predictably addresses the multifaceted unhappiness with her summer at home by withdrawing from her disempowered, enervated embrace within the warm, "motherly breath of the suburbs" and *not* eating (113, 130).

Plath's technique of matching Esther's negative emotional responses with food moments retains a consistent pattern throughout the work. In using the strategy in this way, Plath provides *The Bell Jar* with one of several effective structural spines for the narrative. The approach offers narrative continuity as the practice mirrors Esther's continuing mental decline through the arc of the story. Forced to live with her mother, Esther sees her mother's anxious face "sallow as a slice of lemon" (131). Seated on a park bench reading a newspaper article about a suicide attempt, Esther "cracked open a peanut from the ten-cent bag . . . and ate it. It tasted dead" (136), clearly associating food/eating with death. Scheduled for shock therapy by her psychiatrist at his private hospital, Esther, barely able to speak, "stared at the smiling, familiar face that floated before [me] like a plate full of assurances" (142). Wandering around the outer coastal suburbs of Boston thinking about suicide, Esther is struck by the "fancy blue and pink and pale green shanties . . . on the flat sands of the Point like a crop of tasteless mushrooms" (151). Set up by a friend with a date to the beach, Esther "managed to cook my hot dog. . . . Then, when nobody was looking, I buried it in the sand" (155). Motivated to visit her father's gravesite, she finds his stone is "a mottled pink marble, like canned salmon" (167). Recalling that neither she nor her mother cried at her father's funeral, Esther cries unashamedly, laying her face on the smooth marble, howling her loss into the "cold salt rain" (167). Subjected to the indignities of life inside a public mental hospital, Esther lashes out and kicks a Black male server who places two kinds of beans on the patients' table, because one should know "perfectly well you don't serve two kinds of beans together" (179). In the end, facing a tentative, fragile recovery, Esther reprises her reliance on the central metaphor of the novel, thinking that for the person under the bell jar, life is a blank, stopped like a dead baby, but also not able to forget the negative experiences. Thus, she free-associates Marco and his diamond, the sailor she meets on Boston Common, her psychiatrist's "wall-eyed" nurse, and—naturally—the story of the fig tree and the two kinds of beans (327). Food and negative experience fuse in the narrative of Esther's struggle, a significant deployment of food moments that entails strategic association of mood, plot, and character to achieve a convincing realism. Plath's use of food references, scenes, and food-related passages, like Roth's, intentionally incorporates significant uses of food to support theme, narrative, and character development within the framework of her story.

John Updike's *Rabbit, Run*

Rabbit, Run (1960), the first and most critically acclaimed of Updike's five books recounting the life of Harry "Rabbit" Angstrom, his most famous creation (McMartin B4), is another twentieth-century experiment in American realism that incorporates food in a significant way. As Updike acknowledges, he wrote narratives realistically because he wanted "to give the mundane its beautiful due." Updike writes crystalline sentences filled with period detail to achieve a realistic rendering of the life of his fictional Everyman, Rabbit, and his fictional setting, the conjoined towns of Brewer and Mt. Judge, amidst his fictional re-creation of 1950s working/lower-middle-class white America. Food references feature prominently in the details that make Rabbit's fictional adventures and travails credible, the primary—if often underappreciated—goal of literary realism that continues to make realistic writing immensely popular.

Updike's use of food may be contrasted effectively with both Roth's and Plath's techniques in *Goodbye, Columbus* and *The Bell Jar*, respectively, in one important respect. While any writer attempting to tell a story realistically must select language, plots, archetypes, and characterizations that plausibly conform to a given setting, era, and culture, there is still substantial potential variation in the choice of means to achieve such a realistic effect. Roth, as we've seen, uses food in *Goodbye, Columbus* primarily to highlight the social class gap between Neil and Brenda, allowing their socially distant orientations to upwardly mobility and status aspiration to dictate the trajectory of their relationship and support the book's core theme. His use of food, however, plays only a limited role in sketching out the realistic background upon which the narrative rests. While Plath certainly uses food in relation to Esther Greenwood's struggles with achievement goals and class status as well, her use—like Roth's—plays a marginal role in fashioning the realistic foundation upon which the story rests. Plath employs food moments more strategically than Roth with regard to Esther's mood, though, so that Esther's associations with food, and her fictional experiences with food, mirror the emotional trajectory of her decline, page by page, by day, week, and month, as her mental health deteriorates. Plath also uses her food scenes and mentions as companions, like Roth, to major themes, in Plath's case to Esther's ambivalent anxiety over the tension between traditionally feminine 1950s dreams and her own desires for personal achievement.

In *Rabbit, Run,* by contrast, Updike inserts food moments consistently to fulfill literary realism's functional requirements, although—like Roth and Plath—he also uses food to support his plot and themes. Fashioning a story about a married, lower-middle-class/working-class white male protagonist in a decidedly second-rate eastern US city in the late 1950s, Updike is compelled by realism's strictures to portray a place, a time, and a palette of character motivations and experiences that the reader can plausibly imagine. Having committed to realism, he must construct a seemingly realistic world. Although many, perhaps most, of Updike's food references are used to construct narrative background in *Rabbit, Run,* these references do not subside into *mere* background. Rather, Updike's food references are integrated into what might be called a seamless tapestry in the novel, so that the food references coalesce with other period and location details to convey realistic depth, as opposed to mere superficial illustration. Arguably, Updike's use of food details in this way, create what we might characterize as *"significant background,"* rather than what we might label as "mere background." Updike's use of food is, thus, a more crucial element than the merely superficial backdrop to the primary focus of the novel's contemplation. Used in this way, background becomes *more than* the equivalent of stage scenery, which is known to be just painted canvas. To achieve this effect, Updike quietly, almost surreptitiously, paints a picture so intricate that his incorporation of food as a major part of the whole creates an indispensable feature of the narrative, one that makes the appearance of food-related scenes a critical component of the structural framework that anchors his narrative realistically. Indeed, Updike's adoption of food moments is so pervasive that even this rather plebian purpose makes his appropriation of food mentions a significant one in *Rabbit, Run*.

Although Updike's use of food moments is often for the purpose of creating a densely layered background, his use of food also has intricate ties that support the plot, themes, and characterizations. This, too, is a vital factor in his use of food in *Rabbit, Run*. Thus, Updike incorporates food scenes in ways that map changes in the plot by marking transition points or creates scenes leading to character development. Notably, the novel's dramatic climax—in which Rabbit's wife, Janice, accidentally allows baby Rebecca to drown in an overfilled bathtub (267–79)—is driven by drink, tying consumption to character to plot to fate. This scene, and others, when examined in a close reading, disclose that Updike uses food and eating both to connect the narrative solidly back to the place, time, and culture he is attempting to depict *and* to advance major plot and thematic lines. That is, even when Updike uses a food moment to go beyond realism's core requirements, he generally does so in a way that includes cementing his story back to the context of realism he has created. In this way, Updike makes food and everything associated with it akin to other cultural signifiers such as music, clothing, media, infrastructure and geography, religion and spiritual belief, sexual behavior, nature, and foreign words. Used alone and together, these elements of culture form a mosaic that is densely, plausibly real. And one of Updike's prominent qualities as a novelist is to create complex language pictures that seldom interrupt the realism he is creating while at the same time furthering characterization, plot, and theme.

Rabbit, Run is the first installment of the well-known story of Rabbit Angstrom, twenty-six-year-old former high school basketball hero (and B-league scoring champion!), whose early success of cheering crowds and a girlfriend who waits outside the gymnasium has not prepared him for the less glamorous life of demonstrating a "kitchen gadget" in local "five-and-dime stores" or a marriage that Rabbit himself describes as a second-rate mess (9). The book is, like other examples of American realism, firmly anchored to a very specific time and place—the late 1950s in a second-rate town next to a second-rate small city in eastern Pennsylvania—and even more firmly connected to lower-middle-class/working-class culture of the period. Rabbit, the son of a printer and a housewife, has fled his wife, Janice, the daughter of a used car dealer and a housewife, from the life he feels is trapping him in search of some indistinct "thing that wasn't there" (Updike 140). Scared, like a rabbit, he runs until it seems like he has made an ambivalent peace with his life—but then he runs some more, seeking an answer to questions about life and commitment he cannot even articulate. Rabbit's run takes him along Pennsylvania's two-lane highways, through rural towns, amidst the trappings of American popular culture, and deep into his memories, and the dregs of his vaguely articulated dreams. During this beautiful yet tragically rendered journey, Updike routinely uses food as one element of the realistic detail that serves as the background to Rabbit's struggle to achieve some transcendent moment in an otherwise quotidian, socially and culturally impoverished landscape. In this way, a background that might seem of little interest becomes the symbolically empty receptacle that represents his own empty experience of life.

As the novel opens, Rabbit inserts himself into a group of kids playing pick-up basketball, reminding himself of the days when he did something really well, first-rate. Reaching his home, he stands in the vestibule, inhaling the same smell as always, sometimes like "cabbage cooking" but sometimes like "the furnace's rusty breath" (7). The pungent smell of cabbage cooking is both a comfortable reminder of home and an unpleasant odor of a constrained, lower-middle-class culture. Inside, he "sees his wife sitting in an armchair with an Old-Fashioned" (7), watching a popular children's show of the era starring the Mouseketeers with "Darlene and Cubby and Karen" (9). Here, Updike's intricate use of period detail is on display along with food moments (cabbage cooking, an old-fashioned) that quietly infiltrate and support his finely detailed description.

Rabbit's present unhappiness is an opportunity for Updike to use

Rabbit's reveries for literary effect. Thinking back to when he was younger, Janice was his girlfriend, working at Kroll's department store "selling candy and cashews in a white smock with 'Jan' stitched on her pocket" (14). This association is with something pleasant: after work they would retire to her girlfriend's apartment in Brewer and make love on her "[p]ipe-frame bed" (13). Dragged back to the present moment, he hears Janice—who has gone into their kitchen to prepare dinner—"drop . . . something metal, a pan or cup" (14–15)—returning him to baleful thoughts of the "tightening net" he perceives strangling his life (15). Leaving to pick up his two-and-a-half-year-old son, Nelson, at his mother's house, Rabbit peers in "the lit kitchen window" and "sees himself sitting in a high chair" (22), neatly tying together Rabbit's past, present, and foreseeable future with a kitchen window and a high chair at a kitchen table. The tableau of Nelson being cared for in the kitchen by his mother, father, and younger sister lets Rabbit reflect that the comparison of the two kitchens means "this home is happier than his" (23). Stealing away without notice, Rabbit decides to pick up their car from in front of his mother-in-law's house, which reminds him "for some reason of an abandoned ice-cream stand" (24). Once in the car, he drives out of town, trying to avoid the "supper-time traffic" as he listens to a "Negress" sing "A field of corn," her voice dark and warm (25). Yet a pleasant, musical food association turns rancid. He thinks "Supper music. Music to cook by," imagining, as he runs, "Janice's meal sizzling in a pan, . . . the grease-tinted water bubbling disconsolately, the unfrozen peas steaming away their vitamins" (25). Here, the major plot and theme—Rabbit runs—is nestled among memory of a candy and nut counter at a department store; Janice starting dinner in their kitchen; observing his son through the kitchen window at his mother's house; comparing his in-laws' house to an ice-cream stand; and hearing a "Negress" sing "A field of corn," which reminds him it is the dinner hour—that it is akin to music to cook by.

Harry Angstrom, like Esther Greenwood, has many experiences and memories that he regrets. However, unlike Plath, Updike is not telling a story where dissatisfaction predominates to the same degree. Thus, Updike does not use food mentions solely to mirror and signal negative emotional moments. Continuing to flee his unsatisfying life "into orange groves and smoking rivers and barefoot women" (26), Rabbit stops at a diner where he eats two hamburgers, a glass of milk, and a piece of apple pie: "the crust is crisp and bubbled and they've had the sense to use cinnamon. His mother's pies always had cinnamon" (31–32). He leaves "feeling pleased," because "the hamburgers had been fatter and warmer than the ones you got in Brewer, and the buns had been steamed" (32). In short, Updike does not solely use food as a marker for another desultory moment in a continuing downward trajectory. Rather, for Updike a food moment can equally be used as part of a paradisical dream fantasy or evidence that "things are better already" (32).

Updike's approach to using food in a significant fashion is perhaps most easily recognized when it is used in close connection with other literary techniques, like lists scattered throughout a text, often in the form of free association. Thus, as Rabbit drives south through the night, he reads the names of "Bird in Hand, Paradise" on his map and has an urge to go there imagining "candy houses in lemon sunshine" (31). Quickly, though, his attention turns to the radio, reciting the details of songs that are played ("If I Didn't Care" by Connie Francis), commercials (for Rayco Clear Plastic Seat Covers), news (President Eisenhower and Prime Minister Macmillan begin talks), sports (Yankees over Braves in Miami), and weather (fair and seasonably warm; spring scheduled to arrive tomorrow) (32). Nestled neatly among what he hears is "a commercial for Lord's Grace Table Napkins and the gorgeous Last Supper Tablecloth" (33), reintroducing another food moment and spearing religion in a "two-fer" in one fell swoop. Turning his distracted attention back to his driving, Rabbit notes along the highway "hot-dog stands and Calso signs and roadside taverns" (33). In just three pages, Updike has introduced highway food culture (hot-dog stands, roadside taverns), several specific foods (hamburgers, coffee, pie, candy), and common items related to serving food (napkins, tablecloth) commingled with other common 1950s signifiers. This effective use of food references to help densely pack what would otherwise be mere background is a distinctive technique that makes Updike's use of food in this way significant.

For Updike, the point has always been to highlight through his writing the ethereal beauty and spiritual basis of existence buried within the grubby and tragic moments found in mundane reality. Food, and everything related to food, its preparation, and its consumption, is simply one more element of the everyday for Updike to insert, note, celebrate, and critique, but because of its ubiquity in his writing, and in reality, food becomes a significant feature. When, as above, a food moment can do "double duty" by serving the goals of realism and still offer sly, subtle reference to a character, an attitude, or a theme ("Lord's Grace Table Napkins"), Updike shows little compunction, but much skill, in conscripting a food moment into a second, rather unrelated purpose, but still making it work. When Rabbit's dream of escaping the invisible net that traps his existence by driving south fails, he returns to Mt. Judge and looks up his old high school basketball coach at the neighborhood Sunshine Athletic Association. Coach Tothero, waking Harry where he has been permitted to sleep in his old coach's bed, tells him "To eat Harry, to dine. D.I.N.E. Rise, my boy. Aren't you hungry? Hunger. Hunger" (51). As soon as Updike inserts eating into the story, though, Updike uses Tothero's rhapsodic declamation to introduce a different kind of hunger vital to the narrative:

> "Whatsis girl business?" [Harry asks.]
> "What is it, yes, what is it? Cunt," Tothero exclaims in a stream. (51)

Uniting the two forms of hunger more closely, Rabbit and Tothero proceed to meet and escort Ruth and Margaret to a restaurant, setting up the story within a story of Rabbit and Ruth, itself an opportunity for Updike to reflect on the intersection of man's purpose, traditional religion, and things of the spirit. Moreover, Updike uses the interlude between Rabbit and Ruth to reengage reflections about Rabbit's decision to leave his wife, Janice, and tie both together with food and drink.

We should recall that when Rabbit returns home in the first few pages of the novel, Janice is "sitting in an armchair with an Old-Fashioned, watching television turned down low" (7). Rabbit, unhappy with his life, is infuriated at his wife's advanced pregnancy; he tells Janice she's "a mess" when he learns she has left their car at *her* mother's and their son, Nelson, at *his* mother's house. Rabbit, gesturing at her old-fashioned, asks, "How many of those have you had?" (10–11). Distressed by her drinking and listening to her explanations, Rabbit concludes, "There seems no escaping it: she is dumb" (13). Later, when his old coach asks him what has happened to his home, Harry invokes his wife's drinking as the explanation for his situation.

"It was a mess. . . . My wife's an alcoholic," but he quickly adds, "God she's dumb. She really is" (45). When Rabbit moves in with Ruth the following night, he rises (on Palm Sunday) to go back to his own house to pick up his clothes. Wandering about—"trying to gather up the essence of what he has done"—he finds in the kitchen "the pork chops never taken from the pan, cold as death, riding congealed grease" and smells "something sweetly rotting" in the paper bag under the sink when he disposes of them (104). Taking desultory measures to clean up the "mess" by putting the now-empty pan into soak, Rabbit hears the "the breath of steam" from the scalding water as a "whisper in a tomb" (104), thereby uniting wasted food, garbage, Janice's oversight and her faults, the "mess," their kitchen, his abandonment of his home, the death of his marriage, and yet, amidst the despair, Rabbit experiences a sense of hope akin to the welcoming of Jesus as he enters Jerusalem. Here, food and the kitchen support the plot, act as reminders of Rabbit's unhappiness and his existential dilemma, and refer obliquely to a major religious theme in the work. When Rabbit returns to Ruth's apartment, he goes across to the convenience store to get food, which Updike recites in another list: Rabbit "brings back eight hot dogs in cellophane, a package of frozen lima beans, a package of frozen French fries, a quart of milk, a jar of relish, a loaf of raisin bread, a ball of cheese wrapped in red cellophane, and, on top of the bag, a Ma Sweitzers' shoo-fly pie" (97–98). When Ruth makes lunch, "he sees she is a better cook than Janice" (99), turning the shopping list of frozen, processed, and prepared 1950s staples into one more justification for finding Janice a failure as both a wife and a woman.

What has been said so far also demonstrates Updike's use of food to support his depiction of a highly gendered portrait of gendered 1950s America. Marriages are traditionally heteronormative; women are housewives or, in the alternative, casual prostitutes and loose women like Ruth; women cook and either like cooking (Ruth) or are failures at cooking as well as failures as housekeepers (Janice), that other requisite role for 1950s women. Men, meanwhile, don't cook (Rabbit; his father; Eccles, the pastor) but, rather, eat and play the traditional male role of "breadwinner" (Rabbit, for both Janice and Ruth; Rabbit's father for his mother; Janice's father for her mother; Eccles, for his wife, Lucy). Indeed, Janice's failure at caring for their children and caring for their apartment is fused with her drinking to dramatize her ultimate failure as a woman—her accidental drowning of their infant daughter, Rebecca (267–79). Serving the gendered story further, Updike uses food to subtly announce Ruth's pregnancy. Ruth notices she is "crying easily at work and must "rush into the john like she had the runs" (153). And then there is the other telling fact that she is hungry all the time: "For lunch an ice-cream soda with the sandwich and then a doughnut with the coffee and still she has to buy a candy bar at the cash register" (153).

In sum, Updike's use of food in *Rabbit, Run* is significant because his process is carefully intertwined with the narrative requirements of realism and the intrinsic demand of any novel for good storytelling. Food is a natural feature of the everyday, mundane world that is Updike's forte, yet, when necessary for the story, it is also a strategically placed detail in the novel. In essence, Updike's use of food is significant because his form of writing and storytelling could not be achieved without significant food moments skillfully incorporated into the flowing narrative structure he creates, in addition to its recruitment for service in relation to his themes of gender relations, marital discord, abandonment, religious quest, and mortality.

As a method and technique of literary criticism, studies of significant moments of eating, food mentions and references, food preparation, consumption, distribution, and related uses offer a flexible and innovative means for investigating American literature. Birkenstein, a strong advocate of studying "significant food," argues that this is so because "in some fiction, food is much more than itself" (80). He urges that literature which treats food in such a way "demand[s] to be read through the lens of food and food issues" (90). Other literary critics have adopted the study of significant food for much the same reason. Smith, as one example, argues that throughout *The Bell Jar*, Plath appropriates food moments to underscore the intense hold that behavioral models set up by women's magazines have on Esther's sense of self (4). For Esther, an intelligent, ambitious, educated achiever, relegation to household manager—the limited role for women of the 1950s she fears—was identified principally with the acquisition, preparation, consumption, disposal, and clean-up of food, a future too painful for her to bear. Smith recognizes that Plath's use of food is thus tied intimately to one of the novel's central themes. Moreover, as I have shown, food associations are specifically tied to Esther's psychic experience in confronting her journey to adult womanhood in the novel. These are the reasons that Smith (and I) can call Plath's use of food a "significant moment," in light of food's utility in revealing theme and character.

Arguably, Philip Roth in *Goodbye, Columbus* and John Updike in *Rabbit, Run* have each used food moments in significant ways as well. Roth, like Plath, intricately ties food moments to Neil's struggles with social class, Jewish American striving in the 1950s United States, and upward mobility—the core interwoven themes of his narrative. Updike's insertion of food and eating-related moments serves his overall purpose of depicting a plausible setting for his examination of post-World War II American values through the fictional life of Harry "Rabbit" Angstrom. Eschewing the approach where a central grand theme drives the narrative and food references are bound closely to this theme, Rabbit's quest, rather, is more vaguely polymorphic, and the narrative pinballs from exuberance, hope, and celebration through tragedy, disappointment, and loss, only reaching an unresolved endpoint where Rabbit simply "runs. Ah: runs. Runs" (Updike 325).

Taken together, these three well-known twentieth-century novelistic examples of American realism suggest not only that the concept of "significant food" offers a valuable critical tool but implicitly proposes the idea that realism as a genre may be especially amenable to incorporating significant food moments.

WORKS CITED

Baumgarten, Murray, and Barbara Gottfried. "The Suburbs of Forgetfulness: *Goodbye, Columbus* (1959)." *Understanding Philip Roth*, University of South Carolina Press, 1990, pp. 21–42.

Birkenstein, Jeff. "Teaching Significant Food in Carver's Fiction." *Carver Across the Curriculum: Interdisciplinary Approaches to Teaching the Fiction and Poetry of Raymond Carver*, edited by Paul Benedict Grant and Katherine Ashley, Cambridge Scholars, 2011, pp. 79–92.

Bundtzen, Lynda K. "Lucent Figs and Suave Veal Chops: Sylvia Plath and Food." *Gastronomica*, vol. 10, no. 1, 2010, pp. 79–90.

Bylund, Sarah. "Merry Levov's BLT Crusade: Food-Fueled Revolt in Roth's *American Pastoral*." *Philip Roth Studies*, vol. 6, no. 1, 2010, pp. 13–30.

Dowbnia, Renée. "Consuming Appetites: Food, Sex, and Freedom in Sylvia Plath's *The Bell Jar*." *Women's Studies*, vol. 43, no. 5, 2014, pp. 567–88.

France, Alan W. "Philip Roth's *Goodbye, Columbus* and the Limits of Commodity Culture." *MELUS*, vol. 15, no. 4, 1988, pp. 83–89.

Friedan, Betty. *The Feminine Mystique*. Norton, 1963.

Kutlu, Filiz. "Philip Roth's *Goodbye, Columbus*: Neil's Farewell to the American Dream." *Interactions*, vol. 17, no. 2, 2008, pp. 57–64.

Lannum, George. "The Evolution of Howells's Realism: 'Suburban Sketches.'" *American Periodicals*, vol. 12, 2002, pp. 34–39.

Leach, Laurie F. "Sylvia Plath's *The Bell Jar:* Trapped by *The Feminine Mystique* (1963)." *Women in Literature: Reading through the Lens of Gender*, edited by Jerilyn Fisher and Ellen S. Silber, Greenwood Press, 2003, pp. 35–37.

Leonard, Garry. "'The Woman Is Perfected: Her Dead Body Wears the Smile of Accomplishment': Sylvia Plath and *Mademoiselle* Magazine." *College Literature*, vol. 19, no. 2, 1992, pp. 60–82.

McMartin, Pete. "Rabbit's Run Ends, and So Does Updike's World." *Vancouver Sun*, January 29, 2009, p. B4.

Perloff, Marjorie. "'A Ritual for Being Born Twice': Sylvia Plath's *The Bell Jar*." *Contemporary Literature*, vol. 13, 1972, pp. 507–22.

Plath, Sylvia. *The Bell Jar*. 1963. HarperCollins, 2006.

Roth, Philip. *Goodbye, Columbus*. 1959. Vintage International, 1993.

Sceats, Sarah. *Food, Consumption, and the Body in Contemporary Women's Fiction*. Cambridge University Press, 2004.

Séllei, Nóra. "The Fig Tree and the Black Patent Leather Shoes: The Body and Its Representation in Sylvia Plath's *The Bell Jar.*" *Hungarian Journal of English and American Studies,* vol. 9, no. 2, 2003, pp. 127–54.

Smith, Caroline J. "'The Feeding of Young Women': Sylvia Plath's *The Bell Jar, Mademoiselle Magazine,* and the Domestic Ideal." *College Literature,* vol. 37, no. 4, 2010, pp. 1–22.

Updike, John. *Rabbit, Run.* 1960. Random House, 2012.

Valverde, Mariana. "The Class Struggles of the Cosmo Girl and the Ms. Woman." *Heresies,* vol. 5, no. 2, 1985, pp. 78–82.

Modernism, the Grotesque Body, and Food in Anderson, Kafka, and Hemingway

JEFF BIRKENSTEIN AND
ERICKA BIRKENSTEIN

> When you spend many hours alone in a room
> you have more than the usual chances to disgust yourself—
> this is the problem of the body, not that it is mortal
> but that it is mortifying.
> —Lucia Perillo, "Again, the Body"

> Beauty is truth, truth beauty,—that is all
> Ye know on earth, and all ye need to know.
> —John Keats, "Ode on a Grecian Urn"

Perhaps.

Surely truth and beauty are sometimes aligned, as the ancient ode indicates. But this is not all of the story, for truth may also be found in people and things not perceived to be beautiful. Indeed, truth may be found, we argue in this essay, in that which is thought to be grotesque. Examining this alternative to the enduring and seemingly straightforward words in Keats's poem, we will first consider contrasting perspectives on the grotesque as contemplated by two modernist authors, in Sherwood Anderson's 1919 short-story sequence *Winesburg, Ohio* and in Franz Kafka's 1922 short story "A Hunger Artist" (Ein Hungerkünstler). While Anderson's characters become grotesques as a result of their choices, Kafka's implicit assertion is that the human condition is innately grotesque and that this state, as Perillo suggests, is as inescapable as it is fatal.

Using what we have learned from these two authors, we will then consider how food plays a role in the grotesquerie that is Jake Barnes and his world in Ernest Hemingway's 1926 novel *The Sun Also Rises*. In the book, the divide between gluttony and abstemiousness, between the physical acts of eating and (not) having sex, is an important narrative use of food and food spaces, ideas also intimately connected to the supposedly modern world that came to the fore with the conclusion of World War I. Again and again in the novel, Jake and those around him weave in and out of significant scenes that both confirm and challenge these important cultural signifiers of eating and not eating. In turn, these food scenes are at almost all times connected to the grotesque specter of Jake's inability to move on, both physically and psychically, from the trauma of his war wounds. The alienation that we observe in Jake is the creation of an irresoluble divide: he identifies within himself, and cannot reconcile, that which is intolerable about society as well as his place in it. He must either opt for, or be forced into, exile by his inability to conform and/or perform. Ultimately, Jake remains in stasis throughout the novel. And while he valiantly, if futilely, uses food and drink as tools to conquer, or at least dull, the pain of his injuries, like many in his so-called Lost Generation, he is simply unable to make any significant forward progress.

Sherwood Anderson's *Winesburg, Ohio*

The concept of the grotesque in literature is an old device and has been conceptualized in many forms. In *Winesburg, Ohio,* one of the first works to identify its characters as grotesques in a modern literary sense,[1] the many characters are typified, with rare exception, by their total lack of "depth or breadth, complexity or ambiguity; they are allowed no variations of action or opinion; they do not . . . grow or decline" (Howe 200). Stasis is key here, expounding more than anything else the one-dimensional caricature of a community that has come to a developmental full stop due to, as Howe further explains, "some crucial failure in their lives, some aborted effort to extend their personalities." In *Winesburg,* the characters have *become* grotesque; their "humanity has been outraged and . . . to survive in Winesburg have had to suppress their wish to love" (201). We see their decline within the text most acutely as we read through the stories; the parade of grotesque characters takes on ever more meaning as we see that these feelings of emptiness and disconnectedness begin, indeed, to connect them all, even while they do not, cannot, see this as the reader does.

Anderson's book begins with a discussion of *The Book of the Grotesque,* about one of the "great" hinted-at masterpieces of American literature that will forever be unpublished and thus unread. Of course, it's not a "real" book, but only a tome described briefly in Anderson's foreword (subtitled "The Book of the Grotesque") to *Winesburg, Ohio.* Still, we are told that it was a *real* thing by the foreword's unnamed narrator.

The supposed "proof" is that the narrator claims to have seen a manuscript of the book: "It was never published, but I saw it once and it made an indelible impression on my mind" (3). The narrator cannot shake the main idea of the book, and he attempts to explain it:

> That in the beginning when the world was young there were a great many thoughts but no such thing as a truth. Man made the truths himself and each truth was a composite of a great many vague thoughts. All about in the world were the truths and they were all beautiful.
>
> The old man had listed hundreds of the truths in his book. I will not try to tell you of all of them. There was the truth of virginity and the truth of passion, the truth of wealth and of poverty, of thrift and profligacy, of carefulness and abandon. Hundreds and hundreds were the truths and they were all beautiful.
>
> And then the people came along. Each as he appeared snatched up one of the truths and some who were quite strong snatched up a dozen of them.
>
> It was the truths that made the people grotesques. The old man had quite an elaborate theory concerning the matter. It was his notion that the moment one of the people took one of the truths to himself, called it his truth, and tried to live his life by it, he became a grotesque and the truth he embraced became a falsehood. (3–4)

This story and this understanding about the grotesque, then, acts as a frame for all the stories of the inhabitants of Winesburg that follow, some characters and stories connected directly to others, some not, but all connected thematically.

"The Book of the Grotesque" speaks to the rest of the volume in myriad ways. In it, we see an author who seeks out the stories of others. One such story grows from an exchange where *The Book of the Grotesque*'s author, who has always constructed stories with written words, employs a carpenter, who uses wood to elevate the writer's bed so that he, infirm and old, may see outside his window and to the larger world. Instead of working, the two begin talking, during which time the carpenter tells the story of himself and his brother during the Civil War, which is then related by the story's author character:

> The carpenter had once been a prisoner in Andersonville Prison and had lost a brother. The brother had died of starvation, and whenever the carpenter got upon the subject he cried. He, like the old writer, had a white moustache, and when he cried he puckered up his lips and the mustache bobbed up and down. The weeping old man with the cigar in his mouth was ludicrous. (1)

A curious and sad anecdote, loaded with details unstated and meanings unexplained, this story nevertheless impresses itself upon the story's narrator, the *Book*'s author, and the reader as being one of central import to the entire narrative of the carpenter. It is a story that hinges upon food or, rather, its absence. Death by starvation is an ugly, obscene way for a person to die, both the wasting away that occurs but also because elsewhere, usually nearby, there are other people with plenty to eat. This soldier's death, which then impacts the life of his brother forever, is all the more awful because it was a deliberate act, a choice made for and to the imprisoned soldier(s) as a kind of retribution for being on the wrong side of the Civil War. The narrator's use of the term "ludicrous" establishes the grotesqueness of the original act, its memory, and its enduring influence on the life of the carpenter and, now, the story's writer and the reader of this story.

Winesburg is not a town filled with stories of light and hope: "*Winesburg* is a book largely set in twilight and darkness, its backgrounds heavily shaded with gloomy blacks and marshy gray—as is proper for a world of withered men who, sheltered by night, reach out for that sentient life they dimly recall as the racial inheritance that has been squandered away" (Howe 200). Moving through the dark spaces of many of the stories is the town's young newspaperman, George Willard. He is obsessed with learning the stories of as many people as he can in Winesburg, even as he is determined to leave the town behind for the Big City, where, his clung-to truth grotesquely encourages him, a productive future surely lies. Despite collecting the stories of so many spent lives, or perhaps because of it, George believes that living one's entire life in a small agrarian town at the dawn of a new, more technological age affords little future for someone such as himself, someone who is determined to make what he understands to be forward progress. Howe sums up the trouble that might face the unsettled and out-of-place young Willard if he holds on to this truth too tightly: "Like most fiction, *Winesburg* is a variation on the theme of reality and appearance, in which the deformations caused by day (public life) are intensified at night and, in their very extremity, become an entry into reality."

In *Winesburg, Ohio*'s many stories, the included details from the lives of the townspeople are small yet meaningful. The Winesburgers we meet may be broken, yet, somehow, they remain ever hopeful that just around the corner lies something better, renewal or redemption. This is true also for George, whose story ends ambiguously. In the collection's penultimate story, "Sophistication," George goes to Helen White's house to, perhaps, woo her. He asks her to walk with him, and they head down to the fairgrounds. Helen is a young woman from a wealthy family who might even believe, as her mother bluntly states, that "[t]here is no one here fit to associate with a girl of Helen's breeding" (214). Helen overhears this remark and is burdened by its implications, and so she goes willingly when George comes to call in a seeming small sign of rebellion against her parents:

> In the darkness under the roof of the grand-stand, George Willard sat beside Helen White and felt very keenly his own insignificance in the scheme of existence. . . . The presence of Helen renewed and refreshed him. It was as though her woman's hand was assisting him to make some minute readjustment of the machinery of his life. . . . He had reverence for Helen. He wanted to love and to be loved by her, but he did not want at the moment to be confused by her womanhood. In the darkness he took hold of her hand and when she crept close put a hand on her shoulder. . . . In that high place in the darkness the two oddly sensitive human atoms held each other tightly and waited. In the mind of each was the same thought. "I have come to this lonely place and here is this other," was the substance of the thing felt. (216–17)

Both Helen and George are at the crossroads that young lives often face, of sexuality, of growth and development, of gender and related expectations, of career and hope for the future. Helen will stay in the small town for now, but she lives with the grotesque knowledge that her parents believe she is too good for it and for the townspeople.

In the book's final story, "Departure," we see that George, despite a deep connection with Helen, does leave, believing, even as he holds Helen in his arms, that the small town holds nothing for him. On the train out of town, George leans back and reflects:

> The young man, going out of his town to meet the adventure of life, began to think but he did not think of anything very big or dramatic. . . . The young man's mind was carried away by his growing passion for dreams. . . . Winesburg had disappeared and his life there had become but a background on which to paint the dreams of his manhood. (222)

This open-ended yet seemingly hopeful moment is tempered by several sentences that close out the book. The conductor of the train, who knew George, "made no comment," for "Tom had seen a thousand George Willards go out of their towns to the city" (221). If George has hope for his future, this is not shared by the conductor, who knows better than to think society outside of Winesburg is much different than within. Further, as George contemplates the stories of the many Winesburgers he has come to know, he thinks also of "Helen White standing by the window in the Winesburg Post Office and putting a stamp on an envelope" (222). The narrator tells us that, at this moment, "[o]ne looking at him would not have thought him particularly sharp." And so George embraces this "truth" of leaving, despite the emotional tolls that must be paid by many (himself, Helen White, his parents), because he is determined to believe that there is always something better over the horizon, and that this act is how he may best express his manhood, thereby becoming the final grotesque in the book. Ultimately, George is unwilling to consider any alternate paths for himself despite what damage his leaving may cause, as he uncritically embraces the "truth" that he must leave. Important characteristics of the grotesque are rigidity and stasis, both of which Geoffrey Harpham believes are the antithesis of "a flexible, complete human spirit" (465). Despite George's ostensible forward motion (to the big city), his choice is itself a kind of stasis of personal growth (away from a significant interpersonal relationship). Harpham posits that the "subdivisions" of the grotesque can be crudely represented in four categories: caricature; comic grotesque (ludicrous or satiric); fantastic grotesque (terrible); and, gothic-macabre (464). Of course, these demarcations are not mutually exclusive of each other, but they each "testify to a sense of inner disruption, to a self radically alienated from a dissolving social structure, an increasingly pointless world" (467), an overarching idea central to *Winesburg, Ohio,* a book that came to influence much of the literary modernist movement that followed.

Franz Kafka's "A Hunger Artist"

If Winesburg is comic grotesque, then Kafka's "A Hunger Artist" falls squarely under the gothic-macabre. The grotesque here functions as metaphor for, in Harpham's words, "confusion, chaos, insanity, loss of perspective . . . or angst. The plain assumption of the grotesque is that the rules of order have collapsed" (466). Over the course of the story, the hunger artist seems, both to his spectators and to us as readers, to defy the logical dictates of survival by subsisting without food or water, with only brief periods of exemption, for years on end. For comparison, Anderson's primary characters are effectually Kafka's background characters: unselfconscious witnesses to his protagonist's decay. The crowds of onlookers are static, base, and undesirable, representative of the worst of society while thinking they are the best of it. The nucleus of Kafka's stories, though, is not those characters who are unselfconsciously grotesque, but rather those who have, by degrees, become aware of their own innate grotesqueness. Implicitly argued here is that grotesques are born, not made—that human nature is, by definition, grotesque. "A Hunger Artist," then, operates in reverse of Anderson's structure: where his characters become grotesques through their choices and are then rendered static, Kafka's characters realize they have always been grotesque and endeavor to change, though futility fundamentally unites both visions of the grotesque. Harpham's collapsed rules of order are not indicative of a shift in the societal dynamics of their worlds, as in *Winesburg*, but rather that the disillusioned hunger artist is newly aware of the falsity of his contexts, that his individuality has been a sham.

Harpham writes that "[e]ach age redefines the grotesque in terms of what threatens its sense of essential humanity" (436), and, for the hunger artist, it is the mindless ignorance of his audience and keepers that is unacceptable. They do not understand his objective:

> [I]nitiates knew well enough that during his fast the artist would never in any circumstances, not even under forcible compulsion, swallow the smallest morsel of food; the honor of his profession forbade it. Not every watcher, of course, was capable of understanding this. . . . Nothing annoyed the artist more than such watchers; they made him miserable; they made his fast seem unendurable. (245)

The "honor" refers here to the artist's higher purpose of transcendence. He disdains his audience for their inability to recognize the absolute necessity of his fast, stating that "[a]nyone who has no feeling for it cannot be made to understand it" (254). That is, these watchers have no awareness of their own grotesqueness, and thus no sense of urgency to escape it. Later, he subtly mocks them for their decadence: at his own expense, his watchers are brought a hearty breakfast after an overnight shift, "on which they flung themselves with the keen appetite of healthy men" (245). His use of the word "healthy" is fascinating, as we know that the artist considers himself to be quite well from the way that he derides the "exaggerated caution" of his attendants, claiming that they "secretly [give] him a shake so that his legs and body tottered and swayed" (248), as if, without these measures, he would appear to be in perfect health. His description of the watchers as "healthy men," then, is deeply sarcastic: if the artist, who does not eat, is to himself the very picture of wellness, then any man who flings himself brazenly into excess—who proves by his appetite his base humanity—is profoundly inferior.

The artist fasts with the goal of undoing his humanity—not overcoming it, but negating it altogether to become something new, something free from the affliction of grotesquerie. This rebellion against human nature, against "*Sove'a* . . . the Hebrew term for eating until one is satisfied" (Crane 331), may be likened to a "redemptive processes" in which, "repelled by the physical world and . . . intent on 'cutting' himself free from it," he seeks "another purer state of being" (Satz and Ozsváth 210, 204). Satz and Ozsváth argue that the artist becomes a parody of this process, his practice of "self-denial solely for its own [*sic*] sake," a "mere purposeless feat of a circus performer" (204). In this last, Satz and Ozsváth miss the mark: quite the contrary, the artist's fast is not for "its own sake" but for *his* own sake, a matter of survival. Self-starvation becomes a defense mechanism: the artist feels he must "defend and assert himself, [as independent of human grotesquerie] or else be lost" (Sokel 40).

The artist's efforts, inevitably, only *expose* his grotesqueness to increasing degrees and offer a direct challenge to the traditions of Jewish consumption, traditions with which Kafka would have been aware: "If extreme eating—too little or too much—is meant to be both highly regulated and only occasional, how are Jews to eat during the rest of the calendar year when no special celebrations require peculiar eating practices? What is a Jewish eating ethic that applies to everyday life?" (Crane 330). Again, Harpham's grotesque rigidity: by all accounts the artist is only as adaptive as is necessary, and for the minimum amount of time. He will tolerate being paraded down to grandiose feasts at the end of his fasts despite the fact that the thought of it makes him violently nauseated (248), but only because he knows these will be "small regular intervals of recuperation," after which he returns to the safety of his unyielding cage with its straw litter and harsh light (244–45). That the artist can, after everything, consider feeding recuperative suggests, at best, the trauma of delivering oneself from an ever-judging society, and more likely that he hasn't bought into the possibility of liberation as completely as it seems at first. Indeed, any deviation from the prescription of the grotesque is so inane as to hardly be called a variant at all. Even so, he vehemently denies complicity and balks at the surrender of autonomy: "never yet, after any term of fasting—this must be granted to his credit—had he left the cage of his own free will" (246).

The hunger artist sees himself as nearing an ideal, a state of existence in which he has no mundane, human needs. He exalts himself to the reader in a monologue careful to relay puissance and surety. Yet he cannot completely mask the truth of his condition. The artist is withdrawn "deep into himself," sitting "with his ribs sticking out so prominently, not even on a seat but down among straw on the ground . . . stretching an arm through the bars so that one might feel how thin it was . . . staring into vacancy with half-shut eyes" (247). He is like a circus animal for the ghoulish pleasure of the crowd, and we have no sense of the artist possessing characteristics that would make him a whole, actualized individual. His interests, ambitions, and defining characteristics are singular, and he is so physically revolting that his fasts are limited, not for his own safety, but because experience dictates that after forty days "sympathetic support" from the spectators wanes, as they are unable to further endure the sight of the artist (247). But despite the objective horror of his physical condition, finally, the artist decides to continue with his fast, effectively sealing his fate: "When the hunger artist because of worldly indifference is freed to fast interminably, he achieves only external acknowledgement of his own isolation, and ultimately his own destruction" (Satz and Ozsváth 207). Yet, in his mind, it is a calculated thwarting of public interest in order to realize his potential as an individual. Submitting to the forty-day time limit feels like a continued bowing to the inclinations of the grotesque; winning total autonomy in his profession will, he believes, fully purge him of his impure human nature. Inauspiciously, he is permitted the continuance of his fast only if he agrees to move his cage into the menagerie, which is a decision he rationalizes easily: "his cage should be stationed, not in the middle of the ring as a main attraction, but outside, near the animal cages, on a site that was after all easily accessible" (252). He asserts that he has not "lost his sense of the real situation" (251), and that the spectators "might even have stayed longer had not those pressing behind them in the narrow gangway, who did not understand why they should be held up" (252).

The artist's understanding of grotesqueness is fully realized in this final scene, but in a moment of sweeping, tragic irony the artist finally recognizes the immutable futility of his efforts to transcend his own nature. The scene unfolds: "Only too soon—not even the most obstinate self-deception, clung to almost consciously, could hold out against the fact—the conviction was borne in upon him that these people, most of them, to judge from their actions, again and again, without exception, were all on their way to the menagerie" (252). His language is jerky and unsettled, and he withdraws completely into himself, wishing that his cage was not so near the animals, after all, because "that made it too easy for people to make their choice" (253). He is indistinguishable from the other animals, except so far as to be overlooked for those neighboring animals with more flashy characteristics, and at last he understands this. As the artist nears his end, the carnival overseer questions him, "Are you still fasting? . . . when on earth do you mean to stop?" (254–55). The artist, distraught, begs, "Forgive me, everybody," and laments that he has done nothing to be proud of, that he simply had no choice but to fast (255). The overseer cannot understand, even after the artist explains his dissatisfaction:

> "What a fellow you are," said the overseer, "and why can't you help it?"
> "Because," said the hunger artist, lifting his head a little and speaking with his lips pursed, as if for a kiss, right into the overseer's ear, so that no syllable might be lost, "because I couldn't find the food I liked. If I had found it, believe me, I should have made no fuss and stuffed myself like you or anyone else." These were his last words, but in his dimming eyes remained the firm though no longer proud persuasion that he was still continuing to fast. (255)

In the face of full, excruciating comprehension, the hunger artist knows that he would have been happier to have lived out his life in the same mindless ignorance as the other grotesques, those who have not been awakened to the truth of the human condition. In his desperation he apologizes for his derisiveness, for judging the masses when he understands now that he should have been so lucky as to escape such keen awareness of reality. His "firm . . . persuasion that he was continuing to fast" is because, of course, he can do nothing else—there is no returning to a state of ignorance, after recognition occurs. Yet he sees now that grotesqueness is insurmountable and that his herculean efforts have been totally, and inevitably, fruitless. He cannot reconcile his true nature, particularly in relation to the society that he loathes. That he ultimately achieved no ground at all in his quest for transcendence is the final blow, and so he resignedly succumbs to starvation.

Ernest Hemingway's *A Sun Also Rises*

Artists, authors, and critics alike have long been fascinated with the grotesque in art and culture because it seems at first so contradictory to the idealized purpose of the strived-for beauty and excellence that are supposedly the goals of humans at their best. But we know by now that most of the best art is created within the friction of liminal spaces, areas of discomfort and discord in which the grotesque lurks, something akin to what Virginia Woolf "saw as an artificially polarized order, by means of the defamiliarization inherent in grotesque aesthetics . . . [through which] society's foundations can be definitely eroded" (Rodríguez Salas and Andrés Cuevas 141). The grotesque, then, destabilizes the artificially perverted and reductive reality that society seeks ever to foist upon us: good and bad, beauty and ugliness, truth and ignorance, and on and on. Trying to define this state of being, Luis Puelles explains:

> Whether it is the frog who exploded while trying to look like an ox—when you are not an ox, all you can do is puff yourself up—or the vast belly of the Minister of War, bursting his belt during Chaplin's first speech in *The Great Dictator*, the grotesque begins with an accident. Such is its origin, its beginning and its very constitution: an abrupt, unwanted accident whose irremediable and painfully irreversible consequences *become* grotesque, or lead to it. (20)

While a particular instance of the grotesque, a grotesque thing, may be the unintended consequence of some other action or decision, what of an accident that is almost not an accident, and which happens repeatedly and without end throughout history, an accident laid out across time in an unceasing display of permutations and obscenities? We are speaking here about war and the unintended consequences that result from the usually intentional act of going to war. In the violence of war, many truths exist, perhaps highest among these being that humans are ready and willing to destroy and maim other humans for goals both righteous and banal, selfish and magnanimous. Humans have always used the grotesquerie of war as a tablet on which to write about the extremes in all forms of the human experience.

Hemingway encapsulates this in a way few other American writers do, from his service as an ambulance driver in World War I to his war correspondence, his novels and stories located in wars, and his various nonfiction and edited collections about war. "The editor of this anthology," Hemingway writes in the introduction to his 1942 anthology *Men at War*, "who took part and was wounded in the last war to end war, hates war and hates all the politicians whose mismanagement, gullibility, cupidity, selfishness and ambition brought on this present war and made it inevitable" (xi). Hemingway hates all the truths that those pulling the levers of society claim for their own in order to justify the grotesqueries of war. Nevertheless, he immediately follows up these caveats with the following rallying cry: "But once we have a war there is only one thing to do. It must be won. For defeat brings worse things than any that can ever happen in a war." But even in winning a war on a grand scale, of course, countless individuals on all sides will end up losing, and sticking to the we-must-win-at-all-costs mentality just ensures that more people will lose their lives and limbs. Ib Johansen argues that "the grotesque can be located at the centre of the American literary canon" and that "the grotesque rather tends to establish a situation, where the high and low change places and the material bodily lower stratum triumphs over an allegedly superior spiritual sphere (just as the stomach triumphs over the head, the id over the superego)" (13). These ideas can be applied to war as well as, if not better than, any other human realm, for, clearly, one of the most obvious places to encounter, locate, and study the grotesque is in the act of warfare.

All war is composed of examples of the monstrous and obscene, of grotesqueries piled upon indignities piled upon injustices, of those in charge maintaining their truths at the expense of people around them. Importantly, this is true even when a war is justified historically, such as when the Allied powers went to war against the Axis in World War II. But it is from the world war that preceded this one—first called the Great War, it only retroactively came to be known as World War I—in which our so-called modern age was born, and from which so many of the great authors that helped define the rest of the twentieth century had come. The Great War, a hellscape that destroyed and maimed so many bodies for so little purpose, was itself a conflagration set in motion by a series of accidents and coincidences, all stemming directly, but not only, from an at-first rather obscure assassination in southeastern Europe. While this clash of empires and nations seemed initially to arise from a past era—one of men fighting with weapons that were not so much larger or more destructive than themselves—it soon became clear that the wholesale annihilation of vast armies of men who could not in any way compete with the modern weapons of war was something new. Up-ending old systems of government and society and culture and narrative, the Great War destroyed the Victorian world once and for all, and gave rise to a world in which machines and weapons of war held sway, a world where human bodies were destroyed and maimed on a vast scale never before experienced, and new levels of bodily disgust and anomie arose.

From this horror arose a novel built around perhaps the most serious war wound that the famously virile, and famously self-promoting, Hemingway could imagine: impotence. As countless critics and uncertain undergraduate students have pointed out for years, Jake Barnes's war wound is never explicitly explained, diagnosed, or demarcated in the text. Perhaps this is because major publishers would not allow such explicitness to be published in the 1920s, and/or perhaps Hemingway was writing to his own belief of what's been called his "iceberg" theory of writing (Hemingway, *Death* 192), but at this point, if the exact physical nature of his wound is murky, the resulting impotence is well established. By way of summary for our purposes here, Elizabeth Klaver hits the key points in *The Sun Also Rises*, an excerpt that also serves to explicate the nature of the grotesque wound with which Jake must deal every minute of every day. We'll quote a longer section from Klaver in order to quickly bring us up to speed on the physical manifestations of Jake's wound:

> In the course of *The Sun Also Rises*, Hemingway never fully reveals the scope of Jake's injury, preferring instead to circle the issue. There are several key points, however, that enable an estimation of the extent and nature of the injury. One of them occurs early in the novel [see chapter 3] in the taxi with the prostitute, Georgette. When she "touches" Jake, he removes her hand, explaining that he is sick. Perhaps realizing that he has implied venereal disease, he quickly amends it to war injury. Late that evening, Jake and Brett suddenly break off some passionate kissing and touching. The sudden interruption and subsequent conversation not only point to an impotence problem, but again indicate a physical injury. Jake's line, "there's not a damn thing we could do," suggests that his problem is beyond the capacity of the talking cure or even the technological devices such as the vacuum pump which were available at the time. Later that night, as Jake is undressing for bed, he catches a glimpse of his body in the mirror, and thinks wryly "[o]f all the ways he was wounded." He reveals that the injury occurred on the Italian front, and that, while recovering in the hospital, an Italian colonel made a sentimental speech about "hav[ing] given more than your life," a remark that is usually interpreted as referring to his "manhood." (90)

Considering these scenes, it is easy to return to them in the book and find more that is relevant to our thesis. The scene with the prostitute, for instance, begins before she and Jake board the horse-drawn taxi. In fact, the chapter begins with Jake sitting "at a table on the terrace of the Napolitain" (22). Robert Cohn has left, and Jake sits alone watching street life, as one does in Paris. He studies the "*poules* going by, singly and in pairs, looking for the evening meal" (italics in original). Literally, *poules* means "hens" in French, but the *OED* tells us the word, indeed borrowed from French, is from the longer *poule de luxe,* slang meaning "A girl or young woman, *esp.* a promiscuous one," and "a prostitute, a call girl." The first written instance of the word being used in this way is, interestingly, from a Hemingway letter, dated 1924, in which he wrote the following: "The plage [beach] and the poules at San Sebastián [Spain] are both great." This was two years before *The Sun Also Rises* was published, though Hemingway wrote the book in the summer of 1925, while he was back and forth between Paris and the Basque Country in Spain (Meyers 189). Clearly, the situation in which Jake finds himself was long on the author's mind.

Hemingway's use of the "the evening meal" here is perhaps not what it first seems, and we learn more after Georgette walks by repeatedly, catches Jake's eye, and sits down at his table. In Paris, as in many places in Europe, you can sit at a restaurant table for hours if you desire; the table becomes yours for as long as you want it, and the server will leave you to it. But, ever watchful in case you might want something, the server is likely to reappear when needed, as happens here. As soon as Georgette sits down, the waiter appears, awaiting an order. A conversation ensues between Jake and the woman, the waiter patiently waiting, no doubt fully aware that a prostitute has just sat down with one of his customers. There is no mention of scorn or derision on the waiter's behalf, just one worker ready to serve another, and, besides, there is clearly a paying customer involved in the equation. This transaction is, ultimately, the same one on which all commerce is based: goods and/or services are provided in exchange for money. The conversation:

> "Well, what will you drink?" I asked.
> "Pernod."
> "That's not good for little girls."
> "Little girl yourself. Dites garçon, un pernod."
> "A pernod for me, too."
> "What's the matter?" she asked. "Going on a party?"
> "Sure. Aren't you?"
> "I don't know. You never know in this town."
> "Don't you like Paris?"
> "No."
> "Why don't you go somewhere else?"
> "Isn't anywhere else."
> "You're happy, all right."
> "Happy, hell!"

Pernod is greenish imitation absinthe. When you add water it turns milky. It tastes like licorice and it has a good uplift, but it drops you just as far. We sat and drank it, and the girl looked sullen.

"Well," I said, "are you going to buy me dinner?" (22–23)

At this point, and significantly *without* ordering dinner, they leave the table and catch the taxi, which leads to an interrupted—or, really, not even begun—sexual encounter between Jake and Georgette.

But, why? Why does Jake get into the taxi with Georgette? What is his goal, his plan? He knows both that she is a prostitute and that he is unable to consummate a sexual encounter because of his war wound. He knows, too, that prostitutes, like all working people, work for money that buys, among other things, food. Clearly, Jake desires companionship, but why do they not stay for dinner, an experience that would probably be welcomed by Georgette, even if the act of companionship, as well as the meal, must also be paid for? Just eating a meal together would not lead to the awkward exchange they have in the taxi. And why, just before they leave the restaurant, is it Jake who asks Georgette if she is going to be the one to buy him dinner? This appears to be quite the reversal of what Jake should expect in such a situation, if, that is, dinner means dinner.

There are immense cultural power structures at work here in this simple exchange between Jake and Georgette, consumer and provider of services, and yet Jake seems to be doing his best to reverse the traditional roles of such a transaction. He has money yet asks for dinner from the prostitute, though a meal of food is not what he is after. Is he referring to sex as dinner? But why ask if it is she who will make the purchase for him, as Jake cannot use the would-be purchased item because of his infirmity? "The body," Lorna Piatti-Farnell writes, "occupies a privileged position to any representation of food in its relations to power. Nonetheless, the ways in which the consuming body interacts with hierarchical systems are multiple. Food articulates the corporeal side of existence—the body that turns food into nourishment—with distinct formations of race, class, and gender" (150). Jake's deliberate conflating of dinner and sex is, then, perhaps a way of clinging to the consumption of something—food—that is still consumable and thus not traumatic for him, when sex—in a traditional heteronormative capacity—is no longer available.

As chapter 4 begins, we encounter another taxi ride. Jake and Brett are in a taxi, "lips tight together" (33), when she pulls away from his embrace:

"Don't touch me," she said. "Please don't touch me."

"What's the matter?"

"I can't stand it."

"Oh, Brett."

"You mustn't. You must know. I can't stand it, that's all. Oh, darling, please understand!" (33–34)

Jake does know but wants to avoid the reality of the situation. Brett looks at him in a way that no one else in the world looks at him, with love and understanding and with the frustration that comes with knowing such feelings cannot be fully satisfied in a way that both of them want. Jake then admits as much, acknowledges that his damaged body is the greatest impediment to their attempts at forming a more perfect union: "'And there's not a damn thing we could do,' I said" (34). For her part, Brett thinks that Jake's inability to perform is some grotesque retribution from the universe: "When I think of the hell I've put chaps through. I'm paying for it all now." She throws this possible reason out as something of an aside, but she is serious about how she feels toward her past actions, even if, whatever they were, we would today want her to be more forgiving of herself. But Jake appears to be less than honest as seen in his immediate retort, and Brett's counter:

"Don't talk like a fool," I said. "Besides, what happened to me is supposed to be funny. I never think about it."

"Oh, no. I'll lay you don't."

"Well, let's shut up about it."

"I laughed about it too, myself, once." She wasn't looking at me. "A friend of my brother's came home that way from Mons. It seemed like a hell of a joke. Chaps never know anything, do they?"

Jake and Brett approach the grotesque humor of the situation in different ways. This is a humor that is not in any way funny except in the way that tragedy can sometimes be absurdly ridiculous, and when laughter is a kind of survival against harsh reality. Jake claims his impotence is supposed to be funny and that he never thinks about it, which we see again and again is a lie. Brett once laughed off the idea when hearing about such a war trauma that didn't seem to affect her directly, but now, with Jake, she believes the joke is over. Crucially, she is herself now a part of this farce (hoping against reason that things were as they are not) and thus implicated in its grotesqueness.

Jake rushes to the end of the conversation with Brett, even as he knows that nothing is solved and his, and their, stasis remains:

> "No," I said. "Nobody ever knows anything."
>
> I was pretty well through with the subject. At one time or another I had probably considered it from most of its various angles, including the one that certain injuries or imperfections are a subject of merriment while remaining quite serious for the person possessing them.
>
> "It's funny," I said. "It's very funny. And it's a lot of fun, too, to be in love."
>
> "Do you think so?" Her eyes looked flat again.
>
> "I don't mean fun that way. In a way it's an enjoyable feeling."
>
> "No," she said. "I think it's hell on earth." (35)

Shortly thereafter, we have the scene when Jake is alone in his room undressing. Lying in bed, he revisits the scenes surrounding his trauma.

Throughout the novel, food (or the idea of food, the discussion of food) is used as a substitute for resolving Jake's sense of alienation. Food fills gaps. Food is a default when conversations halt and ideas clash or just as a fallback when there is nothing else to suggest to do, and there are many instances throughout the novel of this occurring. For instance, upon returning to his hotel, Jake runs into Robert Cohn, who ambushes him:

> "Hello, Jake," he said. "Going out to lunch?"
>
> "Yes. Let me see if there is anything new."
>
> "Where will we eat?"
>
> "Anywhere."
>
> I was looking over my desk. "Where do you want to eat?" (45)

Cohn is grilling Jake about Brett and not liking Jake's answers, what Cohn calls "bitter" talk (46). Everyone is in love with Brett, but Jake believes, as does just about everyone else even if it might only be true for Jake and *because* of his wound, that he has some sort of special dispensation over/with her, and he resents rivals grilling him for information on her. He resents this most of all because he is not able to perform sexually, and yet he hopes against hope that this will not matter in the end, even though he knows better.

Jake appears to display his anti-Semitism when interacting with Cohn, but where does this grotesque line end? Wolfgang Rudat argues that though Jake is not Hemingway, Jake's apparent anti-Semitism "is too complex to be attributed to the narrator alone" (264). Further, Rudat explores the ambiguities in the text by alleging that "Hemingway is satirizing his narrator for racism in the satirical remarks about Robert Cohn, and thus presenting his narrator as a 'Satirist Satirized'" (264). At the very least, Jake responds acerbically to Cohn for what might be multiple reasons, including anti-Semitism, but probably also due to resentment of everyone's attraction to Brett and his own inability to act on his love for her. Cohn calls out Jake on the nature of his responses:

> "You say such damned insulting things, Jake."
> "I'm sorry. I've got a nasty tongue. I never mean it when I say nasty things."
> "I know it," Cohn said. "You're really about the best friend I have, Jake."
> God help you, I thought. "Forget what I said," I said out loud. "I'm sorry."
> "It's all right. It's fine. I was just sore for a minute."
> "Good. Let's get something else to eat." (47)

Again, they default to food, and it is this stilted communion at the table, again and again, that is a replacement for solving the obvious problems.

Tellingly, the absence of food, too, is an important indicator of greater problems avoided, especially when food is replaced with alcohol. After his meal with Cohn, Jake sees Harvey Stone (who might also be Jewish) at the Select, outside and alone and sitting morosely, with a "pile of saucers in front of him, and . . . need[ing] a shave" (49). "Do you want to know something, Jake?" Harvey asks. "Yes," Jake answers. "I haven't had anything to eat in five days," Stone admits. For Stone, there is an obvious connection between a lack of sustenance and the depressed state in which he now finds himself.

In part because of his relationship with Lady Brett, Jake is constantly sought out by the other men in her sphere. As a result, Jake plays the part of the savior or martyr; the line between such roles is often blurred. Jake is the wise one, the one with the clear thinking, the one who can help others. Seeing Harvey down and out, he gives him money and cajoles him into seeking food:

> "Would a hundred help you any, Harvey?"
> "Yes."
> "Come on. Let's go and eat."
> "There's no hurry. Have a drink."
> "Better eat."
> "No. When I get like this I don't care whether I eat or not." (50)

Calling to mind the Hunger Artist, Harvey's disgust with his present circumstances expresses itself through the desire to avoid food in order to punish his corporeal reality, to seek out the dissolution of the self, if only for a short time. While Jake eats and drinks to forget his problems, Harvey starves, the better to contemplate his own.

Related examples come fast and furiously. When Frances complains to Jake about Robert Cohn not wanting to marry her and wanting instead to return to New York so that when his book comes out all the little "chickens" (interesting term, given Jake's earlier use of "*poule*") can flutter around him, Jake says the requisite "It's a rotten shame" (55), to which she responds by saying that "there's no use talking about it. . . . Come on, let's go back to the café."

Later, Brett, Jake, and Count Mippipopolous (the latter being one more person who is in love with Brett) consider what to do next:

> "We'll want to ride out to the Bois for dinner?"
> "If you like," Brett said. "I couldn't eat a thing."
> "I always like a good meal," said the count. (64)

Later that evening, amidst a nice party and food, the count asks Jake and Lady Brett why they do not get married, and they offer only deferential banalities in response. Jake says, "We want to lead our own lives" (68); Brett immediately follows with, "We have our careers," before pleading to "get out of this." The avoidance drags on.

Significantly, as the book concludes, an updated version of the repeated taxi scene plays itself out again, showing for the last time Jake's lack of substantive forward movement. He ends the book partially where he begins, physically still emasculated, yet psychologically his trauma is even more acute, more real, as, having come so far in his own story of futility, he seems to realize with a kind of finality the interminability of his wounded condition.

The end—the very last line, in fact—of *The Sun Also Rises* is famous beyond the text itself. We have all probably heard the line quoted in various contexts, often, perhaps, without the speaker even being aware of the line's origin. If you've made it this far, then you, dear reader, probably already know it before we quote it here. This time Jake is not in a Parisian taxi with a *poule* but in a Madrileño (i.e., in Madrid, Spain) taxi with, once again, Brett. Everything and nothing has changed. Jake is still unable to perform as he wishes to, an inescapable burden that is always glaringly obvious, and therefore remains in a kind of life stasis, unable to move beyond his war wound. Despite so many conversations and (non-) events happening throughout the course of the book, Jake's every dream remains thwarted:

> The driver started up the street. I settled back. Brett moved close to me. We sat close against each other. I put my arm around her and she rested against me comfortably. It was very hot and bright, and the houses looked sharply white. We turned out onto the Gran Via.
>
> "Oh, Jake," Brett said, "we could have had such a damned good time together."
>
> Ahead was a mounted policeman in khaki directing traffic. He raised his baton. The car slowed suddenly pressing Brett against me.
>
> "Yes," I said. "Isn't it pretty to think so?" (251)

Much is clear and much is not from this open-ended ending. Their bodies fit together naturally, and they appear to be relaxed with each other, if only for a moment. But reminders of what could be, and what is not, are always close at hand. It was Madrid-in-the-summer hot, with the sun so blinding that one would need to squint at reality. At first, the taxi seems perhaps to be a refuge, but as they turn onto Madrid's most famous street, the Gran Vía, the great way of Jake's trauma and life after war cannot be avoided. As if all of this wasn't enough, the penultimate paragraph gives us an image of exactly what Jake can no longer do: raise his "baton." And, then, the final line, stated with a clarity and finality that needs nothing after it.

And yet, if we return to the pages just preceding this ending, we find Jake attempting to take solace in food and drink, even as there are hints present indicating that Jake knows the jig is up. Jake had retreated to San Sebastián in the Spanish Basque Country to recover from the endless partying at the fiesta, the excessive drinking, and the relationship drama that played out amongst the main characters. After this refractory period, Jake intends to return to Paris but is called to Madrid by Lady Brett, who is now alone and seeking solace after the dissolution of her short relationship with the young and no doubt virile matador, Romero.

Perhaps the most grotesque aspect of the entire story is that a war-wounded body need not also be seen as grotesque, except insofar as society decides that it is grotesque. This perspective is a collective choice, though one certainly defaulted to by most people throughout most of history. There are infamous stories of Joseph Stalin shipping out grievously injured World War II vets to distant locations (that is, away from

Moscow and Leningrad) because he didn't want their broken bodies seen publicly in a recovering Russia. Ultimately, society is grotesque, and thus humanity is grotesque. Jake was comfortable enough, we can assume, as a member of that society until his wound alienated him from it. Now, unlike George Willard and like Kafka's protagonist, Jake is aware of his grotesqueness and, as such, cannot rejoin society. George hungers futilely for a bigger, more promising society; the hunger artist does not even try; but, Jake *wants* to be reintegrated. While the hunger artist starves to ensure his own alienation, Jake eats to maintain his positioning within, his place in, the social milieu—or, at least, to pretend that this is possible.

Willard believes that liberation from the grotesque, as he understands it, means leaving Winesburg society, even if nothing but more grotesque humanity awaits him (as the conductor knows) in the big city. How could this possibly be better? George does not allow himself to consider it critically, even as the truth he has embraced for himself is that he is the most enlightened citizen of Winesburg. By contrast, Jake's final approach in the novel is to continue to try not to know what he already knows. He has not succeeded, cannot, but he *wants* to not think about it, he wants to be done talking about it. Brett also stops herself from discussing the problem—she doesn't want to know that she is a grotesque, either. So, Jake eats, participates in the same sort of shared meals so derided by the hunger artist as the ultimate expression of grotesqueness—of humanness—and with every meal he reestablishes his membership in a grotesque society of avoidance and overindulgence, the same society that has determined his body is grotesque, and with which, sadly, he agrees.

Human nature is inalienable, these stories tell us. The bastardization of appetite, the isolation, the absolute futility of efforts to overcome human nature all indicate that humanity is grotesque innately, a fate so foul and inhibiting that those few self-aware enough to uncover the truth of the human condition are violently divorced from all by which they had identified themselves, left without recourse to struggle in vain to escape the fundamentally inescapable, both incapable of progressing beyond the limitations of human nature and unable to return to a state of ignorance. As the hunger artist starves himself to death, there can be, ultimately, no satisfying conclusion for Jake or Brett in *The Sun Also Rises*, and the inadequacy of the choice to cease struggling against the grotesque is as much a nepenthe as it is a damnation.

NOTE

1. Ray Lewis Wright writes, "There is no certainty where Anderson found the word grotesque to describe the figures in the mind of the old writer; perhaps the word came from Edgar Allan Poe's 1840 *Tales of the Grotesque and Arabesque*, or perhaps from discussions about art among Anderson's Chicago Renaissance friends" (Anderson 22).

WORKS CITED

Anderson, Sherwood. *Sherwood Anderson's Winesburg, Ohio: With Variant Readings and Annotations*. Edited by Ray Lewis White, Ohio University Press, 1997.

Anesko, Michael. "The Torments of Spring: Jake Barnes's Phantom Limb in *The Sun Also Rises*." *Literature and Medicine*, vol. 33, no. 1, 2015, pp. 52–69.

Conway, Juliet. "'To Hell with Women Anyway': Flirtatiousness and Male Entitlement in Hemingway's *The Sun Also Rises*." *Hemingway Review*, vol. 40, no. 2, 2021, pp. 23–38.

Crane, Jonathan K. "A Satisfying Eating Ethic." *Fasting and Feasting: The History of Ethics and Jewish Food*, edited by Aaron S. Gross, Jody Myers, and Jordan D. Rosenblum, New York University Press, 2019, pp. 330–38.

Goody, Alex. *Modernist Articulations: A Cultural Study of Djuna Barnes, Mina Loy and Gertrude Stein*. Palgrave Macmillan, 2007.

Harpham, Geoffrey. "The Grotesque: First Principles." *Journal of Aesthetics and Art Criticism*, vol. 34, no. 4, 1976, pp. 461–68.

Hemingway, Ernest. *Death in the Afternoon*. Scribner, 2002.

———. "Introduction." *Men at War*, edited by Ernest Hemingway, Crown, 1942, pp. xi–xxxi.

———. *The Sun Also Rises*. Scribner, 2006.

Howe, Irving. "The Book of the Grotesque." *The Grotesque*, edited by Harold Bloom, Bloom's Literary Criticism, 2009, pp. 188–207.

Johansen, Ib. *Walking Shadows: Reflections on the American Fantastic and the American Grotesque from Washington Irving to the Postmodern Era*. Brill Rodopi, 2015.

Kafka, Franz. "A Hunger Artist." *The Story and Its Writer: An Introduction to Short Fiction*, edited by Ann Charters, 10th ed., Bedford/St. Martin's, 2019, pp. 450–57.

Klaver, Elizabeth. "Erectile Dysfunction and the Post War Novel: *The Sun Also Rises* and *In Country*." *Literature and Medicine*, vol. 30, no. 1, 2012, pp. 86–102.

Meyers, Jeffrey. *Hemingway: A Biography*. Macmillan, 1985.

Ngai, Sianne. *Ugly Feelings*. Harvard University Press, 2005.

Piatti-Farnell, Lorna. *Food and Culture in Contemporary American Fiction*. Routledge, 2011.

"Poule." *Oxford English Dictionary Online*. www-oed-com.stmartin.idm.oclc.org/view/ Entry/148987. Accessed August 24, 2022.

Puelles, Luis. "Nothing under One's Feet: Approaches to an Aesthetic of the Grotesque." *The Grotesque Factor*, Museo Picasso Málaga, 2012.

Rodríguez Salas, Gerardo, and Isabel María Andrés Cuevas. "'My Insides Are All Twisted Up': When Distortion and the Grotesque become 'the Same Job' in Katherine Mansfield and Virginia Woolf." *Katherine Mansfield and Literary Modernism*, edited by J. Wilson et al., Bloomsbury, 2022, pp. 139–48.

Rudat, Wolfgang E. "Anti-Semitism in 'The Sun Also Rises': Traumas, Jealousies, and the Genesis of Cohn." *American Imago*, vol. 49, no. 2, 1992, pp. 263–75.

Sanchez, Rebecca. "Shattering Communicative Norms: The Politics of Embodied Language in *Winesburg, Ohio*." *Modern Language Studies*, vol. 43, no. 2, 2014, pp. 24–39.

Satz, Martha, and Zsuzsanna Ozsváth. "'A Huger Artist' and 'In the Penal Colony' in the

Light of Schopenhauerian Metaphysics." *German Studies Review*, vol. 1, no. 2, 1978, pp. 200–210.

Sokel, Walter H. "Beyond Self-Assertion: A Life of Reading Kafka." *A Companion to the Works of Franz Kafka*, edited by James Rolleston, Boydell & Brewer, 2002, pp. 33–59.

Von Cannon, Michael. "Traumatizing Arcadia: Postwar Pastoral in *The Sun Also Rises*." *Hemingway Review*, vol. 32, no. 1, 2012, pp. 57–71.

Southern Comfort in the Age of Jim Crow

Representing Soul Food in Ralph Ellison's *Juneteenth* and Beyond

ANTON L. SMITH

Defining the relationships among food, spirituality, representation, and identity has been a formidable but necessary undertaking in African American literature. Exploring such connections involves reconfiguring traditional boundaries, specifically those related to America's reductive notions about the consumption patterns and religious beliefs of African Americans. Arguably, soul food—which derives from the historical circumstances African Americans experienced during slavery—involves more than the pleasure of eating and feeding. African Americans use soul food as an essential tool to trace their "roots" and forge communal ties.

Soul food emerged as a culinary practice in the United States in the context of a society that historically devalued African American humanity, experience, and intellectual abilities. In two sermons from Ralph Ellison's second novel, *Juneteenth* (1999), the preachers embrace soul food to salve their congregations by inspiring them to remember the fevers and deaths of the Middle Passage, recall the subsequent destruction of African language and culture, yet also celebrate the acquisition of a new identity that would incorporate these elements of their shared history. In doing so, Ellison represents soul food as a form of southern comfort and cultural resistance. Through this culinary practice, Ellison illustrates how African Americans creatively took care of their souls while they combatted discrimination and second-class citizenship. Although Ellison was unsparing in his depiction of African American subjugation, he believed that African Americans could persevere, even thrive, in spite of racism and inequality. From Ellison's point of view, African Americans had a rich culture that deserved recognition, admiration, respect, and, above all, remembrance. Soul food distilled African American culture and experience into a shared cuisine that was emblematic of their past. Ellison uses it to show that without soul food, African Americans would not be who they are today.

Soul Food:
Some Origins and History

With respect to soul food, do Black folks eat to live or live to eat? The answer to this question depends primarily on both historical and cultural contexts. Scholars contend that the cuisine that Black folks consumed revealed the intricate process by which they preserved their body, mind, spirit, and identity in the face of adversity. Upon coming to the new world, people of African descent did not arrive empty-handed. Contrary to popular belief, they struggled to hold on to their African cultures and their souls through the foods they prepared in an attempt to adapt to the challenging conditions of the Americas.

The saga of soul food is one of affirmation, resistance, and resilience. Looking back from the twenty-first century, Kimberly D. Nettles offers some intriguing insights on the origins of soul food. Nettles observes that

> Contemporary memories of soul food or black southern cuisine are linked to notions of family, love, and community—to the idea that black people, struggling under the yoke of slavery, and the post-slavery experiences of sharecropping, Jim Crow racism, migration North, and more contemporary forms of discrimination could at least rely on the comforts of the traditional foods that solidified their relationships with one another in the face of adversity. (Nettles 108)

The meat used was usually the least desirable cuts, and the vegetables, some bordering on weeds, were all that was available for Black slaves to prepare nutritious meals for their families during the colonial era. In the southern states, African slaves began to cook with new kinds of greens (collards, mustard, and kale), turnips, beets, and even dandelions. Slaves were also given pigs' feet, beef tongue, ham hocks, chitterlings, pig ears, and tripe to cook with, as they were considered the unwanted meat products of the pig and cow. To flavor their recipes, Blacks added garlic, thyme, onions, and bay leaves. Early soul food recipes also included wild game, such as rabbit, and raccoon that slaves caught on their own (Burns). From these meager ingredients evolved a cuisine that was simple yet hearty and delicious.

For Blacks living in pre-twentieth-century America, subsistence eating was the norm. Striking a balance between physical health and emotional well-being was no easy task. This challenge continued on into the new century. Laretta Henderson acknowledges the cultural and historical trajectory of soul food promoted by Nettles but adds a class dimension:

> In its culinary incarnation, "soul food" was associated with a shared history of oppression and inculcated, by some, with cultural pride. Soul food was eaten by the bondsmen. It was also the food former slaves incorporated into their diet after emancipation. Therefore, during the 1960s, middle-class blacks used their reported consumption of soul food to distance themselves from the values of the white middle class, to define themselves ethnically, and to align themselves with lower-class blacks. Irrespective of political affiliation or social class, the definition of "blackness," or "soul," became part of everyday discourse in the black community. (81–82)

The consumption of soul food, as suggested by Henderson, involved a solidarity that transcended both racial and class difference.

In some intellectual circles, the development of soul food provided an outlet for community building that combined nationalism with aesthetics. Drawing on the scholarship of Stephan Palmié and Jessica Harris, Jennifer Jensen Wallach argues that Black aesthetics were supportive of separatist politics and a Black nationalist ideology:

> In the aftermath of the civil rights movement many activists used food habits to reimagine their relationship to the U.S. nation-state. They embraced what Stephan Palmié has labeled "culinary identity politics" where "black collective selfhood" became rooted in a matrix of particular food practices. Jessica Harris claims that "eating neckbones and chitterlings, turnip greens and fried chicken, became a political statement" in the late 1960s. (qtd. in Wallach)

Furthermore, rebelling against the mainstream society by being essentially anti-white, anti-American, and anti-middle class, artists such as Amiri Baraka (also known as Leroi Jones) viewed soul food as expression of Black art. For Baraka, there was something identifiably Black about African American–derived creations like soul food. His insistence on the projection that this cuisine was a tool to fight racism and advance racial pride was a core tenet of his belief in the need for cultural autonomy.

In essence, food is not simply for food's sake but for claiming social and political identity. Soul food represents a poignant pathway for framing affirmation to, or alienation from, one's place in our society. According to Sheylah Brown, in 1962 Baraka ("Soul Food") observed: "Recently, a young Negro novelist writing in *Esquire* about the beauties of America mentioned that one of the things wrong with Negroes was that, unlike the Chinese, Black people have neither a language of their own nor a characteristic cuisine. And this to me is the deepest stroke, the unkindest cut, of oppression, especially as it has distorted Black Americans. . . . There are hundreds of tiny restaurants, food shops, rib joints, shrimp shacks, chicken shacks, 'rotisseries' throughout Harlem that serve soul food" (qtd. in Brown). Here Baraka positions soul food as the center of cultural understanding and transmission. From Baraka's point of view, it is insulting to dismiss the presence of soul food in the life of Black folks. More precisely, such a "cut" only compounds the marginalization of Afro-Americans. He passionately defends soul food as a traditional cuisine that deserves recognition, admiration, and respect.

Juneteenth and Soul Food

Juneteenth centers on two characters: a racist white U.S. senator, Adam Sunraider, who is fatally shot on the Senate floor sometime in the 1950s, and an older African American minister, Rev. Alonzo Z. "Daddy" Hickman, who, we learn, raised the future senator as a boy preacher, Bliss, in his congregation. The protagonist Bliss (as Senator Sunraider, his older alter ego) struggles with his identity—as a man caught between his African American and his Caucasian backgrounds. Reverend Hickman travels to Washington, D.C., with some of his parishioners to foil an assassination attempt on his adopted son, Sunraider/Bliss. No one pays Hickman or his parishioners any heed, until the gravely wounded senator is taken to the hospital and requests that Hickman be allowed to come to his hospital room. There, Hickman and the senator work together to reconstruct their past. Through their recollections, readers can piece together the events of their story.

To the reverend, soul food was not just food such as ham hocks and collard greens traditionally eaten by southern U.S. Black people. Rather, Hickman's meditation on soul food and the survival of African American culture during the Juneteenth celebrations incorporates the principles Baraka, and others, have raised about the African American experience and cultural authenticity. Consider the following excerpt taken from one of Hickman's Juneteenth sermons that situates soul food as an integral part of the religious experience of Black Americans:

> We learned that all blessings come mixed with sorrow and all hardships have a streak of laughter. Life is a streak-a-lean—a streak-a-fat. Ha, yes! We learned to bounce back and to disregard the prizes of fools. And we must keep on learning. Let them have their fun. Even let them eat hummingbirds' wings and tell you it's too good for you.—Grits and greens don't turn to ashes in anybody's mouth—how about it, Rev. Eatmore? Amen? Amen! Let everybody say amen. Grits and greens are humble but they make you strong and when the right folks get together to share they can taste like ambrosia. So draw, so let us draw our own wells of strength. (Ellison 129)

From Hickman's perspective, soul food placed Black people in touch with themselves and their culture. Hickman reminds his audience that African Americans struggled day to day to make it in the New World. Good food, as history tells us, was hard for Black Americans to secure; indeed, any food was not easy to secure at times. When Hickman says, "Life is a streak-a-lean, a streak-a-fat" and "We learned to bounce back and to disregard the prizes of fools," he re-creates through metaphor the cuisine developed by Africans, a cuisine fashioned from the meager ingredients available to the slave and sharecropper Black families. Moreover, colorful phrases such as "sorrow and hardship have a streak of laughter" and "Ha, yes!" poignantly capture the spiritual humor as well as signify the resilience and strength of Black folks. Grits and greens were humbling because such food may seem to offer scant nutritional appeal, but in fact these items kept the stomachs of Blacks full so they would not starve and die. Spiritual laughter enables people to experience the word of God and have fun while doing it. Through Hickman and preachers like him, Ellison implies that a healthy part of stepping out on faith includes laughing out loud. Furthermore, Hickman suggests grits and greens were not only sources of energy for the body but also fuel for regenerating and preserving Black folks' culture and souls. Just as ambrosia conferred immortality to Greek and Roman gods, grits and greens conferred immortality to the Black community of the United States (Kelly). Hickman celebrates the faith of African Americans that permits them to take a bad situation and transform it into something positive and edifying. In a sense, Ellison implies that the consumption of grits by African Americans parallels the grit, or indomitable spirit, of the Black family and the Black community.

A few pages later in the narrative, Hickman continued to express his zeal for soul food in a discussion regarding the festivities of the June-teenth Day festival:

> Lord, we et up to fifteen hundred loaves of sandwich bread; five hundred pounds of catfish and snapper; fifteen gallons of hot sauce, Mr. Double-Jointed Jackson's formula; nine hundred pounds of barbecue ribs; eighty-five hams, direct from Virginia; fifty pounds of potato salad and a whole big cabbage patch of coleslaw. Yes, and enough frying-size chicken to feed the multitude! And let's not mention the butter beans—naw! And don't talk about the fresh young roasting-ears and the watermelons. Neither the fried pies, chocolate cakes and homemade ice cream . . . (Ellison 133)

Indeed, Hickman truly believes that there is an intimate relationship between soul food, the body, and the spirit as they relate to the well-being of African Americans. This passage illustrates that the church is not the only place that Black people attend to nourish their spirit and reinvigorate their soul. While soul food serves as an intricate part of the fellowship of some Black parishes, its consumption outside of the Black church is just as important as it fulfills the same function. Ellison shows that Black people do not necessarily have to go to church to know their God and express their spirituality. The sharing of soul food demonstrates the resolution and fortitude of African Americans to forge communal ties, with or without the facilitation of the Black church. In describing the communal aspect of soul food, Hickman states, "I'm not just talking about eating. I mean the *communion,* the coming together—of which the eating was only a part; an outward manifestation, a symbol, like the Blood is signified by the wine, and the Flesh by the bread. . . Ah yes, boy, we filled their bellies, but we were really there to fill their souls and give them reassurance—and we *filled* them" (Ellison 133). Without specific reference in Ellison's novel, it is easy to see by extension that in biblical times, meals meant more than just eating food: they were important in Jewish life, and in Jesus's ministry as a celebration of God's sustenance and saving presence (Mark 2.18–20; Mark 6.31–44; Mark 8.1–10; Luke 7.31–35). Meals were also seen as a tangible demonstration of God's acceptance of and reconciliation with humankind, and they signified a foretaste of the abundant blessings that communion with God would one day yield. In particular, the Last Supper is an occasion when the Christian church remembers how the risen Jesus broke bread with his disciples (Luke 24.30–31), and how the Church "feeds" on him by faith and so has communion with Jesus. Hickman's use of food symbolism in *Juneteenth* is simply Ellison's way of inserting Black American cuisine into this well-known history of religious allusions to the inextricable ties between feeding the body and feeding the soul.

The theme regarding the relationship between soul food, the image of man, and God reemerges as Bliss, the protagonist of the novel, preaches in the manner of Reverend Eatmore, a fiery traveling preacher. Bliss improvises on Eatmore's delivery and shows that creation in the Bible means more than bringing something into being; it portrays humanity as a reflection of God. Human beings are created in God's image, and they share, in a finite and imperfect way, the communicable attributes of God. Among these attributes are personality, spirituality (John 4.24), rationality, including knowledge and wisdom (Colossians 3.10), and morality, including goodness, holiness, righteousness, love, justice, and mercy (Ephesians 4.24). These attributes in turn give human beings the capacity to enjoy fellowship with God and to develop personal relationships with one another. In the following passage, Bliss gives a sermon on the power of God's images as it relates to the development of African American spiritual sensibilities:

> For although in his pride, Man had sacrificed whole generations of forests and beasts and birds, and though in the terror of his pride he had raised himself up a few inches higher than the animals, he was moved, despite himself he was moved a bit closer, I say to the image of what God intended him to be. Yes. And though no savior in heathen form had yet come to redeem him, God in His infinite mercy looked down upon His handiwork, looked down at the clouds of smoke, looked down upon the charred vegetation, looked down at the fire-shrunk seas with all that broiled fish, looked down at the bleached bones piled past where Man had fled, looked down upon all that sizzling meat and natural gravy, parched barley, boiled roasting-ears and mustard greens. . . . Yes, He looked down and said, Even so, My work is good. . . . Yes, it will take him a few billion years before he'll discover pork chops and perhaps two more for fried chicken. It will take him time and much effort to learn the taste of roast beef and baked yams and those apples he shall name Mack and Tosh. (Ellison 139–40)

The rhythm and structure of Bliss's sermon reflects an African American interpretation of Genesis and God's creation of the world. By referencing soul food (i.e., pork chops, fried chicken, roast beef, and yams), Bliss not only humanizes Black people but also celebrates their sense of humor. Drawing upon the talent of Reverend Eatmore, an itinerant preacher who "was a joke to some but a smart wordsman just the same" and "knew the fundamental fact, that you must speak to the gut as well as to the heart and brain," Bliss shows that people of African descent are indeed civilized and can think on their own and create amazing things (Ellison 140).

Preaching is no task for the timid or the faint of heart. Consider what a preacher affirms when he comes to his or her pulpit to preach. Preaching with all its variations ultimately rests upon the claim that preachers can know what God is and what a man or woman may become. The preacher claims to know the will and word of God and to proclaim it in relation to the options and situations of his time.

The preached word is the heard word, and each hears with his own experience. The preacher must consider that he is engaged not in monologue but in a conversation. At points in his preaching, his sermon needs to reflect the reaction of those to whom he is preaching. This is an important part of the sensitivity of the preacher. He must show that he knows the hearer as well as the word. Not only must he be aware of God's disclosure, but he must also be sensitive to the acceptances and resistances that are in the listener. So, the worshiper must feel that in the preacher he (or she, as the first case indicates) too has a voice. He or she should feel an active part of the conversation, a subject acting, not an object acted upon (Smitherman 211).

Part of a preacher's function is to find words that will convey the essential truth to those who are outside looking in. In a sense the preacher is not unlike the translator who must take the original language and restate the truth in a way that will be understood by the people. Obviously, without words preachers would not be able to impart the word of God and acknowledge his presence. Linguist and educational activist Geneva Smitherman observes in *Talkin That Talk*, "When the preacher is 'taking his text' a hushed silence falls over the whole congregation, and it is most out of order to get up, move around in your seat, talk, or do anything until he finishes this brief ritual in the traditional structure of the sermon" (211). She notes that "taking a text" consists of (1) the act of citing the scriptural reference from which the message of the sermon is to be taken, followed by (2) the reading of the passage, and concluding with (3) a usually cleverly worded statement articulating the "theme" (message) of the sermon (406). By extension, the sermonic dialogue of

Ellison's *Juneteenth* not only celebrates and valorizes the power of the spoken word but also reflects the degree to which language nourishes and humanizes Black people. One could say that the preacher is setting the table for a feast, where the preacher's words attempts to bridge the gap between the sacred and secular worlds of Black folks.

The Norton Anthology of African American Literature characterizes vernacular as "the church songs, blues, ballads, sermons, stories, and in our own era, hip hop songs that are part of the oral, not primarily the literate (or written-down) tradition of black expression" (Gates and McKay 3). As general editors of this volume, Henry Louis Gates Jr. and Nellie McKay maintain that "the vernacular encompasses vigorous, dynamic processes of expression, past and present. It makes up a rich storehouse of materials wherein the values, styles, and character types of black American life are reflected in language that is highly energized and often marvelously eloquent" (4). Such is the vernacular of Ralph Ellison . . . and then some. Ellison's *Juneteenth* is thus more than a novel. Part song, part spiritual, part record of oral performances, part sermon, part street speech—it exceeds all of these constituents. Blues, folk sermons, street jive—the salient events of contemporary history—are all media of serious expression for Ellison, and all collaborate to produce dramatic effects.

Charting Soul Food beyond Ellison's Representations

Soul food has built African American communities from one generation to the next. Through soul food, Black folks ate not only to satisfy their hunger but also to eat for pleasure and companionship, to celebrate and console. Writers like Ralph Ellison based their fictional representations of soul food on real spaces where the cuisine evolved and thrived. Cookbooks and restaurants are two such sources.

Cookbooks serve as blueprints for documenting the creativity and spirit of the Black community. Rosalyn Collings Eves comments on the rhetorical function of cookbooks, observing that they are memory texts that "memorialize both individuals and community," invoke "memory beyond mind," and "generate a sense of collective memory that in turn shapes communal identity" (Eves 281). For Eves, cookbooks are rich repositories that provide opportunities for cultural preservation, exchange, and meaning-making. She suggests that cookbooks not only mark the presence of Black culture but highlight how Black women were at the forefront of building African American communities: "The potency of food memory makes recipes an ideal text for the counterme-morial function they serve within the community of African American women invoked by these cookbooks. Not only does the collection of indi-vidual memories serve as a memorial of the community as a whole, with each individual voice embodying a representative perspective within the community, but also the sum effect of these collected memories gener-ates sense of collective memory" (293). Singer Patty LaBelle, meditat-ing on her own cooking experiences in *LaBelle Cuisine: Recipes to Sing About,* remarks: "I realized why cooking has always been such a labor of love for me. Because it's as much about friendship and fellowship as it is about food. Because, behind the whole process—the shopping, the plan-ning, the preparing, the serving—cooking—is really about love. Cook-ing is a way to show it, share it, serve it. Cooking is as much about nour-ishment for the soul as it is the stomach" (LaBelle and Lancaster 21). Whether the recipe is "Say-My-Name Smothered Chicken and Gravy" or "Aunt Hattie's Scrumptious Sweet Tater Bread," LaBelle shows that soul food brings people together, and shared intimacy becomes part of the meeting.

Restaurants, like cookbooks, offer avenues to explore how soul food forges Black solidarity and commitment. Consider the develop-ment of Sylvia's Restaurant, a soul food establishment in Harlem, New York: "During the turbulent 1960s when Black Nationalism and self-determination were the buzz words, Sylvia's Restaurant was in a prime position to attract patrons, particularly with its delectable fried chicken, ribs, collard greens, cornbread and an assortment of mouth-watering desserts" (Boyd 26). Sylvia Woods didn't lose sight of the fact that cook-ing engages all of your senses and can be a very pleasurable activity. For Woods, soul food was a mobile, flexible cuisine that could exist be-yond the American South: "No sooner had the first helping of ribs, fried chicken, waffles and grits been served was the word out, and the mo-ment you stepped into the restaurant, you were taken aloft by an aroma of down-home cooking that typified Woods' upbringing in South Car-olina" (Boyd 26). Woods urges us to take a moment to smell the aro-mas and enjoy the sight of soul food dishes before we consume them. Furthermore, Woods not only owned a restaurant, she wrote two cook-books: *Sylvia's Soul Food: Recipes from Harlem's World Famous Restau-rant* and *Sylvia's Family Soul Food Cookbook: From Hemingway, South Carolina, to Harlem.* In short, soul food cookbooks and restaurants highlight how Black folks perceive and conceive their world; they sym-bolize the values that people of African descent prioritize as they continually adapt to changing realities. Woods united soul food's mission of solidarity through each.

Barry Ulanov frames the senses of tradition and community that are reinforced by the sharing of soul food. "What has not always been noted about the soul-food experience," he maintains, "is that those who provide it, in home or in restaurant, do so with an unmistakable inflection of psyche, conscious or unconscious. Sitting down to or getting up from the soul-food table, you know you have been made welcome, a message clear from the very first, from those in the kitchen filling the dishes to the filled dishes in front of you. It is a message that must be taken up by those who work with the psyche and the spirit professionally" (3). From Ulanov's point of view, then, the psychological and physiological responses to soul food complement each other. He implies that soul food consumption among Blacks results in a fascinating choreography between emotion and motion, observing:

> We can make fun or even feel offended by the somewhat simple-minded categorizing of the black world as one where "all God's chillun got rhythm." Extend the phrase to cover all of us who have in any way caught the defining beat of a fully-lived life and you must see—and hear and taste and touch and smell—the reach into that collectivity of the senses of body and soul where we share a delight in being alive by welcoming others to our table, literal or metaphorical. That is how healing begins—with a beat. A-one, a-two. (Ulanov 3)

The psychic power and cathartic potential of soul food for Black folks are tremendous. Set the mind at ease, and the body will follow.

As the twenty-first century unfolds, the frontiers for soul food continue to expand, with virtual landscapes and food trucks leading the way. These new venues expand the soul food universe that Ellison captures in his novelistic portrayal of the previous century. Other contemporary means arising from new technology do nothing to alter the fundamental relationship between soul food, African American families, and Black communities because the symbolic meaning for Black folks remains the same. The website for Sylvia's Restaurant, for example, enables customers to purchase products such as Sylvia's Kickin' Hot, Hot Sauce and Sylvia's Sweet Cookin', Dippin' & Moppin' Sauce (sylviassoulfoodbrand.com). These items allow people from all over the country to infuse their meals with a bit of pizzazz and enjoy soul food from their own home. As one of the online pages suggests, folks can discover that "a little comfort can go a long way" and can "get inspired" as they "explore [a] range of spices and breakthrough flavors." Heavy's Food Truck (heavysfoodtruck.com) and J & J Food Truck (jandjsoulfoodtruck.com) in Florida represent the mobility of soul food in the modern era. Both offer affordable meals on the go and enable businesses to showcase their passion for cooking and connecting with people in an outdoor setting.

Conclusion

African Americans today, like their ancestors, are not monolithic in terms of their spiritual expression. They do share, however, a spiritual temperament that was born from enslaved Africans and preserved and transformed by their children in succeeding generations. Ralph Ellison believed that African Americans could persevere, even thrive, in spite of racism and inequality. Ellison felt that Blacks were more than the sum of their circumstances. From Ellison's point of view, African Americans had a rich culture that deserved recognition, admiration, respect, and, above all, remembrance. Soul food shows the genius of a supposedly powerless people in dire circumstances and the skill with which they thwarted them. In essence, soul food is as much about the cerebral as it is about physical comfort. Ellison knew this and made it a symbolic centerpiece of his book.

WORKS CITED

The Bible. New Oxford Annotated Version, 3rd ed., Oxford University Press, 2001.

Boyd, Herb. "Queen of Soul Food Sylvia Woods Passes at 86." *New York Amsterdam News,* vol. 103, no. 29, July 26, 2012, p. 26.

Brown, Sheylah. "Soul Food: A Medley of Flavors, Full of History and Celebration." NorthJersey.com, www.northjersey.com/in-depth/life/2020/12/03/soul-food -medley-flavors-history-celebration/3507617001, accessed May 10, 2022.

Burns, V. M. "What Is Soul Food, Anyway?" VM Burns—Mystery Writer, www .vmburns.com/what-is-soul-food-anyway, accessed June 21, 2022.

Ellison, Ralph. *Juneteenth.* Vintage Books, 1999.

Eves, Rosalyn Collings. "A Recipe for Remembrance: Memory and Identity in African-American Women's Cookbooks." *Rhetoric Review,* vol. 24, no. 3, 2005, pp. 280–97, www.jstor.org/stable/20176662, accessed May 10, 2022.

Gates, Henry Louis, Jr., and Nellie Y. McKay. *The Norton Anthology of African American Literature.* 2nd ed., Norton, 2004.

Henderson, Laretta. "'Ebony Jr!' and 'Soul Food': The Construction of Middle-Class African American Identity through the Use of Traditional Southern Foodways." *MELUS,* vol. 32, no. 4, 2007, pp. 81–97, www.jstor.org/stable/30029833, accessed May 10, 2022.

J & J Soul Food the Food Truck. https://jandjsoulfoodtruck.com, accessed June 22, 2022.

Jones, Leroi. *Home: Social Essays.* William Morrow, 1966.

Kelly, Sean. "Ambrosia and Nectar: The Food and Drink of the Gods." *Classical Wisdom*

Weekly, October 27, 2021, https://classicalwisdom.com/mythology/ambrosia-and
-nectar-the-food-and-drink-of-the-gods, accessed June 22, 2022.

LaBelle, Patty, and Laura Randolph Lancaster. *LaBelle Cuisine: Recipes to Sing About.*
Broadway, 1999.

Nettles, Kimberly D. "'Saving' Soul Food." *Gastronomica*, vol. 7, no. 3, 2007, pp. 106–13,
https://doi.org/10.1525/gfc.2007.7.3.106, accessed May 10, 2022.

Smitherman, Geneva. *Talkin That Talk: Language, Culture, and Education in African
America.* Routledge, 2000.

"Sylvia's Harlem Restaurant: Queen of Soul Food." *Sylvia's Soul Food Brand,* https://
sylviassoulfoodbrand.com, accessed on June 22, 2022.

"Three Important Guidelines We Live By." Heavy's Restaurant and Take Out | Best Soul
Food Truck in St. Petersburg, Florida, www.heavysfoodtruck.com, accessed on June
22, 2022.

Ulanov, Barry. "Soul Food, Psyche Food." *Journal of Religion and Health,* vol. 38, no. 1,
1999, pp. 3–4.

Wallach, Jennifer Jensen. "How to Eat to Live: Black Nationalism and the Post-1964 Culinary Turn." *Study the South,* 2014, pp. 5–14, https://southernstudies.olemiss.edu
/study-the-south/how-to-eat-to-live, accessed June 21, 2022.

PART II

Children Eat, Too

Wild or Wilder Food

Subsistence Eating in
American Children's Literature

GREGORY HARTLEY

One of the primary purposes of literature for children is to transmit values (Crippen). As children read, they learn about their own culture and the cultures of others. Hence, it's no real wonder that children's books overflow with cultural knowledge. Of course, food's place in cultural folkways stands as possibly the most relatable of all values to transmit. This is because everybody eats, but since every culture eats in a different way, children can access a wide range of learning through their food preferences. This learning extends to literary eating as well. Bethany Schneider argues that authors who know this fact can "intervene in the childhoods" of their readers by tying values to cultural foodways (69). Notable American authors Velma Wallis and Laura Ingalls Wilder treat the acts of gathering and eating food in precisely this manner.

These authors grant special significance to how characters collect food: Wilder's settler family and Wallis's native Alaskans both eke out their existence through subsistence, a life in which the opportunistic collection of food marks the difference between life and death. On one hand, this focus emphasizes the value of communal survival, but on the other, it also stresses rugged individualism. Americans enthusiastically embrace both values, in spite of their apparent contradiction. Each figures prominently in the American collective consciousness and finds thematic purchase in numerous titles. A simple survey of the last century of American children's literature—as represented by Newbery Award winners and nominees—demonstrates this special significance in novels with subjects similar to Wilder and Wallis, focusing on some combination of western expansion, either via the Indigenous diaspora or the American pioneer experience that drove it forward.[1]

National interest in this trend peaked in the 1930s, triggered by the Great Depression and renewed interest in western expansion (Maher and George). During that decade, nearly one-quarter of all Newbery honor books—twenty out of eight-five total—addressed the lives of pioneers and Indigenous peoples, and with that resurgence came interest in the now-old-fashioned hunting and cooking techniques practiced by both settlers and Native Americans ("John Newbery Medal").[2] By the 1930s, the Old West had closed, and the frontiersmen, with what Frederick Turner dubs their "stalwart and rugged qualities," had receded from popular experience by a full generation (15). This was sufficient time to generate romanticized myths, especially within the confines of the Depression and its taxing privations. Writers like Laura Ingalls Wilder—who wrote four of the twenty novels during the 1930s—led a vanguard of literature intended to pass on these historical experiences to new generations (Tharp and Kleinman 55). Subsistence eating played a central role in these books. As the twentieth century gathered speed, and such practices became a quaint historical artifact rather than a physical reality, nostalgic revivals of Indigenous and pioneer literature continued to keep the trend active, with a new wave emerging about once per decade ("John Newbery Medal").

Regardless of this popular focus on subsistence living, very few residents of the United States still engage in such a lifestyle, thereby relegating it to fictional portrayals that make it seem increasingly distant and inaccessible. And because the U.S. Indigenous population has shrunk to a minor fraction of what it once was, far too few books from the last hundred years give an authentic voice to Indigenous peoples. Of the books that do correlate to Native folkways, few were actually authored by Native Americans and none by Natives actually still practicing subsistence ways of living. This is precisely why Velma Wallis stands as an important representative of Indigenous subsistence. Her small but vibrant pocket of traditional subsistence still functions today. That she lives in Alaska helps explain why. While authors of historic fiction may use food to glance nostalgically at lost ways of living, Native Alaskan authors show young people how shared practices of gathering and eating impact real life and transmit cultural values.

Wallis's work also gives voice to the voiceless. Native Alaskan authors are possibly the most underrepresented of all Indigenous authors, even within the narrow genre of Alaskan fiction. None have ever drawn the attention of the ALA for a Newbery, and only recently has a Native Alaskan—or any Indigenous person—been honored with a Caldecott medal (Egan). Too often, writers representing the cultures of European settlers have instead imitated the voice of the Alaska Native cultures. The resulting works, such as Lide and Johansen's *Ood-Le-Uk the Wanderer* (1931) and Jean Craighead George's *Julie of the Wolves* (1973) do not accurately represent the values, much less the culture, of Alaskan Natives, in spite of having received Newbery honors.

This study addresses this deficiency by drawing attention to the subsistence values of Wallis's Gwich'in Athabascan tribe. Wallis grew up in the rural village of Fort Yukon, fishing, hunting, and crafting in a tiny community of just a few hundred. Her life in the tundra informs her writing, lending it an authenticity that colonial-minded writers reaching for "multiculturalism" cannot touch. For comparison with the legacy of colonial American writing, this essay will also examine Laura Ingalls Wilder's work, since she is the dominant figure representing the Euro-American colonial presence. Both authors wrote about the subsistence lifestyle, using food to regularly demonstrate its joys and challenges. Both authors also lived the life they write about, contributing authenticity to their fiction. Most importantly, both authors share explicit and implicit values through the food and meals they portray in their books. In what follows, I will compare subsistence eating in Wallis's first novel, *Two Old Women* (1993), and Wilder's first novel, *Little House in the Big Woods* (1932), in order to show that Wallis's Gwich'in Athabascan values demonstrate to young readers how to preserve land resources whereas the consumer values transmitted by Wilder lead to exploitative agricultural practices.

Previous Study

While articles regarding this specific topic are uncommon, recent scholarship has visited Indigenous subsistence eating in children's fiction at least once. Kara Keeling and Scott Pollard devote an entire chapter of their book *Table Lands* to a comparison of the eating habits portrayed by Laura Ingalls Wilder and Louise Erdrich. They start the conversation by contrasting Erdrich's "anti–Little House" approach with Wilder's more traditional pioneer food (64). Decolonialist in nature, their study attempts to show that the American elevation of the pioneer experience took place at the expense of the Native way of life. Keeling and Pollard call out Wilder for her ignorance regarding Native resettlement via the "Trail of Tears" and the implicit racism in the Little House series. They also correctly identify subsistence patterns shared by both pioneer and Indigenous cultures alike. Both Erdrich and Wilder preserve historical foodways, present gathering food as a "central structuring activity," and use specific foods and their preparation as a means of transmitting cultural values (66). However, the authors remain silent as to just what values may be transmitted through such eating. This might partly be because both Erdrich's Ojibwe and Wilder's Sooners are relics of the nineteenth century. Since no practitioners of these precise cultures remain, understanding the values upheld through food often amounts to cultural guesswork.

This becomes one more reason to explore Native Alaskan subsistence as the primary Indigenous culture here. Unlike the vast majority of tribes in the contiguous United States, a large percentage of Alaska's Indigenous peoples still reside on their native lands, practice subsistence hunting and gathering much as they have done for thousands of years, and thus maintain cultural practices related to food storage, preparation, and consumption that are traditional and historically accurate in nature.

Alaskan Reliance on Subsistence

Alaska remains one of the last bastions of active subsistence living in the United States. As Rachel Ramsey points out, however, colonial contact with European expansion permanently altered Alaskan Native culture, especially Wallis's Athabascans (24). Prior to Western contact, the Gwich'in peoples roamed nomadically, following caribou herds and targeting salmon runs along the Yukon River and its many tributaries in north central Alaska (Inoue 184). Modern Gwich'ins are no longer nomadic, living in villages so that they retain access to federal services like public schools and post offices. And as Ramsey points out, this Western contact also had the negative effects of washing the culture in alcoholism and welfare-induced lethargy, common afflictions of modern North American Natives (24). However, it's not accurate to say that their subsistence way of life has been erased due to this contact. All residents of Alaska have certain subsistence privileges, and traditional practices are the origin and source of contemporary hunting and fishing regulations (Alaska Department). In general, Alaskan residents may forage, fish, and hunt as a means to supplement or—in Native villages—utterly replace their reliance on store-bought food. The government grants Native Alaskans much broader permissions for subsistence than in many states, extending towards otherwise protected wildlife such as walrus, seal, whale, and otter (Alaska Department). Native Alaskans also are exempt from hunting permits, and several state fisheries are limited to subsistence use only. Notably, however, the federal government regulates Alaskan subsistence now, whereas prior to statehood, Native Alaskans could practice subsistence at will, with only other bands of Natives to contend with for control of resources (Norris 16–17).

Since Wallis positions her Gwich'in Athabascans far earlier in history, colonial settlers are nowhere to be seen in *Two Old Women*. The story unfolds with a nomadic band moving into the winter after a particularly poor season of hunting and foraging. The tribal chief makes the brutal decision to abandon the two oldest members of the tribe, the old women of the book's title: Ch'idzigyaak (whose name means "Chickadee") and Sa' (or "star"). The old women say goodbye to their children and grandchildren, urging them not to fight the chief's decision and reminding them that survival depended on cooperation and obedience. After the original shock of this cruel utility, meant to ward off starvation, the novel shows how the women rediscover their subsistence skills and live for a full year off the land, hunting and trapping small game. The women survive their abandonment and begin to thrive, storing up a large cache of food that, in a twist of dramatic irony, actually saves the tribe itself from a second disaster one year later.

Alaskan Emphasis on Native Values

The core narrative of Wallis's tale provides sufficient fodder for a closer look at Native Alaskan tribal values. To this day, the Gwich'in Tribal Council GTC) maintains a list of the ancient values carried forward by the tribe, including this list practiced by its members:

Gwich'in Athabascan Values

Respect	*yiinjinihłetr'ichil'eh*
Honesty	*chigwijuu'ee tr'igwindaii*
Our Stories	*nakhwigwandak*
Honor	*yiinjitr'ichil'eh*
Laughter	*tr'eedlaa*
Kindness	*zhuh ghat t'igwidich'uu*
Sharing & Caring	*nihk'atr'inaatii*

Immediately following the list of values, the council offers the following principles that flow outward from them:

- Our Elders play a crucial role as teachers. They are the keepers of our knowledge, history, language, protocol, and culture.
- Our Youth are the future of our Nation. We must listen and hear their perspectives and provide opportunities for them to learn, understand and develop into our future leaders.
- Our way of life is based on a unique and special economic and spiritual relationship between each other and the land, air and water.
- The preservation and respect for the land are essential to the well-being and subsistence lifestyle of our people and our culture.
- Our family history and linkages to our relatives in the Northwest Territories, Yukon, and Alaska is important to our identity.
- We all have a role to play in revitalizing our culture and language.
- Cross-cultural understanding and awareness between Gwich'in and non-Gwich'in is essential in building a new relationship based on respect, reconciliation and cooperation. (GTC)

As the basic plot of *Two Old Women* shows, Wallis seeks to reinforce these core Athabascan values. Her elderly characters serve as teachers for the impulsive and cruel tribal chieftains. The young people of the tribe receive protection as an investment in the future. Their food comes exclusively from the land without interference. They must find it and catch it to eat it, creating a deeply spiritual relationship between the land and themselves.

Since this study examines values transmitted through eating narratives, it is important to specify how deliberate each author is about their respective value system. To this day, the contemporary Gwich'in tribal council actively collects knowledge from elders about caribou, wolf, bears, and other mammals crucial to the tribe's survival (GTC). They not only make this knowledge public but archive it to preserve the wisdom of elders for future generations in a time when oral transmission is breaking down due to diaspora and other social disruptions. As a member of the tribe, Wallis expresses the same intent to pass a story "given by an elder to a younger person" (xvi), which aligns with the approach preferred by tribal councils across the state. Elders teach the next generation how to catch and prepare foods. Their stories establish the value placed on hunting and gathering skills as well as on the wildlife they catch, kill, prepare, and eat to sustain their own lives.

The character arcs Sa' and Ch'idzigyaak follow emulate these values deliberately. After their ejection, the old women rediscover their own value through their isolation. They recall skills they had nearly lost as they hunt and build their own shelters. They realize they had become soft in their old age, believing that their worth had been used up, and they reverse their error just in time to preserve their own lives. Armed with this self-discovery, they are able to reciprocate when the band approaches them the next year nearly starving to death. The women share their abundant food, tell their story, and teach a new appreciation for respect (115, 118). The tribal leaders realize that they did not correctly value the wisdom of their elders and nearly paid the ultimate price. The novel functions as an explanation for why the Gwich'in value elders so highly and as a strong rationale for why values and survival are intertwined. The tribe has been instructed to respect their elders from childhood, but on the occasion when the women get ejected and abandoned, the chieftains had decided that "they knew more than the older ones" (91).

Wilder, on the other hand, does not adhere to such a clearly defined values system, nor does she explore the gruesome reality that too often attends subsistence living, even though her portrayal showcases the very mechanisms by which Native Americans were subjugated and replaced. Her first book, *Little House in the Big Woods,* serves as a veritable how-to primer for pioneer living. Technically the story of Charles Ingalls moving his family onto a homestead in the Big Woods of Wisconsin, the episodic plot really just moves from meal to meal, with Ingalls lavishing the reader with procedures detailing food production. Since the novel is told from daughter Laura's perspective, Charles's—or Pa's—exploits hunting in the forest largely get passed by in favor of kitchen prep. This means Ingalls keeps even animal death at arm's length. Tharp and Kleiman argue that this portrayal misrepresents the real frontier. They refer to the *Oxford Companion to Women's Writing* for a list of values expressed by Wilder's works: "family, community, landscape, history, *and American myth*" (Tharp and Kleiman 55; Bosmajian 922, emphasis mine). While one may certainly find similarities with Wallis and her Athabascan values, the inclusion of myth calls attention to the fictitious nature of Wilder's portrayals and begs the question of what purpose such fiction serves, especially since Wilder's fictions are so vivid that young readers literally "internalize the remembered past as an experience and a truth" divergent from actual facts and experiences (Bosmajian 922).

The remainder of this study will seek to explore just such inquiries. We may at this point turn our attention to how each novel expresses its values by intertwining subsistence eating with a unique message about how a culture should view food collection and consumption. This will be mapped out as a series of contrasts inspired by the Gwich'in principles enumerated above: Wallis elevates interdependence while Wilder glorifies independence; Wallis's characters only seek survival while Wilder's want to thrive; Wallis's Athabascans must remain attentive whereas Wilder's allow distractions to blur their focus. The final comparison will examine how both use story differently to transmit subsistence values.

Interdependence vs. Independence

Athabascan values show how elders and youth must interact to keep its people culturally healthy. Wallis embroiders this group dynamic into *Two Old Women* by showing how food collection always must be a team effort. The band may live apart from other bands, but they are interdependent. Hunters move out together and work as a team. Children observe and learn both in the field and at home after the hunt, helping to collect babich, the dried sinews of moose (7–8). Bringing food to the band is the path to gaining social status (55). The old women themselves, once abandoned to the elements, cling to each other for literal warmth and emotional support, helping each other remember long-forgotten skills for snaring rabbits and spearing squirrels (50). Sa' sums up the instinct in a single sentence: "The body needs food, but the mind needs people" (59). Genie Babb claims that this reading of the novel must come deliberately since the collectivism and reciprocal power structures endemic to Native cultures strike westernized readers as counterintuitive. Young readers instead are much more likely to respond to the old women's achievements as acts of tremendous self-reliance (308). Babb hints that the chief reason for this is simply because most of Wallis's readers are not Gwich'in, so they must learn to value elders and recognize that the reunion with the tribe at the conclusion of the novel restabilizes the band rather than the opposite. Therefore, a proper reading of the novel cannot include a celebration of self-reliance. Instead, it is Wilder who celebrates such individualism.

Wilder's protagonists choose the independent eating of the separatist rather than Wallis's tribal collectivism. Charles Ingalls deliberately isolates his family within untamed territory away from organized civilization. Instead, he sets out with his family on his own, celebrating the mythical value of individualism and finding one's own way (Tharp and Kleiman 56). He keeps his family in minimal contact with both European colonials and the Indigenous people with whom he shares the wilderness. When Charles goes hunting, he is not preserving a group identity for himself or his family; instead, he becomes the stereotypical pioneer, the "rugged individual." In the course of doing so, Charles, like other American settlers, discards, adapts, innovates, and ultimately changes his practices at will. One moment he wants to live in the forest, next on the prairie. One moment he builds a log cabin and hunts game, the next he abandons the same cabin and embraces the new agricultural technology of the threshing machine. He longs for a crop of European wheat and expresses disgust with "old-fashioned ways" of killing animals for food, declaring instead his adherence to "progress" and lauding the "great age" in which he lives (228).

Unlike Indigenous peoples, many European-American settlers neither had a definite legacy to convey nor any real commitment to passing on their traditions. Rather, by constantly leaving their former way of life—either in Europe itself or on the progressive march westward through American territories—they signaled their readiness to dispense with any traditions that proved difficult or even just inconvenient. Holly Blackford indicates that the episode of the threshing machine not only underlines Pa's self-reliance but also ultimately contradicts it, for immediately after that moment Charles experiences the existential crisis of being unable to kill a deer he finds in the forest, since it, like him, is "strong and free, and wild" (233; Blackford 151). This, according to Blackford, actually breaks the myth by representing its inherent contradiction: in order to survive, settlers must kill animals and clear the forest, but doing so destroys the land lifestyle the novel exists to celebrate. The center cannot hold, and the Ingalls must depart, showing that Wilder's central value of individualism is unsustainable.

Nevertheless, Wilder's young readers apparently miss this contradiction, or are not troubled by it, evidenced by the popularity of Wilder's books despite the destructive forces they unleash. Wilder's settlers bring with them nonnative crops, which they force the land to produce. They slash and burn old-growth forests and deep-rooted prairie grass, not knowing that this exact cascade of mismanagement would lead to the Dust Bowl in less than half a century (Hurt). The Ingalls' settler mentality pushes boundaries while maintaining a tether to the civilization from which they fled. The irony that Charles must travel to a town called "Independence" in order to procure his European luxuries and staples is almost certainly not intentional, but the act represents a similar cultural lifeline that nearly all settlers maintained. Charles eventually must become more and more dependent "on distant markets and distant suppliers" (Holtz 84). The scenario is in fact a predecessor to the modern industrial supply chain. Such towns are always on the fringes of the Ingalls' life, always there when needed or when the hardships of settler life gain reprieve by European luxuries. Settlers cannot break with this chain or they will perish, if not from hunger then from shame. After all, Ma needs her white sugar to save face when company comes.

Nomadic Indigenous tribes, however, do not have such safety nets. As Inupiaq scholar Cana Uluak Itchuaqiyaq reminded University of Alaska faculty at a recent seminar, there is no "rugged individualism" in subsistence hunting. No Charles Ingalls who fetches all the family's protein alone and unaided. Collaboration is absolutely necessary. Children in Alaskan Native households have memories of watching parents cutting up a seal. The kids watch, and go play, watch, and go play. As the cycle repeats, eventually the skill gets transferred and children can try cutting up the seal for themselves. The work is hard. Hunting is hard. Cleaning is hard. A bearded seal (*ugjuk*) weighs two hundred pounds. Properly cleaning it requires teamwork from men catching the seal and women cutting up the seal. The whole group brings it in to shore. The whole group cleans it. Children cannot do this work alone, but they can cut meat in small pieces and put the cubes into buckets; they can remove fly eggs from the meat to prevent maggots; they can scrape skin in preparation for tanning. And they can expect sharp criticism. An outsider may find cause to criticize, but survival is at stake and the harshness aligns with the environment's reality, a reality westernized children can only imagine.

Survive vs. Thrive

While Wallis's Athabascans have no lifelines or source of leisurely indulgence, it should come as no surprise that colonial culture and Native culture experience tension when juxtaposed. The land provides or the people die. Wallis knows that Alaska stands on the outer edge of the global supply chain, which is why the state can still be called the Last Frontier. A primary value for both Wallis and Wilder, survival, emphasizes how characters choose to engage in risk in order to acquire food. Wallis says that the high priority of survival sometimes forces the band of humans to behave more like animals, appearing to sacrifice reason and virtue to allow the larger portion of the group to live. This is the practice that leads the chief in *Two Old Women* to abandon the protagonists in winter (5).

Survival requires struggle in the face of circumstances that can lead to death. The Athabascans constantly teeter on the brink, and Wallis centers her story around this determination to survive. The Athabascans must rely on a hierarchy of rationing nutrition. Hunting males must eat first since they support the caloric needs of the band (2). This leaves women and children on the lower end of the spectrum, and therefore hovering near starvation in the winter. This hierarchy, driven by necessity, leads to the corresponding value of obedience. Since hunters keep the band alive, their decisions must be followed without question (9). The harsh social structure might seem too extreme for a young audience, but Wallis frames the narrative as a partial critique of how the old women were devalued, showing that if elders are ignored, then the survival of the culture is also at stake (Inoue 186). The novel's protagonists occupy the lower hierarchy within the band, yet they still manage to find ways to survive by relying on their cultural knowledge. So, while subsistence forces a harsh focus on survival, the elders' wisdom actually increases the whole group's chances. Ch'idzigyaak, one of the two old women, stubbornly declares that they "have earned the right to live," which inspires them to survive or "die trying" (14).

Wilder's survival value contrasts sharply with Wallis's. Winters are harsh on the prairie, but the pioneer spirit and the impulse to store up abundance creates a caloric savings account the Ingalls family can draw from throughout the winter months. The goal of storing up food for the winter involves creating plenty rather than just enough to survive. Therefore, the novel emphasizes comfort and pleasure rather than the harsh realities of starvation (44). Because of this, winter is not particularly hard; just restrictive, and sometimes even cozy. Death is present—such as when the family pig is slaughtered—but its harshness is distant and the family focuses more on the delights of ham and bacon rather than the process of killing a pig. Laura simply covers her ears and the narrator passes the moment by letting Pa say, "It doesn't hurt" (13). Just a few pages later, the girls are gleefully playing ball with the inflated pig's bladder, the macabre nature of the moment evidently lost on both characters and narrator, vanished in what Blackford calls "the poetics of labor" (160).

Although they work hard, they still have some time during the evening for leisure, so Laura's memories are filled with Pa's fiddle playing and songs. The subsistence life led by the Ingalls family has far fewer risks. If Pa cannot catch enough game in the forest, the family can always fall back on store-bought cornmeal to get them through lean months (Holtz 86). In fact, Holtz argues that complete subsistence by settlers was simply impossible. The ultimate goal of the pioneer movement was not to create myriad independent homesteads but to generate commerce and growth for the local towns that supported them. The Ingalls family has chosen to mostly live apart from Eurocentric city life, yet they nevertheless bring vestiges of it with them, and the foods they eat demonstrate this. The girls suck peppermint candy at Christmas (74), Ma bakes Swedish crackers (62), and Pa's primary objective is to grow wheat, a European transplant crop (228; Crosby xxiv).

Charles Ingalls yearns for more than merely surviving. He strives for abundance, constantly reaching to acquire more land and bigger crops. His impulse embodies the colonial urge to dominate and possess. One prime example is when Charles finds a huge beehive in the Old Forest. Rather than taking only what he needs to provide for his family's immediate needs, he gathers every bucket and tub they own and destroys the hive that had stood for generations, taking every last drop of good honey. Laura laments that the poor bees have lost their home and their honey, but as with the death of the pig, Pa casually assures Laura that the bees will just rebuild in a new stump and "have plenty of honey again, long before the winter" comes (198). Pa assumes bees seek abundance just as he does, but we never find out what becomes of the homeless bees.

The divided emphasis between surviving and thriving influences how the authors treat death. Set within the harsh Alaskan winter, Wallis keeps death ever present. The two old women are essentially victims of euthanasia. In both human lives and animal lives, death figures prominently, and even the animals the women kill receive detailed death narratives, like the rabbit caught in a snare that lays trembling and "partially strangled" until Sa' squeezes it until its pulse disappears (20). Death's reality pounds at the Athabascans, driving them to migrate in search of game, forcing them to make horrific decisions like the one the chief makes to abandon the women (4). But the end result does not shock or traumatize. Instead, it teaches readers to trust in the wisdom of elders and to be grateful for the bounty of the land. The land provides, but its rules must be obeyed, lest "quick and unjudgmental death would fall upon the careless and unworthy" (38). The connectivity gained by such an emphasis not only builds cultural strength but allows readers to confront—and make peace with—the reality of death.

Wilder takes a far different approach, shunning death as any imminent reality and focusing instead on the joie de vivre despite the harsh pioneering conditions of the Big Woods and the Oklahoma prairie. Famine never really touches the Ingalls family and cookery, which, while simple by modern standards, is embellished by all kinds of culinary flourishes and treats. The episodes regaling crispy pig's tail, white sugar, Christmas peppermint, and gathering maple syrup signify a pleasure aesthetic that stands partly in denial of the death and risk surrounding the homestead. Wilder repeatedly remarks that indulgences were exceedingly rare, but in the accelerated pace of the narrative, to the reader they seem to occur at least once every chapter. Obsessing over such joys and pleasures feels stoutly "American" and previews the culture of indulgence to which such attitudes inexorably led. In those sugary treats lay hidden the looming epidemic of diabetes and other diet-related ailments that arise from a way of life that seeks unrestrained pleasures.[3]

Attentive vs. Distracted

Wallis's Athabascans know the land intimately, paying attention to its rhythms and contours, and are able to read the seasons like an actual daily calendar. The characters model the Gwich'in value of awareness. This gives their subsistence activities precise timing and increases their chances of success. Sa' and Ch'idzigyaak know the uses of every part of every creature and plant in their environment. When rabbits run scarce during the winter, they know to boil spruce branches to extend their own energy and prolong life. When the rabbits return, they also know that the diet of spruce tea has "made the stomach sour," so they only sip the broth from the kill at first, reacquainting their systems to avoid a negative reaction after their near-starvation diet (62).

The old women create food security through their attentiveness as well. In childhood, they had learned how to set snares for rabbits, as all members of the band do. But they also learned from their elders that one must check the snares regularly and attentively because "neglecting your snareline brought bad luck" (63). As a result, they eventually build a stockpile of food to store in a surplus cache, which they share once they rejoin the starving band, saving their lives as well.

On the other hand, the Ingalls family seems to suffer from a veritable plague of troubles caused by distraction, inattention, and misidentification. Charles certainly makes for a competent carpenter and hunter, but he and his family are newcomers to the lands they invade, so he does not possess intimate land knowledge like the Athabascans. Ma and the girls live under a form of patriarchal rule and so are not permitted to possess the knowledge that even Charles has for the family's survival, keeping them relatively ignorant compared to Charles (Holtz 82). As a result of these cultural conditions, the family continually makes dangerous mistakes. In one episode, Ma mistakes a large bear for the family cow, smacking it on the rump in an attempt to open a gate. Her action endangers her daughters, who stand defenselessly nearby as their mother accidentally provokes a wild animal (104). They survive simply because the bear decides not to retaliate. Charles makes a similar blunder on his return from a hunting trip. He mistakes a tree stump for a bear and attacks it ferociously—with no provocation from the perceived bear (112). He retells his adventure to his family as a humorous foible, but the outcome of both encounters could have been fatal if fortune had turned against them.

Stories vs. Episodes

Not every value expressed by Wallis and Wilder stands in opposition to each other. Both authors are female, telling their stories from a female point of view within a patriarchal society. They both value land-based living away from high-density population centers. They both highly value the family unit. And, as evidenced by their occupations, storytelling represents a central value, specifically food narratives. Both novels exist because of these shared values, and both authors understand that folkways about food get transmitted to the next generation through the power of storytelling. The authors do offer contrasting approaches on how to tell food stories, however.

Wallis's approach is to emphasize stories within her story. When the two old women join back up with the rest of the band of Athabascans, the elders tell the full story of their adventures in the wilderness, and when the conversation turns to the many food caches the women have stored in areas nearby, "their visitor's eyes became alert" (109).

Wilder chooses a first-person narrative. She is herself the elder telling the food stories. This causes some chapters to become almost like cookbooks, with prescriptive instructions for how to perform culinary tasks like smoking bacon or pounding hominy corn. But since Laura the child never accompanies her father on hunting excursions, the narratives exclude instructions for how to catch game. Pa just brings home meat that he always successfully catches, creating a noticeable gap in Wilder's instructions. Her readers not only receive an idealized portrait of the realities of pioneer life but also witness highly polarized gender roles (Blackford 171). Laura does not hunt because that task is men's work.

Wallis's tale does open with similar gender conventions, but the narrative works to deliberately undermine these (8; Ramsay 35). The tribe may be led by males, but the old women can hunt just as well as the men and are sometimes more successful (55). But rather than idealize her protagonists in service of her gender politics, Wallis portrays her hunting scenes with clear-eyed realism. Wallis's old women snare rabbits and stalk moose, but they do not always succeed, bringing them closer to starvation. When Sa' uses her bow and arrow to hunt moose, her craving for moose meat causes her to impatiently fire her arrow too soon, so the women do not eat that night (80). In contrast, Charles Ingalls always succeeds. His masculinity dominates the narrative just as it does the countryside he inhabits. Wallis the storyteller obeys the laws of the land in a way that Wilder conveniently ignores.

Conclusion

Robin Wall Kimmerer speaks of the "honorable harvest": the practice of taking just enough, leaving some for others, and expressing gratitude for what one has received (183). Her advice comes from the wisdom of Indigenous cultures worldwide, the key to successful subsistence. While subsistence practitioners face tremendous physical duress at times, they also create sustainable partnerships between humans and the land. In turn, this fosters generational transitions, as elders teach youngsters to rely on tribal practices, just as Sa' and Ch'idzigyaak remind their own band.

Wilder specifically teaches younger generations as well. Her values ring true to the pioneer spirit, mythologized as it has become. Yet the ways of Charles Ingalls—exploiting land for resources only until they run dry, then moving on to a new location to start the process again— are reminiscent of what Dr. Seuss's *Lorax* calls "biggering":

> But I had to grow bigger. So bigger I got.
> I biggered my factory. I biggered my roads.
> I biggered my wagons. I biggered the loads
> Of the Thneeds I shipped out. I was shipping them forth
> To the South! To the East! To the West! To the North!
> I went right on biggering . . . selling more Thneeds.
> And I biggered my money, which everyone needs. (61)

Seuss succinctly captures the expansionism of the pioneer spirit while offering a satirical critique of American capitalism. And, of course, the

Lorax's story ends in personal and ecological disaster. Wilder's books do not follow to this logical conclusion, largely due to her own romanticized values and the fact that her narrative occurs very early in the cycle, but one hundred years later, the cycle is plainly visible for all to see.

Wallis writes much later than Wilder and knows more about where Wilder's values will lead, so she offers an alternative by calling readers back from this death spiral. By giving readers values that honor the land, Wallis offers a chance to renew what Kimmerer calls the "ethic of reciprocity" that has largely gone extinct from the planet, especially within the United States (200).

NOTES

1. I will not be using the term "Indian" in this study unless required by reference to a source. My stance on the term aligns with that of Alfred Crosby, author of *The Columbian Exchange*, who found the term "ambiguous and inaccurate" and its adoption into American nomenclature an "egregious error" (xxvi).

2. By comparison, an analysis of all 430 Newbery honor and medal winners from 1922 to 2022 shows only forty-eight books with pioneer/Indigenous subject matter have been honored by Newbery in its hundred-year history. In other words, nearly half of the total books on this subject were authored in the 1930s, demonstrating a trend in both the preferences of the ALA and in American readers and authors ("John Newbery Medal").

3. In 2017 the Centers for Disease Control reported that the number of Americans suffering from diabetes exploded between 1958 and 2015, increasing by 1,500 percent from 1.5 million to 23.3 million (CDC). Laura Ingalls Wilder herself died in 1957 of undiagnosed diabetes, one of the early casualties of the epidemic.

WORKS CITED

Alaska Department of Fish and Game. "Subsistence in Alaska Overview: Definition, Responsibilities, and Management." *ADF&G Home*, www.adfg.alaska.gov/index.cfm?adfg=subsistence.definition.

Alaska Native Knowledge Network. "Alaska Native Values for Curriculum." University of Alaska Fairbanks, 2006, http://ankn.uaf.edu/ANCR/Values/index.html.

Babb, Genie. "Paula Gunn Allen's Grandmothers: Toward a Responsive Feminist-Tribal Reading of *Two Old Women*." *American Indian Quarterly*, vol. 21, no. 2, 1997, pp. 299–320.

Blackford, Holly V. "Civilization and Her Discontents: The Unsettling Nature of Ma in *Little House in the Big Woods*." *Frontiers*, vol. 29, no. 1, 2008, pp. 147–87.

Bosmajian, H. "Wilder, Laura Ingalls." *The Oxford Companion to Women's Writing in the United States*, edited by C. N. Davidson and L. Wagner-Martin, Oxford University Press, 1995, p. 922.

Centers for Disease Control. "Long Term Trends in Diabetes," *CDC's Division of Diabetes Translation*, April 2017.

Crippen, Martha. "The Value of Children's Literature." *Oneota Reading Journal*, www.luther.edu/oneota-reading-journal/archive/2012/the-value-of-childrens-literature.

Crosby, Alfred W. *The Columbian Exchange: Biological and Cultural Consequences of 1492*. Praeger, 2003.

Egan, Elisabeth. "This Indigenous Author and Artist Team Have an Important Message." *New York Times*, February 25, 2021, retrieved June 24, 2022.

George, Suzanne, and Susan Naramore Maher. "Children's Literature." *The Encyclopedia of the Great Plains,* University of Nebraska–Lincoln, 2011, http://plainshumanities .unl.edu/encyclopedia/doc/egp.lt.010.

Gwich'in Tribal Council. "Mission, Vision, and Values." Gwich'in Tribal Council (GTC) website, www.gwichintribal.ca/mission-vision--values.html, accessed June 23, 2022.

Holtz, William. "Closing the Circle: The American Optimism of Laura Ingalls Wilder." *Great Plains Quarterly*, vol. 4, no. 2, 1984, pp. 79–90.

Hurt, R. Douglas. "Dust Bowl." *The Encyclopedia of the Great Plains,* University of Nebraska–Lincoln, 2011, http://plainshumanities.unl.edu/encyclopedia/doc/egp .pe.022.

Inoue, Toshiaki. "The Gwich'in Gathering: The Subsistence Tradition in Their Modern Life and the Gathering against Oil Development." *Senri Ethnological Studies*, vol. 66, 2004, pp. 183–204.

Itchuaqiyaq, Cana Uluak. "An Inuk in the Institution: Centering Clanwork and Community as a Matter of Course," University of Alaska Anchorage, April 8, 2022.

Keeling, Kara K., and Scott T. Pollard. "Food of the Woods and Plains." *Table Lands: Food in Children's Literature,* University of Mississippi Press, 2020.

Kimmerer, Robin Wall. *Braiding Sweetgrass: Indigenous Wisdom, Scientific Knowledge, and the Teachings of Plants*. Milkweed, 2013.

"John Newbery Medal." *American Library Association,* March 24, 2021. www.ala.org /alsc/awardsgrants/bookmedia/newbery, accessed June 14, 2022, document ID 4c554695-91d6-4e23-8299-49318b08dbbb.

Norris, Frank Blaine. *Alaska Subsistence: A National Park Service Management History.* Alaska Support Office, National Park Service, US Department of the Interior, 2002.

Ramsay, Rachel. "Salvage Ethnography and Gender Politics in *Two Old Women*: Velma Wallis's Retelling of a Gwich'in Oral Story." *Studies in American Indian Literatures,* vol. 11, no. 3, 1999, pp. 22–41.

Schneider, Bethany. "A Modest Proposal: Laura Ingalls Wilder Ate Zitkala-Ša." *GLQ*, vol. 21, no. 1, 2015, pp. 65–93.

Seuss, Dr. *The Lorax.* Random House Children's Books, 2010.

Tharp, Julie, and Jeff Kleiman. "*Little House on the Prairie* and the Myth of Self-Reliance." *Transformations*, vol. 11, no. 1, 2000, pp. 55–64.

Turner, Frederick Jackson. *The Frontier in American History.* Holt, 1921.

Wallis, Velma. *Two Old Women: An Alaska Legend of Betrayal, Courage and Survival.* 1993. Harper, 2013.

Wilder, Laura Ingalls. *Little House in the Big Woods.* 1932. Harper, 1953.

Kogi, Tía Perla, and KoBra

Food Trucks and Identity in Texts for Young Readers

KATY LEWIS

Literary food studies, as a field, examines how literature takes up food as an aspect of human identity. Gitanjali Shahani emphasizes in *Food and Literature* that "[f]ood is memory, food is irony, food is drama, food is symbol, food is form" (3). Literary food studies focus on the multifaceted nature that food plays in our lives, the role it takes as a literary device, and the way it works as an expression of our identities. In American literature, texts for young audiences depicting cultural diversity often use food to approach this topic, as many readers, no matter how young, can recognize how food is central to who we are. Like texts for their adult contemporaries, texts for young audiences discuss how identity and food are connected, which mirrors the ways food influences how we see different communities and how they see themselves.

This connection between food and identity, in general, has been discussed by children's literature scholars like Kara Keeling and Scott Pollard. In their book *Table Lands,* Keeling and Pollard argue that "comprehending the sociocultural contexts of food reveals fundamental understandings of the child and children's agency and enriches the interpretation of such texts" and that "the harvest, preparation, and consumption of food is such a central human activity that it permeates literary texts at all levels" (6). Literary texts often address the ways humans eat and share food; in doing so, the texts implicitly suggest that cuisine is an important activity involved in developing one's identity. Keeling and Pollard reaffirm how "[f]ood and foodways are rich with interpretive possibilities," acknowledging that, "[g]iven the omnipresence of food, cooking, and eating in children's literature, the worlds within texts for children are indeed table lands, and children's literature invites us as scholars to the table to taste, chew, and discuss the stories" (10). Certainly, there have been countless children's and young adult (YA) texts published about food that all draw connections between food and identity. My essay, then, extends these ideas about food in literature for young audiences and focuses specifically on food trucks in three books: Jennifer Torres's middle-grade novel *Stef Soto, Taco Queen* (2017), Maurene Goo's YA novel *The Way You Make Me Feel* (2019), and Jacqueline Briggs Martin and June Jo Lee's nonfiction picture book *Chef Roy Choi and the Street Food Remix* (2017). I will explore how food trucks represent complex identity conflicts, as they are central to each text's plot and serve as motifs for the multicultural identities of the protagonists and their families. I argue that, as places and spaces that are never (or, not usually) permanently stationary, food trucks signify the liminality, movement, and dynamism associated with understanding identity in complex rather than reductive ways. As such, I also explore how the places the trucks go in these books represent something positive for each of the principal characters because they are critical spaces where they come to better understand themselves. Moreover, the settings of different scenes where the trucks show up connect to the larger identity conflicts that the books discuss. Food trucks in these American texts thus help uniquely portray food and culture as they honor the complicated and situated nature of identity.

Connections between Food Trucks and Literary Food Truck Spaces

Food trucks, as we may currently know them, trace their histories to taco truck culture. In *The Taco Truck: How Mexican Street Food Is Transforming the American City,* Robert Lemon argues that there is a slight difference between food trucks and taco trucks, especially based on their history (8–9). Lemon specifies that he uses "*taco truck* or *lonchera* to describe a food truck that is owned and operated by someone who migrated from Mexico and prepares traditional Mexican street foods (such as tacos, tortas, and huaraches) mostly for other Mexican immigrants to consume" (8). In the books I analyze, the trucks share similar features to taco trucks, including the salient fact that they are mobile.[1] Food trucks (and taco trucks), then, are complicated spaces with complicated histories. Lemon argues that "[t]aco trucks are by-products of the capitalist mode of production" as well as "an economic response to a cultural demand" (3). He adds that they "are foremost emblematic of Mexican cultural identity" because "Mexican immigrants who may or may not have U.S. citizenship typically own taco trucks" (3). These immigrants "serve inexpensive, traditional-style tacos primarily to Spanish-speaking, low-wage, mostly male, Mexican day laborers" (3). In this way, Lemon also connects cultural and ethnic identity with class and immigration status, emphasizing how taco trucks and, by extension, food trucks are sites where multiple identity categories intersect.

Food trucks have not always been nationally recognizable or accepted, though, a tension highlighted in some of the books I analyze. In "Twenty-First-Century Food Trucks: Mobility, Social Media, and Urban Hipness," Lok Siu states that "[f]ood trucks seem to have exploded on the national stage in the late 2000s" (232). "While the previous generation of food trucks was quite diverse," Siu notes, "in general they were perceived as offering cheap, 'authentic' (often read as 'ethnic' or 'low culture') food consumed primarily by the working class or sometimes thought to be the only option available in the area" (232). Like Lemon, Siu connects food trucks with identity, cuisine, ethnicity, and class, all elements that point to a space defined by connections and movement. Siu adds that this "low-brow" image, so to speak, has changed in recent years: "although food trucks still have a reputation for being affordable, they have been transformed into something modern, hip, cutting-edge, and mainstream" (232). Even as food truck spaces have become fancier or more gourmet (a word that Lemon uses), food trucks, like other service industries, are still associated with hard work, especially in the texts I examine in this essay.

This intense labor stems not only from the kinds of owners and workers that food trucks have; the need to move from place to place adds another layer of labor to maintaining a food truck. This mobility is what distinguishes food trucks from other eateries: many scholars and eaters compare food trucks to their "brick-and-mortar" cousins (i.e., stationary restaurants in buildings), and they highlight how food trucks embody fluidity in response to their environment (Irvin 44). For instance, with current technology, many eaters can locate where food trucks are and will be, which becomes a defining characteristic for how many modern food trucks interact with their customers. Siu contends, too, that "[w]hat sets [these trucks] apart from their restaurant counterparts is their mobility" and that "this style of food service and consumption, in addition to their food" is what "attracts people to food trucks" (235). Moreover, this mobility creates unique opportunities to think about space because food trucks can occupy so many different geographical spaces. In the texts I analyze, these locations and scenes signal to the reader important ideas about the characters' identities and conflicts, as the texts often detail the geography and circumstances surrounding the trucks when they are parked. Food trucks also consider where customers will be. Siu asserts, for instance, that "the mobility of food trucks offers a different commensality from conventional restaurants" *because* "[f]ood trucks go to where their consumers are likely to be found" (235). The trucks can become predictable, though, as they "usually move around within a circuit of designated sites in a city" (236). Food trucks, then, respond to their environment, community, and the desires of their eaters in ways simply not possible with brick-and-mortar restaurants.

Setting, too, including the place and space surrounding the trucks, is an important part of understanding how these trucks operate. "Through a taco truck's mobility," Lemon writes, "any given space can become a temporary place for people to eat tacos" (3). This ingenuity represents how "[t]aco trucks are capable of persistently producing new social spaces and ascribing additional meanings to places, which can challenge the ways in which people come to understand such spaces and places." Taco trucks act on the spaces in which they exist as much as those settings impact the trucks' existence. Through this mobile aspect, Lemon comes to "define *taco truck space* as an evolving cultural and culinary environment in which influences of local life continually converge with economic, political, and social forces at myriad scales" (3). Lemon highlights how "[t]aco trucks are dynamic spaces, because not only do they create a convivial atmosphere by linking place and time through culinary customs, they are also mobile" (3). I extend Lemon's ideas to consider literary food truck spaces in these texts, which are physical, psychological, and temporal spaces where characters work through their identities. Literary food truck spaces, then, are defined by a variety of contexts that surround the food trucks, including the places where they end up; we can better conceptualize the fluidity of these spaces by recognizing where and when the food trucks appear in the narratives. Moving from place to place, with the number and identities of customers changing each time, food trucks are an inherently fluid space where identity work occurs through culinary mechanisms. This fluidity underscores how food trucks require intentional, thoughtful labor—just like remaking oneself requires intentional, thoughtful reflection. Thus, food trucks, as mobile entities, represent how understanding and developing one's identity is a process constantly in flux and inherently defined by negotiation. Food trucks help readers see how identity development functions, especially as it is informed by class, ethnicity, culture, and cuisine.

I begin my analysis with how each book establishes the importance of a food truck to the plot and how this truck is connected to character identity. Understandably, each truck means something different to each of the characters, which is sometimes positive, sometimes not. I then focus on how the books highlight the manner in which food trucks connect place and identity since they can only inhabit certain spaces because of various city regulations, their size, and traffic, among other factors, even as the trucks are known for their mobility. Ultimately, these texts encourage readers to see each food truck almost as a character, with its own personality and importance as well as a unique identity that flows specifically from its owners' personalities and histories. These food trucks represent more than a space where culture and identity meet: each serves as a place where the characters learn to better understand themselves and navigate different conflicts. The surface function of the food trucks (i.e., serving food) recedes into the background while the significant roles they play moving the plot forward and supporting character development become more prominent. Certainly, this latter focus makes up much of the action of these books since the trucks serve as settings for character interactions or are themselves part of the plot's conflict. These plot points related to the food trucks are important, but the figurative role that these food trucks play is thus even more critical: in each book, the food truck symbolizes how food and culture intersect in different ways, especially as these intersections connect back to the protagonists' identity conflicts.

Tía Perla in Torres's *Stef Soto, Taco Queen*

In Jennifer Torres's middle-grade novel, *Stef Soto, Taco Queen*, the protagonist, Stef, is constantly ashamed of her family's taco truck, Tía Perla—the truck is old, worn down, and smells like old tacos. New city regulations are proposed because of health and safety concerns surrounding the food trucks in their area, although the book does not make clear who specifically has raised concerns (Torres 59). Like other truck owners, Stef's family is worried about how they will make a living when new regulations are proposed. Meanwhile, Stef struggles with how other students see Tía Perla and, by extension, her. Along the way, other middle school problems pop up, but, in each scenario, Tía Perla comes to save the day. In this book, the taco truck is both the catalyst for the protagonist's identity issues *and* the solution for those issues.

The first page of *Stef Soto, Taco Queen* opens with Stef lamenting that her father always brings Tía Perla to school. This scene immediately establishes Stef's antipathy toward Tía Perla:

> Papi had pretty much promised to stop bringing Tía Perla to Saint Scholastica School, but when the last bell rings on a Monday afternoon, there she is just the same, waiting for me in the parking lot: Tía Perla, yet again. Tía Perla, like always. Tía Perla, huffing and wheezing and looking a bit grubby no matter how clean she actually is. Tía Perla, leaving anyone who comes near her smelling like jalapeños and cooking oil, a not-exactly-bad combination that clings to your hair and crawls under fingernails. Tía Perla, Papi's taco truck, stuffed into a parking space meant for a much smaller car. A normal car. A station wagon! Something beige or black or white, with four doors and power windows. (Torres 1)

Stef provides rich detail about Tía Perla as she communicates her frustrations about the taco truck. First, Stef implies that Tía Perla is an unwanted constant in her life: "yet again" and "like always" establish, in an exasperated tone, how Tía Perla is never far away. Next, Stef personifies Tía Perla negatively, suggesting it is run-down and unpleasant to look at. At the same time, Stef contradicts these sentiments when she allows that "smelling like jalapeños and cooking oil" is "a not-exactly-bad combination" (1). Even so, she follows this up by observing that the smell "clings" to her body, implying that Tía Perla is an unwelcome constant, even when she is not in the vicinity of the truck (1). Stef's initial lack of appreciation and embarrassment over her family's taco truck become a central conflict in the book and ultimately something with which she must reconcile. To do this, Stef must renegotiate her relationship with not only her parents but also the truck, as their identities are inextricably linked together.

As Stef suggests in the opening scene, Tía Perla is her father's truck, and she later describes how Papi's childhood experiences informed his decision to start his taco truck. Stef narrates how Papi's "mother, my abuelita, had taught him to cook when he was my age. She didn't know where he might travel someday, she told him, but wherever he went, he would have her recipes to bring him back home. Now, nothing made Papi happier than sharing that warm at-home feeling with others" (14). Stef highlights how the recipes Papi grew up loving are the basis for the foods he serves from Tía Perla. Several words signal a flow of identity between individual eating experiences and sharing food with other people, even if through a business. Both *travel* and *wherever he went* imply a sense of movement, signaling a flow of identity from one space to another. *Her recipes* emphasize how these foods are unique and specific to Papi's childhood experiences and his mother's cooking. Papi then shifts from enjoying these foods with his family to *sharing* with others (his customers, including Stef's friends) the importance of what these foods mean to him. Thus, Papi's personal taste is what he shares with others while making food on Tía Perla. Through his unique family history and experiences with cuisine, Papi creates a unique space to share the tastes of his home.

Much of the novel focuses on Stef's frustration with her parents, especially her father, and how Tía Perla consumes their lives. The places and spaces where Tía Perla shows up reveal how important the truck is to Stef and her family: the truck does not just appear in places only for financial gain but also in spaces where "she" is needed. Across the book, Tía Perla appears outside of Stef's school (1–2; 32; 93; 158–60); across from the library in a local neighborhood (6); in a park next to Stef's friend, Amanda's, soccer game (37–8; 112–20); at a flea market (45); at a gas station where Stef, her father, and other food truck owners find a notice about the city's taco truck rules and regulations changing (58; 68–71); outside the Viviana Vega concert that Stef wanted to attend, where Viviana Vega actually ends up buying food from their truck (77–83); at the commissary, with other truck owners (94–98); and at the school dance (157–60). Some of these places are first about earning money, as generating revenue is Tía Perla's most important contribution to the family. Even so, each place has strong ties to Stef, her friends, and her family at different moments in their lives, especially moments defined by conflict.

For instance, Stef desperately wants to go to Viviana Vega's concert, but her parents are worried about letting her go by herself, claiming she is too young. They ultimately decide she cannot go, but, much to Stef's chagrin, Papi takes Tía Perla to the concert because the spot will drum up good business (77). Stef is devastated that she cannot attend the concert but still works the truck alongside her father. Though she does not know it at the time, one customer, "with the hood of her sweatshirt pulled low over her forehead" (79), is Viviana Vega, who is photographed by paparazzi buying food from Tía Perla. Once the other students find out that Viviana Vega visited Papi's truck, Stef instantly becomes popular because her fellow students now believe that Stef is able to bring Viviana Vega to perform at the school dance. When Stef eventually tells the truth, that Viviana Vega is not coming, she feels embarrassed about letting everyone down.

Tía Perla eventually "saves the day," though, on the evening of the school dance. When the school gym loses power, Stef asks her father, who has been waiting in the parking lot, "Can we fire up Tía Perla, like, right here?" (157). Her father enthusiastically agrees, and Stef works the truck with him as "[s]tudents tap their feet as they wait in line for nachos, quesadillas, tortas, and—for Arthur—the wheat-free, dairy-free, egg-free, nut-free, meat-free specialty of the house super burrito that Papi and I slide through the window as fast as we can" (159). Working with her father that night (and, later, pleading for the city to reconsider the new regulations that would endanger her father's business as well as many others), Stef learns to love Tía Perla and appreciate the role that it plays in her life. Even as Stef sees Tía Perla as the source of her constant misery, the truck provides a certain sense of community and connection that she comes to understand and eventually appreciate. The book ends with Stef repainting Tía Perla in the middle of the night, giving it a new life, and accepting how important it is to their family.

KoBra in Goo's *The Way You Make Me Feel*

In Maurene Goo's YA novel *The Way You Make Me Feel,* Clara Shin is sentenced, as she puts it, to her father's Korean Brazilian food truck Ko-Bra for the summer with her enemy Rose after they cause a scene at the prom a few weeks earlier. A prank gone wrong—involving a fight, fake blood, and fire—dooms them to the rhythm of cooking and prepping in the food truck throughout the rest of the summer.

As they work on the truck together, the novel makes clear that Clara's major identity conflicts stem from her relationships with others. First, she struggles with how Rose just seems to do everything differently than Clara does. Clara's second conflict comes when she finds herself liking Hamlet, a boy she meets while working on KoBra. Having sworn off love and relationships, Clara cannot seem to take her feelings for Hamlet seriously—nor his feelings for her. Lastly, her relationships with her parents are unequal: Clara lives with her father, Adrian (who she calls Pai), and they interact well. Her mother, Juliana, on the other hand, is absent—as an influencer, she is often whisked away to new locations without many thoughts for Clara. Clara is supposed to visit her mother in

Tulum at the end of the summer, but her sentence on KoBra threatens the trip; her punishment, serving on KoBra, causes unease in her relationship with her father and leads her to make rash decisions. Ultimately, working on KoBra forces Clara to face her relationship conflicts and their effects on her identity, and the novel focuses on how spending time on KoBra and making her father's food enables Clara to better understand herself.

Early in the novel, Clara explains how she enjoys the food her father makes on KoBra, but she is not interested in the truck itself—not because she is embarrassed by the truck but because she dislikes the idea of working on it: "Ever since he first started running the KoBra, my dad had been trying to get me to work on it. But the idea of being stuck in a hot, cramped truck for hours on end literally made me want to die" (Goo 3). This comment foreshadows what ends up happening a few chapters later. After Rose and Clara get into a fight the night of the prom, Adrian decides that, as punishment, "You're going to pay back the damages for the cafeteria. And you're going to do it by working the KoBra. *All summer*," effectively ruining Clara's summer plans, including her trip with her mother to Tulum (35). As the last few weeks of school pass, Clara laments the time because "I knew it brought me closer to my KoBra prison sentence with Rose" (40). Yet this prison sentence turns out differently than she imagines—Clara ends up enjoying her time on KoBra, and working on the truck is ultimately what allows her to resolve her relationship conflicts.

Clara explains how her father created the idea for KoBra:

> My dad, Adrian, was always experimenting with recipes. As the owner and chef of a food truck, that was pretty much his job. Since before I was born, he'd always worked at various restaurants, starting off as a busboy when he first immigrated here from Brazil ("Adrian" was the Americanized "Adriano"). My clearest childhood memories were the nights when, after his late shift, my dad would pick me up from my babysitter's and carry me home on his shoulders as I dozed off. Finally, two years ago, he had saved up enough money to open his own food truck, the KoBra—a literal and metaphorical merging of Korea and Brazil. My grandparents had made the trek from Seoul to São Paulo, a city with an established Korean immigrant population, where my dad was born. Months before I was born, my parents packed up for L.A. (13)

KoBra, as it brings together characteristics of Korean and Brazilian cuisines (both in name and in taste), represents the different aspects of

Adrian's identity. Pai combines his Korean and Brazilian heritages to make a space where both cuisines can coexist and intermingle, mirroring how he, too, experiences the mixing of those heritages. As Clara says, "The food was symbolic of my dad's upbringing" (13).

Clara's experiences on KoBra help her develop better relationships, though not without difficulty. Clara and Rose have a massive fight their first day on the truck; when they return the next day, KoBra finds its way to "an office park filed with grass, big shady trees, and depressing 1980s architecture" (70). This setting is where Clara first meets Hamlet, who is twirling a sign for a coffee shop called Java Time. Later that day, KoBra makes its way to "a bar in Echo Park where [they'd] catch the happy hour and evening crowd" (76). Clara explains: "Things went smoothly for a while—I realized that working in KoBra was almost like a finely choreographed dance. Because the space was so small, the three of us had figured out a way to stay in our little spheres" (77). Clara uses a simile about dancing to underscore how she, Rose, and Pai have to navigate KoBra's literal tight spaces, which also hints at how they must work through emotional spaces as well, especially since Clara and Rose fight so often. For instance, Clara's insensitivity toward food preferences, sensitivities, and intolerances angers Rose, and they eventually fight over cleaning pans between foods since Clara attempts to cook a vegetarian dish in a meat pan (79). Over time, though, working together helps them understand how to be friends. The two agree to secretly enter KoBra into a food truck competition (134–35), and Clara even invites Rose over to help her pick out her outfit for her date with Hamlet (145).

All this progress reaches a breaking point, however, when Pai discovers that Clara entered the competition without his permission, making him very angry. "My emotional investment in this truck came crashing down on me," Clara narrates, "as if to say, 'Ha-ha, this is what happens when you care'" (245). Clara has always kept people at a distance, and this moment reiterates how she is not ready for the emotional fallout that conflict brings. Later, Clara takes out her anger at her dad on Hamlet, declaring, "I'm going to Mexico" and "Screw my dad. Screw the competition. My mom wants me there so I'm going" (249). Hamlet finally calls Clara out, saying, "While you've never told me why you like me, I have my own theories—the main one being that you've surrounded yourself with people who enable this side of you, and I don't" (250). "The side of you that can't handle being real," Hamlet explains, "that thinks it's not special to care. . . . But Clara, it's the least special thing about you. It's the exception" (250).

Hamlet sees Clara for who she is—a girl scared to care and scared to deal with the aftermath of what caring entails. When the first sign of negative emotion occurs, Clara does not stick around to deal with the consequences; much like her mother, Clara escapes to Tulum after this argument with her father about KoBra. During this trip, she confronts some of the hard truths about her relationship with her mother. She begins to understand all the ways her mother is absent and all the ways in which their relationship is superficial. Clara finally realizes what is important to her while sitting in front of her meal: "When I took a bite of the food, I immediately thought of how much Pai would like the seasoning. Sitting there eating fish on a white sand beach with a cool breeze drifting over me, more than ever I wished I were on the KoBra—enclosed in an overheated truck with my dad and my best friend" (289).

When things become rough, Clara immediately thinks of KoBra and the peace it brought during the past summer as she grew in her different relationships. With this realization, she decides to go home immediately, especially "because the food truck competition is tomorrow" (296). Hamlet joins the KoBra crew for the food truck competition, and, together, Clara, Pai, Rose, and Hamlet try to win the $100,000 grand prize for funding to start Pai's restaurant. While KoBra does not win, one of the judges approaches Pai to invest in his restaurant idea (314). The four of them spend the book's last moments sitting atop the food truck looking out over LA, celebrating the experience. Clara sums everything up: "I looked over at the KoBra crew and felt so grateful for the small part of the universe I had" (317). Thinking about what the truck brought her, she ends with, "In this huge city, there were three people in this truck who mattered a lot to me. I'd protect that little part of the universe for as long as possible" (319).

Before working on KoBra, Clara keeps people at a distance and checks out of any kind of emotional labor. By the novel's end, Clara cares not just about her father, her best friend, and her boyfriend, but also about the truck and the space it created for her to establish these relationships. KoBra, thus, serves as a space where Clara learns that give and take are natural parts of learning about identity.

Kogi in *Chef Roy Choi and the Street Food Remix*

Jacqueline Briggs Martin and June Jo Lee's nonfiction picture book, *Chef Roy Choi and the Street Food Remix*, features real-life Chef Roy Choi and his journey to making Kogi, a famous family of taco trucks that combine Korean and Mexican cuisine. Roy starts as a chef working in restaurants but soon learns that the traditional restaurant scene is not the setting in which he loves to cook food. A friend suggests starting a taco truck, though Roy rejects the idea at first. Eventually, though, Kogi is born, a place where Roy learns to remix the flavors of his family and home with the flavors he ate and loved on the streets of Los Angeles while growing up. Unlike the other two books I discuss, Kogi is a real taco truck that exists outside of the story world: in the narrative (and in real life), the taco truck symbolizes finding one's identity.

Unlike Clara and Stef, who are the daughters of food truck owners, Roy Choi owns his own truck, Kogi. The double-page spread where Kogi is first featured emphasizes this pride, despite initial doubt and obstacles to their success. On the left side of the spread, the page focuses on the critics who think that Kogi's flavor combination does not make sense. The text reads:

> Roy and his friends rolled down the streets of L.A. in their Kogi BBQ truck, looking for hungry people.
> "Move on," people said.
> "Korean guys can't do tacos."[2]

Two people are pictured walking away from Kogi; one person has a thought bubble reading "No way." Their bodies and faces turn away from the truck, reinforcing how they dismiss Kogi. The food truck itself sits in the center of the image on the right page, the bright-white color of Kogi contrasting with the darker, more intense colors in the spread. The page with the truck reads: "Roy kept cooking inside the truck while his friends hustled outside, finding people to buy their tacos." Molly Bang, in *Picture This: How Pictures Work*, argues that "The center of the page is the most effective 'center of attention.' It is the point of greatest attraction" (76). Kogi, situated in the middle of the image, attracts readers' attention in this way, exemplifying the way in which the narrative emphasizes how important the food truck is, as if itself is a protagonist. Centering Kogi this way also points readers to the struggle Roy faces when customers turn from the idea of combining Korean and Mexican cuisines, while the following pages celebrate Roy and Kogi's ultimate success in converting people's palates.

For Kogi, Chef Roy Choi builds upon his experiences of eating Korean food made by his mom as well as tasting the street foods of LA. The idea begins when "a friend said let's open a taco truck, put Korean barbecue in a taco," which contrasts with the narrative explaining that people believed "Chefs cook in kitchens, not on trucks!" But, then, "Roy said yes! He wanted to remix the tastes he loved on the streets that were his home." His home and community foods thus inform Roy's cooking, which he recognizes. The word *remixing* here also reinforces a sense of movement, especially as this word is depicted in one illustration: Roy Choi creates food and adds flavor in a setup that looks like a mixing board used in producing music, although he is working with food. A note from author June Jo Lee specifically comments on this motif: "When Roy created the Kogi Korean taco truck, he mixed together two very different and delicious cuisines—Korean and Mexican." Mixing and remixing become Kogi's signature style and, ultimately, the processes that satisfy Choi—both what he makes and how he makes it.

Roy and his friend search for customers, waiting to see how people will respond to Kogi. When Kogi is first introduced, the text reads: "And when they did . . ." This pause creates a tension for the reader, which is satisfied by the page turn: in the next double-page illustration, readers find an image of Kogi serving a long line of customers. The text describes how "Kogi tacos taste so good—sweet, tangy, so much savory— eaters ordered more, took pictures to share with friends." This scene implies that Kogi's success at finding customers results from Kogi's ability to move since, in one location, there were not interested customers and, in another space, customers abound. Moreover, the remixed food receives a warm welcome from a diverse community: the text clarifies how "Strangers talked and laughed as they waited in line—Koreans with Latinos, kids with elders, taggers with geeks."

Oliver Wang, in "Learning from Los Kogi Angeles: A Taco Truck and Its City," describes "how Kogi's mélange of flavors reflected Los Angeles's larger social/cultural mixtures. As Roy Choi told *Newsweek*, 'These cultures—Mexican and Korean—really form the foundation of this city. Kogi is my representation of L.A. in a single bite'" (qtd. in Wang 80). And Choi's passion for representing LA is emphasized throughout the narrative. In one spread of the picture book, for instance, the text reads:

> Roy found his place, back on the streets feeding hungry people, cooking up joy. He was home. He was living his best good time.
>
> Kogi tacos made Roy famous. Kogi trucks showed people that fresh food, full of flavor, chopped, mixed, and seasoned by hand, didn't need fancy restaurants.

The mobile nature of Kogi, the ability to interact with lots of different people, enables Roy's new understanding of his career and role in food through "living his best good time." Without Kogi, Roy may have had nowhere to belong; with Kogi, he not only remixes his cuisines but also his life and those of his customers.

The mobility of the truck and its ability to attract customers enable readers to see how the Roy's identity is based in lively experiences with and through food. The authors' notes provide additional information about Roy and how important making Kogi was to him. One note from author Jacqueline Briggs Martin states that "After the Kogi trucks became so popular, Roy could have chosen a path toward fame and wealth. Instead, he chose to cook good food, with love, for people who might not be famous or wealthy. Sharing good food on the street is sharing care. And that is Roy's path." Overall, Kogi provides a space for Roy Choi to be the kind of chef with whom he most identifies, the kind who can remix cuisines as he wants, and the truck comes to represent how exchanging food (serving and eating), even when this occurs through a capitalistic mechanism, still informs an important identity experience.

Literary Food Truck Spaces and Identities in Flux

Overall, food trucks, as mobile spaces, replicate and host the contexts for each protagonist to come to understand themselves and their identity better. The food trucks in these narratives sit in the center of each story's conflict in different and overlapping ways. Though Stef struggles with Tía Perla itself (especially regarding how others respond to her cultural roots), the truck comes to her rescue on more than one occasion. Stef eventually advocates for Tía Perla, underscoring how important the truck becomes to her and those she cares about. Likewise, Ko-Bra is the catalyst for Clara to understand the kinds of relationships she appreciates and wants with others. Even though she initially sees the truck as a prison, Clara arrives at a place where she not only accepts the truck but loves what it has brought into her life. Lastly, Kogi helps resolve Roy Choi's questions about *how* he wants to cook and what kind of chef he wants to be. Throughout these conflicts based in and around food trucks, the characters must rethink and renegotiate their identities and relationships. These new identities are possible with connections between culinary and cultural spaces. Through their food truck experiences, the protagonists gain a better understanding of who they are, who matters, and how food is able to bring disparate people together.

NOTES

1. In this essay, I will use the term that the characters use for the truck.

2. *Chef Roy Choi and the Street Food Remix* is unpaginated, so no page citations will be provided.

WORKS CITED

Bang, Molly. *Picture This: How Pictures Work.* 25th anniversary ed., Chronicle Books, 2016.

Goo, Maurene. *The Way You Make Me Feel.* Square Fish, 2019.

Irvin, Cate. "Constructing Hybridized Authenticities in the Gourmet Food Truck Scene." *Symbolic Interaction,* vol. 40, no. 1, 2017, pp. 43–62. *JSTOR,* www.jstor.org/stable /90000407, accessed May 14, 2021.

Keeling, Kara K., and Scott T. Pollard. *Table Lands: Food in Children's Literature.* University Press of Mississippi, 2020.

Lemon, Robert. *The Taco Truck: How Mexican Street Food Is Transforming the American City.* University of Illinois Press, 2019.

Martin, Jacqueline Briggs, and June Jo Lee. *Chef Roy Choi and the Street Food Remix.* Illustrated by Man One, Readers to Eaters, 2017.

Shahani, Gitanjali G. "Introduction: Writing on Food and Literature." *Food and Literature,* edited by Gitanjali G. Shahani, Cambridge University Press, 2018, pp. 1–35.

Siu, Lok. "Twenty-First-Century Food Trucks: Mobility, Social Media, and Urban Hipness." *Eating Asian America: A Food Studies Reader,* edited by Robert Ji-Song Ku, Martin F. Manalansan, and Anta Mannur, New York University Press, 2013, pp. 231–44.

Torres, Jennifer. *Stef Soto, Taco Queen.* Little, Brown, 2017.

Wang, Oliver. "Learning from Los Kogi Angeles: A Taco Truck and Its City." *Eating Asian America: A Food Studies Reader,* edited by Robert Ji-Song Ku, Martin F. Manalansan, and Anita Mannur, New York University Press, 2013, pp. 78–97.

Bad Children and Hungry Women

Food and "Hansel and Gretel" in the
Later Work of Shirley Jackson

SHELLEY INGRAM

At a dinner party hosted by Shirley Jackson, a friend told her that he was carrying a dead baby in his bag, which he would eat after it was "roasted over a campfire." Jackson replied, "It's always nice to have a little snack along in case you get hungry" (Oppenheimer 67). This exchange, recounted in Judy Oppenheimer's 1988 biography of Jackson, exemplifies some of the most prominent themes in Jackson's writing: food and mothering and witchcraft, monstrous consumption, subversive womanhood. Jackson grapples in her fiction with both the 1950s ideal of domestic bliss via the perfect mother/housewife and the Romantic construct of the pure and innocent child. As such, aberrant mothers, wicked children, and the food that binds them are central points around which much of her work revolves. Here I explore a narrative motif that weaves itself around these points, giving notice to the power of food, houses, witches, and folklore—namely, maternal consumption. Or, more precisely, the tale of "Hansel and Gretel."

I begin with a review of Jackson's play *The Bad Children* (1959), a retelling of "Hansel and Gretel" she wrote to be performed by the students in her daughter's school. The play has not been considered by scholars, as it is not in wide circulation and is a mash-up of Jackson's own writing and her children's musical numbers (Oppenheimer 222). However, *The Bad Children* clearly shows that "Hansel and Gretel" was of interest to Jackson, as it explicitly links food, witchcraft, uncanny children, and ambivalent mothering. Coming as it does between her writing of *The Sundial* (1958) and *The Haunting of Hill House* (1959), the play reveals how "Hansel and Gretel" gives shape to Jackson's particular desires concerning motherhood and domesticity. I then move to map Jackson's engagement with the fairy tale in *The Sundial, Hill House,* and *We Have Always Lived in the Castle* (1962). I argue that "Hansel and Gretel" is an avenue by which Jackson explores domestic and familial feeding and consumption, constructing counternarratives to both the tale itself and the decade's formulations of womanly domesticity. "Hansel and Gretel" provides a template for Jackson's negotiation of feeding mothers and eating children who live together in unsettled and sequestered homes.

Food matters, in life and in literature. Food brings the past forward, it connects us to those in our present, it marks boundaries between insider and outsider, between parent and child, between friend and foe. Fictional characters, unlike their physical counterparts, do not have to eat to live. That they do so says to the reader: pay attention, this is important, *it signifies.*[1] Food certainly seemed to be important to Jackson.[2] Both Oppenheimer and Franklin note that Jackson set a rich table, and concerns about food and overconsumption, including her weight, followed her for most of her life (Oppenheimer 219–20; Franklin 371–76). Jackson wrote in an unpublished essay that the reason was rather simple: she loved "the beautiful and lovely and fascinating foods mankind has devoted himself to inventing since he first learned to heat up meat. . . . The wonderful imported candies, the elaborate desserts, the rich sauces, the cheese and potatoes and creams and sweets" (Franklin 374). This fascination with food and eating makes its way starkly into her fiction.

One of the ways it does so is through Jackson's use of fairy tale motifs that involve food. Maria Tatar notes that "Food—its presence and its absence—shapes the social world of fairy tales in profound ways." Food in children's fairy tales, Tatar adds, centers on two things: the threat of cannibalism and food as literal wish fulfillment, and both are laid out explicitly in "Hansel and Gretel" (*Classic* 179). Susan Honeyman sees the "practical basis" of the tale as "a premodern story about controlling basic hunger" (196). Another folklorist has said that the tale is specifically "about conflicting family loyalties expressed in terms of sharing and hoarding food," as "Hansel and Gretel" begins with famine (Taggart 435). In the tale, a man and his wife live with their two children, and the wife—the Grimms change the character, as they often did, from "mother" to "stepmother" in their second edition—demands that her husband take their children into the woods and leave them with only a scrap of bread, because there is not enough food to feed the whole family.[3]

Then Hansel drops his famous trail of breadcrumbs, and as the children look for the path home, they find that the birds and mice have eaten the bread, leaving them lost and hungry. It is then that they find a house "built entirely from bread with a roof made of cake," with "windows made of clear sugar":

> Hansel reached up above, and broke off a little of the roof to try how it tasted. . . . Then a soft voice cried from the room,
> "Nibble, nibble, gnaw. Who is nibbling at my little house?"
> The children answered,
> "The wind, the wind,
> The heaven-born wind"
> and went on eating without disturbing themselves.[4] (64–65)

The woman, the witch, a figure with whom Jackson identified her whole life, had "only built the little bread house in order to entice them there" as she brings the children in to "fatten" them up for a good meal. Eventually, Gretel pushes the witch into the oven, saving herself and her brother. They take treasure from the witch's house and finally make their way home. The mother/wife/stepmother, importantly, has died while they were away, and the father welcomes them back with open arms. "Then all anxiety was at an end," the story says, "and they lived together in perfect happiness" (69).

Jackson wrote that she "resented violently the fact that Hansel and Gretel eat the witch's house and never get punished for it" (Oppenheimer 222). It's true that the children in "Hansel and Gretel" are unusually active for fairy tale protagonists. They are working against the plan of the mother and the father all the way through, and they trick and vanquish the witch themselves without any human or supernatural aid (Lüthi 63). But we can also see how they ignore the "soft voice" that protests their eating of the house and gorge themselves on the sweets—as Bruno Bettelheim once said, showing "how ready [children] are to eat somebody out of house and home" (161). Jackson decided to rewrite the tale, turning it into a musical called *The Bad Children* to be performed by students at her daughter's school. The children in the play were "whiny brats," and she said that "every time I [think] of something my children do that I can't stand—and there's a lot—I put it in for Hansel and Gretel" (Oppenheimer 222).

Jackson's play begins with the Witch leaving her gingerbread house one morning to have breakfast with her neighbor, the Enchanter. The Witch and the Enchanter are eating a stolen-by-magic breakfast of "griddle cakes and maple syrup and sausages and orange juice and coffee" when they hear voices and scurry off to hide. The voices belong to a family of wood gatherers: Mother, Father, Hansel, and Gretel. In Jackson's version of the story, the mother and father abandon their children near the witch's house because the children are, quite simply, very bad, particularly in their cruelty to forest animals. As soon as Hansel and Gretel find themselves alone, they rush to the witch's house and begin to "eat greedily," including the bricks, vines, and windowpanes. When the witch comes out of hiding to demand an explanation, Hansel says, "We're eating this little house, stupid" (16). Their actions are not precipitated by the fact that they are hungry, as it is in the traditional tale, but because they are gluttonous and *bad*. The children's disregard for the Witch's privacy and autonomy is represented through their eating of her home.

What follows is a give-and-take between Witch and children, with the children demanding that they be incorporated into the familiar tale. In what is perhaps the most telling of lines, Gretel says, "We've got a *right* to eat this house" (17). The children's entitlement drives the rest of the story, and the Witch cannot wait to give them back to their parents. When the mother and father pass the gingerbread house again, they are asked if they have lost their children. "Oh no! No, no, no!" says the mother. "Children? What are children?" says the father (22). After finally acknowledging Hansel and Gretel as theirs, the adults all argue about who should keep them. Eventually they scare the children into being good:

> HANSEL: Think how it sounds.
> GRETEL: All that mean talk.
> HANSEL: Why don't you be like *us*?
> GRETEL: Always nice and sweet? [*Smiles prettily*]
> . . .
> HANSEL *and* GRETEL: We're *good* children [*both smile broadly*].
> MOTHER: Children—please stop smiling like that!

The play ends with these creepy, uncanny children playing nice while the adults lament the magic's failure. Hansel and Gretel, says Jackson, "stay horrible until the end" (Oppenheimer 222).

At one point, Gretel says, "you can just go ahead and catch us if you can, because *everyone* knows what is going to happen *then*, and I get to watch Hansel push you in the oven" (17). The children's desire to become actors in the familiar fairy tale suggests that Jackson saw fairy tales as a way children understood their lives and made sense of their place in the world. The feeding/not-feeding mother in traditional tales existed primarily as an object for children to reject in order to develop their sense of difference, of "inside/out, self/other, good/bad," functioning as one-dimensional foils for the children's burgeoning self-awareness (Daniel 102). However, *The Bad Children* rejects this premise, as Jackson's version allows the adults to express a sincere longing to claim an identity beyond the domestic and familial foil. The Witch and the Enchanter spend much time discussing their unconventional breakfast in the beginning of the play, joyfully debating whether to magic it in from the Castle or the Waldorf Astoria, free of the burden of cooking and feeding and pleasing anyone other than themselves. The play makes explicit that women are not always happy to give up their own house, or their own *food*, to children. When the Witch is attempting to return the children to their parents, the Mother refuses by saying, "We're going to have fried chicken for dinner every night and *we* are going to get the drumsticks" (23). While the traditional "Hansel and Gretel" is a condemnation of the mother who will let her children starve, Jackson's play instead highlights children's insatiable hungers, as their devouring of the witch's home stands in for their overall monstrous entitlement and lack of empathy.

The Bad Children thus brings to the fore the connection between children, food, and the houses in which women live. Jackson wrote this play after she completed *The Sundial* and at the same time as she was writing *The Haunting of Hill House,* which suggests that she was not only concerned with the children's or the witch's point of view but also *the house's,* with what it would feel like to have children nibble at your walls. Angela Hague argues that in Jackson's fiction, houses "function as places of entrapment and incarceration for the women who visit or live in them" (82). However, I do not think that the houses are so easily classified as purely malevolent in their entrapment. If we trace the contours of "Hansel and Gretel" as they manifest in Jackson's later novels, a more complex view of the connections between food, houses, and mothering emerges. It is telling that all of Jackson's great houses are attractive or compelling from the outside, standing apart from their surroundings and very rarely entered by outsiders. In fact, it is often the threat of invasion by the outside that reveals the various powers that the houses possess. Plots are set in motion because someone, somewhere could not resist the lure of these (gingerbread) houses and the mother/witch inside.

The Sundial and Gingerbread Houses

The Sundial, first published in 1958, directly engages the "Hansel and Gretel" story. The novel follows the Halloran family and their hangers-on one summer as they prepare themselves and their large estate for what they believe will be the end of the world. It opens with the family's return from the funeral of Lionel, the only child of Richard and Orianna Halloran. Lionel had met a suspicious end, falling down a flight of steps to his death, and most of the Hallorans assume that he was murdered by his mother, Orianna, in a bid to secure the Halloran estate for herself. Meanwhile, Richard's sister Fanny receives multiple messages from their deceased father instructing the family to prepare for an unidentified apocalypse. What awaits them after is a new earth full of plenty, washed clean of society's ills. The rest of the novel follows the Hallorans and a select number of followers as they turn the house into a stronghold against the outside world. As the novel ends, the windows are boarded up as a great storm rages outside, though we never know whether this is the end of the world or merely an afternoon thunderstorm. What we *do* know is that Orianna is dead from a fall down the stairs. Her young granddaughter Fancy, Lionel's only child, follows Orianna's body down and laughingly assumes the mantle of regent, removing the crown that Orianna had recently taken to wearing and placing it on her own head. Fancy had previously asked her grandmother when she could have her crown, and Orianna had answered, "when I am dead" (200).

With a push, the mother kills the son, the granddaughter kills the grandmother.

The novel is actually a dark and wickedly funny comedy. There are moments of pathos, however, in which we are also meant to see the Hallorans, and Orianna specifically, as more than caricatures of upper-class midcentury isolationism. The story of "Hansel and Gretel" provides one such moment. Orianna is the "predatory and tyrannical" mother whose iron-fisted control of the family speaks to her desire to remake the world as she sees fit (Rubenstein 315). She, the murdering mother, has a dream:

> A place of my own, Mrs. Halloran thought . . . a place all my own, a house
> where I can live alone and put everything I love, a little small house of my
> own . . . no one will talk to me, and no one will hear me; there will be only
> one of everything—one cup, one plate, one spoon, one knife. Deep in the for-
> est I am living in my little house and no one can ever find me. (101)

Orianna then hears a boy's voice in her dream: "See, sister? I told you we
would find some place here in the forest." When the sister expresses fear
of approaching the house, the boy says, "Don't be silly . . . we're only children." Once they discover the house is made of candy, they begin to eat
voraciously. Mrs. Halloran, then "feeling the roof being eaten away over
her head," thinks, "Stop it at once! This is *my* house" (101–2).

In the dream, Orianna begs them to stop eating what she *feels* as an
extension of her body—she will put them in cages, but only until they
promise to stop eating her and her house. She calls to them, addressing
them as "son" and "daughter." But in a further revision of the traditional
tale, the children's mother storms into the clearing and rescues them.
The children lie and tell her:

> "—and she was going to cook us and eat us because she's a witch, and she
> offered us pieces of her house and said there was licorice in the closet and
> there wasn't because all she wanted to do was get us inside and then she
> locked us in and she said she was going to cook us and eat us . . . and she's a
> witch because she said there were cream cakes in the cupboard" . . . the lit-
> tle girl snatched away a fragment of the window frame and stuffed it into her
> mouth. (103)

The children intentionally assert power over the witch, her home, and
her body, manipulating the adults through an exploitation of their position as children and their need for food. They are a direct challenge to
the Romantic notion of childhood, which holds that "the near perfect
child" has a goodness "only matched by a purity, innocence, and innate
wisdom that redeems the errant souls of the fallen adults." Such romanticized children have a unique "ability to maneuver the world untouched
by its corruption" (Clark 193). Jackson is blatantly pushing back against
this construction of childhood innocence: these children are horrible, as
they lie, bully, and consume the witch and her home.

The Sundial thus explicitly references "Hansel and Gretel" as a way to
explore Orianna's movements through a space governed by what Elaine
Tyler May calls the "ideology of containment," which had developed in
the United States during the 1950s. This era was full of contradictions:

economic prosperity for many coupled with Cold War anxiety, a dedication to the nuclear family alongside a struggle against its constraints, the chafing of the American Dream against the reality of the growing Civil Rights Movement. Consequently, coming as it did after two decades of upheaval in the family and social structure, the 1950s saw a reinscription of traditional gender roles in an effort to define and "to embrace domesticity in the midst of the terrors of the atomic age" (May 26). The decade's modern home was supposed to provide stability at a time when people feared nuclear annihilation, a clear concern of *The Sundial*, and midcentury culture had decided that such stability required a full-time caretaker: thus, "the object of a woman's efforts" turned toward pleasing "husband, children, and friends" (McFeely 101). Traditionally, the story of "Hansel and Gretel" was a way to express, among other things, a fear of children's hunger and the moral judgment and defeat of women who let their children starve so that they themselves could be fed. As a morality tale, the story nestles easily into the 1950s iteration of the cult of domesticity. *The Sundial,* however, offers a counternarrative. Orianna sees the Halloran estate as hers and hers alone, something to which others, including her husband and child, have no right, disturbing the era's valorization of the nuclear family. Their nibbling away at the house/body comes at the cost of Orianna's own selfhood. It is a consumption that she tries to stop but cannot, and it ultimately consumes Orianna completely.

Furthermore, Orianna is almost entirely removed from the domestic realm, being what James Egan calls "a monstrous parody of the nurturing mother" in direct contradiction to the decade's feminine ideal (20). She takes care of her ailing husband sporadically, and she leaves cooking to the staff. She is now a mother without a child, monstrous particularly if she is the one who pushed her son down the stairs. Tatar has said that adult women in fairy tales are often "alien intruders" who "disturb the harmony among blood relations" (*Hard Facts* 142). Orianna functions in much the same way. She controls the people in the house but not the house itself, because her precarious position as a woman and an outsider who simply married into the family prevents it. The witch in the traditional "Hansel and Gretel" tale is also a monstrous inversion of the domestic ideal: she provides food and shelter for the children, but only so that she can one day eat them. And even then, what she offers the children is not the wholesome food of a healthy home but the food of decadence. Egan thus calls Orianna's dream of being the witch in "Hansel and Gretel" more evidence of her role in the "horrifically inverted familial" pattern of the novel (20).

And yet Orianna's fantasy is achingly domestic. She wants to have a home and food and peace and quiet. The story of "Hansel and Gretel" is outlined clearly in *The Sundial:* the murderous mother, who is in turn murdered by her offspring, fantasizes about being the witch in this enchanted forest, living in her *own* house, one made of food, a position Jackson seemed to identify with, only to be disrupted by both children and an idealized, rescued version of motherhood that turns the mother into the leader of a mob—a role, as is clear in her biography, Jackson also relished.[5] In *The Sundial*, Orianna is construed from the beginning as an "unmotherly monster" who felt driven to kill her own child out of fear that the house would be lost to her. It is not only the children, then, who are lured by the house and the rich food it promises. The witch is as well, but for her the lure is a house existing outside of the prevailing domestic constructs of her era.

The Haunting of Hill House and Hungry Mothers

Jackson's last two novels, *The Haunting of Hill House* and *We Have Always Lived in the Castle,* engage "Hansel and Gretel" motifs in more figurative ways, signaling Jackson's evolving concerns for women and their homes. *Hill House,* like *The Sundial,* finds its thrill constructing domesticity as a source of terror. And since *Hill House* suggests that the woman and the house are not easily cleaved apart—"the house is Eleanor," Jackson writes in her notes (Franklin 415)—we can see the shape of "Hansel and Gretel" continuing to provide Jackson a way to explore the consumption of a woman by her children, particularly since we know that she was writing *The Bad Children* at the same time. But here Jackson asks, What happens if that process is reversed? What happens if the mother eats the child?

Critics have often read the novel in two complementary ways: as a comment on the constraining horrors of domesticity and as a representation of the mother as monstrous consumer. In the novel, Eleanor Vance is looking for a purpose after the recent death of her mother, so she travels to Hill House to be part of a supernatural group experiment run by Dr. Montague. Hill House hails Eleanor, with the words "HELP ELEANOR COME HOME" appearing on its walls. The house sometimes embraces Eleanor so that she feels like "she was held tight and safe," while at other times it makes her think that it "is monstrous . . . cruel." In perhaps the novel's most revealing scene, Eleanor awakens, disoriented, calling out, "Coming, mother, coming . . . It's all right, I'm coming." She hears a loud knocking and thinks, "my mother is knocking on the wall." Eleanor carries a heavy guilt from her mother's death: "'It was my fault my mother died,' Eleanor said. 'She knocked on the wall and called me and called me and I never woke up'" (156). Indeed, it is possible for the reader to infer that Eleanor intentionally let her mother die. Hill House, then, knows its prey, as Eleanor is both motherless and childless and looking for absolution through maternal love.

Deane Curtin argues that "eating is like childbirth in the way it threatens a sense of self as absolutely autonomous. . . . The mother's body is food for the child" (9). If we read "Hansel and Gretel" as a search for the perfect mother who will feed her children the food of their dreams rather than abandon them because of her own hunger, then we see its echo here, because Eleanor is also looking for a mother who will invite her in. She is lured by the house and the promises it makes, including a restitution of the original mother/child bond that is connected intimately to feeding. After one particularly harrowing encounter, during which the house knocks on the walls and tries to get into the room that Eleanor and fellow participant Theo share, the women describe the phenomenon to Dr. Montague and Luke, the final member of the group. Theo says, "Someone knocked on the door with a cannon ball and then tried to get in and eat us" (98). Eleanor believes that eat "was exactly the right word. The sense was that it wanted to consume us, take us into itself," a reversal of the traditional mother/child feeding dynamic (102). The house, a representation of the mother, herself represented by the witch in the traditional tale, is seeking to consume its child.[6]

In "Hansel and Gretel," it is fairly clear that the witch and the mother are one and the same—that when the children kill the witch, they also kill the mother. Thus, "the death of the mother eliminates the twin dreads of starvation and the fear of being devoured" (Tatar, *Classic* 182). Lisa Chinitz argues that in "Hansel and Gretel," "the complete merging of inner and outer psychical life with the mother . . . comes to represent the threat of the loss of self," which makes the resulting assertion of autonomy that comes from killing the witch/mother necessary. In the house in the woods, Hansel and Gretel are able to find a home with a mother who they think will feed them, in a house which itself can be and is eaten. They trespass into her space and then consume her, overcoming the witch/mother in order to procure their own autonomy. This allows them to return to the father, vanquishing the mother who both feeds them and denies them food.

In Jackson's notes is a sketch of Hill House that seems to suggest a picture of herself, so that Hill House is the body is Shirley Jackson,[7] the mother of four who is also writing *The Bad Children,* a play whose very title strips Hansel and Gretel of differentiated selfhood. And in *Hill House,* the house wins, ultimately refusing Eleanor's autonomy. The house had seemed to promise a restitution of the mother/daughter feeding bond by asking her to come home, offering to ameliorate the loss that arose after the death/murder of her mother. Hill House beguiles Eleanor with hallucinations and fantasies that assure a reunion with some kind of womb, much as the gingerbread house lured hungry children who were met with a witch who plotted to cook them in an oven. Thus, when Eleanor drives herself into a tree rather than be rejected from Hill House, it signals her ultimate unwillingness to give up the merging of her own "inner and outer psychical life" with the mother. She does not reject the mother in order to enter a motherless, patriarchal world, an entrance that in "Hansel and Gretel" is signaled by pushing the witch/ mother into the oven and emerging as autonomous and triumphant. In the end, Eleanor is consumed and *not* incorporated, as she does not become part of the house; she is not embraced by the mother, she does not achieve differentiated selfhood. Instead, she is erased, because in Hill House, "whatever walked there, walked alone" (182). In this novel, unlike in *The Sundial* or "Hansel and Gretel," the witch wins.

We Have Always Lived in the Castle and Evil Witches

In Jackson's final complete novel, *We Have Always Lived in the Castle,* eighteen-year-old Merricat lives with her sister, Constance, in Blackwood Manor, their home behind a gate and beyond the village. This marks the Blackwood sisters as aloof and set apart from their mostly working-class neighbors, who in turn treat the sisters with unconcealed hostility. Six years prior, someone had poisoned the family sugar, and the mother, father, aunt, and ten-year-old son died after eating dessert. We find out toward the end of the novel that the then-twelve-year-old Merricat was the murderer, though Constance had stood trial and was acquitted of the crimes.

Very little motive is given for the murders except that Merricat was punished for being, in Constance's teasing words, a "wicked, disobedient child" who was sent away from the table without her supper. Daniel argues that "the primal experience" between mother and child "also involves absolute fulfillment," and that once the absence of food is realized, "desire for [its] restoration" swiftly follows (88). For Hansel and Gretel, this abandonment and hunger manifest in their instant succumbing to the lure of a house made of food and in their entering the witch's home, looking for a restoration of the mother. For Merricat, the only person in her family who had succeeded in feeding and caring for her was Constance, who would "go up the back stairs with a tray of dinner for [Merricat] after [their] father had left the dining room" (34). The moment when food is withheld forces a realization: with the rest of the family gone, Merricat could finally restore and then strengthen the primal, infantile bond with her sister.

Constance has spent the years since her acquittal retreating into a kind of hyperdomesticity, taking care of Merricat and the only other survivor of the poisoning, their sickly uncle Julian. Constance is strongly associated with food and nurturing, always cooking and baking and gardening and canning. She took over the role of family cook long before her parents' death, because the (absent) mother was simply uninterested in domestic chores. Constance exhibits the skills her own mother seemed to lack, and she is all that Merricat wants in a mother, a figure out of fantasy who comes to power through a monstrous act of violence. With food and family annihilation, Jackson situates *Castle* within in the world of the fairy tale.

While in *The Sundial* the house is barricaded against outsiders and stocked with provisions, in *Castle* the seemingly impenetrable walls are eventually breached, making the house susceptible to invasion as the contents of the home are laid bare. The sisters engage in a final confrontation with both their cousin Charles, who had come to marry Constance and send Merricat away, and the villagers. The community picks up where a fire has left off, stoning the house and destroying the interior. In their attack they pay particular attention to the kitchen, emptying out the stores of food and breaking almost all the dishes. In *The Sundial,* the children nibbling at Orianna's walls reinforce her desire for isolation and, most of all, control of the Halloran estate. This desire is never fulfilled, as she is foiled by the actions of a wicked child. In *Castle,* though, when the sisters return to their home the next day, they clean the kitchen and barricade the windows and eat and drink from the few dishes and the two cups that survived the assault. They sit in their house in the woods that now decidedly belongs only to them, the fruition, down to the singularity of cups, of Orianna's "Hansel and Gretel" dream.

A new order is established in *Castle.* Uncle Julian has died, and the sisters now live alone in their home as witches, whose existence is sanctified by the action of the villagers. The women of the village make offerings of food to the sisters in penance for their violence, and the sisters live off these goods. Merricat and Constance have become a story that parents tell their children, achieving what Gretel in *The Bad Children* so desperately demanded as they are incorporated into local lore. Julie Carr argues that "[t]he woman in [Hansel and Gretel], as in so many [fairy tales], is the regulator and distributor of food. Fairytale wives, mothers, and witches feed, or do not, and when they do feed, they often poison" (19). In *Castle*, a mother tells her son that the sisters are scary women who will "hold you down and make you eat candy full of poison," warning that they capture the little boys who get too close to the house and eat the little girls (141). Masking evil with sweetness, feeding to kill instead of nourish, and threatening not just death but cannibalism: these traits all position Merricat and Constance as outside the natural domestic and maternal order and connect them to the witch of "Hansel and Gretel."

As Merricat and Constance sit in their house discussing the omelets to be made from a young boy's offering of fresh eggs, Merricat wonders if she "could eat a child if [she] had the chance." "I doubt if I could cook one," says Constance, though she is not denying cannibalism so much as lamenting her lack of a good recipe (146). Both of these responses clearly reject a particular ideology of domesticity and mothering. Merricat could, and in fact *did,* kill a child, but as of yet has not consumed one like she is about to consume the boy's eggs. And when Constance rejected Charles's offer of marriage, she rejected the possibility of biological reproduction, and eggs for her are now only to eat.

We see the shape of "Hansel and Gretel" in this new world that Merricat and Constance inhabit. After their home has been eaten away by the villagers, they contemplate their roles as women in this particular place and time. In the novel are ovens and wombs, eggs and baked children, and since the threat of cannibalism is ever present in fairy tales about witches, children, and food, this scene reinforces the sisters' witchy dyad. But the readers I have encountered through teaching this novel many times generally have no problem morally recouping Merricat's character and rooting for her happiness. That so many readers feel connected to, and empathy for, a fictional character who murdered her father, mother, aunt, and ten-year-old brother is an integral part of the novel's meaning-making.

Partly, this has to do with Merricat's compelling first-person narration, as we see through her eyes the hostility of the villagers and their children. But I would also suggest that it is a testament to the power of the witch and the lure of her gingerbread home. Jackson's fiction suggests that children do indeed "stay horrible until the end" and that witches are women whose sometimes destructive desire is simply to live an undisturbed life with a power that is fully their own, unconstrained by socially enforced notions of femininity and domesticity. Her later novels find meaning through motifs culled from "Hansel and Gretel," as they are full of food both nourishing and poisonous, sinister children like Fancy, devouring mothers like Hill House, and witches like Merricat, who as a child kills her family yet gets, in the end, everything she wants. There are hungry women and the bad children who eat away at their homes and their bodies, who refuse to stop because of their own insatiable desires. Jackson's novels reveal how witchcraft is a peculiar longing for her, and how a woman's desire to exist in a space without children there to consume her—and her desire, in fact, to consume—is figured and refigured in Jackson's era as monstrous. In reality, Jackson's witch only wanted a little house to herself with food enough to eat as she so pleased, worried of neither scarcity nor gluttony. Jackson thus capitalizes on the enduring power of "Hansel and Gretel" to offer up subversive versions of both womanhood and childhood that challenge the era's criteria for happily ever after.

NOTES

1. Food, as Roland Barthes says, "sums up and transmits a situation; it constitutes an information; it signifies" (29).

2. Cf. Ingram and Mullins.

3. For a brief discussion of this change, see Tatar, *Classic* 180, *Hard Facts* 142–43, and Harries 225–27.

4. This is from the 1884 *Grimm's Household Tales*, translated by Margaret Hunt with an introduction by Andrew Lang. I do not know if this is the version that Jackson was familiar with, but as Jackson's husband, Stanley Edgar Hyman, a folklorist and myth critic, was very interested in Lang's work, I could imagine this version in their library. Other textual clues include Jackson's repetition of the word "nibble" in her version of the tale in *The Sundial*.

5. Franklin recounts a story about Jackson fighting to have a teacher at her daughter's school fired for abuse and being portrayed as part of a "small band of upstarts who flouted the chain of command" (378–81).

6. Much of the criticism concerning the novel *Hill House* focuses on the notion of a "devouring mother." See Rubenstein, Newman, Lootens, and Kahane.

7. See Hattenhauer 164.

WORKS CITED

Barthes, Roland. "Toward a Psychosociology of Contemporary Food Consumption." *Food and Culture: A Reader,* edited by Carole Counihan and Penny Van Esterik, 2nd ed., Routledge, 1997, p. 29.

Bettelheim, Bruno. *The Uses of Enchantment: The Meaning and Importance of Fairy Tales.* Knopf, 1976.

Carr, Julie. *Someone Shot My Book*. University of Michigan Press, 2018.

Chinitz, Lisa G. "Fairy Tale Turned Ghost Story: James's *The Turn of the Screw*." *Henry James Review*, vol. 15, no. 3, 1994, pp. 264–85.

Clark, Dorothy G. "Edging toward Bethlehem: Rewriting the Myth of Childhood in Voight's *Homecoming*." *Children's Literature Association Quarterly*, vol. 25, no. 4, 2000, pp. 191–202.

Curtin, Deane W. "Food/Body/Person." *Cooking, Eating, Thinking: Transformative Philosophies of Food*, edited by Deane W. Curtin and Lisa M. Heldke, Indiana University Press, 1992, pp. 3–22.

Daniel, Carolyn. *Voracious Children: Who Eats Whom in Children's Literature*. Routledge, 2009.

Egan, James. "Sanctuary: Shirley Jackson's Domestic and Fantastic Parables." *Studies in Weird Fiction*, vol. 6, 1989, pp. 15–24.

Franklin, Ruth. *Shirley Jackson: A Rather Haunted Life*. Liveright, 2016.

Hague, Angela. "'A Faithful Anatomy of Our Times': Reassessing Shirley Jackson." *Frontiers*, vol. 26, no. 2, 2005, pp. 73–96.

Harries, Elizabeth. "Hansel and Gretel." *The Oxford Companion to Fairy Tales*, edited by Jack Zipes, Oxford University Press, 2000, pp. 225–27.

Hattenhauer, Darryl. *Shirley Jackson's American Gothic*. SUNY Press, 2003.

Honeyman, Susan. "Gingerbread Wishes and Candy(land) Dreams: The Lure of Food in Cautionary Tales of Consumption." *Marvels and Tales*, vol. 21, no. 2, 2007, pp. 195–215.

Jackson, Shirley. *The Bad Children: A Play in One Act for Bad Children*. Dramatic Publishing, 1959.

———. *The Haunting of Hill House*. 1959. Penguin, 2006.

———. *The Sundial*. 1958. Penguin, 2014.

———. *We Have Always Lived in the Castle*. 1962. Penguin, 2006.

Kahane, Claire. "The Gothic Mirror." *The (M)other Tongue: Essays in Feminist Psychoanalytic Interpretation*, edited by Shirley Nelson Garner, Claire Kahane, and Madelon Sprengnether, Cornell University Press, 1985, pp. 334–51.

Lootens, Tricia. "'Whose Hand Was I Holding?': Familial and Sexual Politics in Shirley Jackson's *The Haunting of Hill House*." *Shirley Jackson: Essays on the Literary Legacy*, edited by Bernice M. Murphy, McFarland, 2005, pp. 120–34.

Lüthi, Max. *Once Upon a Time: On the Nature of Fairy Tales*. Translated By Lee Chadeayne, Indiana University Press, 1976.

May, Elaine Tyler. *Homeward Bound: American Families in the Cold War Era*. Basic Books, 1988.

McFeely, Mary Drake. *Can She Bake a Cherry Pie? American Women and the Kitchen in the Twentieth Century*. University of Massachusetts Press, 2001.

Newman, Judie. "Shirley Jackson and the Reproduction of Mothering: *The Haunting of Hill House*." *American Horror Fiction: From Brockden Brown to Stephen King*, edited by Brian Docherty, Palgrave Macmillan, 1990, pp. 120–34.

Oppenheimer, Judy. *Private Demons: The Life of Shirley Jackson*. Fawcett Columbine, 1989.

Rubenstein, Roberta. "House Mothers and Haunted Daughters: Shirley Jackson and Female Gothic." *Tulsa Studies in Women's Literature*, vol. 15, no. 2, 1996, pp. 309–31.

Taggart, James M. "'Hansel and Gretel' in Spain and Mexico." *Journal of American Folklore*, vol. 99, no. 394, 1986, pp. 435–60.

Tatar, Maria. *The Classic Fairy Tales*. W.W. Norton, 1999.

———. *The Hard Facts of the Grimms' Fairy Tales*. Princeton University Press, 2019.

PART III

The Salad Bowl and American Immigrants

The Ingredients of an Emblematic Personal Self

Autobiographical Memory and Autonoetic
Consciousness in Diana Abu-Jaber's
The Language of Baklava

SANGHAMITRA DALAL

The recent surge of food memoirs, sometimes called culinary life-writing, by ethnic and multicultural authors highlights the significance of food as a metaphorical cultural identifier. These texts are able to signify one's origin, heritage, tradition, and identity, both for an immigrant or an immigrant-descendant who is fractured by multiple selves and numerous notions of home.

However, writing about food, cooking, and sharing meals together is not just a recent phenomenon. While Claude Lévi-Strauss argues that cooking is "a truly universal form of human activity" (40), Roland Barthes observes that food can also be recognized as "a system of communication, a body of images, a protocol of usages, situations and behaviour," where information could be gathered not just by direct observation but also by indirect observation "in the mental life of a given society" (24). Louise Vasvári rightly notes that sharing recipes with one another has its roots in oral storytelling, where memories, histories, and stories blend together to re-create "the fiction of one's memories through food" (2). Likewise, David Sutton argues that food memories constitute a "form of historical consciousness" (26), as culinary life-writing and cookbook memoirs acquire an increasing relevance when myriad modes of transnational and transcultural migrations have become a widespread reality. Similarly, Linda Murray Berzok concludes that "[f]amily recipes offer us a glimpse into our pasts—a way to understand who we are by exploring who we were. . . . They serve up real connection and history no matter how far we've travelled since we first tasted these dishes" (xix). In this context, I will read American author Diana Abu-Jaber's memoir *The Language of Baklava* (2005) as it effectively transcends from a simple recollection of cooking and sharing meals together to a symbolic narrative of auto-evaluation. I will argue that Abu-Jaber's memoir can be read to suggest that the culture of cooking and sharing meals together can pave the way for an emblematic construction of the personal self, by a process of fusing disparate ingredients into a delicious concoction of transcultural belongingness.

Born in Syracuse, New York, to an American mother and a Jordanian father, Diana Abu-Jaber had to move homes between Jordan and the United States a number of times throughout her childhood and was compelled to learn how to be an Arab at home and American in the street.[1] In spite of the proliferation of important Asian American food memoirs like Abu-Jaber's as well as scholarly studies on Asian American foodways and food literature, a specific focus on the food writing of Middle Eastern immigrants in America is arguably rare. Carol Bardenstein, in an exploration of cookbook memoirs of Middle Eastern exiles, observes that the particular nature of food often acts as a "carrier" of individual and collective memory, which is articulated "retroactively, after displacement" ("Transmissions" 358). She argues that cookbook memoirs produce a rich site for exploring relationships between food and memory, and the ways "nostalgia mediates between the past and the present, shaping and reshaping both in the process" ("Transmissions" 358). Therefore, recollecting, cooking, and sharing the foods of one's homeland in a new country can be simply seen as restoring the chasm of displacement, of acknowledging that one is caught between two different worlds. However, in a later article, she rightly notes that Abu-Jaber's *The Language of Baklava* is distinctively different. She evaluates Abu-Jaber's memoir as not just a plainly nostalgic register of home-cooked dishes and their recipes, the kind signaling a straightforward binary of then and now or loss and recuperation, but rather "a sustained portrayal of a poignant, dialectical, and constantly evolving relationship between its protagonists on the one hand, and the places and cultures they inhabit in Jordan and the United States, on the other" ("Beyond" 161).

Cooking is arguably one of the more significant identifiers of Middle Eastern cultural legacy. Preparing and sharing food, interspersed with long sessions of storytelling, dominate Middle Eastern cultural practices. While this may be true of some other cultures to a degree, Abu-Jaber uses this recognition to describe how the metaphor of food practices transforms one's understanding of the self, thereby helping one evolve through the unrestricted preparation and consumption of food beyond the limits of racial and cultural stereotypes. Therefore, *The Language of Baklava* is prompted by and woven together with shards of memory—of specific dishes and their ingredients. Each chapter reflects on what the memory of that particular dish recalls, either in Jordan or in America, and articulates the stories and recipes associated with it, all in a quest to discover one's personal notion of the self. In an interview, Abu-Jaber recalls the process of writing the memoir as one that involved a constant struggle of reevoking and reliving the past. She eventually realizes the fascinating power of memory, and memory repression, asserting: "[I]t seems like a kind of magic to me, the way we can lose things that we've lived through, and then, almost ineffably, rediscover them, sometimes years later, again" (Mackintosh). She contends that each dish referred to in her cookbook memoir summons up memories and stories of her food-obsessed family, thereby also symbolizing "a different stage in our evolution as a family, as immigrants" (Shalal-Esa). In sum, the concept of autobiographical memory is a complex construct that integrates past experiences into the present, while envisioning the future and the future self. In doing so, she examines the idea of autonoetic consciousness, a process of investigation that interrogates a conscious experience of the self while recalling the past even as the self is reformed. Consciously reliving the memories and experiences of her earlier self not only enables her to be aware of her predicament of fractured belonging and straddling multiple homes, but also emancipates her with a choice of conceiving and shaping her future self of her own volition.

Autobiographical Memory and Autonoetic Consciousness

Robyn Fivush defines autobiographical memory as a unique type of human memory that "moves beyond recall of experienced events to integrate perspective, interpretation, and evaluation across self, other, and time to create a personal history" (560). Hence, autobiographical memory can be perceived as one of the major components in constructing an introspective life-narrative. Fivush has differentiated autobiographical memory from episodic memory, a concept popularized by Endel Tulving. Tulving's idea of episodic memory includes both the notion of consciousness and autonoetic consciousness. Rather, I propose that both concepts—autonoetic consciousness and autobiographical memory—are operating simultaneously in constructing Abu-Jaber's personal self-narrative as she recalls and relives her past.

According to Tulving, autonoetic—which means, essentially, self-knowing—is a kind of human consciousness that "mediates an individual's awareness of his or her existence and identity in subjective time extending from the personal past through the present to the personal future" (2). Tulving asserts that the functioning of episodic memory is closely related to evoking consciousness. However, he also argues that even though remembering is a conscious experience, all kinds of consciousness are not the same, and there is a difference between consciousness and conscious awareness, which he defines as autonoetic consciousness. He explains that while consciousness identifies "a particular capability of living systems," conscious awareness signifies "the internally expressed outcome of exercising this ability in a particular situation" (3). In other words, consciousness in episodic memory involves the memory of a specific incident, whereas autonoetic consciousness necessitates an awareness of the self as having undergone, through narrative memory, the experience of that specific incident. Fivush rightly points out that there is a need to distinguish between episodic memory and autobiographical memory. According to her, even though autobiographical memory utilizes the concept of episodic memory, it develops its own characteristics in three specific ways. First, autobiographical memory is not only distinctively marked by its inclusion of the self as the subject of the event, thereby evoking autonoetic consciousness, but also, as Fivush elucidates, is characterized by its ability to establish a connection between the self's experiences and visualization of its past, present, and future. Fivush further extends this function and identifies a significant shift in the operation of autobiographical memory, maintaining that "autobiographical memory goes beyond the episodic memory function of guiding current and future behaviour to serve social and emotional functions, including self-definition, self-in-relation, and self-regulation" (560–61). She contends that autobiographical memory, along with its close association with experiencing autonoetic consciousness, is complex in its ability to harbor "long developmental history" and shape itself as a form of cultural activity specific to certain "local and cultural forms of social interaction" (561). Consequently, drawing from Fivush's proposition, I submit that exercising autobiographical memory purposively is crucial in conceptualizing one's life-narrative. An integrated frame of reference depends on a self-referenced and self-experienced memory of specific sequences of individually perceived events. The creation of a co-herent self must incorporate action from one's past through the present to the future, and be effective in constructing both a reflective space for appreciating the event and the lived experience of those subject to the event.

In its attempt to contrive an emblematic personal self, the construc-tion of such a contemplative space accentuates the role of autonoetic consciousness in autobiographical memory. As Fivush points out, re-calling any past incident and remembering the self-experience of that particular incident highlights autobiographical memory as advancing a dual layer of representation. The presence of autonoetic consciousness while autobiographical memory is in action ensures that the memory not only represents what happened but also what the experiencer felt when it happened. Therefore, connecting the self in the past with the self in the present, and experiencing and recalling the event as well as the self's involvement in that event, encourages the self to engage in a critical, evaluative function. Autobiographical memory, then, establishes a continuous link between an earlier self as a subject who experiences an event and a present self as an appraiser of the same event. The ability of invoking the self as "a continuous being in time" with "a past, present and future that links specific episodic representations into a meaningful sequence of events" is, according to Fivush, not only "the crux of auto-biographical memory" but also a phenomenon that "define[s] a person and a life" (563). Herein lies the significance of autobiographical mem-ory and autonoetic consciousness in fashioning a life as well as a life-narrative. The memoirist constantly looks back in order to look forward, recollecting the fragments of the past in the quest of shaping a meaning-ful entity for the continuous self, one thriving in the present and primed for the future. Abu-Jaber's text, then, uses autobiographical memory and autonoetic consciousness to align with her fragmented self, as she recalls specific incidents in her life, particularly through her memory of tasting distinctive dishes associated with these incidents, while shifting between different continents and cultures.

Tracing the Recipes of Reconciliation between Fragmented Selves

Spanning twenty-four chapters and forty-three recipes, *The Language of Baklava* traces what Abu-Jaber's explains as "the ways we grew into our-selves" (xi). The undertaking, which is simultaneously marked by flights of fantasy interspersed with nightmarish ordeals, could be a story of episodic disintegration. As she traverses oceans and continents, the narrator's memories and stories of self and home become fragmented and indistinct. Her disorientation raises the dangerous possibility of fostering and re-creating competing, diverging selves and a conjoined sense of never being at home. However, reminiscing and delineating her father's nostalgic experiences and her mother's diverse cultural roots, as well as her real-life memories and stories recollected over the long and joyous gatherings at dinner tables, signal the possibility of a greater reconciliation between her Jordanian and American selves. Thereby, Abu-Jaber prioritizes the need to safeguard the emotional core of her memory, irrespective of it being private and flawed, outlandish or idiosyncratic. As she maintains that "memories give our lives their fullest shape, and eating together helps us to remember" (xi), the metaphor of food in her cookbook memoir transforms as we read from being simple ingredients and recipes to signifying "something much larger: grace, difference, faith, love" (xi). Having united the various strands that constitute herself through food, she has a place from which to launch into a place where she is able to find herself: "The fruits and vegetables, the dishes and the music and the light and the trees of all these places have grown into me, drawing me away. And so I go. Into the world, away" (328).

Diana's initial recollection of her father, Ghassan Saleh Abu-Jaber, fondly called Bud by all in America, is invariably marked by his cooking and serving of elaborate Arab dishes to a large number of family and friends on the weekends. Even though she can specifically relive the aroma and the taste of the amazing meals of her childhood—shish kebob, pita bread, salty braided cheese, and hummus—she also remembers the uneasy feeling that such family gatherings induced in her. As she fails to comprehend what her father and his extended family are pining for, she realizes that in spite of being a close-knit family, they all inhabit different worlds: "I was born into this snowy Syracuse world. I have no inkling of what other worlds are like" (20). Abu-Jaber's confusion over belonging to fragmented worlds is enhanced by her mother's roots in multiple cultural strands, as opposed to her father's distinctively secure historical antecedents. Along with her extended Irish-German-Catholic family, her mother grew up in New Jersey and was not particularly concerned with meticulously identifying the origin of her forefathers. Even though Bud is determined to cook only Arab food at home, as he is single-minded about bringing up "good" Jordanian girls, Abu-Jaber also finds solace in the simple foods prepared by her mother when Bud is away, such as grilled Velveeta sandwiches.

Abu-Jaber's struggle with her conflicting identities continues outside of her home as well. She remembers the foods served in her school cafeteria as "a congealed, mealy, gray mass that gazes sadly up at the ceiling" (22), in contrast to her bagged lunch of garlicky chicken kabobs, crunchy falafels, or fresh spinach pies. However, in her zeal for becoming an American, she recalls that she has forced herself to appreciate "instant chocolate pudding in single-serving aluminum tubs" or "crystal cups of gummy eggnog from a carton" that the mother of her then best friend, Sally Holmes, serves (73). Abu-Jaber's perpetual and exhaustive struggle with and against how to be an Arab at home and an American in the streets reaches a crescendo during her teenage years when she rebels against her father and refuses to return to Jordan.

However, as she recalls and relives her first visit to Jordan when she was seven years old, she discovers that the perception of native lands or native foods does not necessarily need to be identified with either America or Jordan. Essences of home and belonging can be carved out distinctively through a fusion of disparate identities. She recalls a remarkable pancake breakfast in Jordan. While a young Diana and her mother strive to prepare pancakes with scant ingredients available, their experimental pancakes turn out to be "dense and chewy and smack of fried butter, wheat, olive oil and scorched iron" (38). Yet the breakfast is amply appreciated by the neighbors, who not only enjoy their "burnt American flat food" but generously share their "bread with sesame seeds and fresh hardboiled eggs and tomatoes warm from the garden, fragrant mint and tubs of rich yogurt and salty white cheese and olives and pistachios" (38). Even as a young girl, Diana innately comprehends that different types of foods prepared and consumed together across apparent cultural and geographical gulfs could smoothly be digested and absorbed within one's own shifting and evolving self. Thus, her memories of her initial struggle to conform, along with her re-creating the experiences of how she reconciles her fractured and fragmented identities, appropriately symbolize the significance of autobiographical memory and autonoetic consciousness in reinscribing a sustainable life-narrative.

Unfolding the Layers of Baklava, Unraveling the Mystery Filling

Diana's interaction with the presumably authoritarian Auntie Aya during her visit to America marks the crowning experience of *The Language of Baklava*. First, Auntie Aya calms Diana with her version of "shaking tea" when a thirteen-year-old American Diana defiantly attempts to overpower "the Jordanian 'Dee-ahna'" (58). As the infusion of water, dried ginger, whole cloves, cinnamon, and anise seeds, simmered with a pinch of salt, garnished with chopped almonds or pistachios, and served with sugar or honey "mingles with the brown melancholy inside . . . and releases particles of sleeplessness and sadness embedded within" (184), Diana eventually submits herself to Auntie Aya's proposition of baking together. The choice to make baklava together ultimately transforms into a moment of truth for articulating an emblematic construction of personal self, a self no longer fractured and fragmented but a tranquil fusion of similarities and differences.

Baklava is therefore both symbolic and significant, as this popular dessert—made with layered and buttered phyllo dough and fillings of ground walnuts, cinnamon, sugar, splashes of lemon juice, and dressed with cooled syrup—has a long, contested history of origin. Baklava cannot be attributed to any single country, as different evidences suggest that even though it could claim having both Turkish and Greek origins, historically, it could also be traced back to the Assyrian or Ottoman Empires (Arvela 76). Diana starts learning how to prepare different kinds of cream puffs, layered cakes, tortes, strudels, kolaches, and cookies—"voluptuous pastries from a variety of ethnicities" (Abu-Jaber, *Language* 186)—before tasting Auntie Aya's famous baklava, her specialty. As Diana gapes at the phyllo dough layers turning flaky and buttery in the oven, at the central core of pistachios roasting fragrantly being sweetened and perfumed "like a baby with an attar dashed with sprinklings of orange blossom and rosewater," she intuits that the smell of freshly baked baklavas could herald an abstract feeling that is "too dear for this world [containing] the mysteries of time, loss, and grief, as well as promises of journeys and rebirth" (191), and thus signifying endless connections and continuity. The family dinner table graced by her Auntie Aya's "Poetic Baklava (for when you need to serenade someone)" unearths crucial moments of recognition (192). Bud promises, while holding a half-eaten baklava between his fingers, that he will never send his daughter away. Diana is not only assured that she is finally home for good, but the luscious and fragrant fillings of the delectable pastries unpeel the deep-rooted intricacies of her convoluted sense of home and self to reveal what her Auntie Aya suggests: "It's never a bad idea to put a secret in your filling" (187).

The autobiographical memory of such significant incidents, which Diana relives through her autonoetic consciousness in her cookbook memoir, thus repeatedly unravel themselves even as they become harbingers of personal truth that signal an emergence within her of a unique awareness of home and self. The journey from Diana's initial queries—from "What sort of person am I? Where are my loyalties?" (51), to the more formless wonderings about whether people must decide who they are or where their home is, to witnessing disintegrating distances and dissipating geographical strictures where "there is something in us connecting every person to every other person" (229)—dissolves into reaching out to simple *lebeneh* (yogurt drained and thickened to become mild and rich and then drizzled with a pinch of salt and good olive oil), as she mysteriously suffers and recovers from her psychosomatic nausea and sleeplessness. Her literal passage of growing up, through childhood to her writerly and professional self, is replete with her metaphoric flights of homecoming as realized through her conscious experiences: "Each event is one piece in the path of claiming myself" (233). When she applies for a Fulbright fellowship in order to research a new novel set in Amman, she recognizes that, in contrast to her father's obsessive belief in Jordan as their true and essential home, her self-chosen journey to Amman for a year would be her tentative attempt toward the "self-excavation, recovery, and reconciliation" of her fractured selves and cultural ambivalence (235). By reminiscing about her memories and stories through the lenses of particular dishes, plus settling on visiting Jordan on her own with an eye toward resolving her conflicting cultural identities, Abu-Jaber eventually evokes Fivush's view on the significance of autobiographical memory in exploring and claiming self-definition, self-in-relation, and self-regulation.

However, Abu-Jaber's cookbook memoir, paradoxically, also reveals a different kind of discernment, which is appropriately expressed by her auntie Aya: "People say food is a way to remember the past. Never mind about that. Food is a way to forget" (189). She further clarifies that Bud's passion for cooking Arab food in order to zealously preserve the memory of his Jordanian home is ironically drawing him further away from reality: "He thinks he cooks and eats Arabic food, but these walnuts weren't grown from Jordanian earth and this butter wasn't made from Jordanian lambs. He is eating the shadow of a memory. He cooks to remember, but the more he eats, the more he forgets" (189–90). Moreover, "Jordan is not the place he thinks it is. It won't save him; it can't even save itself" (186). Bud eventually discovers this painful schism from his own family at home in Jordan when he realizes that his brother, Frankie, is trying to exhort him to buy his old, decayed house without a kitchen at an incredibly exorbitant price, thereby exploiting Bud's perennial obsession with his dream of setting up a family restaurant. Abu-Jaber's cookbook memoir, therefore, traces not only her own journey through disparate cultures but also her father's evolving journey through his memories and ideas of home. Bud finally acknowledges: "I'm never coming back to Jordan again. . . . Time to go home" (307–8).

The acts of recalling and delineating performed in Abu-Jaber's autobiographical memory and autonoetic consciousness do not, however, amount to it being a manual of selecting between multiple homes and selves in transit. Rather, as proposed earlier, it is an attempt to carve out a route through an evolved understanding of the intricate relationships between memory and perception, past and present, and toward envisioning an ever-expanding future. Through re-creating past incidents and reviving forgotten sensibilities, *The Language of Baklava* manifests the idea that constructing lives and life-narratives reflects singular moments on the move, moments out of time where the autonoetic consciousness of one's past endeavors to stimulate the dynamic faculty of autobiographical memory in order to adapt to changing circumstances as well as to foresee and equip oneself for an indefinite and uncertain future. The final chapter of *The Language of Baklava* is thus appropriately titled "The First Meal," indicating this steadfast association between the past, present, and future. Bud's compulsive desire to run a family restaurant serving foods from home eventually materializes into a small hut by a driving range for golfers where he serves "rows of burgers, sizzling French fries, blistering hot dogs, and grilled cheese sandwiches" (324). Abu-Jaber realizes that such basic foods recall her father's first meal in America: "a daily regime of hamburger and Coke—that began all his other American meals." Tracing lives though foods, therefore, reveals that even though biological life follows a temporal, chronological pattern, the personal perceptions and (re-)constructions of life's stories instinctively meander through manifold layers of cracks and fissures, continuities and connections. Consequently, Abu-Jaber consciously embraces her legion of myriad selves that symbolically converse with each other within the folds of the shadows of silent nights, which she perceives as "more than *looking*: the elements of darkness and distance release my mind like a dash of sugar on the surface of hot water" (327, emphasis in the original). Her inner self envisages that "the purple black glisten of an eggplant skin within the night air" or the calling out for a spread of tea, mint, sugar, dark bread, and oil is able to reassure her other self that "it owns nothing, and it wants nothing, only to see, to taste, and to describe." Ultimately, not only the dish and its ingredients but also the taste of memory, emotions, and sensibilities eventually pave the way to unravel the layers and intertwining of myriad selves and homes—transient and ephemeral—drifting forever through similarities and differences.

NOTE

1. Currently, a professor and writer-in-residence in the Department of English at Portland State University, Diana Abu-Jaber is the author of six novels including *Fencing with the King* (2022), *Silverworld* (2020), *Birds of Paradise* (2011), *Origin* (2007), *Crescent* (2003), and *Arabian Jazz* (1993); and two memoirs, *Life Without a Recipe* (2016) and *The Language of Baklava* (2005). *Birds of Paradise* won the 2012 Arab American Book Award, *Crescent* won the PEN Center Award for Literary Fiction and the American Book Award, and *Arabian Jazz* won the Oregon Book Award for Literary Fiction and was a finalist for the PEN/Hemingway Award. *The Language of Baklava* won the Northwest Booksellers' Award and has been translated into many languages.

WORKS CITED

Abu-Jaber, Diana. *Arabian Jazz*. Harcourt Brace, 1993.
———. *Birds of Paradise*. W.W. Norton, 2011.
———. *Crescent*. W.W. Norton, 2003.
———. *Fencing with the King*. W.W. Norton, 2022.
———. *The Language of Baklava: A Memoir*. Pantheon, 2005.
———. *Life Without a Recipe*. W.W. Norton, 2016.
———. *Origin*. W.W. Norton, 2007.
———. *Silverworld*. Random House, 2020.
Arvela, Paula. "Pastel de Tentúgal: Serendipity or Cultural Syncretism?" *Wrapped and Stuffed Foods*, edited by Mark McWilliams, Prospect, 2013, pp. 68–81.
Bardenstein, Carol. "Beyond Univocal Baklava: Deconstructing Food-as-Ethnicity and the Ideology of Homeland in Diana Abu-Jaber's *The Language of Baklava*." *Journal of Arabic Literature*, vol. 41, 2010, pp. 160–79, https://doi.org/10.1163/157006410 X486792, accessed February 26, 2022.
———. "Transmissions Interrupted: Reconfiguring Food, Memory, and Gender in the Cookbook-Memoirs of Middle Eastern Exiles." *Signs*, vol. 28, no. 1, 2002, pp. 353–87, https://doi.org/10.1086/341011, accessed February 26, 2022.
Barthes, Roland. "Towards a Psychosociology of Contemporary Food Consumption." *Food and Culture: A Reader*, edited by Carole Counihan and Penny Van Esterik, 3rd ed., Routledge, 2013, pp. 23–30.
Berzok, Linda Murray, ed. *Storied Dishes: What Our Family Recipes Tell Us about Who We Are and Where We've Been*. Praeger, 2011.
Fivush, Robyn. "The Development of Autobiographical Memory." *Annual Review of Psychology*, vol. 62, 2011, pp. 559–82, https://doi.org/10.1146/annurev .psych.121208.131702, accessed February 26, 2022.
Lévi-Strauss, Claude. "The Culinary Triangle." *Food and Culture: A Reader*, edited by Carole Counihan and Penny Van Esterik, 3rd ed., Routledge, 2013, pp. 40–47.
Mackintosh, Angela Miyuki. "Diana Abu-Jaber Discovers Her True Identity with Origin." *WOW! Women on Writing*, June 2007, www.wow-womenonwriting.com/10-FE -diana-abu-jaber.html, accessed February 26, 2022.
Shalal-Esa, Andrea. "Diana Abu-Jaber: The Only Response to Silencing Is to Keep Speaking." *Al-Jadid*, vol. 8, no. 39, 2002, www.aljadid.com/content/diana-abu-jaber -only-response-silencing-keep-speaking, accessed February 26, 2022.

Sutton, David. *Remembrance of Repasts: An Anthropology of Food and Memory.* 2nd ed., Berg, 2001.

Tulving, Endel. "Memory and Consciousness." *Canadian Psychology / Psychologie Canadienne,* vol. 26, no. 1, 1985, pp. 1–12. https://doi.org/10.1037/h0080017, accessed February 26, 2022.

Vasvári, Louise O. "Introduction to and Bibliography for the Study of Alimentary Life Writing and Recipe Writing as War Literature." *CLCWeb: Comparative Literature and Culture,* vol. 17, no. 3, 2015, https://doi.org/10.7771/1481-4374.2781, accessed February 26, 2022.

Kitchen Secrets

Food Stories and the Politics of
Silence and Voice in Ana Castillo's
Black Dove: Mamá, Mi'jo, and Me

MÉLINÉ KASPARIAN-LE FÈVRE

As Patricia Montilla explains, many Latina artists incorporate food in their work, drawing from the culinary realm in order to tell stories and make political statements:

> In their works [food] becomes a key to Latino storytelling and imagery. . . . For many Latina women, cooking itself is an important artistic outlet. It is part of their daily routine that serves as a means of creative expression that may not exist for them otherwise. In literature the connection between the creativity of food preparation and art results in its frequent utilization as metaphor for the creative process itself. . . . The writer as cook finds in the culinary an inspiration, a muse from which to make revelations about personal or social space. (420)

The connection Montilla makes between the culinary and the act of making revelations, both about personal stories and about more collective, sociopolitical issues, provides an interesting lens to view Ana Castillo's 2016 memoir *Black Dove: Mamá, Mi'jo, and Me*, in which explorations of the domestic space and images of food are linked to the sharing of personal and familial stories that touch on societal and political issues. As a political autobiography, *Black Dove* is reminiscent of the tradition of *testimonios*, or personal narratives that speak to broader social forces and issues while narrating the experiences of marginalized people. *Testimonios* are centered on a "story that needs to be told—involving a problem of repression, poverty, subalternity, exploitation, or simply survival" (Beverly 73). In *Black Dove,* Castillo evokes stories from her own life and her relatives' lives that speak to the experiences Beverly lists, such as the subaltern status of migrants in the United States and women's oppression in a patriarchal society. *Black Dove* therefore intersects with the tradition of *testimonios* but also with a different genre, one that at first glance appears very far from the political narratives of oppression that *testimonios* represent: the genre of the culinary memoir. Indeed, *Black Dove* exhibits a mix of food and autobiographical storytelling that is at the heart of the culinary memoir. Traci Marie Kelly, for example, suggests that a culinary memoir constitutes a personal narrative in which food appears as a recurring, significant theme (255). *Black Dove* seems to fit with such a definition. Even if it does not contain recipes, as some culinary memoirs do, food figures as a prominent theme within the memoir, which evokes food memories, the sensorial pleasures of gastronomy, and the role of food in the family. *Black Dove* merely adds food as a cultural marker and makes the link between food-work and women's oppression a focal point of the story. Whether one considers *Black Dove* as a food memoir, *testimonio,* or both, as I would contend, the text clearly establishes a connection between food and autobiographical storytelling, between the culinary and the sharing of the self, which warrants analysis.

Castillo's interest in food is evident from her many texts that describe the cultural and symbolic value of food, its role in caring relationships and in the family, and its ability to underpin memory (Herrera; Salazar; Steere). While critics have explored the theme of food in Castillo's novels *Sapogonia* (1990), *So Far from God* (1993), and *The Guardians* (2007), the role of food in her memoir *Black Dove* is distinctive and equally deserving of critical attention. *Black Dove* is an autobiographical text explicitly concerned with the value and difficulties of autobiographical narrative, and such concern is reflected in the way Castillo writes about food. Indeed, in *Black Dove,* food is clearly linked to a reflection on the importance of sharing one's life stories but also (and this brings us back to the tradition of *testimonios*) on the politics of speaking and silence. Who has the right to tell their own story? Who is silenced? Such questions pervade *Black Dove,* and they have gendered answers. Throughout *Black Dove,* Castillo denounces the way women's stories are silenced, unheard, or unlistened-to in a patriarchal society that tries to keep their mouths shut, depriving them of the nourishing and healing process of sharing one's story. In patriarchal cultures, including Latin American ones, cultural norms prevent certain stories from being told and listened to; this is perhaps especially true for stories regarding sexual violence and women's oppression. In her memoir, Castillo breaks the silence regarding these stories and provides a commentary on the harm caused by silencing victims. Conversely, she emphasizes the power of writing and telling one's most painful stories and experiences.

In the text, food plays an important role in this reflection about silence, both as a consequence and a cause of women's oppression. The activity of cooking, which encourages conversation, contrasts with a patriarchal society in which women are discouraged from telling their own story. In *Black Dove*, food appears as a possible answer to this dilemma, facilitating women's self-expression in several ways. First, the memoir highlights the way the space of the kitchen or the moment of food preparation can facilitate conversations in which women's stories are told, listened to, and honored. Second, Castillo's own self-expression through autobiographical writing is facilitated by food, as she uses food symbolism and metaphors to convey central themes and ideas, including, perhaps most importantly, the healing value of autobiographical storytelling. If, as Cherríe Moraga puts it, "silence is like starvation" (44), *Black Dove* suggests that when the mouth that has been closed finally opens to share painful stories, the sharing of words is as nourishing as any meal. Thus, in *Black Dove*, both the theme of food and food symbolism are connected to a reflection on women's stories and storytelling.

Stories and Silences from the Kitchen

"Food is never just food," Molly Wizenberg writes. "It's also a way of getting at something else: who we are, who we have been, and who we want to be" (2). Food can be a means of exploring one's own story, and this connection between food, self-exploration, and self-narrative is central in *Black Dove*. Food appears in *Black Dove* as a way of getting at the heart of who Castillo is and has been. Many references to food or the kitchen point to what seems to have been a defining aspect of Castillo's life: her struggle to speak her own story, to find ways to communicate and share, and her hunger for intimacy and honest dialogue, especially with women (and most importantly with her mother). Throughout her memoir, Castillo tries to fulfill that hunger for stories and honest dialogue in the space of the kitchen.

Feminist food studies have demonstrated that the space of the kitchen holds an ambivalent place in women's lives; often a place of oppression, it has also been shown to provide a space of comfort, creativity, and community. Tracy Marie Kelly, for instance, has suggested how the kitchen can be a place where women can express themselves and tell their own stories, a tradition on which the culinary memoir builds: "The culinary autobiography is unique because it is almost a natural extension of an oral storytelling tradition that has been playing itself out for generations in our very own kitchens" (253). Such conversations in the kitchen can be a source of bonding, an important aspect of what makes the kitchen a positive space for women, as Arlene Voski Avakian observes: "While most women do agree that cooking has been compulsory for women and has signified and constructed their oppression, many also assert that their mothers and grandmothers created authority and control in their kitchens, which often became a space where they bonded with other women" (261). Rocío del Aguila and Vanesa Miseres argue that the kitchen is an important bonding space for women and that a nuanced narrative about the role of food in women's lives is needed to account for the positive role of cooking for many women: "The relationship of women with food and the kitchen seems to constrain them within traditional female domestic roles but, at the same time, it provides them with a sphere in which they can find freedom and cultivate their creativity and sorority" (8). Castillo's text resonates with this idea of the kitchen as a space of bonding and sorority between women, as it insists upon the liberating potential for conversations women share in the kitchen and at the kitchen table, over shared meals or through cooking together. In such conversations, women are able to tell their own lives and stories to one another in a safe space, partaking in the oral tradition of storytelling in the kitchen that Kelly describes. For instance, Castillo recounts how her friendship with her aunt was forged through moments of dialogue and conversation in the kitchen: "We were friends, confidantes, as I have already mentioned, mostly in the way traditional married women with children had friends—in the kitchen while preparing meals, quick chats on the phone between chores, at family gatherings when others' ears were not close enough to pick up private anecdotes" (34). In effect, shared moments in the kitchen while cooking become one of the rare occasions during which women are not interrupted and can enjoy some privacy to swap stories and bond. Meals and moments shared at the kitchen table allow for the recovering and sharing of intimate memories and stories from women's lives. The kitchen appears as a space associated with memory and stories of a past, too, a place where women can share their life story through reminiscent storytelling, which would likely not be honored in the same way if men were present.

For John F. Carafoli, "food will always be a powerful magnet to draw out buried memories" (55). In *Black Dove,* this process, both by the individual and by the collective, often happens through shared food and food spaces. When Castillo recounts those conversations she had in the kitchen with her relatives, what clearly emerges is her desire to unearth and to bring to light repressed memories, especially those from the lives of ordinary women. Castillo's memoir is nourished by myriad such conversations at the table and/or in the kitchen, all of which allow her to glean material and write the family history into her narrative. For instance, a substantial portion of the memoir focuses on the story of Castillo's mother and aunt, who grew up in Mexico and became domestic workers at a very young age. Castillo explains that she was only able to learn about their stories through kitchen chats. While she doesn't know much about her uncles, the conversations she has with her mother and her aunt Flora in the kitchen prove crucial to providing her more details about her family's history: "But I know about the daughters—Raquel and her younger sister, Flora—because when they grew up and became women, they told me in kitchens, over meals, and into late evenings, that by the time they were ten years old, they worked as live-in domestics" (15). In this passage, Castillo highlights the idea that the space of the kitchen facilitates a dialogue between women but also the importance of such kitchen chats for the writing of her memoir. What she knows of the family history, she learned in the kitchen, thanks to the intimacy allowed by this space. The kitchen as a space of conversation thus plays a pivotal role in Castillo's ability to even write the memoir we are reading, which is in large part concerned with tracing her family's history. The kitchen is not only the place where stories are told orally between women but also the space from which the written story, the memoir *Black Dove,* emerges, a place that houses the stories from which the memoir is woven.

The stories that are told in the kitchen in *Black Dove* reveal the impact of patriarchal norms and violence on women's lives. They are stories about women's vulnerability and victimization, but also about women's resilience and efforts to assert their own voices and to fulfill their own appetites, if sometimes through subversion and concealment. An example of such a story would be the one Castillo heard from her aunt Flora at the kitchen table, when Flora told her about what she did when her husband forbade her from going to a concert. Flora announced to her husband that she would cook a special meal for him that night. She told her husband that she would have to go to the market so that he should not stay at home waiting for her, but rather go to the bar, where she would send someone to get him once supper was done. Instead of going to the market, she goes to the concert:

> In apron and chanclas, Flora caught a cab right quick that zoomed her across town to the Celia Cruz concert. . . . An hour later she jumped back in the cab and went home. "What happened to the groceries you had gone for?" I asked. "What happened to the special meal you said you would prepare?" "Egh" my tía Flora responded with a toss of a hand as if she couldn't have cared less. "I simply said that the market was closed when I got there." (37)

This story speaks to the domestic realm both as a space of women's oppression (a space where Flora's husband tries to control her comings and goings and expects home-cooked meals from her every evening) but also as a realm of clever subversion. Flora enacts a hidden form of resistance, concealed in the garb of the perfect housewife (literally, as she wears her apron and house slippers to go to the concert). Flora takes advantage of her husband's lack of knowledge and curiosity about the details of what goes into producing the meals he enjoys, as she knows she can just say the market was closed and he will not ask any follow-up questions. Here, Castillo's text underlines the way women's association with food and the kitchen can be oppressive but also appropriated as a source of empowerment, while staying protectively within the limits imposed by a patriarchal society. This story exemplifies the idea that the domestic space can conceal acts of resistance by women who appear to conform to patriarchal norms but are actually exploiting the constrained space in which they find themselves. As Brinda Mehta suggests, "female power in the kitchen lies in its invisibility, that is, in its ability to transform an unfavourable situation to the advantage of women through strategies of subversive affirmation" (115). The idea of an invisible rebellion that women enact without outwardly taking a stand against their relegation to the domestic space resonates with Flora's story. Secrecy, concealment, and invisibility are tools Flora uses in her rebellion. In this story, told at the kitchen table, silence and secrecy are necessary, emancipatory tactics for a woman who rebels within the constraints of her patriarchal world and family instead of overhauling them. However, silence and secrecy are also shown in Castillo's memoir to be extremely damaging, when they are not embraced voluntarily as tactics but merely imposed onto women. The space of the kitchen, while often positively connoted, also at times embodies this patriarchal silencing of women.

Black Dove explores the possibility that the kitchen, and food, can loosen tongues and facilitate a healing, bonding process of conversation between women, but it also evokes the idea that patriarchal norms infiltrate the domestic space and create barriers that prevent women from experiencing sorority and open communication. As Abarca argues, while recognizing the fluidity of the kitchen as a space that can be reappropriated by women, it is important not to idealize "the conversion of a patriarchal kitchen into a feminist site and ignore that this ideological reconstruction is also fluid and not a complete or permanent block to the power of the male gaze, at times manifested in some of our own (women's) actions" (138). *Black Dove* represents precisely such ambivalence. Instead of painting an idealized picture of the reappropriation of the kitchen and the culinary realm as a space for sorority and emancipation, it gives an honest account of the obstacles such conversion faces, including women's own complicity with patriarchal norms. This means that the kitchen is not only a space for conversation and sharing but also, sometimes, a space where women's voices are silenced by other women, women who participate in the (re-)production of patriarchal tradition. For example, the kitchen in Castillo's childhood home, as described in the memoir, is a place associated with a toxic silence that her mother imposes on her, preventing her from speaking about painful experiences in her life. It is from the kitchen that Castillo's mother shouts at her daughter to act more normally and threatens to commit her to a psychiatric hospital if she doesn't, instead of letting her talk about her feelings of depression (58). It is also in the kitchen that her mother refuses to let Castillo talk about her experience of an attempted rape by a male relative:

> A day or so later when my mother was in the kitchen preparing supper after work, heating up the pot of beans and tortillas, adding something else to pep up the meal, I tried to tell her what had happened. She did not stop her tasks. She did not look me in the eye. She had no questions, nor did she even seem surprised. She simply advised, "A man is a man before anything else," as if she had had that line memorized since the time of her own girlhood. I never brought it up again, not when X later spied on me as I dressed in my room or when he tried other things we can justifiably call inappropriate. (77)

Here, Castillo's mother forces her into a poisonous secrecy, refusing to let her share the details of what happened to her, denying her the comfort and healing such sharing might have provided—especially when it seems as if Castillo's mother has her own story of gendered oppression and violence to share. Her silence and lack of surprise are telling, revealing how accustomed she seems to have become to the pervasiveness of sexual violence against women, even within the home, so much so that she normalizes it. Thus, Castillo's mother's silencing of her daughter is accompanied by a toxic communication of gendered norms as she suggests that men's violent desires should be expected and accepted, not denounced. Instead of being a space in which women may share their stories through an open and supportive dialogue, the only communication that happens in this kitchen is this one-way communication of poisonous norms that ends up, as we learn later on in the memoir, compounding Castillo's trauma and suffering.

This episode in the kitchen is a pivotal one in the memoir, which becomes, in part, the story of how Castillo managed to turn that culturally imposed silence about women's experiences into talk and text. The silence between Castillo and her mother revealed in those kitchen scenes is perhaps the central drama of the memoir, as Castillo reckons with her mother's withholding and silencing ways, despite continually trying to engage her mother in sincere conversation: "My attempts to have open conversations almost always failed. I'd catch her at her house chores in the evenings or in the kitchen before or after we had supper. I might be put to cleaning the beans or drying dishes as she swept, and I'd attempt to have a meaningful conversation with her, woman to woman" (81–82). It seems as if Castillo will never manage to get the intimacy she craves from her mother, to share moments of conversation like those she enjoys with her aunt in the kitchen. The kitchen of Castillo's childhood home therefore appears as the place where her mother denied her the nourishment that talking about her experiences could have brought, the place where a poisonous silence was imposed onto Castillo, a place of oppression through silence. As these passages exemplify, Castillo's narrative does not idealize relationships between women: yes, it evokes the bonds that can be forged between women over food and in the kitchen, but it also suggests that women can sometimes deny each other the nourishment of honest dialogue because of the gendered norms they have interiorized. Instead of a romanticized, idealized portrayal of the kitchen as a space of unrestrained female support, *Black Dove* provides a powerful and political reflection on the stakes and the difficulty of finding a safe space to tell one's own story as a woman.

Ultimately, Castillo finds a space to tell and write her own story, even if that space is not her childhood kitchen. Literature provides her with a medium to tell her own narrative, one in which she finds a voice, a language, to communicate her experiences, through a style that makes frequent use of food as a source of imagery and symbolism. As Roland Barthes reminds us, food is "not only a collection of products. . . . It is also, and at the same time, a system of communication, a body of images" (24). This conception of food as a system of communication applies to *Black Dove,* in which food provides a "body of images" that Castillo deliberately and carefully uses to communicate certain ideas and experiences that are at the core of her memoir. Castillo uses food as a language, as a shorthand to convey certain ideas and emotions more easily and effectively to her readers—namely, her concern with the harms of imposed silence and the healing potential of autobiographical storytelling.

Stories Like Prickly Pears: Food Metaphors and Narrative in *Black Dove*

Thus far, this essay has examined food as a theme in *Black Dove* by looking at passages in which Castillo explores the role of food and food spaces in facilitating women's autobiographical storytelling. But food also plays a central role in the memoir as symbol and metaphor. Food symbols and food metaphors facilitate Castillo's own autobiographical storytelling through her memoir. Just like the people in her memoir use food and food spaces to tell their stories (even when not listened to), Castillo uses food imagery and food metaphors in order to express herself, convey meaning, and communicate central ideas.

More specifically, food imagery helps Castillo to capture the experience of being a woman and to reflect on the societal factors that contribute to the reality of violence against women. For instance, when writing about her experience of sexual assault, Castillo uses food imagery to convey the idea that violence is not about a sexual hunger but more about a desire to control and to inflict suffering:

> X threw me over his shoulder, just as that gangbanger Shadow would do a year later. I hardly knew Shadow. He never flirted or spoke so much as two words to me. These were not the only times in my life when men picked me up out of the blue, held me high like a ballerina in the air, or tossed me over their shoulders like a sack of potatoes. They never asked permission. . . . "You see? You can't get away," X taunted as he made his way directly to my bedroom with me in tow, begging to be let down. I wonder if these are the very thoughts that animals have when they catch their prey: You see? You can't get away. We'd like to think they only hunt smaller creatures for food to survive, but anyone who has spent time in nature knows there is a sport to it.

Sometimes, they enjoy taunting the prey before they finally kill it. I have two splendid ranch dogs, a pair of mixed-breed sisters. When they were young, they teamed up to chase rabbits and caught birds in midair. They mutilated cats. The dogs were well fed. They obviously chased, tortured, killed, and ate animals for pleasure. Pleasure, or was it their nature? (74)

Food imagery enables Castillo to write about sexual violence as the upshot of a sexist culture in which women are objectified and denied agency and control over their own bodies (treated as "sacks of potatoes") and as directly linked to a desire to intimidate and scare women: her aggressor is compared to an animal who taunts its prey before killing it and who hunts even when not hungry, for pure sport and for love of cruelty. Through food imagery, Castillo expresses an idea that is central to feminist theories of rape: the idea that rape is not only about sexual desire but mostly about power, as Shana L. Maier summarizes: "rape is used to exert power and control" (47). Through food-based analogies, Castillo provides accessible, clear images for the power dynamics involved in women's victimization and denounces a culture in which women fall prey to men's violent hungers.

This story of violence, but also of survival, proves to be healing in its recounting, as writing it after decades have passed and after Castillo has come to an understanding of patriarchy enables her to move through trauma and make sense of what happened to her. It provides a fitting example of the kinds of stories Castillo tells in *Black Dove*, stories that she herself describes, through a food-based comparison, as prickly pears: "And when the world so big becomes a small windowless room for me . . . I write poems. . . . I talk to my son, to a lover, and with my compadres. I tell a story. I make a sound and leave a mark—as palatable as a prickly pear, more solid than stone" (25). Here, Castillo suggests that telling stories, talking and sharing about her experiences, or channeling her feelings into narrative is a healing process, as nourishing as a prickly pear. Her choice of this particular food to describe the stories she tells as part of her healing process, or as a coping mechanism against anxiety, is particularly eloquent. Delicious inside but thorny outside, and an emblem for the possibility of surviving and finding nourishment within a harsh, desert landscape, the prickly pear is a perfect emblem for the stories Castillo tells within *Black Dove*. Indeed, these stories have their thorns (as they are often about experiences of suffering, violence, and oppression) and may seem unappealing, but they are actually nourishing and a source of strength. The sharing of those stories by Castillo is part of a healing process both for the writer but also, potentially, for the readers who may have gone through similar experiences and might find a sense of comfort and solidarity reading her memoir. Lastly, as a fruit that thrives in the desert, the prickly pear also symbolizes the resilience at the heart of many of the stories Castillo tells. In this passage, food imagery plays a metatextual role, providing an image that allows Castillo to talk about her own narrative process and to communicate what is perhaps the central concern of her memoir: the idea that solace can be found in speaking and writing one's own stories, even when those stories are thorny and painful.

Perhaps ironically, another food-related image that plays an important metatextual role in Castillo's memoir is the image of the closed mouth. While the prickly pear encapsulates the healing, nourishing value of telling stories, the closed mouth represents the toxicity and danger of not speaking, of not sharing one's stories. Castillo explains that the silence she felt she had to maintain around her experiences of sexual violence and her own emotions led to depression, and that, at times, she would shut down completely and refuse to speak: "I didn't know why I couldn't talk at times. I just couldn't and wouldn't. When I shut down, you could come at me flailing a medieval spiked ball and my lips wouldn't have parted" (59). The image of the closed mouth suggests how Castillo used silence as a defense mechanism, as a way to protect herself by erecting boundaries, fences, between herself and the world. The image of medieval torture that she uses exposes the suffering and violence associated with her experiences; instead of conversation, what she imagines here is an interaction based on a threat of violence, on one hand, and on silence, on the other. Relationality appears difficult. Closing the mouth represents Castillo's refusal of being in relationship with others (as those relationships have so far in her life been a source of suffering) and of revealing herself and her feelings to others. Revealing herself to others is, however, precisely what she comes to do with her memoir, which can be read as the narrative of how she came from that place of silence to one of speaking, how she managed to move from silence to sharing, how she found the courage to finally open her mouth to tell her story and denounce the violence that was done to her, as well as the painful silencing she experienced. In this food-centric memoir, the image of the closed mouth, which cannot take in any nourishment, acquires a painfully ironic connotation as it embodies the psychic starvation created by enforced silence. The image of the closed mouth gestures toward the central dialectic of speaking and silence that structures the whole memoir. Indeed, the dialectic of opening and closing, retaining and releasing, which is associated with the mouth, points to the central concern of *Black Dove*, which constantly underlines the hurtfulness of imposed silence (retention) and the healing potential of sharing one's own story (expression). Such autobiographical sharing, in *Black Dove*, seems to be facilitated by food as material, metaphor, and process: the alimentary realm provides a context and a language that assists in the healing process of telling one's stories.

According to Carole Counihan, "food-centered life histories . . . can provide a voice for women who have not had a chance to speak publicly and provide a weapon against the silencing that has always been a central weapon in women's oppression" (201). The idea that food can provide a medium for women to tell their stories and to counteract their cultural silencing provides an interesting lens through which to view *Black Dove*, in which the culinary realm is linked to the autobiographical one in two principal ways. In *Black Dove*, conversations in the kitchen, over meals, and in between meal preparation allow Castillo to recover stories from the women in her family, stories that speak to their oppression but also to their resilience. Moreover, food becomes an idiom for Castillo's own self-expression, a language she uses to symbolize some of the most important things she has to say in her memoir, which powerfully speaks back to a patriarchal culture that silences women. In Castillo's memoir, the kitchen is described as a space that should serve to recover forgotten or marginalized stories, not hide them; the language of food provides a symbolic shorthand method to communicate such stories effectively and to reflect on issues of violence and the cultural silencing of victims. A feminist, food-centered memoir that evokes the healing potential of putting one's story into words, *Black Dove* suggests that food can facilitate autobiographical storytelling, providing both a context and a language through which stories can be communicated and shared.

WORKS CITED

Abarca, Meredith. *Voices in the Kitchen: Views of Food and the World from Working-Class Mexican and Mexican American Women.* Texas A&M University Press, 2006.

Barthes, Roland. "Toward a Psychosociology of Contemporary Food Consumption," *Food and Culture: A Reader,* edited by Carole Counihan and Penny Van Esterik, 3rd ed., Routledge, 2008, pp. 23–31.

Beverly, John. *Against Literature.* University of Minnesota Press, 1993.

Carafoli, John F. "Amarcord: The Flavour of Buried Memories." *Food and the Memory: Proceedings of the Oxford Symposium on Food and Cookery 2000,* edited by Harlan Walker, Prospect, 2001, pp. 49–56.

Castillon, Ana. *Black Dove: Mamá, Mi'jo, and Me.* Feminist Press at CUNY, 2016.

Counihan, Carole. "The Border as Barrier and Bridge: Food, Gender, and Ethnicity in the San Luis Valley of Colorado." *From Betty Crocker to Feminist Food Studies: Critical Perspectives on Women and Food,* edited by Arlene Voski Avakian and Barbara Haber, University of Massachusetts Press, 2005, pp. 200–217.

Del Aguila, Rocío, and Vanesa Miseres. "Towards the Construction of a Latin American Gastronarrative." *Food Studies in Latin American Literature: Perspectives on the Gastronarrative,* edited by Rocío del Aguila and Vanesa Miseres, University of Arkansas Press, 2021, pp. 3–21.

Herrera, Olga L. "Geographies of Latinidad in Ana Castillo's 'Sapogonia.'" *Confluencia,* vol. 31, no. 1, 2015, pp. 159–69, www.jstor.org/stable/44075001, accessed Sept. 21, 2020.

Kelly, Tracy Marie. "'If I Were a Voodoo Priestess': Women's Culinary Autobiographies." *Kitchen Culture in America: Popular Representations of Food, Gender, and Race,* edited by Sherrie A. Inness, University of Pennsylvania Press, 2000, pp. 251–69.

Maier, Shana L. *Rape, Victims and Investigations: Experiences and Perceptions of Law Enforcement Officers Responding to Reported Rapes.* Taylor & Francis, 2014.

Mehta, Brinda J. *Diasporic (Dis)locations: Indo-Caribbean Women Writers Negotiate the "Kala Pani."* University of the West Indies Press, 2004.

Montilla, Patricia. *Latinos and American Popular Culture.* ABC-CLIO, 2013.

Moraga, Cherríe. *Loving in the War Years: What Never Went through His Lips.* 1983. South End, 2000.

Salazar, Anthony. "Commodifying Food and Maintaining Culture along the Border in Ana Castillo's *The Guardians.*" *Humanities Bulletin,* vol. 4, no. 1, 2021, pp. 202–14.

Steere, Elizabeth Lee. "'Because Feeding Is the Beginning and End': Food Politics in Ana Castillo's *So Far from God.*" *Rethinking Chicana/o Literature through Food: Postcolonial Appetites,* edited by Nieves Pascual Soler and Meredith Abarca, Palgrave Macmillan, 2013, pp. 79–95.

Voski Avakian, Arlene. "Shish Kebab Armenians? Food and the Construction and Maintenance of Ethnic and Gender Identities among Armenian American Feminists." *From Betty Crocker to Feminist Food Studies: Critical Perspectives on Women and Food,* edited by Arlene Voski Avakian and Barbara Haber, University of Massachusetts Press, 2005, pp. 257–80.

Wizenberg, Molly. *A Homemade Life: Stories and Recipes from My Kitchen Table.* Simon & Schuster, 2009.

PART IV

Food, Race, Sex, and Queer Identity

Food and the Public/Private Body in Nella Larsen's *Passing*

MOLLY MANN LOTZ

> The trouble with Clare was not only that she wanted to have her cake and eat it too, but that she wanted to nibble at the cakes of other folk as well.
> —Nella Larsen, *Passing* (35)

Food is the frequent and daily disruptor of the discrete con-
tainers of our bodies. Nothing else is ingested, digested, and expelled by
us multiple times a day. This is why Julia Kristeva chose food as an example to illustrate her theory of abjection, the idea that what is object
becomes subject once incorporated into the body, and then abject again
once it leaves the body. For Kristeva, the abjection inherent in eating
and digesting arouses horror because it recalls all the other, more violent ways our bodies can be disrupted and made permeable. For Kyla
Wazana Tompkins, food also carries erotic power because of its interaction with the site of the mouth, which she calls its "orality" (16). Food
navigates between the otherwise continent boundaries of our bodies and
the world around us. It is a constant reminder to us that the categories
of self and other, public and private, are easily transgressed and therefore destabilized.

The event of eating is also a site where private needs and public space
converge. Meals are often social occasions, requiring us to venture outside our homes, perhaps to visit others' homes, and to negotiate our own
hungers and tastes with what is available for us to eat. If we entertain
others for meals at our own homes, we invite them into what is otherwise considered our own private space. Behavior at meals is codified according to an agreed-upon set of social values known as etiquette. In or-

der to feed ourselves, we must learn how to interact according to these rules, and, even if we dine alone, the choices we make about what and how much to eat are influenced by availability and social mores surrounding food and diet.

Food reminds us of the many other ways our bodies are deployed in the negotiation between public and private spaces; it operates along a spectrum of bodily disruptions that include injury, penetrative sex, and childbirth. Categories of race, sexuality, and even class have all been constructed as legible on and within the body. Since the eighteenth century, race has been understood as a primarily embodied state, one that manifests through skin color and other distinguishing physical characteristics. Judith Butler's work to establish gender as performative emerges in resistance to persistent beliefs that gender has its basis in biology (*Gender Trouble*). Sexuality, another category of identity, seeks out publicly available evidence of how bodies conduct themselves in the sex act, one that is historically understood as private and intimate. In more subtle ways, class is also associated with physical markers, including body weight, teeth, cleanliness, and clothing. Interpreting all these categories of identity requires reading the body for signifiers. Thus, internal characteristics are understood as publicly visible qualities, and, conversely, what is legible on the body is understood to indicate internal states and characteristics.

Food is thus a mediator between public and private spaces, one that both engages and challenges all the categories of identity that also circulate around and through bodies. In Nella Larsen's 1929 novel, *Passing*, moments of eating and drinking are also moments of heightened racial and sexual anxiety, points where categories of public and private are interrogated and destabilized. *Passing* foregrounds taste as the deft navigation between public and private space, revealing public/private to be a false construction upon which the corollary constructs of race, sexuality, and class precariously rest.

Taste functions to distinguish and uphold boundaries around groups of people. Thorstein Veblen and Pierre Bourdieu both observe the way that taste and social status co-constitute each other. According to Veblen, the so-called leisure class is indicated by conspicuous leisure, or nonproductive use of time meant to display social status, since productive work signifies the absence of disposable income. Because of the limited efficacy of conspicuous leisure in urban areas, the leisure class also engages in conspicuous consumption—or the display of purchasing power—to impress their status upon others. Those in other social classes are influenced by this behavior and seek to emulate it as an approximation of social mobility. Bourdieu furthers this argument to assert that those with cultural capital, or access to social mobility, determine what constitutes taste, a kind of cultural hegemony. The inability to access dominant forms of taste further separates ruling and working classes. Because taste is learned at such an early age, it becomes deeply internalized and difficult to recondition, naturalizing apparent class distinctions. In her writing on the "taste work" functions of lifestyle blogs, Minh-Ha T. Pham moves the scope of taste beyond class distinctions and includes race and gender in the cultural constructions co-constituted with taste (5). As taste operates in culture to establish and maintain boundaries between classes, racial groups, and genders, it also forms the boundary between the public and private self; taste is the public presentation of one's private desires. At the same time, as Veblen and Bourdieu show in their work, those private desires are equally constructed through the cultural hegemony of taste.

Larsen's *Passing* explores this false binary between public and private space, and how one is required to daily pass through categories of public and private, often in the act of eating. The novel takes place in Harlem in the 1920s and focuses on the reunion of two childhood friends, Clare Kendry and Irene Redfield. Irene discovers that Clare has been "passing" as a white woman, and Irene's obsession over Clare and her ability to move fluidly through racially defined spaces occupies much of the novel's focus. Ostensibly concerned with racial identity and how to identify someone as belonging to one racial category or another, Larsen's novel is more deeply concerned with the instability of racial categories and with categories of identity altogether. Some scholars, such as Judith Butler and Deborah E. McDowell, also read *Passing* as a queer novel, arguing that it encodes queer desire between Irene and Clare. I am concerned with how race and sexuality function in the novel as fluid, mutable states that move through public and private visibility, identity, and consciousness, much like food. Scenes of eating and drinking in *Passing* offer moments in the text of heightened racial and sexual anxiety, during which the body's abject state reveals the fragile and permeable nature of its other identifiable characteristics. In these scenes from the novel, public ideas intrude on private space, revealing both categories to be mutually constituted and mutually complicated.

"Passing" presupposes category and boundary, and Larsen's novel reveals, repeatedly and finally, that categories of identity and their imagined boundaries are both unstable and unsustainable. The act of consuming food—incorporating objects into the subject body to create an abject other—interrogates all the other ways that discrete categories of public/private and self/other are revealed as fragile constructs. Consequently, binaries of race, gender, and sexuality all come into question through the events of eating.

Passing and the Porous Body

Passing is a novel about racial identity, and more specifically the act of passing between racial categories, thereby fundamentally destabilizing those categories. In my reading, I identify moments of eating and drinking in the novel as sites of liminality between public and private spheres. Through these moments, Larsen's characters navigate complex issues of visibility, identity, and consciousness specifically related to race and sexuality. *Passing*'s food-related scenes feature a heightened racial and sexual anxiety, during which the body's visible porousness in eating reveals the fragile and permeable nature of these other categories of identity.

In *Passing*, Irene Redfield, a well-to-do Black woman living in Harlem, reunites with a friend from her childhood, Clare Kendry. Clare, who passes as white and has married and had a child with a white man who does not know of her racial background, begins spending more time with Irene and Irene's husband, Brian, going with them to teas and dances around Harlem. Clare falls to her death from a sixth-story window at one such party, and many critics understand Larsen's text to mean that Irene, tortured by jealousy and annoyance, pushes her. While the exact cause of Clare's death is unclear, what is certain is that Irene's feelings toward Clare are agonizing and violent, and that they have something to do with both racial identity and sexuality. Throughout the novel, Irene repeatedly attempts to maintain boundaries between public and private life, and her frustrations at doing so—which emerge especially at mealtimes—reveal the futility of policing these mutable categories. Food interacts with bodies in a way that is ever-changing and unstable, and Larsen uses food and drink in *Passing* to show that race and sexuality operate similarly on the bodies they encounter.

Whereas Irene's skin color is a "warm olive," Clare's white husband, John Bellew, describes his wife as "white as a lily" (Larsen 7, 29). The name Clare comes from the Latin *clarus*, which means light, an appropriate name for Larsen's light-skinned character. Irene reencounters Clare at a moment when she herself is passing, having escaped from the hot summer streets of New York to the roof of the Drayton Hotel for tea.

She sees Clare there with a man who is not her husband, and as the two women drink their tea together, Irene reflects on both the precariousness of Clare's passing and her own:

> White people were so stupid about such things for all that they usually asserted that they were able to tell; and by the most ridiculous means, fingernails, palms of hands, shapes of ears, teeth, and other equally silly rot. They always took her for an Italian, a Spaniard, a Mexican, or a gipsy. Never, when she was alone, had they even remotely seemed to suspect that she was a Negro. No, the woman sitting there couldn't possibly know. Nevertheless, Irene felt, in turn, anger, scorn, and fear slide over her. It wasn't that she was ashamed of being a Negro, or even of having it declared. It was the idea of being ejected from any place, even in the polite and tactful way in which the Drayton would probably do it, that disturbed her. (10–11)

Irene's anger comes from understanding the impact of racial categories even as she simultaneously realizes that these categories are arbitrary and rooted more in social constructions of race than any deeper truth about human nature. Clare's passing, even more than her own temporary movement into white space, reveals that space itself cannot be white or black. The Drayton, a hotel, offers a liminal space between public and private, and for Irene and Clare, it serves as a liminal space between their public selves (which present as white) and what is in this moment a privately shared history.

White people are "stupid" to Irene because they understand race to be a discrete category that is visible publicly as "finger-nails, palms of hands, shapes of ears, teeth, and other equally silly rot," as a kind of knowledge gained from interrogating the body (10). In this moment, Irene exhibits what W. E. B. Du Bois calls a "double consciousness":

> . . . this sense of always looking at one's self through the eyes of others, of measuring one's soul by the tape of a world that looks on in amused contempt and pity. One ever feels his two-ness, an American, a Negro; two souls, two thoughts, two unreconciled strivings; two warring ideals in one dark body, whose dogged strength alone keeps it from being torn asunder. (2–3)

Irene feels this "two-ness" on the roof of the Drayton, and indeed, Clare—a woman with both a public and private racial consciousness and identity—represents it for her. At the same time Irene understands herself to be passing as "an Italian, a Spaniard, a Mexican, or a gipsy," she also imagines "the polite and tactful way in which the Drayton would" eject her (11). Deeply uncomfortable with this doubling, Irene's "colour heighten[s] under the continued inspection," and she rejects for herself the fear of discovery—the fear that public and private selves will confront each other—that Clare feels at all times (10).

Carla Kaplan finds parallels between *Passing* and the 1925 *Rhinelander v. Rhinelander* case (xviii). Wealthy socialite Leonard "Kip" Rhinelander filed an annulment suit, at the urging of his parents, to end his marriage to Alice Jones, a domestic servant with whom he had eloped, on the grounds that she had deceived him into believing she was white (xviii). As a result of the marriage, Alice Jones Rhinelander became the richest woman in the United States, and yet the annulment trial included a spectacle in which she was required to strip naked to the waist in court so that the jury could determine whether Rhinelander could have been deceived about his wife's race (xviii). The trial was, unsurprisingly, sensationalized in the press. Kaplan argues that, in contrast to the Rhinelander case, Larsen's novel—published only four years later in 1929—treats Clare's passing as morally complex rather than as a straightforward act of betrayal, as it was understood in the Rhinelander case (xix). Both instances, however, situate race as the triumph of public over private identity. Alice Jones's baring of her private body and, contextually, her intimate moments with her husband, was meant to make visible the public categorization of race on the uncovered parts of her body. For Irene, Clare's presence and her passing, especially the ease with which she performs it, threatens to destabilize racial categories and the boundary between public and private altogether. Irene and Brian have achieved the education, citizenship, and economic independence that are the goals of racial uplift, which some Black leaders offered in the post-Civil War period as a response to continued racial injustices. Their lives depend upon this structure of racial category to provide context for "uplift," and Clare's disruption of category also undermines that structure.

Before Clare's reappearance in her life, Irene lived quite comfortably within an economic system that rests upon categories of difference. Zulena, the Redfields' maid, "a small mahogany-coloured creature," offers another external double consciousness for Irene throughout the novel (38). Whereas Clare, due to her light skin, can pass as white and move through white spaces, the dark-skinned Zulena is employed as a domestic servant, one of the limited forms of labor available to women of color at the time. Between 1890 and 1920, women's participation in the U.S. workforce had increased by more than 25 percent, but the 40 percent of those women who were Black faced greater employment discrimination than white women and were limited to jobs as domestic servants in mostly white households (Patterson 12). Margaret Cheney Dawson notes Larsen's radical move in writing the scene where Irene and her husband, Brian, a doctor, sit down for breakfast, for "Nothing startles the white man so surely as the discovery of a simple, dignified routine in the life of educated Negroes. . . . This technique has been used in Negro fiction before, but not, I think, in the unselfconscious, taken-for-granted way in which Miss Larsen uses it in 'Passing'" (Dawson 87). Yet, this "simple, dignified routine," requires Zulena's silent labor:

> They went into the dining-room. He drew back her chair and she sat down behind the fat-bellied German coffee-pot, which sent out its morning fragrance, mingled with the smell of crisp toast and savoury bacon, in the distance. . . . Zulena, a small mahogany-coloured creature, brought in the grapefruit. (Larsen 38)

Mary Wilson identifies Zulena's "silent servitude" as revealing the fraught nature of domesticity for Black women (980). Zulena, Wilson argues, represents the uneasy intersection of middle-class domesticity with domestic service and servitude. In contrast to Clare, who worked as a maid before marrying a white, affluent husband, Zulena's "legible blackness" legitimizes her labor as a domestic servant (982). Indeed, Clare's and Irene's social mobility is predicated upon Zulena's domestic service, because there are no tea parties and quiet breakfasts without someone to set the table. At the same time, Zulena's presence is also destabilizing, because where Clare is a visual reminder for Irene of the possibilities of passing, Zulena offers another version of Black female selfhood within a white, middle-class model (984). Although Irene is haunted by jealous ideas of Brian having an affair with Clare, Zulena more closely embodies Brian's avowed preference: "I like my ladies darker" (Larsen 19). It isn't, then, Clare's passing that threatens Irene's comfortable middle-class existence, as she fears, but, rather, Zulena's silent presence at the tea table and the structures of racialized labor she represents in Larsen's novel.

Brian's statement about attraction to skin color underscores the way that race and sexuality are bound together in *Passing*. Both intersect on the body as private knowledge that threatens to emerge publicly and, conversely, public interrogation of private life. Butler argues that "queering is what upsets and exposes passing," because it requires an understanding of race, sexuality, and sexual difference as categories that converge, constitute each other, and, ultimately, destabilize each

other ("Passing, Queering" 427). In a break from previous critical interpretations of the novel, Deborah E. McDowell's introduction to the 1986
reissue of *Passing* and *Quicksand* situated the novel's apparent concern with racial passing as a rhetorical cover for encoded lesbian desire. McDowell argued that the "more dangerous story" is "Irene's awak-
ening sexual desire for Clare" (xxvi). At the same time, Irene is aware
that Brian "doesn't care for ladies. . . . I sometimes wish he did. It's South
America that attracts him" (Larsen 31). Within a queer reading of the
text, Brian's attraction to South America appears as encoded homosexual desire and threatens the Redfields' marriage as uncovered homosex-
uality would:

> That strange, and to [Irene] fantastic, notion of Brian's of going off to Bra-
> zil, which, though unmentioned, yet lived within him; how it frightened her,
> and—yes, angered her! . . . [he] had even hinted at a dissolution of their
> marriage in the event of his persistence in his idea. (40)

Rather than a story of wifely jealously directed at Clare, McDowell's
reading offers instead a novel in which queer desire on both sides of a
marriage threatens to explode the marriage itself as well as the institution of homosexual marriage and the social system it supports. Irene's
"fright . . . like a scarlet spear of terror leaping at her heart" is over private desire menacing the public—and therefore social and economic—
structure of her married, middle-class, life. (62)

Irene's attempts to police the boundaries between private and public life become most apparent at mealtimes. Shortly after her realization
that something—whether her desire for Clare or Brian's—poses a real
threat to her marriage, she descends to tea, where she reasserts her self-
identification as a middle-class woman who performs a kind of domestic service separate from the waged domestic labor Zulena performs:

> Downstairs the ritual of tea gave [Irene] some busy moments, and that, she
> decided, was a blessing. She wanted no empty spaces of time in which her
> mind would immediately return to that horror which she had not yet gath-
> ered sufficient courage to face. Pouring tea properly and nicely was an occu-
> pation that required a kind of well-balanced attention. (63)

In this passage, Irene echoes the views of another proponent of racial
uplift for Black women: Margaret Murray Washington, the wife of ed-
ucator and author Booker T. Washington. In "The New Negro Woman,"
Washington describes a division between kinds of Black women, arguing that those with more education and financial means should lift up

Black women of another "class" (57). Although Washington concedes that "we are a race of servants," she also argues that Black women, who were especially "helpless" during "all the black days of slavery," lacked:

> Lessons in making home neat and attractive; lessons in making family life stronger, sweeter, and purer . . . lessons in tidiness of appearance . . . lessons of clean and pure habits of everyday life in the home, and thus bringing to women self-respect and getting for them the respect of others . . . need to be given to this class of women to-day. (56–57)

Although Washington challenges racial distinctions by arguing for Black women to access the benefits of middle-class domesticity (and therefore property ownership), she upholds class distinctions between Black women who have achieved the level of education and financial means to cultivate "clean and pure habits" and those who have not. Irene, too, regards Zulena as a different class from herself, and, like Washington, her understanding of race relations and her own position as a Black woman require upholding this class boundary. Yet Irene's "well-balanced attention" in pouring tea cannot withstand the force of her repressed understanding that, within the context of Clare's complete disruption of racial categories, class categories are similarly unstable and prone to fracture:

> Rage boiled up in [Irene]. There was a slight crash. On the floor at her feet lay the shattered cup. Dark stains dotted the bright rug. Spread. The chatter stopped. Went on. Before her, Zulena gathered up the white fragments. (Larsen 66)

Even sentence structure is disrupted in this passage, as Larsen's text becomes shorter and more abrupt, reflecting Irene's fractured and intense thoughts. This moment, immediately after which Hugh Wentworth—a white man who takes part in Irene's social circle and enjoys discussing race relations with her—apologizes to Irene because he "must have pushed you," foreshadows Clare's fall out the window (66). It also leaves Zulena to pick up the "white fragments" of the teacup (a literal white fragility), which Irene tells Hugh "was the ugliest thing that your ancestors, the charming Confederates ever owned" (66). Here, one kind of racist structure—the Confederacy—is broken but replaced with a new kind of racialized power structure, one in which Zulena, the dark-skinned servant, is left to pick up the pieces. In the falling of the teacup, an ironic reversal of "racial uplift," Larsen reveals to her readers that pursuing Black equality through white, middle-class structures will always leave some bodies of color upholding those structures with their labor. The disruption of a boundary between public and private space also undermines any sense of division between professional and laboring Blacks.

The falling and breaking of the teacup is a "passing" through both physical and social space. The cup breaks with a "slight crash. On the floor at her feet lay the shattered cup. Dark stains dotted the bright rug. Spread" (66). This teacup, which recalls the tea Irene and Clare shared on the roof of the Drayton Hotel at the beginning of the novel, suggests a fracture of both their relationship and Irene's brief embrace of passing herself. It also foreshadows Clare's fall, associating it with a domestic object that represents the delicate kind of femininity to which Irene aspires as part of her middle-class values. Its breaking into "white fragments," allowing the dark liquid to spill out onto the carpet, similarly represents the disrupted boundary between public and private, Black and white (66). Irene seems relieved that the cup, "the ugliest thing that . . . the charming Confederates ever owned. . . . I've never figured out a way of getting rid of it until about five minutes ago. I had an inspiration. I had only to break it, and I was rid of it for ever. So simple! And I'd never thought of it before" (67). This epiphany could also follow Clare's fall out the window as another aspect of U.S. racial history that Irene can be "rid of . . . for ever." The crossing of boundaries in passing requires discrete boundaries to cross, thereby upholding racial distinctions. By removing Clare, the passing figure, from view, Irene begins to allow for the end of these distinctions. Similarly, by breaking the teacup and ending the presence of artifacts of a racist past in her home, Irene welcomes an end to racial categorization and the separation of the public from the domestic spheres. In the instance of the teacup, however, this welcoming is supported by Zulena's labor as she picks up the "white fragments" (67).

The breakfast scene in which Zulena silently brings in toast and grapefruit features a moment between Irene and Brian in which racial and sexual anxieties intersect in a discussion that is ostensibly about skin color. Brian understands passing as a biological imperative similar to sex: "we disapprove of it and at the same time condone it. . . . We shy away from it with an odd kind of revulsion, but we protect it" (39). He considers it an "instinct of the race to survive and expand," the same instinct exhibited by the "so-called whites, who've left bastards all over the known earth. Same thing in them" (39). What Brian understands—and what Irene rejects as "Rot!"—Butler identifies as the way that race and sexuality both constitute and complicate each other (39). The whites are "so-called" because sex across racial boundaries has resulted in "bastards all over the known earth," undermining the very category of whiteness itself.

Their continued discussion of their son, Junior, reveals Irene and Brian's disparate attitudes about racial identification and sexuality, with Junior's skin as the visible site of this intersection between public and family life. Brian praises their "good, strong, healthy boys, especially Junior," who "tall for his age, was almost incredibly like his father in feature and colouring" (41, 44). Brian, who has expressed a preference for dark-skinned women, appears to value his darker-complexioned son for this reason. Ironically, "mahogany" Zulena remains in the background of this discussion. Irene expresses her concern to Brian that Junior has "picked up some queer ideas . . . from the older boys," and Brian pushes her to clarify that by "queer ideas" she means "ideas about sex" (42). He accuses Irene of "trying to make a molly-coddle out of [Junior]. . . . The sooner and the more he learns about sex, the better for him. And most certainly if he learns that it's a grand joke, the greatest in the world. It'll keep him from lots of disappointments later on" (42). In the context of this passage, Brian's use of "molly-coddle" suggests that Irene is overprotective of Junior, but the term also refers to "an effeminate man or boy," centering queerness in this scene ("Mollycoddle"). Although Brian's overt meaning is that sex is time-wasting and frivolous, a queer reading of the novel places heterosexuality itself as the antecedent to Brian's "grand joke," suggesting that categories of sexuality and sexual identity are meaningless constructs. Brian, who expresses preference for and identification with Junior on the grounds of skin color, also projects his own sense of sex and sexuality onto his son.

Just as conversation about sex at the dinner table makes Irene uncomfortable because it too closely merges public and private spheres of consciousness, she is equally ill at ease with explicit discussions of race during mealtimes. At a family dinner later in the novel, Irene scolds Brian for bringing up the topic of racial violence in front of the children: "I do wish, Brian, that you wouldn't talk about lynching before Ted and Junior. It was really inexcusable for you to bring up a thing like that at dinner" (73). Brian argues with her that it's important for their sons to understand the reality of racial conflict:

> You're absolutely wrong! If, as you're so determined, they've got to live in this damned country, they'd better find out what sort of thing they're up against as soon as possible. The earlier they learn it, the better prepared they'll

be. . . . What was the use of our trying to keep them from learning the word 'nigger' and its connotation? They found out, didn't they? And how? Because somebody called Junior a dirty nigger. (73)

Just as Brian wants Junior to understand sex as much and as early as possible so that he can understand it as a "grand joke," he also wants his sons to understand how race becomes legible on the body and deployed violently, despite being a meaningless category, as he argues previously in the novel. Whereas Irene adamantly polices the boundary between public and private in the Redfield home, and especially at the dinner table—which is idealized as a site of middle-class family values—Brian understands these boundaries to be a false binary, as he also argues about race and sex.

By maintaining a boundary between public and private discussions about both race and sex, Irene is aligning herself most closely with Bellew, who similarly insists upon discrete racial categories to reaffirm his own identity. Butler notes the paradox in that Bellew's boundaries of whiteness require an association with Blacks to provide the circumstances for his constant disavowal of any relationship with them ("Passing, Queering" 421). It is through what Butler calls the "institutionalization of that disavowal" that Bellew's "whiteness is perpetually—but anxiously—reconstituted" (421). Although Bellew "draw[s] the line at . . . niggers in my family," Butler argues that he cannot understand his own identity as white without the constant policing of this boundary (Larsen 29). He calls Clare "Nig" to keep this dangerous attraction close to him and to constantly overcome and resist both Blackness and racial ambiguity ("Passing, Queering" 423). At the sight of Clare falling out the window, he cries, "Nig! My God! Nig!" (Larsen 79). The overt reading here is that Bellew is horrified at the death of his wife, but his use of her pet name also suggests that his true horror is over the loss of a relationship he requires to reify and reassure himself of his own whiteness.

Zulena plays a similar role for Irene that Clare, as "Nig," does for Bellew. Her close presence offers an institutionalized mechanism by which Irene can constantly reassert her own socioeconomic position as a middle-class Black woman. Her domestic role of leisure is defined in relationship to Zulena's domestic labor. And, like Bellew's need to address racial ambiguities, Irene's policing of roles within the domestic sphere reveals anxieties about her own place within it. Uncertain of her marriage because of Brian's desire to go to Brazil and his idea that sex is a "grand joke," Irene adamantly opposes discussion of other relationships to sex and sexuality at the dinner table. She does the same with race, be-cause her own identity depends on a certain attitude of "racial uplift" that Clare's passing and news of lynchings threaten. For Irene, public and pri-vate must remain separate and mutually constitutive spheres, and yet they are repeatedly and necessarily complicated throughout the novel.

Irene's reaction—or apparent reaction—to this anxiety is to push Clare out a sixth-story window to her death. Larsen's novel is full of ris-ing and falling imagery—perhaps an ironic take on the idea of "racial uplift"—and Clare's falling represents a different kind of passing through physical space and bodily state. Irene and Clare reencounter each other at the beginning of the novel on the Drayton Hotel roof, where Irene has escaped from the heat in the streets below, and this high pub-lic space provides a starting point for Clare's descent at the end of the novel. Walking up the steps of the building where Clare will meet her death later that evening, Brian jokingly asks her if she's ever gone "up by nigger-power" (77). Clare has been "uplift"-ed beyond the point where there's anywhere for her to go but down. Irene's pushing Clare out the window gives her agency in this downfall. Just as Irene's own uplift re-quires Zulena's silent presence, it also, apparently, requires Clare's fall.

Moments of eating and drinking in *Passing* are points of racial and sexual ambiguity. Not only do these moments underscore that the body itself is not a discrete entity, that it allows the passing through of nour-ishment and waste, but they are moments where public ideas intrude on private space, revealing both categories to be mutually constituted and mutually complicated. "Passing" between any state requires a firm boundary through which to pass, and Larsen's novel reveals, repeatedly and finally, that false binaries are unsustainable.

Conclusion

Food reveals the porous nature of our bodies, a persistent and delicious reminder that categories of self/other and public/private are inherently meaningless. The event of eating is also a site where private needs and public space—both of which are interconnected with race, sexuality, and class—converge. It requires us to engage in larger systems of agricul-ture, economy, labor, and production as well as to follow social mores in which individual desire and custom merge inextricably. A hunger for eggs and bacon, for example, is heavily determined by whether or not it is Saturday breakfast time, whereas a thirst for a martini with olives similarly depends upon whether it is five o'clock on Friday.

Characters in Nella Larsen's *Passing* all grapple with the instability of public/private categories through the act of eating and the interaction between the individual body and its surroundings. Scenes of eating and drinking in the novel are points of heightened racial and sexual anxiety in the text, moments where binary categories of identity are interrogated and thereby destabilized.

Larsen's novel establishes a connection between food consumption and the interrogation of embodied categories of identity. The act of incorporating food objects into the subject body to create an abject other reveals how binaries of public/private and self/other are similarly porous and unstable constructs.

WORKS CITED

Bourdieu, Pierre. *Distinction: A Social Critique of the Judgement of Taste.* Translated by Richard Nice, Harvard University Press, 1984.

Butler, Judith. *Gender Trouble: Feminism and the Subversion of Identity.* Routledge, 1990.

Butler, Judith. "Passing, Queering: Nella Larsen's Psychoanalytic Challenge." *Passing*, by Nella Larsen, edited by Carla Kaplan, Norton, 2007, pp. 417–34.

Dawson, Margaret Cheney. "The Color Line." *Passing*, by Nella Larsen, edited by Carla Kaplan, Norton, 2007, pp. 85–86.

DuBois, W. E. B. *The Souls of Black Folk.* Dover, 1903.

Kaplan, Carla. Introduction. *Passing*, by Nella Larsen, edited by Kaplan, Norton, 2007, pp. ix–xxviii.

Kristeva, Julia. *Powers of Horror: An Essay on Abjection.* Columbia University Press, 1982.

Larsen, Nella. *Passing*, edited by Carla Kaplan, W. W. Norton, 2007.

McDowell, Deborah E. Introduction. *Quicksand* and *Passing*, by Nella Larsen, edited by McDowell, Rutgers University Press, 1986, pp. ix–xxxi.

"Mollycoddle." Merriam-Webster Dictionary, www.merriam-webster.com/dictionary /mollycoddle, accessed April 14, 2022.

Patterson, Martha H. Introduction. *The American New Woman Revisited: A Reader, 1894–1930*, edited by Patterson, Rutgers University Press, 2008, pp. 1–25.

Pham, Minh-Ha T. *Asians Wear Clothes on the Internet: Race, Gender, and the Work of Personal Style Blogging.* Duke University Press, 2015.

Tompkins, Kyla Wazana. *Racial Indigestion: Eating Bodies in the Nineteenth Century.* New York University Press, 2012.

Veblen, Thorstein. *The Theory of the Leisure Class.* Macmillan, 1899.

Washington, Margaret Murray. "The New Negro Woman." *The American New Woman Revisited: A Reader, 1894–1930*, edited by Martha H. Patterson, Rutgers University Press, 2008, pp. 54–59.

Wilson, Mary. "'Working Like a Colored Person': Race, Service, and Identity in Nella Larsen's *Passing.*" *Women's Studies*, vol. 42, no. 8, 2013, pp. 979–1009, https://doi.org /10.1080/00497878.2013.830541, accessed July 5, 2021.

Queer Hunger, Eating, and Feeding in Toni Morrison's *Song of Solomon*

CARRIE HELMS TIPPEN

Food imagery and scenes of eating appear throughout Toni Morrison's *Song of Solomon* (1977). The women in the novel—especially Ruth, Pilate, and Hagar—are most closely associated with hunger, feeding, and eating. In some ways, they interact with food in traditional domestic activities. They prepare meals for their families and treats for their guests, and meals move the plot forward by marking the passage of time. In other ways, these characters engage in food practices that are unusual and sometimes unsavory. Pilate has a habit of chewing on pine needles and bits of string (*Song* 27, 30). Ruth breastfeeds her son long past the typical weening age (14). Hagar expresses her sexual longing through a food metaphor when she says, "Some of my days have been hungry ones" (49). Lena and Corinthians are described as food that has been "boiled dry" (28). When Lena calls out Milkman for his selfishness, she reminds him twice that his sisters were the ones who fed him (215).

Food images are not exclusive to women, either. Milkman is inordinately attracted to women who can feed him (Hagar, Pilate, Sweet) and just as likely to throw them off when they ask to be fed in return. Macon hungers metaphorically for "a big slice of the pie" or at least the "pie filling oozing around the edge of the crust" (63). Elizabeth House argues that, in Morrison, sweets are symbolic of the "competitive-success dreams engendered by white society" (193), which ultimately lead to

Macon's isolation and pain rather than satisfaction. To Milkman and Guitar, baked Alaska becomes a metonym for all that oppression can deny (60), and cherry jam represents to Pilate a meager substitute for the freedom lost with Lincoln's Heaven (167).

Throughout Morrison's oeuvre, her characters experience transgressive cravings; they feed each other poisons and potions and eat the inedible. In *Paradise*, the town of Ruby goes to the Convent for produce and food, particularly the Convent's sexually fraught hot peppers (1, 11). That book begins and ends with brutality in the kitchen. While Christine and Heed do find resolution and healing at the end of *Love*, Christine purposely feeds Heed foods she does not like and openly hopes that Heed will choke on her dinner and die (24). *The Bluest Eye* opens with a frightening encounter that links food with jealousy and inequality; Claudia and her sister are confronted by a neighbor eating bread and butter, going out of her way to exclude them. The girls react with violence that hints at a worse violence their enemy might be experiencing elsewhere:

> We stare at her, wanting her bread, but more than that wanting to poke the arrogance out of her eyes and smash the pride of ownership that curls her chewing mouth. When she comes out of the car we will beat her up, make red marks on her white skin, and she will cry and ask us do we want her to pull her pants down. We will say no. (*Bluest* 9)

In each of these examples, Morrison presents encounters with food that do not conform to normative scripts for food as a nourishing comfort. The inversion and perversion of foodways in the novels represent the rotting relationships and internal conflicts at the center of each novel.

In this essay, I examine the character of Ruth from *Song of Solomon*, whose appetites and food offerings disgust the men in her life. I describe Ruth's hunger, feeding, and eating as queer foodways: practices that are counter to dominant social scripts for behavior. Ruth's food practices serve as metaphors for her experiences of nonnormative sexuality and gender identity that are impossible for her to articulate or express safely in the boundaries of her cultural world.

Scholarly discussions of food in Morrison's work tend to focus on *Tar Baby*, a novel named after a licorice candy that takes its name from a racist term for Black children, often formed in the shape of Black bodies and marketed with racist Black caricatures. Warnes, Carruth, Hill, and Mayberry all examine Morrison's use of food in this novel in order to direct attention to race and the legacy of slave trading in cuisine and culture. *Beloved*, too, is a common text for examining foodways as the main character Sethe starves herself while she obsessively feeds the bloated ghost *Beloved* (Stanford, Lawrence). Other scholarship on Morrison's novels discusses food as an aspect of motherhood or mothering. In *Love*, L is a professional cook, and Anissa Janine Wardi reads her cooking as "a performance of nurturance that is understood as an act of love." Wardi asserts that "Indeed, throughout Morrison's work, hands that cook and offer food to family and community are depicted as healing figures" (206). Likewise, Manuela López Ramírez centers her reading of *Song of Solomon* on Circe and Pilate, variations on the witch or crone, defined as "the complex old woman (nurturing, both life-giving and destructive, a liminal figure—hovering between life and death—seductive, independent, and self-reliant), who becomes a Daedalic guide for the male hero" (42). While there certainly are Morrison characters who nurture and love and guide with food, even within *Song of Solomon*, what remains underexamined are the exceptions to this generalization who, like Ruth, are unsuccessful at making loving relationships even though they cook and serve food to others.

Queer Foodways

I can't take credit for inventing the term *queer foodways* or the idea of examining food practices as they relate to sexuality or nonnormative behavior, but relatively few scholarly articles in food studies use this particular combination of terms. Julia Erhardt explores the connections between queer theory and food studies in her 2006 essay "Toward Queering Food Studies." Erhardt takes Chicana lesbian writing as her example, examining the use of food and cooking imagery as the expression of homoerotic desire in poetry. Erhardt attempts to "make a foray into queering food studies" by examining how literary works "disrupt, destabilize, and transform" normative beliefs about "heteronormative gender and sexual culinary ideologies" (240). Like the poetry that Erhardt analyzes, *Song of Solomon* presents female-identified characters whose interactions with food challenge stereotyped gender roles and the meaning of food in women's sexual lives.

Queer foodways also appears in a 2020 *Gastronomica* article by chef and community activist Gabrielle Lenart, owner of the small business The Queer Kitchen, who describes the resilience of queer communities during the early days of Covid-19 lockdown in New York. The networks of support and ethics of care established in the "chosen family" of the queer community before the pandemic become a source of strength for enduring this time of physical isolation and economic uncertainty (62). Queer foodways, in this instance, refer specifically to the ways that LGBTQIA+ and BIPOC people demonstrate "passion, willingness, and commitment to each other, with food at the forefront" (63). Foodways here are *queer* because the people using them identify as queer, and because their food practices take place outside of heteronormative spaces and structures. While I, too, consider foodways practiced by a character with nonnormative sexual desires and practices, what makes foodways queer in my study is less about the identity of the practitioner and more about the normativity of the practice.

I refer to Ruth's food practices collectively as queer foodways because they fall outside of normative boundaries for how to interact with food in American culture. I use the term *queer* as Judith (Jack) Halberstam does in *In a Queer Time and Place*. Halberstam extends the term to apply to nonnormative experiences of time and space not necessarily linked to an individual's sexual preferences. Halberstam instead defines "the queer 'way of life'" as all "subcultural practices" and "willfully eccentric modes of being" (2). I use the term *queer* to refer to food behaviors— hunger, craving, cooking, preparing, serving, eating, and digesting—that are nonnormative, "willfully eccentric" uses of foods or foodways.

In *Toni Morrison and the Queer Pleasure of Ghosts*, Juda Bennett also draws on Halberstam's definition and points out the instability of the term, even in the field of queer studies (2). Like me, Bennett does not necessarily apply the term to acts or actors who are "queer in the way we often imagine lesbian, gay, bisexual, or transgender identities" but considers "a broad challenge to all forces of convention and conformity," including those ghostly characters who occupy a space between the living and the dead (2, 3).

I argue that nonnormative food behaviors are used in *Song of Solomon* as metaphors for nonnormative sexuality because both food and sexuality have recognizable hegemonic systems that individuals may "willfully" subvert. The hegemonic food system may not be as obvious as the heteronormative sex-gender system, but there are recognizable "rules" for eating. Cultures place limits on what foods are appropriate for consumption, what portion sizes are expected, who should eat what and how. Carole Counihan argues that "rules about food consumption are an important means through which human beings construct reality. They are an allegory of social concerns, a way in which people give order to the physical, social, and symbolic world around them" (55). The fact that "eating disorders" exist presupposes that eating is an ordered system.

Ruth uses feeding and eating as tools creating feelings of intimacy and connection that are sometimes, but not always, sexual. Ruth describes making her body a dessert or a sweet treat for Macon to consume during sex (16). However, Ruth's attempts at establishing "normal" loving relationships with men fail—usually because of her overwhelming need for affection and their inadequacy or unwillingness to meet her needs—leading her to more dramatic and disruptive activities that conversely disgust the objects of her affection. While she denies that her relationship with her father is anything abnormal, Macon interprets Ruth's action of putting her recently deceased father's fingers in her mouth as evidence of a sexual relationship (73). Certainly Ruth's emotional attachment to her father—described by him as "unsettling," "inappropriate," and "disturbing"—may be out of bounds, but her behavior is motivated by a desire for his love (23). Breastfeeding her son is a ritual that makes her feel connected to him and valuable as a human, but she moves beyond the normative when she describes the experience as ecstatic, even orgasmic (13–14).

While Ruth is not the focus of the novel, her encounters with food highlight the discussion of sexuality that preoccupies the novel, as foregrounded in the title. As Anne Imbrie explains, the title of Morrison's novel refers to "the most explicitly sexual book in the biblical canon, a love poem, written in dialogue, which describes the experience of sexual pleasure" (474). The dialogue between the Lover, the Beloved, and, occasionally, their friends repeatedly uses culinary pleasures as metaphors for sexual pleasures. The first line of the first chapter makes a direct reference to food: "Let him kiss me with the kisses of his mouth—for your love is more delightful than wine" (NIV, Song of Solomon 1.2). Throughout the biblical text, the Beloved most often uses food imagery as a metaphor for sexual pleasure: "Like an apple tree among the trees of the forest is my lover among the young men. I delight to sit in his shade, and his fruit is sweet to my taste. He has taken me to the banquet hall, and his banner over me is love. Strengthen me with raisins, refresh me with apples, for I am faint with love" (NIV 2.3–5). Imbrie argues that Morrison's book is essentially a reversal of the biblical text, with "the relationship between Macon and Ruth as an ironic inversion of the dialogic structure of loving exchange" (474). It is also a reversal of normative expectations for food practices. We will not find love overcoming all odds; we will not find food bringing characters together in love.

Queer Hunger and Craving

Ruth's central conflict is her unmet need to be an object of desire, which appears in the novel as a combination of literal cravings for nonfood items and hunger as a metaphor for unmet emotional and sexual needs. Her mouth—which ought to be used for eating—becomes a tool that she uses to attempt to satisfy these other abstract needs through kissing, sucking, biting, and chewing.

The defining relationship in Ruth's life is with her father, the doctor, whom she adores. Ruth's father describes her affection for him as too intense, "a steady beam of love" that he "chafe[s] under" (23). Even after she is "too old," Ruth insists on a goodnight kiss on the lips. Her "ecstasy" and her resemblance to his dead wife give the kiss a sexual tension that the doctor finds repulsive. He feeds her begrudgingly with weak kisses (23), just as Milkman begrudgingly submits to nursing (13), but her hunger for affection only intensifies. Ruth's intense, devouring love breaks the rules of familial intimacy when her mouth gets involved. The doctor cannot think of her as an adult daughter because her actions are more like those of a wife or a young child. Ruth is neither, and so her actions go beyond the pale of expectations. The doctor is not gratified by Ruth's attempts at love but confused and repulsed. Thus, Ruth's hunger is not satisfied by her father's hesitant playing along.

Ruth's hunger reaches a climax when her father dies. His illness (Macon thinks it is an addiction to ether) has made him bloated and fat but unable to eat properly. He must "drink all his meals and swallow something after every meal" (73). Macon describes finding Ruth literally devouring the doctor with her mouth: "laying next to him. Naked as a yard dog, kissing him . . . she had his fingers in her mouth" (73). Macon implies that Ruth's relationship with her father was always incestuous, though the text neither confirms nor denies the validity of the accusation (74). The image of her sucking on his fingers unsettles Macon so deeply that he refuses to have sex with Ruth ever again and only submits to her desires under the influence of Pilate's potions (131). Ruth describes the episode with her father differently; she was beside the bed in her slip just kissing his hands (126). Even with Ruth's alterations to the story, she is still caught in a nonnormative position, using her mouth to extract love from the ultimate object of disgust, a corpse. Macon sees Ruth's behavior and recognizes it as something queer.

When Ruth and Macon marry while her father is still alive, some of the affection for her father and hunger for reciprocated affection is redirected to her husband. Macon describes their early sex life of long and interesting foreplay in food metaphors, with Ruth being "peeled" and left "naked and lying there as moist and crumbly as unbleached sugar" (16). Macon is assured that Ruth liked the foreplay followed by his quick ejaculation. Perhaps Macon is not flattering himself here; their ritual undressing made Ruth into a dish to be consumed where elsewhere she had always been a diner. Ruth's body is the object of Macon's full attention for as long as the undressing lasts. It is the only part of sex that Macon misses after he withdraws from her (16), and "the nourishment of his outrage" is focused on the memory of that undressing (17). As Ruth explains to Milkman, this consuming foreplay is probably the only part of sex she misses, too (125). After ten years of sleeping in separate rooms, Ruth describes her emotional hunger: "I couldn't stand it anymore. . . . I thought I'd die if I had to live that way. With nobody touching me, or even looking like they'd like to touch me" (125). Once the undressing stops, Ruth is forced into the position of seducer, a position that pushes her out of her proscribed passive gender role and into a role that further alienates her and frustrates her aims. Ruth begins to make regular visits to her father's gravesite in the night when her sexual frustration becomes overwhelming. Ruth explains to Milkman that she goes to "reignite that cared-for feeling" that she got from her father (124). Even as restrained as his affections were, Ruth does not get this feeling elsewhere, and she starves for it: "for that, I would do anything," she tells her son (124), even if it means breaking taboos through queer cravings.

Ruth's hunger during her pregnancy crosses another normative boundary, even though American culture gives a wide berth to the cravings of pregnant women. Pilate gives Ruth cornstarch as a cure for nausea (131). Pilate's feeding brings Ruth relief, but after the cornstarch, Ruth craves anything crunchy: "cracked ice, nuts, and once in a fit she put a few tiny pebbles of gravel in her mouth" (131–32). What Ruth describes is probably pica, defined as a "pathological urge or craving," usually for nonfood items like dirt or clay (Strungaru 32). Carmen Strungaru argues that pica is a form of stress relief through "constant oral stimulation" brought on by the sensation of chewing and crunching (40). It is perfectly acceptable for Ruth's physical distress to be manifested in nausea and craving. In fact, Pilate urges Ruth to eat what the baby craves, "'less it come in the world hungry [sic] for what you denied it" (132). The implication is that Milkman in the womb is hungry for something. However, the things Ruth craves are not foods but physical feelings in her mouth. She craves the chewing and crunching sensation, a feeling that Milkman in utero could not share. Craving a nonfood like cornstarch or pebbles suggests that Ruth's emotional distress is more intense than she is prepared to admit, and oral stimulation appears to assuage those feelings. Ruth's physical hunger and emotional hunger lead her to queer foodways.

Queer Cooking and Feeding

The text introduces Ruth early on as an accidentally bad cook: "She did not try to make her meals nauseating; she simply didn't know how not to" (11). Once again, the lack of "proper" feminine training and nourishment in her childhood leaves her without the tools for successful normative relationships in adulthood. Macon sums up her poor cooking thusly: "Your chicken is red at the bone. And there is probably a potato dish that is supposed to have lumps in it. Mashed ain't the dish" (12). While other female characters in the novel provide nourishing food and earn affection and respect (Pilate's home is a fecund and fermenting paradise compared to Ruth's cold and sterile kitchen), Ruth's cooking and feeding of others break boundaries partly from a lack of skill and knowledge. Rather than inspiring the return of love, her affection tends to elicit as much disgust as her cooking, and it may come from a similar lack of skill with normative practices.

Ruth feeds her husband to manipulate his affections and satisfy her own desires. Ruth tricks Macon into impregnating her by feeding him a potion when her loneliness and sexual frustration after her father's death and Macon's withdrawal overwhelm her. She has been rejected and abandoned by her father and her husband—the only men in her life who could satisfy her hunger in anything like normative ways. Ruth's hunger is not for Macon in particular. She tells Pilate, "I want somebody," and "he's as good as anybody" (125). Pilate validates Ruth's sexual desire; rather than encouraging her to repress her sexuality, Pilate encourages her to normalize it by seducing Macon, not turning to another lover. To get his love back, Ruth feeds Macon a concoction of a powder mixed with rainwater that Pilate gives her. Though Ruth's cooking is notoriously bad, Pilate's magic works, and Ruth gets pregnant after "a few days of sexual hypnosis" (131). Instead of reconciling her to Macon, however, Ruth's stunt drives him further away, and he reacts with violence against her and their unborn child (125). On the same page that Macon remembers the delicious foreplay of their early married life, he declares that his thoughts of her now are always "coated with disgust," a feeling that spills onto his son, begotten "in the most revolting of circumstances" (16). Macon's rejection becomes permanent, and Ruth is left hungrier than before without any normative options for satisfying her appetite for affection. This queer feeding does not engender that emotional exchange that Ruth expects it should because it exceeds the bounds of expectations.

Milkman's birth provides Ruth with an escape, with an acceptable "somebody" to whom she can give her love and who can offer her love in return. However, Ruth's hunger for physical contact leads to a sexually charged, queer feeding ritual. Ruth breastfeeds Milkman until he is almost tall enough for his feet to reach the floor while sitting in her lap (13), long past the normative age for weaning. Ruth's choice to feed Milkman in between cooking and serving dinner to the rest of her family further emphasizes that Ruth's food practices are entangled with her sexuality. Nursing her son becomes a solution for the absence of her father and the abstinence of her husband: "Something else is needed to get from sunup to sundown: a balm, a gentle touch or nuzzling of some sort" (13). She craves the physical pleasure of nursing (132), but the sensation is paired with the fantasy that her breastmilk is a "thread of light" or a "cauldron issuing spinning gold" (13). She fantasizes that she is a person filled with goodness and value. The queer feeding is a way to bring up feelings of love for herself, and for Ruth's body to be consumed by the love of another. Milkman nurses begrudgingly; however, Ruth interprets his hesitation as tenderness for her (14). She reads his compliance as affection well after he has become uncomfortable. His gentleness and deference become part of her fantasy, and the ritual constitutes "fully half of what made her daily life bearable" (14). When the feeding ritual is interrupted, Freddie confirms what Milkman suspected: that the act was taboo. Ruth's attempts at making an emotional connection through queer feeding and nourishing fail again.

Greta Gaard argues that Ruth's feeding of Milkman fails to be nurturing because feeding itself is only half the formula for a mother's love: "Ruth breastfeeds Milkman but is unable to provide the other part of mothering, the wise and affectionate support" (12). Gaard doesn't blame Ruth for this failure, noting that her inability to give love is "possibly because she has never received it herself: there is no mention of Ruth's mother, and Ruth spends her entire life within tightly controlled patriarchal family systems (first with her doctor-father, and then with her husband) so that she is unable to nourish or value herself" (12). The root of Ruth's nonnormative feeding is her unsatisfied hunger, which extends from a lack of loving nourishment from her own parents and, more importantly, a lack of resources for developing her own healthy self-esteem. The narrow constraints of heteronormativity require her to passively wait for affection, but she simply cannot trust that the affection will come. When Ruth turns breastfeeding into a food practice that nourishes herself more than her child, she has broken the rules of the game and moved into the realm of queer foodways.

Outside of the family, Ruth uses feeding to connect with both the Black and the white communities around her, again with little success. Ruth entertains other women in her home, though she feeds them poorly with her bad cooking, like the "baked-too-fast sunshine cake" that sticks to the roofs of their mouths (10). Speaking strictly of class, Ruth is in a borderland, separated from the rest of the women by her "big dark house of twelve rooms and the green sedan" (9). Her father's middle-class profession and her husband's property investments provide enough income to give the appearance of prosperity, though some of the women recognize that "the house was more prison than palace, and that the sedan was for Sunday drives only" (10). Ruth knows that her cooking is bad (Macon reminds her often), but she continues to invite the neighbor women to her home as an attempt to secure her gender identity as well as her class status. Offering her guests food is normative behavior, but the undercooked and substandard fare makes the behavior abnormal. Food stuck to the roof of the mouth often triggers a gag reflex; both Ruth and her food are vomited and rejected. Rather than securing her gender identity, Ruth instead secures her place at the bottom of the gendered social ladder. At the borders of the lower middle class, at the borders of femininity, Ruth is alienated both from the women who hate her out of envy and the women who humor her out of pity.

The one attempt at feeding at which Ruth is successful is metaphorical. On the dining table is a water mark leftover from a centerpiece: "a touch that distinguished [the doctor's] family from the people among whom they lived" (12). This is the only thing that Ruth is described as successfully feeding. Though she has tried many methods to remove the stain, "her glance was nutritious" and it seemed to grow instead of fade (12). The mark is described as animate; it "flourished," "throbbed," and "sighed" (13). The narrator claims that Ruth uses the spot as "a verification of some idea [she] wanted to keep alive" (13). That idea could be her father's wealth and reputation, her father's affection for her, or both. Macon's critique of Ruth's raw chicken and lumpy mashed potatoes follows Ruth's comment on the decorative floral centerpiece she has made for the table to cover the spot (12). She has given her nourishing attention to the symbol of her father's class status rather than the nourishment of her romantic partnership. The table is an unspeaking, throbbing barrier between Ruth and Macon where they play out their conflict. Corinthians notes how her mother used conversation at the dinner table to provoke Macon into violence rather than bringing them closer; Macon has "no exit save violence" in these conversations (64). Ruth's attempts at gaining affection by feeding fail through her queer use of the family dining table as a battleground.

Queer Eating and Being Eaten

Finally, Ruth's own eating habits can be seen as queer, even apart from her temporary pica. One of Macon and Ruth's most intense fights at the dinner table happens after Ruth eats out of bounds. Ruth attends the wedding of the relative of one of her father's "working-class white patients" where she clumsily takes Communion reserved only for Catholics (65). Here, Ruth's eating breaks an ecclesiastical rule, making the act queer (setting aside for a moment the queer implications of transubstantiation, eating the Father's flesh). Ruth takes the host in order to close the distance between herself and the wedding guests; she goes to the altar because the rest of the congregation goes (65). But Ruth's purpose in attending the wedding is to exploit the class distinction that alienates her from the Black community by rubbing elbows with the white community. Ruth leaves the wedding feeling gratified that her father's name still carries weight in white circles (66). Her eating, she thinks, has brought her into community and equity with her perceived "betters."

However, as she retells the story to her family, Ruth's faux pas is interpreted as a humiliating error. Macon is incredulous that Ruth really could have been accepted so readily: "You see them put up their own school, keep their kids out of public schools, and you still think their religious stuff is open to anybody who wants to drop in?" (66). In Macon's estimation, he and his family have been set up as Others to the white Catholic community. Though Ruth assures him that everyone was delighted with her, Macon is convinced she has made "a fool" of herself, "embarrass[ed] everybody at the reception, and come to the table to gloat about how wonderful" she was (67). "You by yourself ain't nobody," Macon tells her. "You your daddy's daughter" (67). He means that she is insignificant in the community except as an echo of her father's memory, merely tolerated for his sake and not loved for her own. Ruth, how-ever, revels in the title "daddy's daughter" because she reads it as proof that she belongs to her father, that her identity has been conflated with his own. Macon reads her pride as proof of the sinister sexual relation-ship he imagines between Ruth and her father.

The motivation behind much of Ruth's behavior is the desire to be an object of desire. This shows up in the novel as a queer desire to be con-sumed and eaten. As established, her preference in sex with her hus-band is to be passively consumed (16). Her breastfeeding Milkman is less about offering him nourishment than it is about offering her body for consumption. Being "nobody" but her "daddy's daughter" is an ac-complishment of which to be proud. Nowhere is this queer desire for annihilation illustrated more clearly than in Milkman's "dream" (that is not a dream) of his mother being devoured by tulips in her garden (104–5). Milkman describes the phallic tulip sprout, growing preternaturally fast and tall, "a solitary thin tube of green, then two leaves open[ing] up from the stem—one on each side," moving "up against his mother's dress" then exposing their "bloody red heads" (105). Ruth is utterly sub-missive to the tulips. They are "bobbing, snapping heads . . . smothering her, taking away her breath with their soft, jagged lips." But Milkman tells Guitar, "She liked it. She was having fun. She liked it" (105). Ruth is covered over and swallowed up by the tulips, and for the first and only time in the novel, Ruth is described in positive terms, playful and smil-ing, having finally accomplished her character's motivating desire.

Conclusion

To finish a queering of foodways, we must show that there is, in the end, nothing queer at all about Ruth's hunger, eating, and feeding. As het-eronormative sexuality is a cultural construction that artificially limits and inhibits both those who conform and those who subvert the norm, so Ruth is limited and inhibited by her culture's norms of relationships between father and daughter, husband and wife, and mother and son. These same limits prohibit the men in her life from being able to recip-rocate Ruth's desires. In the world of the novel, the problem with Ruth's feeding and affection is that it insists on equitable reciprocation. She ex-pects to be fed in return for feeding, to be devoured in return for eating. In short, she expects to be loved equally in return for loving.

Unfortunately for Ruth, these relationships do not permit mutual-ity, and her love is a threat to her partners' experiences of masculinity. As

Guitar explains to Milkman, "Black women, they want your whole self" (222), but men, too, want to own women: The Days must avenge the rape of a Black woman "because she's mine" (223). As long as both parties want to dominate and control the other, neither can. When Ruth's attempts to satisfy her desires in normative ways fail, she turns to queer sexual and food practices. It is not clear that she intends for her love for her father or her son to be sexually expressed until her hunger for affection—caused first by the absence of a nourishing mother, and later by the death of her father and the emotional and physical withdrawal of her only acceptable sexual partner—is so intense that it cannot be satisfied within the dominant script of behaviors. Ruth's queer hunger, feeding, and eating only serve to alienate her further by breaking the rules until she becomes an object of disgust.

Pilate offers a clear contrast to Ruth's queer foodways, but even her food practices cannot be described as healthy. Anyone who enters Pilate's house is fed and satisfied (48). Milkman leaves their first meeting thinking that the "delicious" day had been "the first time in his life that he remembered being completely happy" (49, 47). Even Macon is drawn to Pilate's house at dinnertime. At Pilate's house, there is music and conversation; at Macon's house, there is "his wife's narrow, unyielding back; his daughters, boiled dry from years of yearning; his son to whom he could speak only if his words held command or criticism" (28).

Pilate's feeding is successful in creating connections, however, because unlike Ruth, she lacks appetite and does not require reciprocation. Macon remarks that the women in Pilate's home "ate like children," picking up "what they had on hand or came across or had a craving for" (29). The cravings they have are soft and immediately satisfied; their appetites are not as outsized as Ruth's. Pilate feeds anyone who asks of her, but Hagar and Reba remark that she eats "like a lizard," never eating much herself (48). Patricia Allen and Carolyn Sachs seem to be describing women like Pilate in their article "Women and Food Chains":

> Women's involvement with food constructs who they are in the world—as individuals, family members, and workers—in deep, complex, and often contradictory ways. . . . And although women bear responsibility for nourishing others, they often do not adequately nourish themselves. (23)

Certainly Pilate's identity is structured around her feeding of others. She makes her living on fermenting fruit wine (that she never drinks) and feeding her family (without feeding herself). Ruth's preoccupation with being nourished herself makes her behavior queer: counter to the expectation that her appetites should be as insignificant and unobtrusive as Pilate's.

Still, even Pilate, with her rich and nourishing feeding rituals, is characterized by abnormal appetites and eating. The narrator takes pains to mention Pilate's constant chewing on pine needles (27), pieces of string (30), and bits of wood (186), drawing even more attention to moments when the chewing stops (48–49). This is another version of Ruth's pica, and it seems to be a reaction to the trauma of Pilate's birth and early childhood. Perhaps her supernatural birth and lack of a belly button might explain her lack of appetite (28). Unlike Ruth, who seems to suffer from having no mother figure, Pilate supersedes a need for a mother, birthing herself. Independently taking charge of her own birth may have made her more suited to the job of unreciprocated feeder that the normative script of her gender expects of her. Or perhaps Pilate learned not to be hungry after the death of her father. Young Pilate cries when Circe brings her cherry jam instead of "her own cherries, from her own cherry tree" (167). That craving for cherries and the lost promise of the independence of Lincoln's Heaven "had almost devastated her" (167). Though Pilate is traumatized, a queer eater, and more or less a social pariah, she can more readily conform to heteronormative expectations because she needs nothing from that system. At least she is never hungry.

Paradoxically, Pilate's home on the fringes makes it easier for her to simultaneously conform to and subvert expectations of gender and race. Farid Parvaneh argues that some Morrison characters, like Pilate, "who are rootless drifters . . . [o]utside or beyond all cultures" are allowed greater freedom to "create a new identity for themselves in a new culture of their own making" (37). This is in direct contrast to those still "enslaved" within the dominant culture (37), like Ruth. Pilate, perhaps, occupies this space of freedom outside the community where she can take an action like feeding, which is burdened with overdetermined meaning in Ruth's world, and make it mean something else in her counterculture. Because she lacks a desire for heteronormativity (no male partner and surrounded by her daughters), Pilate can give eating and feeding whatever valence she chooses, including, perhaps, no valence at all. Though Ruth clearly occupies a liminal space between cultures, her position cannot be described as liberated. Parvaneh does not address Ruth's character in his article; however, Ruth may represent what Parvaneh characterizes as "cultural suicide": sacrificing a "unique cultural voice" in order "to fit into the larger cultural context" (37). Perhaps this "suicide" can explain her insistence on passivity and her desire to be annihilated by the consumption of her body.

Deborah McDowell writes in her afterword to *Recovering the Black Female Body* that African American women are regularly portrayed as "simultaneously all bodies and nobodies" (289), making them perfect objects of desire, all object and no identity. Morrison earned McDowell's praise for flouting this narrative with *Sula* in 1985:

> The need to portray their people with honesty and imagination has been paramount for contemporary black women novelists. . . . [T]hey have liberated their own characters from the burden of being exemplary standard-bearers in an enterprise to uplift the race. The result is not only greater complexity and possibility for their heroines, but also greater complexity and artistic possibility for themselves as writers. (287)

Morrison takes on a border-breaking and class-obsessed character like Ruth for the very purpose that McDowell describes: troubling inherited narratives of Black female sexuality. Ruth is certainly no "standard-bearer" for her race or gender, but she is a woman in a crisis of identity who cannot be simply "all body and nobody" because the human condition is far too complex for those proscribed borders. In *The Power of Horror*, Julia Kristeva describes Ruth's crisis exactly:

> If it be true that the abject simultaneously beseeches and pulverizes the subject, one can understand that it is experienced at the peak of its strength when that subject, weary of fruitless attempts to identify with something on the outside, finds the impossible within; when it finds that the impossible constitutes its very *being*, that it is none other than abject. (5, emphasis in original).

In other words, Ruth, "weary of fruitless attempts to identify with something on the outside," finds that she can live within no narrative, within no normative boundaries. Ruth disappears from the novel three-quarters of the way through. She is devoured by tulips and becomes a nobody in Milkman's narrative. The impossible constitutes her very being.

Ruth fails to satisfy the desire that motivates her character in the novel because her identity fails to be constructed in normative ways. Her behavior is not inherently wrong or evil, and in someone else (someone not female, not Black, not newly middle class), in some other time or place, Ruth's motives would be praised or admired. Why shouldn't she be loved by her father, husband, and son? Why shouldn't she be rewarded for communicating her desires and working to satisfying them? But Ruth is the victim of a script that expects her to be a healing feeder and to want no healing or feeding in return. Ruth contradicts this narrative through her pitiful feeding and constant queer hunger. Though she tries to live within the boundaries of her culture's ideals, her behavior is queer because she sees no normative behaviors that will accomplish her non-normative goals, and so she fails in all her roles as a female: daughter, lover, wife, homemaker, mother, woman. At novel's end, she has found no healing in either food or sex. The barrenness of the dining room and the kitchen that refuse to obey her are living images of the barrenness of Ruth's femininity and the culture that refuses to accept her.

WORKS CITED

Allen, Patricia, and Carolyn Sachs. "Women and Food Chains: The Gendered Politics of Food." *Taking Food Public: Redefining Foodways in a Changing World*, edited by Caroline Counihan and Psyche Williams-Forson, Routledge, 2012, pp. 23–40.

Bennett, Juda. *Toni Morrison and the Queer Pleasure of Ghosts*. SUNY Press, 2014.

Carruth, Allison. "'The Chocolate Eater': Food Traffic and Environmental Justice in Toni Morrison's *Tar Baby*." *Modern Fiction Studies*, vol. 55, no. 3, 2009, 596–619.

Counihan, Carole. "Food Rules in United States: Individualism, Control and Hierarchy." *Anthropological Quarterly*, vol. 65, no. 2, 1992, 55–66, JSTOR, accessed April 21, 2012.

Erhardt, Julia. "Toward Queering Food Studies." *Taking Food Public: Redefining Foodways in a Changing World*, edited by Psyche Williams-Forson and Carole Counihan, Routledge, 2011, pp. 239–50.

Gaard, Greta. "Literary Milk: Breastfeeding across Race, Class, and Species in Contemporary U.S. Fiction." *Journal of Ecocriticism*, vol. 5, no. 1, 2013, pp. 1–18.

Halberstam, Judith. *In a Queer Time and Place: Transgender Bodies, Subcultural Life*. New York University Press, 2005.

Hill, Cecily. "Three Meals: Eating Culture in Toni Morrison's *Tar Baby*." *Midwest Quarterly*, vol. 53, no. 3, 2012, pp. 283–98.

House, Elizabeth. "The 'Sweet Life' in Toni Morrison." *American Literature*, vol. 56, no. 2, 1984, pp. 181–202, JSTOR, accessed February 9, 2012.

Imbrie, Anne E. "'What Shalimar Knew': Toni Morrison's *Song of Solomon* as a Pastoral Novel. *College English*, vol. 55, no. 5, 1993, pp. 473–90, JSTOR, accessed April 21, 2012.

Kristeva, Julia. *The Power of Horror*. Translated by Leon S. Roudiez, Columbia University Press, 1982.

Lawrence, David. "Fleshly Ghosts and Ghostly Flesh: The Word and the Body in *Beloved*." *Toni Morrison's Fiction: Contemporary Criticism*, edited by David Middleton, Routledge, 1997, pp. 231–46.

Lenart, Gabrielle. "Adapting Queer Foodways." *Gastronomica*, vol. 20, no. 3, 2020, pp. 62–63.

López Ramírez, Manuela. "The New Witch in Toni Morrison's *Song of Solomon* and *God Help the Child*." *African American Review*, vol. 53, no. 1, 2020, pp. 41–54.

Mayberry, Susan. "Guess Who's Coming to Dinner? Food, Race, and [En]countering the Modern in Toni Morrison's *Tar Baby*." *Toni Morrison: Forty Years in the Clearing*, edited by Carmen R. Gillespie, Bucknell University Press, 2012, pp. 212–35.

McDowell, Deborah. "Afterword: Recovery Missions: Imaging the Body Ideals." *Recovering the Black Female Body: Self Representations by African American Women*, edited by Michael Bennett and Vanessa Dickerson, Rutgers University Press, 2000, pp. 296–317.

Morrison, Toni. *Beloved*. Alfred A. Knopf, 1987.

——. *The Bluest Eye*. Alfred A. Knopf, 1970.

——. *Love*. Alfred A. Knopf, 2003.

——. *Paradise*. Alfred A. Knopf, 1997.

——. *Song of Solomon*. Plume, 1977.

Parvaneh, Farid. "Formation of Identity in Toni Morrison's African-American Characters." *Studies in Literature and Language*, vol. 1, no. 5, 2010, *JSTOR*, accessed February 2, 2012.

Stanford, Ann Folwell. "Death Is a Skipped Meal Compared to This: Food and Hunger in Toni Morrison's *Beloved*." *Contemporary Literary Criticism*, vol. 480, no. 1, 2021, pp. 129–47.

Strungaru, Carmen. "Consuming the Inedible: Pica Behaviour." *Consuming the Inedible*, edited by Jeremy McClancy et al., Berghahn, 2007, pp. 31–42.

Wardi, Anissa Janine. "A Laying on of Hands: Toni Morrison and the Materiality of *Love*." *MELUS*, vol. 30, no. 3, pp. 201–18, *JSTOR*, accessed April 21, 2012.

Warnes, Andrew. *Hunger Overcome? Food and Resistance in Twentieth-Century African American Literature*. University of Georgia Press, 2004.

Appetites and Identity

Mixed-Race Identity Construction
through Food and Sex
in Carmit Delman's "Footnote"

RACHEL FERNANDES

Food and sex are embodied practices intimately tied to one's sense of identity, and this intersection between food, sex, and identity is a well-studied one. The eighteenth-century French gastronome Jean Anthelme Brillat-Savarin was famous for his aphorisms, but perhaps none so popular among food studies scholars as his declaration: "Tell me what you eat: I will tell you what you are" (qtd. in Ashley et al. 161). In her book *Carnal Appetites*, Elspeth Probyn merges the three words of her subtitle into one: "FoodSexIdentities." She also asks, "in eating, do we confirm our identities, or are our identities reforged and refracted by what and how we eat?" (11). She draws the connection between food and sex later in the book: "in eating we experience different parts of our bodies. . . . The same could, of course, be said of sex. Obviously, at times, the corporeal experience of sex also joins us with other bodies as it reworks aspects of our own relations to ourselves, past and present" (62). This essay takes up these questions about food and sex: Can one construct an identity through what one has in one's cupboard? What about our sexual encounters? Do the people we sleep with define who we are?

These questions are interesting to consider for a person of any cultural background but are particularly challenging when applied to people of mixed race. More specifically, can those of us with multiracial backgrounds cultivate a meaningful sense of connection to our various heritages by consuming foods associated with our ancestors' racial and cultural backgrounds? And can we connect to our heritage by becoming closer to the bodies of people who also belong to a particular racial group? After all, as David Parker and Miri Song remind us, "people of 'mixed race' often have distinctive experiences of their parents and family life [and] unique patterns of identity formation" (7). The mixed-race person often faces particular challenges, including "falling outside dominant racialized categories; facing distrust and suspicion from both 'sides' of their family; being profoundly and hurtfully misrecognized by others, enduring the 'What are you?' question; enjoying the potential for multiple allegiances and identities" (7). Using a food studies lens, and by doing a close reading of Carmit Delman's short story "Footnote," I argue that the cultivation of a nuanced mixed-race identity may include these practices of eating or cooking and sexual activity, but in this story these activities ultimately leave the main character unfulfilled. The protagonist's use of food yields only a rudimentary engagement with Indian food culture, and her exploration of sex with a man who recently immigrated from India results in her objectifying and othering her partner because of his "exotic" background, rather than cultivating a meaningful relationship with him. I argue that these brief, hurried engagements with aspects of Indian culture do not leave Angie with a stronger connection to her heritage but rather contribute to the alienation she feels.

"Footnote" is no more than twelve pages long, but the short story is nonetheless complex in its handling of race, food, and sex. The protagonist, Angie, is a young professional living in downtown Boston. The third-person narrator explains that her father's family is white, although the narrator does not provide further detail about his ancestry. Angie's maternal grandfather was Indian, but Angie was almost completely cut off from this part of her heritage while she grew up. In fact, she describes her Indian heritage as "not even a footnote" in her life story, because her parents never discussed her racial background with her, even if she physically presents as "exotic" within her white community (86). Angie is described as having "rum hair and skin" and being darker in complexion than her mother, which made her stand out as a child in their West Virginia town. In spite of her racial difference, Angie makes friends with white children and develops a love of country music and singers like Dolly Parton and Johnny Cash. She even goes as far as teasing her own dark hair and wearing clothes inspired by Parton's signature "cartoonish" look, as Angie's mother describes it (87). During these years, Angie exclusively dates white men, even though they fetishize her as a desirable "other." However, her immersion in white American culture shifts abruptly when she moves to Boston for college and begins working in the city.

As an adult, Angie becomes interested in asserting her Indian heritage one day after observing an elderly Indian couple on a walk. She follows them into an Indian grocery store and immediately feels "parched and anxious and empty" (89). Rather than retreating from her culture, this alienation and anxiety push her to seek a connection to her Indian heritage. Although she has no knowledge of how to cook Indian food, she eats it often, ordering takeout almost every night of the week. At the climax of the story, one night Angie invites an Indian food-delivery worker to come in and eat with her. She asks him about his life in India and his reasons for coming to America, but their conversation is brief. They have sex on her couch. After this, as he flips channels on the television, Angie's impression of the provincial Indian immigrant is shattered: she realizes that he is a prospective college student who watches American basketball and even recognizes Johnny Cash on the TV, which reminds her of her own love of Cash's music. He is suddenly quite different from the "exotic delivery man who had come to the door two hours ago" (95). The story ends as Angie's white American past collides with her present desire to cultivate an Indian identity and the delivery worker leaves Angie's apartment, refusing the money she puts on the table.

I turn to food studies and postcolonial theory to untangle the story's themes of food and sex as connected to identity construction. An important concept in food studies is that food is often connected to a strong sense of nostalgia. Though the word means a longing for the past, it can often imply a yearning for an idealized past that never truly existed. In diasporic South Asian literature, nostalgia features heavily. In his theoretical text *Curry: Reading Writing and Race*, Naben Ruthnum—who writes from a second-generation diasporic perspective—scrutinizes the myriad diasporic novels with mangoes and spices adorning their covers. These books, he says, often contain familiar scenes in which the main characters agonize over their inability to re-create a specific dish that their parents made, which therefore leads to a feeling of disconnection and estrangement from family and culture (20). While Ruthnum sees these novels and their ubiquitous cooking scenes as tedious, he allows that these authors, through these food scenes, address a visceral desire for belonging while they navigate their experiences as immigrants or part of the second generation born outside of South Asia. Although he criticizes the repetitive scenes of cooking, Ruthnum understands that these authors and their readers are searching for something familiar. He admits, "The disconnected experience of being a person in the West, let alone a person of color in the West, doesn't lend itself to a sense of comfort or peace: fitting your own story to a narrative where answers are to be found in a familial, national past can be extremely soothing" (60). Whether or not one should capitulate to this hunger for nostalgia, and how much importance should be attached to these feelings, is a major question for food studies scholars.

As it pertains to the South Asian diaspora, there seem to be two ways of thinking about culinary nostalgia in food studies. Razia Parveen agrees that nostalgia is necessary to create a "renewed cultural experience" that balances reality with a utopic remembrance of the home country (55). In her article "Food to Remember," Parveen is primarily concerned with community and identity creation through oral storytelling and the oral sharing of recipes. She advocates for the importance of romance and imagination in stories about food in the South Asian diaspora because "[i]t is nostalgia, that sense of romance and loss, that makes the individual in diaspora want to recreate a small part of home 'out of place' through culinary practice" (52). This individual longing can then be shared with others, so that "[c]ulinary practice becomes a kind of cultural tissue that binds a community together," even if their remembrance of the home country is skewed by nostalgia (52). Parveen explains that communal cooking, or cooking with family members, is an effective way to engage with nostalgia and thus ease the longing for a lost homeland by re-creating a taste of that home in one's new kitchen.

Conversely, food studies scholar Anita Mannur sees nostalgia as misleading because it so often distorts actual memories that diasporic people bring from their home countries. In her book *Culinary Fictions,* Mannur argues that reading food in diasporic literature as purely nostalgic is to oversimplify its importance in the text (28). She insists that narratives about memory and cooking "must also be read as a metacritique of what it means to route memory and nostalgic longing for a homeland through one's relationship to seemingly intractable culinary practices which unflinchingly yoke national identity with culinary taste and practices" (29). For Mannur, to use such a malleable medium as food as a tool to connect to one's heritage is to attach oneself to something that is ever-shifting and adapting. "Footnote" illustrates this challenge through Angie's failure to attach her individual identity to specific "culinary tastes and practices," which suggests that Delman understands the mutability of food as an expression of culture.

Mannur also introduces the concept of "culinary citizenship": "that which grants subjects the ability to claim and inhabit certain identitarian positions via their relationship to food" (29). However, the danger of using food as a membership card into a culture is that it is an oversimplification of the complexities of cultural identity as well as a continuation of the myth of cultural authenticity. Mannur reminds readers that, in the context of the Indian diaspora, there are endless expressions of identity, and that food preparation and consumption varies based on geographical region, religion, social class, and even personal preference. However, South Asian fiction is still haunted by a desire to "imagine cuisines as authentic manifestations of national essences" (41). Delman's story depicts a character who buys into the idea of culinary citizenship, and Angie attempts to force a superficial connection to her Indian identity through the food she consumes.

Although I argue that Angie's attempts to assert her Indian identity through food are ultimately unsuccessful, it is understandable that she feels a longing to demonstrate her membership in the Indian diaspora, both to acknowledge the fact to herself and to self-identify to others, because she is singled out as nonwhite for most of her life. Her darker complexion marks her as "other" in both West Virginia and in Boston, and she is cut off from her Indian relatives. Aside from her mother, who exclusively engages in cosmopolitan American culture and hosts dinner parties with British-inspired dishes on the menu, like Cornish hen, Angie is estranged from her South Asian roots (86). Angie yearns for a connection to this distant part of her family, and she turns to food to forge this bond. In her memoir *Shame on Me: An Anatomy of Race and Belonging*, multiracial author and librettist Tessa McWatt writes from the perspective of a Canadian woman with multiple heritages, including Scottish, English, French, Portuguese, Guyanese, African, and Chinese. In her memoir, McWatt expresses the longing for simplicity that has plagued her as a multiracial person: "Part of me has longed for a profound connection to a single tradition, one ethnicity or culture or territory to fully inhabit. I long for a simple past" (70). Angie also feels this longing and knows what scholars and cookbook authors also understand: that often in Indian culture, "women are expected to be responsible" for the preservation of the culture, "through their comportment, their adherence to specific caste or religious rules, and their reproduction of culture through food" (Narayan 17). As a young woman with Indian heritage, Angie feels compelled to cultivate her own connection to

Indian culture, and when her clothing and skin color are insufficient, she turns to food for a more visceral connection.

Angie's introduction to Indian food first happens because she follows the elderly couple into the Indian store one afternoon. The aroma of the food is a sensual experience; she first notes "the heavy scent of spices that [sinks] into her hair and skin and mouth all at once" (89). The experience of standing in the store makes her feel "anxious and empty." Angie immediately tries to fill this emptiness with the trappings of an Indian identity. She purchases Bollywood CDs and some randomly selected groceries: a bag of basmati rice, some chili powder, and several prepared dishes from behind the counter. As she continues in her quest for culinary belonging, Angie orders Indian takeout exclusively, eating a wide variety of Indian food without knowing its regional origins (so important in Indian cuisine) or whether or not the dishes would be eaten in her grandfather's home.

While consuming the food may make her feel closer to her grandfather and his culture, her connection is superficial because her interest does not progress beyond a generic appreciation for pan–South Asian cuisine. Angie might develop a stronger sense of her Indian identity by taking more of an interest in the specifics of her ancestry. She might, for instance, learn more about her grandfather's life or study the specific culture of his birthplace. Knowing more about her family history might help her learn about the specific religious or cultural practices common in her ancestral home. She might discover more about her family's social status in India, which would also influence the kinds of food eaten by her relatives. Instead, Angie eats anything from the local Indian store— samosas, aloo gobi, dahl, and chicken tandoori—and is not interested in learning about differences between regional foods.

She also never learns to cook this food herself, which, were she to do so, might help her situate herself more directly and deeply within her Indian heritage. By learning how to cook food integral to her ancestors, she might engage meaningfully with some culinary nostalgia and cultivate the culinary citizenship that Mannur discusses. The process of cooking many kinds of Indian food is often painstaking and requires knowledge of ingredients and cooking techniques. Although her mother may not have learned these skills from Angie's grandfather, Angie might take a more focused interest in her culinary heritage through cookbooks or even cooking shows. Instead, she signals her heritage by dressing in a vaguely Indian manner, wearing clothing with extra lengths of fabric that mimic saris and by eating a wide variety of South Asian food without knowing its origins or how she might prepare it herself (88).

While these more in-depth inquiries into her specific family heritage might help cultivate a more nuanced and solid sense of identity, I also maintain that her membership in the Indian diaspora is not contingent on her knowledge of Indian history, traditions, or even a thorough understanding of how to prepare a regional meal. Her heritage alone should be enough to assert her membership in the diaspora. However, the story suggests that Angie feels forced to identify as South Asian because she does not physically fit into the category of "white," which results in a contrived ethnic performance. It is significant that in "Footnote" the narrator never discusses or qualifies Angie's white heritage. The reader does not know where her mother's white ancestors come from, and her father's background is also never discussed. This serves to highlight Angie's otherness, which is connected to her Indian heritage and the relative darkness of her skin. There are also many instances in Angie's life that contribute to doubting her own legitimacy as an Indian person, beginning with her mother's distance both from her parents and extended family. Angie says that she herself "never felt Indian" as a child, and that she "had never met a single person from the Indian side of her family" (86), as her grandfather died when she was a baby. She is unable to connect directly with her relatives, and her resentment toward her mother only grows as she ages. As a teenager, Angie observes her mother's preparations for a dinner party: as Beethoven plays in the house, her mother cooks Cornish hens. In response, she yells at her mother, "You're disconnected from everything, think you're better than everyone else" (86), which can be interpreted as Angie angrily reminding her mother that she is not completely white and cannot truly fit in among her friends. With all these factors building up over a lifetime, it is not difficult to imagine why Angie would search for a clear, demonstrative way of asserting her Indian identity. However, Angie tries on Indian culture in the same ways that she tries on the white country music culture of Dolly Parton. She first uses clothing and music as primary means of connecting, before shifting to food. Ultimately, she graduates to sexual experimentation with a man who is visibly Indian in the hopes that, if he accepts her, she will finally be accepted as a member of the South Asian diaspora.

Food, sex, and identity are interconnected, embodied experiences. Sex is, after all, often described in terms that are analogous to food: we hunger or have an appetite for sex, it is all-consuming, and often involves many of the same senses we use when we eat. In addition to consuming food, Angie turns to this other form of consumption—sex with an Indian man—as an opportunity to assert her own Indian identity. Unfortunately, Angie's use of sex as a means of identity expression is as unsuccessful as her attempt to use food. The work of Edward Said can help untangle Angie's impulse to seek connection to Indian culture through sex with an Indian man. In his influential text *Orientalism*, Said describes the phenomenon as beginning during British, French, and American colonial rule over various territories in the global East, with echoes of Orientalism continuing to reverberate today. He explains that the Orientalist believes in "a kind of intellectual authority over the Orient within Western culture" (27). The Orientalist creates a certain image of the primitive yet opulent world of the Orient and engages in various contexts with the Orient and its people "without ever losing the relative upper hand" (15). To parse the use of another's body for one's own motives, I turn to bell hooks and her important essay "Eating the Other." Although hooks writes specifically about white supremacy, I think her ideas about sexual intercourse for personal gain can be applied to the mixed-race protagonist here. For hooks, sexual encounters between members of different races are about power. She argues that certain power-seeking white people see black bodies in particular as "sexual playgrounds" that they may visit and rule over without relinquishing their own privilege (367). Delman's story interacts with both Said's and hooks's theories in Angie's encounter with the delivery worker; by attempting to engage sexually with a man of Indian origin, Angie tries—and fails—to physically and psychically absorb some more cultural authenticity to soothe her longing.

Prior to her brief encounter with the delivery worker, Angie exclusively dates white men but finds that they never truly understand her, a sentiment she expresses to her ex-boyfriend Travis. Although Travis cares for Angie, he exacerbates her anxieties about her identity. When Angie discusses her newfound interest in her Indian heritage, Travis responds, "Aren't you only half Indian?" (88), to which Angie replies, "Well, a quarter, but that's not the point" (89). Here, Travis unwittingly polices Angie's membership in the Indian diaspora by invoking mathematical language to quantify her identity. This is a common issue in mixed-race studies, and many scholars argue that identity cannot and should not be reduced to blood quantum or fractions or any kind of racist "one drop rule." As Travis reminds the reader of the long history of white colonizers categorizing and quantifying racial otherness for their own benefit,

Angie begins to believe it is impossible for him to understand her desire to explore her racial background. Travis has also never tried Indian food, and when he does it gives him indigestion. This is the final straw for Angie, and she refuses to see him again, saying, "You don't understand me. I'm different from you." He responds by justifying her concerns: "So you like spicy food. Big deal" (89). Travis ends the conversation by calling her style of clothing and interest in her Indian heritage "crap," compared to his image of her as a country-music-loving American teenager (91). His dismissal is fresh in her mind when the delivery worker arrives. She suddenly decides that her next romantic partner will be someone who understands her better, and, for Angie, this means that her new sexual partner must be Indian.

Although Angie does not seem to seek power over her sexual partner as hooks might suggest, she holds the upper hand throughout the interaction. First, Angie and the deliveryman inhabit the unequal roles of customer and service worker. She invites him into her apartment for a glass of water and both instigates and steers their conversation. Angie is entranced by the young man when he arrives at her door, and her first impression of him is that he has recently immigrated and misses his home country. The first thing she notices about him is the darkness of his skin (92), then the inflection of his speech (93). She also notes that he smells exotic; she leans in to better smell "the spices that came from his pores" (93). This is particularly interesting in that Angie connects the young man with the food he eats: he smells like the food she has been eating, too, which means, she thinks, that perhaps they share some level of cultural understanding. The narrator does not reveal how the deliveryman sees Angie, although Angie imagines that he is beguiled by her, that he can hardly believe "what seemed to be happening here in this clean apartment, with this fragrant girl pressing close" (93). The word "clean" is significant here, as cleanness and whiteness are often associated in the history of American racism. Angie has long been relegated to the realm of whiteness and wants to have an experience with someone who is outside of her sterile, colorless environment. It is unclear whether the young man sees her as a South Asian woman or whether he views her as undeniably American in her sexual aggressiveness. Angie continues to control the interaction as she convinces him, "with a bit of encouragement," to sit on the couch and share the food (93).

Angie steers the conversation as they eat. She asks him about his life in Delhi. He happily obliges her questions about India at first, although he occasionally strays from the topic to talk about his life in America. He begins to mention his aspirations to go to college and his new Nike shoes, which Angie does not like, so she actually "shushes" him and steers the conversation back to idyllic "tales of dusty over-crowded streets where all of humanity was packed together . . . and still you could go to a vendor on the corner and he'd cut open a young green coconut for you so you could drink the sweet water right out of the top" (93). Angie is not interested in the young man's American life, even as this new life appears to be his main interest. She would much rather see him as an embodiment of that "dark continent" of which hooks speaks, and insists on connecting him with a place full of, to her, exotic people, eating exotic foods, indulging in an Orientalist view of the young man and his birthplace.

To return to hooks's concept of eating the other, Angie, in sleeping with the young man, may hope to incorporate some of his exoticism into herself. Delman aligns Angie with hooks's insistence that

> It is precisely that longing for the pleasure that has led the white west to sustain a romantic fantasy of the "primitive" and the concrete search for a real primitive paradise, whether that location be a country or a body, a dark continent, or dark flesh, perceived as the perfect embodiment of that possibility. (370)

Probyn builds on this theory, explaining that the figure of the cannibal eating another's flesh "reminds us of hunger." She writes, "It would seem that we are hungry for difference, more often than not understood in terms of ethnic difference. . . . [W]hiteness is seen as a 'state of incompleteness' that needs to be supplemented by ethnic difference" (83). Angie seeks a solution to her feelings of emptiness and hopes to find it in the body of this young man. His racial difference, she hopes, will help erase her incompleteness, her whiteness.

After the sexual act, it becomes even more clear that Angie's desire for the young man is based on her desire for closeness to someone with a clearly Indian identity. Although their brief encounter seems to be a positive experience, she realizes that she objectifies the young man's racialized body and understands that she tries to use his exoticism to affirm her own membership in the diaspora. In the final scene of the story, one can see that they are not so different; although he is a recent Indian immigrant, he knows all about American culture and the things she knows about as well—he even mentions the death of Johnny Cash, which Angie herself did not know about. Because the text ends in a quiet moment while Angie thinks about her old interest in Cash, who is a symbol of white, rural America, the text suggests that she may eventually conclude that she is a brown woman who also enjoys things that are typically "white" and American, just as the delivery worker can be an Indian man with diverse interests and a focus on his future in America. In this final moment, Angie realizes that sex and food are not the only ways of expressing identity, though they may be integral parts of one's internal sense of cultural identity.

The power dynamic is further complicated because money is involved in their brief relationship. When the young man arrives, Angie does not pay him for the food but rather invites him in. Significantly, when the young man leaves, he does not take the money she puts on the table, although he hesitates for a moment before leaving "every cent of it there" (95). The narrator explains that the young man is conflicted because he thinks it might be fairer to split the cost as they split the food, but I suggest that there might be some more complex dynamics at play. To accept money after sex—even if that money is meant to pay for the food delivery—may reveal to the young man that the sexual experience was obviously transactional. Taking the money would highlight the superficiality of their encounter and cast him as a sex worker, summoned by a lonely American woman. It would also solidify the Orientalist role that Angie assumes in relation to the young man, who is already an Oriental subject in her home; taking the money would amplify his complicity in that relationship.

Although "Footnote" is a very short story, it contains many complex negotiations of food, sex, and mixed-race identity. Angie's connection to her Indian heritage is distant to begin with, but her impulse to develop her Indian identity is valid because it is a vital part of her racial makeup. Her methods of developing this identity, however, are questionable. The ending of the story underscores the futility of searching for identity through superficial means. Angie's interactions with Indian food and her brief encounter with the deliveryman demonstrate that food and sex are merely components of one's identity and that membership in a racial group is not contingent on either of these concepts alone or both of them together. Ultimately, Angie is no closer to her Indian identity after her experience with the deliveryman, nor has she developed a better understanding of her Indian identity through the Indian food she orders. "Footnote" suggests that a more fulsome engagement with one's own family history and geography, and the cultivation of meaningful relationships with people of one's various ethnicities, can help the mixed-race person develop a more well-rounded, more deeply connected sense of identity than through cursory interactions with food and sex.

WORKS CITED

Ashley, Bob, et al. *Food and Cultural Studies*. Routledge, 2004.

Delman, Carmit. "Footnote." *Mixed: An Anthology of Short Fiction on the Multiracial Experience*, edited by Chandra Prasad, Norton, 2006, pp. 83–96.

hooks, bell. "Eating the Other: Desire and Resistance." *Black Looks: Race and Representation*, South End, 1992, pp. 21–39.

Mahtani, Minelle, and April Moreno. "Same Difference: Towards a More Unified Discourse in 'Mixed Race' Theory." *Rethinking "Mixed Race,"* edited by David Parker and Miri Song, Pluto, 2001, pp. 65–75.

Mannur, Anita. *Culinary Fictions: Food in the South Asian Diasporic Culture*. Temple University Press, 2010.

———. "Edible Discourse: Thinking through Food and Its Archives." *American Literary History*, vol. 7, no. 2, 2015, pp. 392–402.

McWatt, Tessa. *Shame on Me: An Anatomy of Race and Belonging*. Random House Canada, 2019.

Narayan, Uma. "Eating Cultures: Incorporation, Identity, and Indian Food." *Social Identities*, vol. 1, no. 1, 1995, pp. 1–24.

Parker, David, and Miri Song. "Introduction." *Rethinking "Mixed Race,"* edited by Parker and Song, Pluto, 2001, pp. 1–22.

Parveen, Razia. "Food to Remember: Culinary Practice and Diasporic Identity." *Oral History*, vol. 44, no. 1, 2016, pp. 47–56.

Probyn, Elspeth. *Carnal Appetites: FoodSexIdentities*. Taylor & Francis, 2000.

Ruthnum, Naben. *Curry: Reading, Eating and Race*. Coach House, 2017.

Said, Edward. *Orientalism*. Routledge & Kegan Paul, 1978.

Recasting the Culinary Arts

Cooking, Ethnicity, and Family in the Queer Novels of Bryan Washington and Bill Konigsberg

EDWARD A. CHAMBERLAIN

In 2020 the Black American writer Bryan Washington published his novel *Memorial*, a narrative that depicts the intimate experiences of two gay men living in the southern United States. Set in Houston, Texas, *Memorial* portrays the interethnic relationship of two young cisgender gay men in the early twenty-first century. Telling the story of a Black gay man named Benson and his Japanese American boyfriend, Mike, *Memorial* weaves a story that connects a myriad of unique foods and characters who cook. Early in Washington's novel, Mike is shown to be a talented professional chef, who also plays the role of cook in the gay couple's apartment. As *Memorial* begins, Mike is "cracking eggs by the stove, slipping yolks into a pair of pans," to all appearances fully at home with his relationship, cooking role, and himself, but he is compelled to travel to where his father lives in Japan because his father is dying from pancreatic cancer (3). For Benson and Mike, change is on the horizon. Unsurprisingly, the writings of people who are lesbian, gay, bisexual, transgender, or queer (LGBTQ+) frequently involve change, such as the reimagining of a common domestic role: the family cook. Instead of depicting the traditional American role of a happy homemaker, queer texts such as *Memorial* will lead readers to ponder the intimate lives of people seldom seen by the public. In this sense, *Memorial* departs from the usual *casting* of present-day cooking shows and storytelling to stage a more inclusive and true-to-life performance of the culinary arts. This culinary performance calls attention to the varied ways that cooks have been enmeshed in sociopolitical norms and systems of privilege that are constructed and naturalized by a broad range of people over time.

As Daphne Brooks observes, the performances of Black artists frequently exhibit the capacity to "confound and disrupt conventional constructions" that have traditionally centered elite heterosexuals and white figures at the core of the storyline (8). Deviating from this well-trod path, Washington's novel *Memorial* delivers a refreshing culinary story that resembles performance. Historically, the process of cooking exhibits a set of commonalities with the creative acts occurring both in theaters and on screens. Much like playwrights, cooks determine a meal's cast of characters, ranging from the recipe's ingredients to who will sit next to whom at the table. At times, too, cooks and directors will *recast* their production for the sake of fashioning an authentic and effective ensemble. Comparably, Washington's *Memorial* exemplifies the conceptual framework of "recasting," in which the performance of the culinary arts is shifted away from the expectation of conventional white domesticity (Pao 389). Notably, Anita Mannur and Kyla Wazana Tompkins underscore the meaningful and varied roles people of color have played in the creation of American comestibles, thereby urging new thought about their contributions (Mannur 5; Tompkins 15). Speaking to such matters, Washington offers a multiethnic ensemble story in his novel, a book that garnered attention after Washington's *Lot: Stories* (2019) was named one of President Barack Obama's favorite books.

Washington's *Memorial* highlights a range of eating experiences and focuses on the pleasures of Japanese cuisine in multiple moments. Interestingly, Washington's storytelling of food and multiethnic experience exhibits several commonalities with another gay American writer, Bill Konigsberg, who similarly recasts the role of the cook in his book *The Music of What Happens* (2019). Konigsberg is a gay white novelist who formerly worked as a sportswriter and now writes young adult novels such as *Openly Straight* (2013), *Honestly Ben* (2017), and *Out of the Pocket* (2008), this last one winning the Lambda Literary Award for best Children's and Young Adult Fiction. As in *Memorial*, Konigsberg's 2019 novel portrays a form of recasting that mirrors the replacement of the familial cook in Washington's novel. In both, readers observe the story of a queer son who experiences a meaningful set of life changes within the context of cooking and their personal relationships.

Instead of staying with their family of origin or peer group, these youths engage in cooking in a new social context and are thus able to find support outside the heteronormative home. In crossing social boundaries, Konigsberg's protagonist, a young gay white character named Jordan, is shown to be an unpopular high schooler, yet one who finds social support from two classmates—Kayla and Pam, whom he jokingly calls his "wives" (23). Beyond these close friends, the poetry-loving Jordan soon begins a friendship with another classmate, a gay Latino youth named Max, who appears to be Jordan's opposite: both a muscular athlete and a gamer. But Max is also more than the popular jock he appears to be. He is a "closet foodie," and his love of cooking becomes a bridge to his friendship with Jordan, who helps Max to come out of the "closet" to more people (3). Konigsberg uses the trope of the romantic relationship in a way similar to Washington's storyline. However, instead of Ben reflecting on his romantic relationship with Mike over the years, Konigsberg's novel tells the story of a budding romance that evolves after Jordan's mother hires Max to help with restarting the family's food truck business, once run by Jordan's deceased father in Phoenix, Arizona. As Jordan's mother is unable to hold a job and struggles to operate the truck, she finds hope in this new collaboration between Max and Jordan. Although ostensibly opposites, Jordan and Max slowly learn to work together with the hope that they can make enough money to pay off the debt of Jordan's family, including "four months of back mortgage," thus revealing the high stakes involved in rebooting the family's food truck (8). As the novel shows, the truck's prior menu of traditional Italian recipes is failing to resonate with their customers, thereby requiring a reinvention that will enable Jordan's family to regain their financial stability.

Analyzing Intersections and Struggles in Culinary Novels

Julian Agyeman, Caitlin Matthews, and Hannah Sobel explain how individuals from a wide range of cultures today are pursuing the American Dream by working on food trucks as a source of income (5). Even so, one of the areas of food trucks that remains undertheorized is the culinary contributions of queer young people such as we see in the case of Jordan and Max. Their personal relationship takes center stage as Jordan deals with familial struggles, including his often-absent mother, while Max contends with the lingering emotional pains caused by a prior toxic relationship. In both *The Music* and *Memorial*, distant parental figures mirror the challenges of social isolation and ostracism that a multitude of queer and transgender youths habitually face during everyday experiences in their homes and communities. Through these portrayals of distancing, the authors enable their readership to understand the social hardships, stigmas, and relationships that queer and transgender youths encounter during a precarious time of young adulthood, a time when people are just beginning to get their footing in the world. To begin making sense of this literary material, it is necessary to build upon the thinking of several fields including ethnic studies, food studies, and queer studies, which offer helpful viewpoints that illuminate the struggles shown in the authors' novels.

Lawrence La Fountain-Stokes and Yolanda Martínez-San Miguel have theorized this distancing as being a kind of "sexile" where queer people are forced out of their homes, states, and countries due to homophobia (La Fountain-Stokes xix; Martínez-San Miguel 814). A similar distancing is shown in the case of Washington's novel *Memorial,* where the book's protagonist Benson (or Ben) becomes distant from his divorced parents after they "kicked him out" for being HIV+ and queer (153). As a contribution to the discussion of sexile, this project explores the queer culinary dynamics that arise when family members break from expected familial roles during acts of distancing. Ben's partner Mike has become distant from his father, who is also a cook and bar owner in the city of Osaka, Japan. Ben and Mike are split apart when Mike leaves Houston to attend to his dying father. Instead of being left alone, Mike's Japanese mother, Mitsuko, moves in with Ben for the short term since she had plans to visit with Mike at this time and elects not to change her itinerary. Mitsuko moving in creates an unexpected social arrangement that is uncomfortable at first due to the fact that Ben and Mitsuko have never met before. Yet Mitsuko begins to cook delicious meals for Ben and herself during Mike's absence. As readers hear of Mitsuko's own separation from her ill husband, Eiju, readers also learn of the relationship between Ben and Mike, a relationship that has been on the rocks and becomes a main cause of reflection for the introspective Ben. Early on, Ben nonchalantly explains, "After the black eye, we stopped putting our hands on each other," an act that remains unexplained yet speaks to a pattern of fighting and discord between the two partners (4). In contrast to this underlying social tension, the two gay men's enjoyment of food and drink creates a counterpoint initiating a bond between them.

A similar separation arises in Konigsberg's *The Music,* in which readers learn about the separation of Max's own parents, who are divorced and living in separate towns. Such acts of distancing serve to heighten the emotionally charged challenges of sexile that the texts' queer figures experience. To mitigate these feelings of sorrow, the authors weave the subjects of food and drink into the novels' plots, thus suggesting that cooking and eating function as a basis for fostering a sense of healing. As a part of this set of social challenges, the books' queers are shown to be culinary successes in their public spheres, thus making visible how queer people are capable of using food as a way to connect with their community, develop deeper social ties, and make money. These capacities are legible as a recasting of scenes shown in mainstream heteronormative representation where queers are cast out of family homes and away from the commensality of the family's table.

As a way of examining the identities being performed in these texts, it is beneficial to think through the critical framework of "intersectionality," which originally developed in the 1990s in the work of researchers such as Kimberlé Crenshaw (1244). Intersectionality occurs in a wide array of forms, such as the conflicting forces and pressures that impose stresses and suffering upon queer people of color and their loved ones. Characters experience intersectional pressures in *Memorial* and *The Music* amidst the collision of homophobia and racism, which collectively imposes psychological stress and harm upon people. In particular, both texts bring attention to a common occurrence in queer communities: the mixing of ethnic and racial identities in acts of dating, hooking up, and long-term relationships. This queer social world has often escaped the attention of mainstream forms of storytelling, which have largely been produced in conjunction with normative practices founded on the problematic ideologies of white, heterosexist supremacy. Amy C. Steinbugler explains how sociologists have studied the intimacies of interracial, or interethnic, coupling by observing that queer interraciality has been overlooked and often remains "invisible" or "unseen" by the public (98). As she explains, the public often makes egregious assumptions about queer interethnic couples, including "supermarket clerks separate their groceries, waiters and waitresses offer to seat them separately, or being hit on by a stranger while their partner stands beside them" (99). In this way, *Memorial* and *The Music* illuminate these lesser-known social phenomena, while these texts specifically make visible these relations through acts of cooking, eating, and selling food, where customers resemble the audiences of public performances. By entwining food with these texts' queer interethnic intimacies, the authors both complicate and reveal these little understood experiences of social life, rendering them more palatable, comprehensible, and relatable for a broader range of readers well beyond that of the assumed queer readership.

To develop the story of his multiethnic cast, Bryan Washington uses several creative approaches, including the portrayal of multiple languages. When Mike's mother arrives, readers see Mike speak with his mother, switching back and forth between English and Japanese, an act known as code-switching, which is common in many novels exploring ethnic identity. In creating depictions that explore ethnic identity, Washington's characters speak to the specificities that intersect with ethnicity, including racial identity. Near the beginning of Ben's reflection on his early days with Mike, the novel depicts how the two young men relate in terms of their identities. In the voice of Ben, readers learn: "It took all of two dates for him to bring up Race. We'd gone to an Irish bar tucked behind Hyde Park. Everyone else on the patio was white. I'd gotten a little drunk, and when I told Mike he was slightly shorter than optimal, he clicked his tongue, like, What took you so long. What if I told you you're too polite, said Mike" (6). These gay men's drinking experience allows them to open up about the stereotypes that are frequently placed upon men of color by varying groups, including the dominant culture. Taking a playful approach to these personal matters, Mike jokes: "I just hope you see me as a fully realized human being, said Mike. Beyond the obvious sex appeal" (6). In the bar's social ambience, the men's date is interwoven with race, including the assumptions, cultural scripts, and stereotypes that habitually influence how myriad people engage in dating. Yet Washington's novel shows a refreshing candor in depicting humanity's complexity, which is reflected in how the characters express themselves unabashedly in scenes across the narrative.

Across Washington's novel, food experience is shown in conventional forms where it is comforting and familial, yet the book also portrays food erotically. This eroticizing of food in a queer context is one of the lesser visible acts within mainstream food representation. As Ben's partner Mike frequently plays the role of cook at the two men's apartment, an unspoken need for a new cook opens when he departs to visit his dying father in Osaka. Ben will prepare food at times, yet he exhibits less enthusiasm for cooking. Mike's mother takes up this role, creating a rearrangement in the gay men's home. Through this reworking of the roles, Ben and Mitsuko become an interethnic couple, albeit a platonic one. As Ben acclimates to Mitsuko living with him, he frequently engages in reflection, showing an appreciation for her cooking. Ben observes Mitsuko by saying, "she fills a bowl with some pickled cucumbers, with a plate for some omelette, leaving another one out for me. We chew hunched over the counter, hip to hip. So, Mitsuko says, how long have you been sleeping with my son?" (25). Her direct language resonates with Ben, who will similarly be candid in his dialogue—a commonality that begins to solidify their burgeoning connection. Ben reflects on her cooking, "The omelette was delicious, the sort of thing Mike would cook, because he did everything in the kitchen" (27). Here and elsewhere, Ben's thinking regularly returns to Mike's cooking, suggesting his love of Mike's culinary creations and similar acts of kindhearted generosity.

Along with his interactions with Mitsuko, readers see imagery of food in social contexts, such as intimate sexual encounters between the gay protagonists. Following one of Ben's memories of his family eating together in a restaurant, Ben delves into another past moment of closeness, in which he and his partner Mike begin to become intimate. Ben says, "We're mashing our chests together, jumbling legs and elbows. . . . I've got one finger in there, and then four. Like I'm kneading dough" (15–16). Using the language of food preparation, including "mashing" and "kneading," transforms this moment of interethnic queer intimacy into a relatable experience. Queer sex is often regarded as an unknown practice in heterosexual circles, however the universal language of food makes this experience feel like less of a threat, thus creating a means for readers across the sexual spectrum to connect with the men's relationship.

The Fallout of Homophobia and Racism in Intimate and Public Life

In a comparable way, Bill Konigsberg's book *The Music* recently came under scrutiny for its depiction of sexual identity, which was deemed a threat by traditionalists. This book was banned during a recent and dismaying purging of libraries, in which hundreds of LGBTQ+ books were pulled from public library shelves, creating a heated debate about the rise of censorship and curriculum bans in U.S. schools and universities. It is worth noting, too, that many books involving matters of ethnicity and race similarly were pulled from shelves, suggesting to the public that these books' topics should be considered too controversial for young readers. Of course, censorship in America has a long-standing history, dating to the 1800s when American legislators passed a puritanical and constraining piece of legislation known as the Comstock Act of 1873, which led to multiple prohibitions on books and mailings. Yet social media apps are not banned from students' phones, even as many of these apps provide students easy access to the same ideas as well as even more graphic material, thereby raising the question of why these books in particular are coming under fire. Is this attack on queer and trans books actually a form of blowback against how today's books present queer and trans people in positive and uplifting ways? Both Konigsberg and Washington lead readers to empathize with the struggles of queers in general, and queer people of color in particular.

To illustrate the problematic impact of homophobia, Konigsberg's book shows the high schooler Jordan internalizing homophobia, such as when he worries that his now-deceased father would not love him. Early on, Jordan reflects on his relationship with his father by wondering how his father would view his struggle to "talk to boys." Would his father be "ashamed" of him, or see him as "not even a real, true boy" (15)? Jordan's interior struggle becomes, remarkably, less of a concern as he gets to know Max during their time on the food truck. Jordan's identity begins to blossom during his time cooking with Max on the food truck, where his developing creativity and humor are just two of the positive results of culinary collaboration.

After struggling at first, the two gay youths expand their food truck's menu by selling "Prickly Pear Frozen Lemonade," which builds upon a popular food trend involving the fruit of the opuntia cactus, a plant known as *nopal* among a segment of Spanish speakers (110). As a popular ingredient of the Southwest, the nopal has a long history of culinary use stretching back to the time before white settler colonialism. Konigsberg's book overlooks this history, yet it brings cultural and ethnic heritage into focus as Jordan learns to be more sensitive to matters of language and its effects on people. In a subsequent scene, Jordan and Max are at a store where Jordan makes a comment that irritates Max, who exhibits a well-developed awareness about the sociopolitical dimensions of language in the context of ethnic and racial identities. While they stand in line at the grocery store, Jordan reflects on the fact that he is "the only white person here," and he comments aloud to Max, "Mucho Latinx," which causes Max to express his ire about the new term "Latinx," then gaining in popularity (124–25). Max responds, "Whatever the hell PC shit that is, is just—grammatically wrong, for one thing" (125). Jordan's words speak to the fact that a growing segment of the population is embracing the "x" as a way of moving beyond the binary of Latino and Latina, which some have seen as limiting, especially in LGBTQ+ contexts. Yet Max's commentary highlights the fact that this identitarian terminology remains a neologism, thus connoting the idea that both Jordan and Max are wrestling with the challenges of change, a subject taking several forms. Among them, Max leans over to Jordan for a first kiss near the narrative's midpoint, and significantly, Max describes Jordan's lips as tasting "like light syrup, sweet and vaguely maple," implying it is a pleasurable step forward (174).

As with Konigsberg's novel, Washington's narrative in *Memorial* portrays the social challenges of change, which arise in the dialogue between the novel's sons and fathers. While Ben visits his aging and retired father, readers observe the father verbalize a set of homophobic and insensitive phrases, all of which depict him as being out of touch. As Ben meets his father for dinner, his father makes a comment on Ben's sexual identity, saying, "It's never too late to change" (78). Ben ponders his father's comment by saying, "From him, this is typical. I've stopped trying to shout him down. Our hands are full of crawfish. Their entrails seep through the newspapers below us" (78). Ben's linkage of the crawfish entrails with the father's unknowing and insensitive comment brings to mind the way that queer people often feel their inside selves or gut feelings exposed during experiences of coming out and similar conversations where their sexuality is questioned or second-guessed. In contrast to the disbelief that Ben faces with his father, Ben intriguingly finds a means of socially bonding with his partner's mother, Mitsuko, during her search for a Japanese food called *natto*. Consisting of soy beans, natto is a popular fermented food that feels sticky in texture and is consumed usually for breakfast. Shortly after meeting, Mitsuko desires to go grocery shopping, so she questions Ben: "You know what natto is, asks Mitsuko, frowning," and Ben replies by saying, "Soybeans, I say, right? Mike uses it" (33). Questioned further about whether Ben eats natto, he replies that he does, prompting Mitsuko to respond, playfully: "I don't believe you" (33). Although their shared interest in Japanese cooking is merely one step toward becoming closer socially, the experience helps the two to break down some of the social walls as they begin to cook and eat together more often.

Through his learning of new recipes as well as trying her versions of classics such as an omelette, Ben comes to admire Mitsuko's techniques. Despite at first thinking they could have no substantive connections, she dazzles Ben and contributes to the household through regular cooking, thus breaking down the wall between them. Like many immigrant cooks who make a living by preparing food for others, Mitsuko enables Ben to consider his life through another lens. Of course, at times Mitsuko experiences challenges requiring Ben's assistance, thereby illustrating the challenges of being a minoritized cook. Such challenges have been identified by researchers, who have theorized the sociopolitical complexities of cooking beyond the boundaries of America's dominant notions of culinary normativity (Halloran 6; Williams-Forson 137). In linking U.S. life to Japanese culture, *Memorial* leads readers to empathize with Mike's struggles as he settles into life in Japan, where he cooks, cares for his father, Eiju, and tends bar at his father's establishment. Along with acclimating to the new terrain, Mike's father makes homophobic comments that are hurtful, such as the moment when Mike comes out to his father, who responds negatively. Translated from the original Japanese into English, the reader sees Mike's Japanese father make statements such as: "You are fucking kidding me" and "So you're a fag" (133). Though hurt by his father's words, Mike takes the high road by showing patience with his father, yet this moment provides social commentary on the challenges of being a gay Japanese American man and one who faces homophobia in his home country as well as racism across the larger public world. Despite this double marginalization, Mike perseveres as he is cognizant that his father's generation has not prepared him to have a gay son, nor has the public fully learned how to address the ingrained social ills of bias.

Unraveling the Novels' Dénouements in Familial and Culinary Terms

Although some imagine that LGBTQ+ communities are more informed and mindful about the problems of ethnocentrism, racism, and xenophobia, a range of problematic assumptions and biases remain in pockets of these communities. As shown in the novels of Konigsberg and Washington, the characters' lives mirror these systemic problems and encourage deeper thinking about how these issues can and should be addressed. In the case of Konigsberg's *The Music*, the narrative revisits Max's past in which he "froze up" and was forced into sex, where he was subjected to racist comments (278). Instead of acting in a consensual way, the gay Latino, Max, felt forced to have sex with a white college student named Kevin, who calls Max "my dark-skinned boy" and "my Arabian prince," terms from Kevin's "fantasy" (34). As Max reminds Kevin, his mother is a Mexican immigrant from Mexico City, and his father is a white man from Indiana, yet for Max, Kevin's words sting because they objectify Max in a racist construct, making Max feel like he is being consumed for Kevin's pleasure. When the two meet to discuss the matter at a café, Jordan unexpectedly appears and plays the role of hero by giving the abusive Kevin a punch in the face. Far from being Max's knight in shining armor, however, Jordan wishes to stand up for Max, thus reworking the dominant "heteronarrative" ideal that people are made to embody in heterosexual narratives (Roof 42). Instead of following fixed roles, the gay youths Jordan and Max recast these experiences by demonstrating greater fluidity, thus mirroring what the scholars Kate Cairns and Josée Johnston have found in their gender-based research, which involves "evidence of more equitable partnerships forged in non-heteronormative couples" (157). This is not to say all nonheteronormative partnerships such as those in the home are predicated on the ideals and realities of equity, however there exists a significant pattern of queer partners who work to create food outside of normative practices associated with heterocentric acts of homemaking.

In similar ways, Washington and Konigsberg utilize textual elements and narrative conventions as a means of emphasizing, or elevating, the queer aspects of their stories. Among their narratives' textual conventions, the books' titles are striking for their significant relation to their sui generis forms of storytelling. In titular terms, Washington's *Memorial* is legible as a way of honoring and remembering Mike's father, although the title also speaks to the relationship between Mike and Ben, which appears to be changing and possibly expanding into a more open relationship by the end of the storyline. *Memorial* may imply a sense of finality, yet it marks a new beginning in much the same way that *The Music* suggests a blossoming of both young men by the story's end, when they are able to express themselves more openly and be seen as a romantic couple in the public eye. Such connectivity is emphasized further in Konigsberg's *The Music*, which is named for a poem created by Jordan, though the words actually originate in an earlier poem titled "Song" by the Nobel Prize–winning Irish writer Seamus Heaney (line 8). Alongside its intertextuality, the title brings Jordan's inner talents and knowledge of poetry to the fore, suggesting a message to Max, who explains it as "we're all connected" (260). Max's enjoyment of Jordan's talents is also a turning point in his friendship with another youth, who sees him "for the first time" (261). Beginnings and endings in *The Music* and *Memorial* arise in multiple forms, which can be seen in the books' conclusions, when the parents in the books are asked to reflect on their earlier actions.

Comparing the endings of *Memorial* and *The Music of What Happens*, the narratives each conclude with the texts' gay sons confronting a parent's decision-making, which read as forms of betrayal, or turning against their children. Near the end of *Memorial*, Mike confronts Mitsuko during a dinner at a Mexican restaurant. With tears "that roll down his cheeks," he asks her to explain her decisions that contributed to the destruction of their nuclear family (298). Noticeably, she cannot eat her meal, signaling that emotional pain has made her lose her appetite. In *The Music of What Happens*, Jordan confronts his mother after learning she has gambled away all the money he accrued from his family's food truck, which means they will likely lose their home. Feeling like he has "been robbed at gunpoint," Jordan decides to listen to his mother, Lydia, who states, "I beyond want to die," which causes Jordan to call 911 out of concern for her life (311–12). Afterward, Lydia remains inactive and silent, inspiring Max to invite Jordan to move in with his family (311). As these queer young people question their parents about damaging decisions, they push beyond their familial role of obedient progeny. As they reckon with the constraining normativities of domestic roles, they undergo considerable change, being recast as the family's culinary hero. In a similar fashion, their culinary contributions are shown to have socially uplifting effects among a broader social circle, such as when Konigsberg's characters disregard the typical pay-for-food approach and serve food to all for free, creating an activist-like moment they call "hooligan do-goodery" (207). With the transformation of these roles, the novels emphasize the meaningfulness of social change, suggesting the importance of reflecting on boundaries and the ways that minoritized chefs sometimes find themselves in a state of culinary otherness, where unbelonging is able to foster new thought and innovation. As these texts connote, queer cooking is a transgressive and spatially inflected act that holds great significance and notable potential. In looking to the aforesaid boundaries and norms, we can begin a movement toward "culinary justice," an experience that the black and gay historian Michael Twitty has envisioned as being the honoring and valuing of contributions from minoritized cooks, including the work of queer cooks of color, who, collectively and individually, share their culinary creativity and inspire positive change courageously (543).

WORKS CITED

Agyeman, Julian, Caitlin Matthews, and Hannah Sobel. "Introduction." *Food Trucks, Cultural Identity, and Social Justice: From Loncheras to Lobsta Love*, edited by Agyeman, Matthews, and Sobel, MIT Press, 2017, pp. 1–20.

Brooks, Daphne A. *Bodies in Dissent: Spectacular Performances of Race and Freedom, 1850–1910*. Duke University Press, 2006.

Cairns, Kate, and Josée Johnston. "Conclusion: Cooking as a Feminist Act?" *Food and Femininity*, Bloomsbury Academic, 2015, pp. 157–75.

Crenshaw, Kimberlé. "Mapping the Margins: Intersectionality, Identity Politics, and Violence against Women of Color." *Stanford Law Review*, vol. 43, no. 6, 1991, 1241–99.

Halloran, Vivian Nun. *The Immigrant Kitchen: Food, Ethnicity, and Diaspora*. Ohio State University Press, 2016.

Heaney, Seamus. "Song." *Opened Ground: Selected Poems, 1966–1996*, Farrar, Straus & Giroux, 1999, p. 173.

Konigsberg, Bill. *The Music of What Happens*. Scholastic, 2019.

La Fountain-Stokes, Lawrence. *Queer Ricans: Cultures and Sexualities in the Diaspora*. University of Minnesota Press, 2009.

Mannur, Anita. *Culinary Fictions: Food in South Asian Diasporic Culture*. Temple University Press, 2010.

Martínez-San Miguel, Yolanda. "Female Sexiles? Toward an Archeology of Displacement of Sexual Minorities in the Caribbean." *Signs*, vol. 36, no. 4, 2011, pp. 813–36.

Pao, Angela C. "Changing Faces: Recasting National Identity in All-Asian(-)American Dramas." *Theatre Journal*, vol. 53, no. 3, 2001, pp. 389–409.

Roof, Judith. *Come as You Are: Sexuality and Narrative*. Columbia University Press, 1996.

Steinbugler, Amy C. "Hiding in Plain Sight: Why Queer Interraciality Is Unrecognizable to Strangers and Sociologists." *Interracial Relationships in the Twenty-First Century*, edited by Earl Smith and Angela J. Hattery, 2nd ed., Carolina Academic, 2013, pp. 89–112.

Tompkins, Kyla Wazana. *Racial Indigestion: Eating Bodies in the Nineteenth Century*. New York University Press, 2012.

Twitty, Michael. *The Cooking Gene: A Journey through African American Culinary History in the Old South*. Amistad, 2017.

Washington, Bryan. *Memorial*. Riverhead, 2020.

Williams-Forson, Psyche A. *Building Houses out of Chicken Legs: Black Women, Food, and Power*. University of North Carolina Press, 2006.

PART V

Significant Food in Classic American Literature

Cultural Dichotomy Crafted through Food in Willa Cather's *My Ántonia*

MARY-LYNN CHAMBERS

A well-set table with food that is familiar brings comfort to the onlooker who reacts pleasantly to the sights and smells, knowing the tasting will be pleasurable. The opposite reaction occurs when we stumble upon food abandoned in the back of our fridge or left too long in the garbage bin. We recoil at the sights and smells that leave a distasteful impact on us. Employing this dichotomy between the agreeably tasteful and what we experience as distasteful and thus disagreeable, disgusting, or downright abhorrent is a literary device used by Willa Cather, in *My Ántonia,* to create a cultural distance between the new immigrant Bohemian family, the Shimerdas, and the older settler family belonging to the narrator, Jim Burden. Although all non-Native Nebraskan families at the end of the nineteenth century had a relatively recent immigrant's heritage, it is crucial to understand that the families who came first and had already begun to put down roots were known as settlers; whereas the newer, just-arrived immigrant families, who were still establishing their position in the community, continued to be treated as foreigners. Settlers were viewed both as stewards and as rightful beneficiaries of the community, but immigrants were targeted by the settlers, who encouraged the newly arrived to complete the assimilation process (Veracini 33). The cultural dichotomy between the so-called settlers and the immigrants is demonstrated through the friendship between Ántonia and Jim. Food discourse undergirds the narrative that addresses the challenges the Shimerdas are experiencing within the assimilation process. Cather crafts the immigrants' tale within *My Ántonia* by establishing a cultural dichotomy, providing evidence of assimilation, while at the same time legitimizing ethnic heritage through food.

Jim Burden, a successful though not happily married man, journeys back in time to share his story related to an immigrant girl and her family, a girl who left a lasting imprint on his heart, a girl he calls "My Ántonia" (Cather xiii). An orphan, Jim traveled as a boy from Virginia to Nebraska to be raised by his grandparents. On the farm outside of Black Hawk, Jim enjoys the benefits of a settler's home with plenty of good food. He is soon introduced to the Shimerdas, whose arrival he had witnessed at the Black Hawk train station (Cather 6). The Shimerdas are immigrants from Bohemia, where the emerging middle class struggled as the Hapsburg Empire collapsed. This Bohemian struggle for autonomy was present during the late nineteenth century when the Shimerda family would have immigrated (Prchal 4). The Shimerdas' ethnicity plays a significant role in the process of othering that was part of the Nebraska experience at the turn of the twentieth century, and Cather clarifies the othering of this immigrant family through literary associations related to food.

Othering, a pattern designed to diminish or devalue a minority group of people, results in social exclusion that creates barriers which often persist over generations (Lonngren 218; AbdulMagied 6). Objectification through othering relegates the Shimerdas into a stereotype of the poor, immigrant family. This mechanism of objectification produces alienation between the Euro-American families known as the settlers who have an established Nebraskan identity and the Bohemian immigrant family. In the opening chapters of *My Ántonia*, the act of othering through food places the Shimerdas in a category of "someone we do not want to be" (Krumer-Nevo and Sidi 300). Out of the Burdens' abundance, Jim's grandmother packs up potatoes, pork, bread, butter, and pies to deliver to the newly arrived Shimerdas (Cather 16). When the Burdens reach the Shimerda place of abode, the immigrant family "fairly snapped at the food. The family had been living on corncakes and sorghum molasses for three days" (19). Another visit soon follows, providing further insight into the immigrant family's meager provisions used to make a style of bread thought by Nebraskans to be foreign. Jim reflects, "I remember how horrified we were at the sour, ashy-gray bread [Mrs. Shimerda] gave her family to eat" (25). Jim describes the crude process of mixing the smear of pastelike dough and the unusual fermenting process. Cather's inclusion of these food discourses establishes the Shimerdas' status within Nebraskan society as foreign and lower class through a food that seems horrifying to the young boy.

Flowers and Swan argue that the production and consumption of food has the potential to create racialization, which they describe as "the politics of 'eating the Other'" (206). The use of food discourses in literature is a technique that can be embedded within othering to help establish identity. Book 1 in *My Ántonia,* entitled "The Shimerdas," includes visual encounters with food that establish the inferiority of the Shimerdas. During the first visit to the Shimerdas' "cave," the Burdens arrive with an abundance, whereas the Shimerdas' fare is limited. The loaf of bread brought as a gift is worthy of examining and smelling and receives high praise of "'Much good, much thank!'" (Cather 19). The pleasing response connected with the Burdens' bread is countered by Jim's horrified response to the Shimerdas' "sour, ashy-gray bread" (25). Almerico explains that "the type of bread consumed by a person has been known to indicate social standing" (6). In this regard, food can, as much as clothing and other material possessions, be a signifier of culture and cultural standing. Yet Cather does not stop at bread to define the Shimerdas' status; she provides an opportunity for Ántonia and Jim to visit two Russian bachelors whose language is close to the Bohemian dialect Ántonia speaks. Upon arrival, Jim discovers that these Russians have a cow, and they use her milk to make butter. They also have a garden filled with watermelons, corn, beans, and cucumbers (29). Unlike Jim's experience with the food eaten by the Shimerdas, Russian Peter splits a ripe melon "with a delicious sound" (30). As the two friends depart, Peter sends cucumbers and milk home with Ántonia (30). The scene effectively communicates that even these bachelors have a better culinary offering than the Shimerdas can afford.

With the first snowfall, Jim's kitchen at his grandparents' house is warm and safe. The food served includes popped corn and taffy on Saturday night. On Sundays, chicken, ham, bacon, and sausage are served with pies, cakes, and pudding with currants (54). In contrast, the Shimerdas are eating prairie dogs and frozen potatoes (54, 60). Jim's grandmother's reaction is, "Josiah, you don't suppose Krajiek would let them poor creatures eat prairie dogs, do you?" (58). Later, she queries Ántonia about the frozen, rotting potatoes that her family are eating, and Ántonia explains, "We get from Mr. Bushy . . . what he throw out" (61). The stark contrast between the food eaten by the two families indicates the disparity between the life of a settler and that of an immigrant. Bezzola and Lugosi acknowledge othering that takes place during exchanges based on food-related social interactions like the ones experienced between the Burdens and Shimerdas where the Shimerdas are the "other." These authors emphasize the propensity for the reader to interpret the scenes through a Eurocentric lens that establishes power relations between those who are engaging within the food-focused scene when there is a clearly established "have" and "have-not" (12).

In a reversal of grub gift-giving, the Shimerdas offer the Burdens a small sack filled with little brown chips that emit a "salty, earthy smell" that is "very pungent" (Cather 63). To affirm that the gift is a good one, Mrs. Shimerda states, "Very good. You have no in this country. All things for eat better in my country" (63). However, the chips were foreign to the Burdens; they were unable to determine "whether they were animal or vegetable" (63). Mrs. Burden's definitive statement was, "I'm afraid of 'em" (64). It is many years later that Jim finally concludes that the chips were dried, wild mushrooms "gathered, probably, in some deep Bohemian forest" (64). In these food-related scenes, the reader witnesses the immigrant family to be eager and accepting of the food offered by the settlers, whereas the settler family is horrified and unaccepting of the immigrant food being consumed or offered. According to Tsank, "Cather . . . fixat[es] on 'foreign' foods through Jim Burden's narration and characterizes immigrants for the benefit of a white middle-class readership, both of which subtly perpetuate nativist ideologies" of othering (39).

Cather also uses food to facilitate conflicting thoughts and to reveal inner turmoil created by displacement anxiety (Dixon 227). As newly arrived immigrants, the Shimerdas navigate cultural issues rooted in their exile from their homeland, which is illustrated through food. Xu recognizes that "Cuisine . . . stratifies us in our food practices" (4), and the class stratification occurring in *My Ántonia* renders the Shimerdas as "other." This stratification creates inner conflict and exacerbates displacement anxiety, which is evidenced especially through the character of Mr. Shimerda. As the timeline within the story transitions from summer to fall to Christmas, the festive fare in the Burdens' house includes gingerbread men "decorated with burnt sugar and red cinnamon drops" (Cather 67). About four o'clock on Christmas Day, after the sausage and waffles had been eaten (71), Mr. Shimerda arrives at the Burdens' front door. He is invited in and offered a glass of Virginia apple-brandy (72). Mr. Shimerda finds the settler's home to be a place of respite where he can experience contentment away from the challenges of immigrant living. He is urged to stay for dinner and, upon leaving, blesses the family for the gift of a few hours where he is once again privileged (72–73). Soon afterward, Mr. Shimerda is found dead, an apparent suicide (79–80). Days later, Jim looks back on the events and concludes: "I remember his contented face when he was with us on Christmas Day. If he could have lived with us, this terrible thing would never have happened" (84). This conclusion is not just about provisions or status but about identity. The othering created through the immigration process moved Mr. Shimerda from a "have" to a "have-not." In Bohemia, Mr. Shimerda "was a weaver by trade . . . a skilled workman on tapestries and upholstery materials" (17). Shimerda's new identity in Nebraska as an unskilled farmer was too difficult for him to bear. Mr. Shimerda exited the status of "other" through death; on the other hand, Ántonia began her exit out of the "other" status by moving into the neighboring town of Black Hawk and working in a settler's home (130).

Ántonia and her female, immigrant peers, Lena and Tiny, soon discover that a way out of immigrant status and into a settler's status is to move into town, to work at jobs that are more closely associated with the settlers, and to learn the settlers' ways. This next step in the assimilation process takes Ántonia into the Harling home, where she spends time in the kitchen learning to make new American dishes. The Harlings, a successful town family, could afford a well-stocked pantry and food delicacies. It does not take long to find Ántonia "beating up one of Charley's favorite cakes in her big mixing-bowl" and "roll[ing] popcorn balls with syrup" (Cather 134). Ántonia›s assimilation begins in the kitchen, Lena's in the sewing room, and Tiny's at the boys' home. In each case, though, these immigrant girls discover the benefits of settlers' food and the prestige that comes with embracing the settlers' dress, mannerisms, and values. For these girls who had been "early awakened and made observant by coming at a tender age from an old country to a new" (165), there were new interests and activities that came with living in town, activities that include dancing and enjoyable visits to the ice cream parlor (171). These girls exchanged hard work in the fields with time to flirt, gossip, and enjoy some sweet treats (179).

Although the assimilation process progressed with the immigrant girls, there was still some resistance indicated with the immigrant farm folk and discrimination evidenced by the Black Hawk settlers. Bohemian discourse from the early twentieth century "included a determined resistance to assimilation" (Prchal 4), and Cather portrayed this resistance through the Shimerdas. Ántonia›s brother, Ambrosch, remains staunchly tied to the farm (Cather 128), and the older settlers are reserved about the dancing and what they viewed negatively as the new male companions being enjoyed by the young immigrant women newly moved into town (174). At times in the storyline, discrimination is evidenced based on Jim's association with the marginalized group (188), a discrimination rooted in Eurocentrism where European values are positioned over the expression of the marginalized culture (Krumer-Nevo and Sidi 301). Although the immigrant girls like Ántonia are embracing many of the settlers' ideologies and assimilating into their practices, there remains an otherness about her that creates distance or barriers. Thus, othering can include the process of attaching a moral assessment of inferiority to the difference between groups as well as condescending evaluations simply based on material success (Pickering 47). One example where the moral code of inferiority is stamped on Ántonia is when she becomes pregnant outside of marriage and returns to the farm to re-enter the immigrant way of life with her daughter (243).

As is true with many childhood friendships, the adult years create a natural distance between Ántonia and Jim. The latter becomes a successful railway lawyer who is stuck in a marriage of convenience (Cather ix–x). In Jim's adult world, he has the opportunity to interact with Lena, a celebrated dressmaker, and with Tiny, who leads an adventurous life and is satisfied with her success (244, 247). However, the collective judgment placed on their friend back on the farm is that of "poor Ántonia" (243). During Cather's chapters relating the activities of these adult years, there is little mention of food. At one point, however, Jim and Lena are passing a candy store, and she exclaims, "Don't let me go in" (229), as she is worried about her weight. No longer is there the immigrant's struggle to find good food; instead, there is a struggle to avoid food, evidence of Lena's assimilation into early twentieth-century American plenty. A research study related to immigrant food consumption concludes that among the Bohemian immigrants in the nineteenth century, there was a higher assimilation process when compared to other immigrant groups (Dirks 93). We see this higher assimilation when Ántonia is in Black Hawk, but Cather retards that assimilation process with the Shimerdas back on the farm.

Jim returns to the Shimerdas' farm for a momentary visit when Ántonia is twenty-four years old. They meet in a field where Jim reaffirms that she will always be a part of him (Cather 263), and Ántonia attests to the truth that she keeps him close every day (265). Then, twenty years

pass without contact until one day Jim finds himself on the road to Ántonia›s own rural farm where she and her husband live with their many
children. Cather situates Ántonia back on the farm without the "oth-
ered" immigrant status but embracing her Bohemian heritage as part
of her American farm wife identity. Mary Dixon, in her article on Cather's use of food strategies in negotiating displacement anxiety, explains
that there is a sacred food heritage that each immigrant carries and that,
optimally, one's food heritage should not be displaced in the assimilation process. Certainly, there are new food customs that come with new
countries and cultures, and food is often used to negotiate what is unfamiliar, yet a sense of ownership and pride in the food heritage of one's
native country needs to be encouraged as an important part of one's new
identity formation (227). For a while in *My Ántonia*, the opportunity for
celebrating the Bohemian food heritage seems to be lost, until we arrive
with Jim at the door of Ántonia›s home and discover that she has kept
the valuable parts of that food heritage alive for the next generation.

Surprised by Jim's appearance at her door, Ántonia heartily welcomes him. After she completes the introduction of her children, she invites him into their parlor while acknowledging the existence of "a nice
parlor for company" (Cather 274). Gone are the days of the immigrant's
"cave" that she endured as her childhood home (19). Cather establishes
a new status of settler for Ántonia through the rooms in the house, the
proper care of many children, and the plentiful food. Conversation is
a priority until the children entice Jim with a tour of their fruit cave.
Flashbacks to the cave home from years ago leave the reader recoiling
at what might be kept in such a cave, but what is tucked away for safe-
keeping is so unlike the rotting, frozen potatoes that were proffered by
Mrs. Shimerda years earlier (60). Jim spies "three small barrels, one full
of dill pickles, one full of chopped pickles, and one full of pickled wa-
termelon rinds" (276), a bounty that will carry them through the winter months without fear of rotting. With a cleaver twist of conversation,
the focus in the next few lines shifts to bread, a theme Cather developed
in the early chapters to indicate the disparity between the immigrant
Shimerdas and the settler Burdens. Yet in this scene, Ántonia enthuses,
"You wouldn't believe, Jim, what it takes to feed them all. . . . You ought
to see the bread we bake" (276). Ántonia is proudly making good bread
for her own family, which is a sign of successful assimilation.

Although Ramli et al. remind us that assimilation can create a new
food identity designed to eliminate the original ethnic identity of the
person (410), Cather's use of bread in the last section of the book keeps

the assimilation process tethered to adequate provisions and comfort rather than extravagance and betrayal of a past. Ántonia lets Jim into her family's food spaces and experiences, yet she does it on her own terms by celebrating what is good from the past rather than longing for what could be. As an immigrant turned settler, Ántonia does not feel the need to defend her past because she is not threatened by the extinction of her heritage. Fabio Parasecoli in his article on food, identity, and culture explains that in the assimilation process experienced by immigrants, there is the "desire to defend an often imagined past that is perceived as threatened with extinction, and to claim roots that are constantly antagonized or negated by the surrounding environment" (431), yet this is not the course of action taken by this mother of many. Rather, Ántonia celebrates the good food founded in a culture she is passing on to her children.

Since food is a cultural marker related to identity formation rooted in history and habit (Ramli et al. 407), the reader naturally searches to see if Ántonia has reserved some of those markers while having yielded to the assimilation process. While still in the fruit cave, the younger girls point out the jars filled with cherries, strawberries, and crabapples, but the exclamation from one of the older boys opens the reader to the possibility that Ántonia has held onto some of her food heritage: "Show him the spiced plums, mother. Americans don't have those. . . . Mother uses them to make *kolaches*" (277). It is significant that the boy separates the family from those outside the familial community by referring to them as Americans. Then Cather inserts a Bohemian word reminding the reader that this now-American farming family still claims a Bohemian heritage. Avoiding the typical approach that "racism and racialization underpin the production, consumption and representation of food" (Flowers and Swan 206), Cather situates the foreign food in the midst of a cave filled with typical American preserves. The dual existence of foreign and American foods together in one cave brings normalcy to the coexistence of the two within one family's eating experience. Gina Almerico acknowledges that "in essence, what one eats defines who one is and is not" (6), and with Ántonia›s family, these foods exist together rather than creating identity isolation. The use of food from both cultures signifies the duality of their cultural identity. Food can be symbolic, and since food has signifying properties, Cather uses those properties to "restore full personhood to those marginalized" (Xu 4), specifically Ántonia. Xu argues that "[h]omogenizing immigrants' and minorities' foodways was part and parcel of the project of assimilation" (5), but Cather's

Ántonia proves to be an exception with a cave that blends both American and Bohemian foods.

On the walk home from the cave, Jim, Ántonia, and her children meander through their many fruit orchards, scattering the fowl, then settling down to milk the cows. Jim concedes, "Everything was as it should be" (Cather 283). Once again, they gather to eat. The dinner table is lined with children and filled with dishes that include kolaches and milk (283). The following day there are "two brown geese, stuffed with apples" for dinner, a hearty family meal to which Ántonia›s traveling husband returns (293). He arrives bearing gifts for the children that include bags of candy, but his gift of candy pales in comparison to the box of candy Jim brought as a gift (292). This reemergence of the American sweets avoided by Lena earlier in the book is a subtle reminder that the American food trends are inserted into the eating experience of this home where the younger children only speak the native language of Bohemia (229, 274), and the rich food heritage is still part of the eating experience. As the book concludes, Jim reflects on his experience of childhood where he was bound to a friendship that brought diversity into his life, a diversity that positively influences him.

In *My Ántonia*, Cather writes an immigrant's tale that highlights the powerful use of food to signify othering. According to Dunbar, these "issues of representation, power, and difference . . . elicit particular responses in readers" (44), and Cather's descriptive use of food elicits emotional reactions that parallel Jim's observations and insights. The danger that Cather navigates throughout the novel is how the act of othering can reduce a rich heritage to a negative stereotype (Santos and Buzinde 324). In the opening section of the novel, there is a clear dichotomy between the immigrants' and the settlers' food experiences, where "[e]ating is a daily reaffirmation of [one's] cultural identity" (Kittler et al. 3). The Eurocentric reader relates to the appeal of the settlers' food while cringing at the meager offerings of the immigrant; however, a shift in food focus occurs when Ántonia moves into Black Hawk and invests in the assimilation process. Cather weaves elements of othering into the introduction of Ántonia without risking what Krumer-Nevo and Sidi claim to be the imprint of inferiority (299). This serves the narrative well as the reader enjoys the sampling of food that Ántonia is learning to prepare in the settler's home, thus marking her progress in assimilating. During the novel's middle section, the author departs from the symbolic use of food only to return to it in the final section of *My Ántonia*, "Cuzak's Boys" (book 5). Cather reengages in the reflection of cul-

ture through the symbolic resource of food with Jim's final visit to Ántonia in her own home. In this last section, we see the encapsulation of
overlapping ideologies through the blending of settlers' food and Bohemian food in the fruit cave (Tsank 39). This food blending legitimizes
Ántonia›s ethnic food heritage that she is passing on to the next generation even as she comfortably embraces the benefits of a settler's status.
Through both the presence and absence of food, Cather, in *My Ántonia*,
creates visual images and cultural impressions that mark the challenges
of othering, the role of assimilation, and the importance of celebrating
cultural heritage.

WORKS CITED

AbdulMagied, Salma. *Othering, Identity, and Recognition: The Social Exclusion of the
Constructed "Other."* Master's thesis, Abo Akademi University, 2020.

Almerico, Gina M. "Food and Identity: Food Studies, Cultural, and Personal Identity."
Journal of International Business and Cultural Studies, vol. 8, 2014, pp. 1–7.

Bezzola, Toya, and Peter Lugosi. "Negotiating Place through Food and Drink: Experiencing Home and Away." *Tourist Studies*, vol. 18, no. 4, 2018, pp. 486–506.

"Bohemia." *Britannica*, 2021, www.britannica.com/place/Bohemia, accessed November
8, 2021.

Cather, Willa. *My Ántonia*. 1918. Macmillan, 2019.

Dirks, Robert. "Diet and Nutrition in Poor and Minority Communities in the United
States 100 Years Ago." *Annual Reviews of Nutrition*, vol. 23, 2003, pp. 81–100.

Dixon, Mary M. "Will Cather's Immigrants: An Aesthetics of Food Strategies in Negotiating Displacement Anxieties." *Journal of American Culture*, vol. 40, no. 3, 2017, pp.
227–34.

Dunbar, Ann-Marie. "Between Universalizing and Othering: Developing an Ethics of
Reading in the Multicultural American Literature Classroom." *CEA Forum*, Winter/
Spring 2013, pp. 26–48.

Flowers, Rick, and Elaine Swan. "Seeing Benevolently: Representational Politics and
Digital Race Formation on Ethnic Food Tour Webpages." *Geoforum*, vol. 84, 2017, pp.
206–17.

Kittler, Pamela G., Kathryn P. Sucher, and Marcia Nahikian-Nelms. *Food and Culture*,
6th ed., Wadsworth, 2012.

Krumer-Nevo, Michal, and Mirit Sidi. "Writing against Othering." *Qualitative Inquiry*,
vol. 18, no. 4, 2012, pp. 299–309.

Lonngren, Ann-Sofie. "Trolls!! Folklore, Literature and 'Othering' in the Nordic Countries." *Rethinking National Literatures and the Literary Canon in Scandinavia*, edited by Ann-Sofie Lonngren et al., Cambridge Scholars, 2015, pp. 205–26.

Parasecoli, Fabio. "Food, Identity, and Cultural Reproduction in Immigrant Communities." *Social Research*, vol. 81, no. 2, 2014, pp. 415–39.

Pickering, Michael. *Stereotyping: The Politics of Representation*. Palgrave, 2001.

Prchal, Tim. "The Bohemian Paradox: 'My Ántonia' and Popular Images of Czech Immigrants." *MELUS*, vol. 29, no. 2, 2004, pp. 3–25.

Ramli, Adilah M., et al. "Food Heritage and Nation Food Identity Formation." *Hospitality and Tourism*, edited by Norzuwana Sumarjan et al., CRC Press, 2014, pp. 407–11.

Santos, Carla A., and Christine Buzinde. "Politics of Identity and Space: Representational Dynamics." *Journal of Travel Research*, vol. 45, no. 3, 2007, pp. 322–32.

Tsank, Stephanie. "The Ideal Observer Meets the Ideal Consumer: Realism, Domestic Science, and Immigrant Foodways in Willa Cather's *My Ántonia* (1918)." *American Studies*, vol. 57, no. 3, 2018, pp. 39–56.

Veracini, Lorenzo. "Settlers Are Not Migrants." *The Settler Colonial Present*, Palgrave Macmillan, 2015, pp. 32–48.

Xu, Wenying. *Reading Food in Asian American Literature*. University of Hawaii Press, 2008.

Katherine Anne Porter's "Flowering Judas"

Mexican Politics, Appetitive
Language, and Alimentary
Religious Symbolism

HEIDI OBERHOLTZER LEE

First published in 1930, Katherine Anne Porter's short story "Flowering Judas" makes extensive use of the possibilities of appetitive language and gustatory imagery to articulate Porter's critique of disembodied socialist idealism and to recommend instead a corporeal, personalized, and humanized doctrine of love. The deployment of a language of the body, and particularly of alimentary religious symbolism, pervades the text as a whole but culminates in a final, climactic dream sequence. In that dream sequence, the protagonist, Laura, imagines a former suitor accusing her of murder and cannibalism as she consumes the bloody flowers of a Judas tree. This essay will offer a reading of the appetitive language and alimentary religious symbolism of this story, situating "Flowering Judas" within its modernist literary context, Porter's socialist milieu, and the early 1920s Mexican political landscape in which Porter set her story.

Porter's identification with Catholicism was complex—often expressed in a strong and explicit anticlericalism—and yet the imagery and vocabulary of the foods and appetites of that faith tradition permeate her text, and she uses them with pointed intentionality. Porter frequently references the body shape and size of her characters, as linked to their appetites, to underscore the changing and problematic expressions of their political ideology. For the final scenes of the story, Porter selects one of the most powerfully symbolic representations of Christian thought—the eucharistic meal—and then rewrites it as a perverse reversal of Christian love in order to redefine what constitutes the betrayal of community and to reiterate what a more honest and effective service to humanity would look like. Porter's story surprises the reader with an unreliable narrator, a villain who unexpectedly proves to be heroic, and a Christic sacrificial lamb who dies on the altar of meaningless politics. I argue that, through the appetitive lens and language of eating, "Flowering Judas" points to the limits of abstract ideology to underscore instead the importance of an embodied and personal connectedness to neighbors and local community as the healthy focal point of ideology.

Though Porter's short story "Flowering Judas" became part of the eponymously named collection of her short stories *Flowering Judas and Other Stories* (1930, reprinted 1935) and "made her literary reputation" (Givner 219), the text has not garnered much recent critical attention. This may be due, in part, to the seeming opacity of its meaning, the complexity of the Mexican political situation in which the story is set, and its reliance on religious symbolism that might at first seem inaccessible to many students in contemporary American classrooms. There is, however, growing interest in understanding Porter as an author whose writings expand the definition of what "counts" as American writing because she did not define herself entirely within national boundaries. Martin Heusser, for example, has explored the relationship between Porter's ethnographic and fictional writings about Mexico, and Emron Esplin has argued for "Flowering Judas" to be recategorized as a work of Latin American magic realism. As early as 1984, Minrose Gwin wrote a short piece for the *Mississippi Quarterly* noting the extent of the food and drink references in the *Flowering Judas* collection as a whole but stopping short of significant analysis of the "Flowering Judas" story itself. Gwin concluded provocatively, but humbly, that "[o]ne could do worse than to approach Katherine Anne Porter's art by way of her tamales" (57). Of course, since the advent of the global Covid-19 pandemic, it is Porter's "Pale Horse, Pale Rider," set in the 1918 flu epidemic, that has attracted both internet buzz and scholarly activity for its potential resonances with readers' recent lived experiences. Perhaps not as obviously, but arguably as deeply, "Flowering Judas" offers pandemic and postpandemic readers an honest meditation on the problems of frustrated idealism and ennui, and simultaneously holds out hope through the promise of the efficacy of authentic love and forgiveness.

The story opens with Porter's protagonist, Laura, listening to the poorly sung, guitar-accompanied serenading of Braggioni, a cruel, arrogant, but "skilled revolutionist" (96), who once led his men sacrificially but who now is characterized more by his self-absorbed excesses of appetite than by his socialist ideals. Porter relentlessly points out the visible signs of Braggioni's hypocrisy and indulgences. While some of his men languish in jail, Braggioni, as Porter describes him, is "heaped upon" a "chair much too small for him" (96). He "loves himself with . . . amplitude" (96). He has an "excess of . . . self-love" and "gluttonous bulk" (96, 97). He "bulges marvelously" in his "expensive," extravagant clothes (98). Porter seems to delight in appetitive language as she describes Braggioni throughout the story. Whereas he used to be called "Delgadito" (or "slender one," in Spanish) when he was young and still passionate for the cause, Braggioni now clearly thinks too much *of* himself and gives too much *to* himself. He is a gross display of excess. Laura, in contrast to Braggioni and his self-indulgence, is, at first blush, a model of self-restraint. Her clothes are "nun-like," and she "has renounced vanities" (97). The young American expatriate teacher, an object both of Braggioni's love and of the love of a young revolutionary named Eugenio, sympathizes with the local socialist politics and even runs errands for Braggioni and his men. She is an idealist, a true believer in the politics that once inspired Braggioni himself. She feels a "sense of grievance" that "she has been betrayed" by how she *must* live in comparison to how she believes she *ought to be able* to live, without the ugly cynicism of others and the compromises she sees them making (97). She politely accepts Braggioni's serenades, but only because she fears the consequences of rejecting him outright (96), and she soundly rejects the love offered her by the wan and dreamy-eyed Eugenio. Interestingly, a bit like Braggioni, who has "a love of humanity raised above mere personal affections" (97), Laura seems far more interested in political causes than in romantic attachment, and, at first, the reader assumes that she is admirable in this devotion. Braggioni, readers initially surmise, is the antagonist here, as he has compromised his principles, while Laura remains the purist.

Soon, though, Porter reveals the cracks in Laura's political idealism, the moments when Laura is perhaps not as consistent as she had hoped to be nor as admirable to the other characters, and eventually to the readers, as we might originally have assumed that she would be. Laura loves handmade lace, rather than that of the "sacred" machines that her socialist comrades would celebrate (98), and she occasionally ducks into a church to pray (98), which again betrays her own inability to hold fast to her socialist, anticlerical, secularist principles. The local people question her presence in their community, assuming that Laura has relocated to Mexico for the sake of a man. However, Laura is not interested in any man and does not even have any affection for the young children she teaches, though they shower affection on her. Ironically, it is Braggioni, the presumed hypocrite, who rightly accuses Laura of a hypocrisy similar to his. She, Braggioni remarks, may be a "lover of humanity," but she loves no man. She is wrong, he notes, in her refusal of love. While the reader might at first assume that Braggioni is merely expressing his frustration at his own rejected advances, the remainder of the story suggests that Braggioni might be right. Porter argues for the healthfulness of moderate, well-fed appetites. Braggioni and Laura are two problematic extremes—overfed and underfed—but two problematic appetites all the same.

It is, in fact, through the two closing scenes of the story that we see just how central this appetitive symbolism is to Porter's argument for the necessity of love and forgiveness in the healing of disillusioned ideology and the cure for ennui. The first of these critical scenes—when Braggioni's wife washes his feet—has elicited almost no scholarly attention, but this scene is an essential piece of the alimentary religious symbolism of the story as a whole as well as an important prerequisite for understanding what Esplin describes as the "bizarre" conclusion to the story (24).[1] In this crucial scene, Braggioni returns home, where his wife awaits him. "[F]or a month his wife has spent many hours every night weeping," and she "is weeping now, and she weeps more at the sight of him, the cause of all her sorrows" (107). She "comes toward him with no reproach except grief on her face," and Braggioni greets her warmly and appreciatively, calling her "good" and a "dear good creature." His wife then kneels before him, removes his shoes, washes his feet, and looks at him with sadness. In response, "he is sorry for everything," begins to weep himself, confesses his hunger, and suggests that they "eat something together," though interestingly it is his wife who asks for forgiveness. This scene clearly draws upon the biblical passage John 13.2–17, wherein Jesus washes his disciples' feet at the Last Supper, or the last meal he and his disciples shared together prior to his crucifixion. Jesus uses this moment both to teach his disciples to serve others, reversing expectations as to hierarchy of master and servant or teacher and student, and to allude to his coming betrayal by Judas. As the disciple Peter responds so enthusiastically to Jesus's teaching in this biblical foot-washing scene, so, too, does Braggioni respond to the foot-washing from his wife. Like the biblical Jesus, Braggioni's wife is blameless and Braggioni the "lesser" and "guilty" party, and, like Judas, Braggioni has clearly betrayed his political cause and his wife.[2] Yet Braggioni is receptive to his wife's teaching. He confesses and repents. He participates in a sacred, ceremonial meal with her as penance for his betrayal and to heal the brokenness in their relationship. This is a brilliant scene of holy and ceremonial dining, a "love feast" of sorts,[3] through which purity is restored and repentance and forgiveness are enacted.

"Flowering Judas" cannot be understood, I would argue, without this foot-washing scene that initiates the so-called "Passion" sequence of biblical references, reinforces the centrality of the themes of love and betrayal in this story, and serves as an illuminating contrast to the dream sequence that concludes the story. In the final two paragraphs, immediately proximate to this scene between Braggioni and his wife, we experience the opposite of the healing and tears of repentance and forgiveness that bathe the foot-washing vignette. Instead, we find a scene of terror and horror. Laura goes to bed, and, as she falls asleep, she counts and thinks "it is monstrous to confuse love with revolution, night with day, life with death—ah, Eugenio!" Eugenio was the revolutionary who had loved her, whose love she had treated indifferently and carelessly, and after whose arrest the one whom she visited in prison. Laura had taken Eugenio narcotics, and eventually he overdosed and died. While Porter allows for ambiguity here, it seems likely Eugenio, whose very name suggests that he is a "good" man or "well-born" (West 184), has committed suicide—brought to despair by his political colleagues, who have largely forgotten him, and by the woman he loves, who delivers to him the very means of his suicide. Laura's thoughts as she falls asleep imply that she has done something terribly wrong by confusing "love with revolution" and suggest that she has not loved properly or well. She has misdirected her passions. She has problematically loved a cause, to the exclusion of loving a person.

Laura's "monstrous" wrong becomes more hideous and disturbing as she moves into full sleep and a disturbing dream. She encounters Eugenio, who beckons to her, and she reaches for him, but he slips away. He calls her a "Murderer," and she moves through several landscapes, at one point clinging to "the topmost branch of the Judas tree" (108). Eugenio says that he will take Laura "[t]o death," whereupon she balks and asks for his hand. Eugenio pityingly replies, "Then eat these flowers, poor prisoner, . . . take and eat," and he pulls "warm bleeding flowers" from the Judas tree and puts them to her lips (108). The story concludes:

She saw that his hand was fleshless, a cluster of small white petrified branches, and his eye sockets were without light, but she ate the flowers greedily for they satisfied both hunger and thirst. Murderer! said Eugenio, and Cannibal! This is my body and my blood. Laura cried No! and at the sound of her own voice, she awoke trembling, and was afraid to sleep again. (108)

What, then, is the meaning of this strange nightmare? Esplin describes these lines as a "supernatural finale" that can best be identified as magic realism (25). Indeed, this passage does point to the supernatural, but not, I would suggest, necessarily as a work of magic realism. Rather, this passage is a continuation of the biblical allusions to the Passion story that the foot-washing scene had begun, but as a perverse and disturbing reversal of the biblical scene that points to what Laura had done wrong. In the Book of Mark's version of the Last Supper scene, Mark records Jesus as saying to his disciples, "Take; this is my body" and, later, "This is my blood of the covenant," as he gives them bread and wine at a Passover meal (14.22–24). Eugenio, a Christ-like figure similar to Braggioni's wife, offers himself to the broken sinner with words that directly echo those of Christ. Laura has rejected his love, though, choosing instead the bloody flowers of the Judas tree, the symbol of betrayal. What should have been a beautiful acceptance of his sacrifice instead becomes a dream in which her conscience accuses her of murdering and cannibalizing Eugenio, betraying his love, and effectively killing him with despair and drugs. This is certainly a horrific eucharistic meal—one that underscores Laura's problematic love of an ideal, a love realized at the expense of the people it was intended to serve.[4] The ennui and disconnectedness, or what Beverly Gross calls the "hopeless monotony" (130), that Laura feels throughout the story seem to be rooted in the distance that she maintains from others. She cannot feel, she does not feed her healthy appetites, and her passions are all wrong. She has not been moderate. Rather, she has starved her soul. She is not the opposite of Braggioni—he the antagonist and she the protagonist; she is, instead, much like him. As the Profligates and the Hoarders shared the same punishment in Dante's hell, Laura and Braggioni have both been excessive in their appetites—he too gluttonous, using his comrades and growing fat on their efforts, and she too restrained—refusing to love others as they waste away with neglect.

Importantly in this scene, Laura clings to the Judas tree, which nearly every literary critic agrees is a symbol of betrayal. Porter herself once wrote, "You don't say, 'I'm going to have the flowering Judas

tree stand for betrayal,' but of course it does" (Liberman 55). That symbolism, according to Porter, drew upon the work of T. S. Eliot and his
poem "Gerontion," which mentions a "flowering judas" tree (Walsh 134–
35). Laura's ennui, disillusionment, and eventual hopelessness suggest
the modernist image of the wasteland that Eliot's poem invokes (West
186). The tree, a redbud, derived its name from the legend that it was
the tree upon which Judas hanged himself after betraying Christ and
whose "buds are red because it actually became the body of Judas, who
is said to have had red hair" (West 184; Rohrberger #10). Thus, remark-
ing that the tree is symbolic of betrayal seems not much of an argumen-
tative risk, though identifying the betrayer in the story is significantly
more debatable. Reading the closing passages of the story through an
appetitive lens suggests that there are two betrayers here—Braggioni,
who repents and receives forgiveness—and Laura, who has not yet done
so. They are foils of each other, and it is Laura, the externally more lovely
of the two, who is revealed to have the heart of a cannibalistic murderer
if she does not learn how to love.[5] Early in the story, Laura had momen-
tarily reflected, "It may be true I am as corrupt, in another way, as Braggioni," but what readers took to be an admirably honest and humble
confession of her humanity turns out instead to be an understatement.
She lacks, to her detriment, Braggioni's self-insight and his ability to feel
true remorse. While Laura's repetition of the word "no" in this closing
dream sequence alludes to the disciple Peter's triple betrayal of Christ in
the Passion story and paints Laura as a similar betrayer (Jiménez-Placer
124), the story's extended focus on Laura's disordered, restrictive, and
ultimately cannibalistic eating underscores the depth and extent of her
traitorous behavior.

"Flowering Judas" is a polyvalent critique—one that asserts with
appetitive language the importance of love for both self-care and care
of the larger community, whether through personal relationship, education, or politics, but one that also very pointedly offers specific comment on the Mexican Revolution. Susana M. Jiménez-Placer states this
viewpoint quite plainly: "'Flowering Judas' is basically an expression of
Katherine Anne Porter's disillusionment with the Mexican revolution"
(114). Indeed, her character Laura "feels betrayed by her revolution that
doesn't fulfill the early idealistic aims of the movement" (Wang 97). We
have explored the importance of the story's clear appetitive language for
the former—Porter's understanding of the place and importance of love
and community—but perhaps less obvious is how this appetitive language helps us to understand Porter's arguments regarding the revolu-

tion. Readers might even wonder whether attention to the political element of the short story is truly a worthwhile endeavor. The specifics of the politics are difficult to follow for those unfamiliar with this portion of Mexican history, but, more troublingly, the Mexican setting could represent an exoticizing, colonizing, and simplistic impulse in the portrait it paints of the country, its people, and its politics. Porter, however, defended herself against such accusations with the claim that she understood herself "never [to have] been out of America," and she located herself in "a borderland" that understood America, including Mexico, as part of *the Americas,* less nationally defined than political boundaries would suggest (870). In doing so, Porter was in keeping with much of contemporary American literary criticism that has sought to understand the United States in the context of the Americas. Significantly, Porter did have more than passing familiarity with Mexico. She repeatedly traveled to Mexico and lived there for almost three years, studying art, teaching dancing, and becoming involved in revolutionary politics. The Obregón Revolution took place while she was living there. The author even offered an account of having witnessed "a street battle between Maderistas and Federal troops" during the earlier Madero Revolution, as well as talking to a nearby "very old Indian woman" (869). The woman, recounted Porter, confidently anticipated that earthly, not heavenly, happiness would be the result of such sacrifice, even as "the dead were being piled for burning in the public square." Reporting witness of the public violence of the revolution was clearly very important to Porter, and, as in "Flowering Judas," she did so by emphasizing the problematics of excess and, in this case, the disturbing images of a seemingly insatiable appetite for death.

While some of Porter's Mexican accounts later proved to be fictive (Walsh 5), Porter did indeed draw upon her own life in Mexico for source material for the protagonist in "Flowering Judas." In 1942 Porter revealed that the short story included autobiographical elements, imaginatively locating her inspiration in a scene the author had viewed while chaperoning a friend of hers, who was serenaded by an unwanted "fat man"; in this moment, Porter said, she saw "symbolic truth," if not the woman's true story (Walsh 122, 128; Porter 716). In subsequent interviews, Porter mentioned the flowering Judas tree being there, though likely it was a reimagined purple bougainvillea, and identified her friend's name as "Mary Doherty," someone who, Porter claimed, did not know how to care for herself (Walsh 122, 135; Madden 177–78). In the 1970s Porter even named a model for Braggioni one "[Samuel] Yúdico," though elsewhere she described Braggioni as a composite character, and she pointed to her own political activities in Mexico, as well as her own dreams (one a marijuana-induced hallucination), as providing additional inspiration for the story; some of these claims, points out Thomas F. Walsh, were not reliable and tell us more about the writer's later remembrances of her motives than the factual original occurrences (122; Givner 155–56).[6] While Walsh documents Porter's fictional reimaginings with regard to what she actually experienced in Mexico and what likely inspired many of the elements of "Flowering Judas," he likewise notes that the foundational truths of her experiences there made their way into the story. As Porter wrote to her friend Doherty, "Mexico was new to us, and beautiful, the very place to be at that moment. We believed a great deal—though I remember well that my childhood faith in the Revolution was well over in about six months" (Walsh 135). Thus, if we are to see continuity between the larger claims of the short story and its more particular contextualization within the Mexican setting, a language of appetites could help elucidate that connection.

Indeed, Porter's short story attributes the failure of revolutionary politics not to complex political machinations or unsuccessful physical conflict, as one might anticipate, but instead to "selfishness, narcissism and self-interest . . . the vices which contributed to the failure of the revolutionary movements" (Jiménez-Placer 114), all of them, we might note, related to appetitive excess. Jiménez-Placer notes that "[i]n Porter's story, the Mexican revolution is devoid of any real revolutionary activity and depends exclusively on the words spoken by its leaders" (115). These words, it quickly becomes clear, are offered to an excessive degree and instead of action. Comrades are left to languish in jail, while the revolutionary leader Braggioni talks, and talks, and talks. Sam Bluefarb, who posits that Laura's presence in Mexico was "in a sense, a sociopolitical extension of her Catholicism," by which Laura hoped to go "into the world to 'do good,'" attributes her disillusionment or what he calls her "loss of innocence," not so much to the verbal excesses on which Jiménez-Placer remarks, but rather to the revolutionaries' "corruption, opportunism, and animal meanness" (256–57). Whichever interpretation one chooses, Braggioni's revolutionary success is hampered by his indulgences. Even the alimentary symbolism attached to Braggioni points to his limitations that result from an overabundance of self-love. As David Madden remarks, Braggioni may be Christ-like in his humble brokenness with his wife, but he is ultimately a false Christ, for his love will never cause him to sacrifice himself (284), just as Laura will never entirely accept the idea of her own guilt (Redden 201, 204). Braggioni loves himself too much, and literally too amply, to embrace self-sacrifice. Braggioni and Laura are, in this sense, gluttons, overindulging the self—he with plenitude and she with anorectic restraint.

Thus, Katherine Anne Porter's "Flowering Judas" makes pervasive use of an appetitive language and alimentary symbolism to underscore the limiting effects that gluttonous narcissism has on the achievement of true revolutionary reform and, moreover, to promote the need for embodied and self-sacrificing love in order to realize individual and communal flourishing. Porter's story transforms traditional Christian corporeal and alimentary ordinances and sacraments—foot-washing and Eucharist—into a salvific redemption in the case of the former, and into a perverse nightmare of horrific and cannibalistic feeding in the latter. She thereby recommends secularized and moderate appetites for the realization of revolutionary change that will rely not on the abstract idealism and practices of fallible leaders, who inevitably disappoint, but rather on the ability of both leaders and followers alike to amend error through listening to and accepting the forgiving love of others as expressed in concrete, personalized, embodied forms of ideology. Porter describes familiarly human betrayals facilitated by the corruption of power or by refusal of human attachments, but her salvations interestingly seem humanly possible as well, as they entail the virtues of humility and selflessness, rather than divine intervention. Porter's alimentary symbolism clearly draws upon the Christian faith tradition, but the author offers a profoundly secular understanding of salvation, a salvation attainable by humans if they would but be moderate in their appetites and focus on honestly and effectively being of service to others. Human connection, Porter insists, preserves us from the monotonous wasteland of purposelessness and ennui that the modernists had so aptly described and redirects us back into a connection with our neighbors that serves as a healthy focal point in which to root our idealism and hope.

NOTES

1. Both Sam Bluefarb and David Madden briefly discuss this scene, but not in terms of its connection to foot-washing in the Passion story. Rather, Bluefarb sees Mrs. Braggioni as representative of "the unlikely domestic side of the revolutionist" and someone who is capable of "trigger[ing]" Braggioni's "frailty" (260). Madden, on the other hand, sees her as a "genuine Magdalene," rather than as a Peter figure (285).

2. Rita Ferrari takes issue with those scholars who "read the scene of Braggioni's reunion with his wife as demonstrating the redeeming potential of love," but her critique of these readings lies in her resistance to the idea of Braggioni as the center of this scene and as a Christic model of love (12). She points to Mrs. Braggioni as an important char-

acter in this scene. My reading, however, answers Ferrari's critique by instead positing Mrs. Braggioni as the Christ-like figure and the true model of love here, with Braggioni being the character in need of forgiveness rather than being the one who forgives.

3. For discussion of the ordinance of the love feast, as particularly linked to foot-washing, see my article in *Food and Faith in Christian Culture*.

4. For an introduction to how fiercely nineteenth- and twentieth-century Christians battled over the meaning of the Eucharist and how freighted were the symbols of wine or juice and bread, see Daniel Sack's *Whitebread Protestants: Food and Religion in American Culture*. For an account of such symbolism reaching even further back into history and into Catholic practice, see Ann W. Astell's *Eating Beauty: The Eucharist and the Spiritual Arts of the Middle Ages*. To explore the sacramental nature of eating in general, not just as located in the Eucharist, see Norman Wirzba's *Food and Faith: A Theology of Eating* and Tish Harrison Warren's "Eating Leftovers" in *Liturgy of the Ordinary*.

5. Susana M. Jiménez-Placer emphasizes not only Laura's betrayal of others and of herself, but also Laura's rejection and betrayal of language, its potential for symbolism, and, by extension, even of the genre of the short story itself (113, 121–22, 123).

6. Walsh points to labor leader Luis Morones as an additional model for the character of Braggioni (135).

WORKS CITED

Astell, Ann W. *Eating Beauty: The Eucharist and the Spiritual Arts of the Middle Ages.* Cornell University Press, 2016.

Bluefarb, Sam. "Loss of Innocence in 'Flowering Judas.'" *CLA Journal*, vol. 7, no. 3, 1964, pp. 256–62.

Esplin, Emron. "Magic Realism in 'Flowering Judas' and the Dual Realities of Katherine Anne Porter's Time in Mexico." *Southern Studies*, vol. 12, nos. 1–2, 2005, pp. 23–46.

Ferrari, Rita. "Masking, Revelation, and Fiction in Katherine Anne Porter's 'Flowering Judas' and 'Pale Horse, Pale Rider.'" *Les Cahiers de la Nouvelle* [*Journal of the Short Story in English*], vol. 25, 1995, pp. 9–20.

Givner, Joan. *Katherine Anne Porter: A Life.* Simon & Schuster, 1982.

Gross, Beverly. "The Poetic Narrative: A Reading of 'Flowering Judas.'" *Style*, vol. 2, 1968, pp. 129–39.

Gwin, Minrose. "Mentioning the Tamales: Food and Drink in Katherine Anne Porter's *Flowering Judas and Other Stories*." *Mississippi Quarterly*, vol. 38, no. 1, 1984, pp. 49–57.

Harrison Warren, Tish. "Eating Leftovers." *Liturgy of the Ordinary: Sacred Practices in Everyday Life*, IVP Books, 2016, pp. 61–73.

Heusser, Martin. "'Why I Write about Mexico': Mexicanness in Katherine Anne Porter's 'Flowering Judas' and 'María Concepción.'" *On the Move: Mobilities in English Language and Literature*, edited by Annette Kern-Stähler and David Britain, SPELL: Swiss Papers in English Language and Literature, vol. 27, Narr, 2012, pp. 69–80.

The Holy Bible: English Standard Version. Crossway, 2001.

Jiménez-Placer, Susana M. "Laura's Unconscious Rejection of the Short Story in Katherine Anne Porter's 'Flowering Judas.'" *Scribbling Women and the Short Story Form: Approaches by American and British Women Writers*, edited by Ellen Burton Harrington, Peter Lang, 2008, pp. 112–27.

Liberman, M. M. "Symbolism, the Short Story, and 'Flowering Judas.'" *Katherine Anne Porter*, edited by Harold Bloom, Chelsea House, 1986, pp. 53–59.

Madden, David. "The Charged Image in Katherine Anne Porter's 'Flowering Judas.'" *Studies in Short Fiction*, vol. 7, 1970, pp. 277–89.

Oberholtzer Lee, Heidi. "Commensality and Love Feast: The Agape Meal in the Late Nineteenth- and Early Twentieth-Century Brethren in Christ Church." *Food and Faith in Christian Culture,* edited by Ken Albala and Trudy Eden, Columbia University Press, 2011, pp. 147–69.

Porter, Katherine Anne. *Collected Stories and Other Writings,* edited by Darlene Harbour Unrue, Library of America, 2008.

Redden, Dorothy S. "'Flowering Judas': Two Voices." *Studies in Short Fiction,* vol. 6, 1969, pp. 194–204.

Rohrberger, Mary. "Betrayer or Betrayed: Another View of 'Flowering Judas.'" *Notes on Modern American Literature,* vol. 2, no. 1, 1977, #10.

Sack, Daniel. *Whitebread Protestants: Food and Religion in American Culture.* Palgrave Macmillan, 2000.

Walsh, Thomas F. *Katherine Anne Porter and Mexico: The Illusion of Eden.* University of Texas Press, 1992.

Wang, Ru. "Symbolism—The Main Artistic Style of Katherine Anne Porter's Short Stories." *English Language Teaching,* vol. 3, no. 3, 2010, pp. 95–97.

West, Ray B., Jr. "Katherine Anne Porter: Symbol and Theme in 'Flowering Judas.'" *Accent: A Quarterly of New Literature,* vol. 7, 1947, pp. 182–88.

Wirzba, Norman. *Food and Faith: A Theology of Eating.* 2nd ed., Cambridge University Press, 2019.

Dial "Saucisse Minuit" for Murder

Nero Wolfe and the Art of Detecting Well

ROSSITSA TERZIEVA-ARTEMIS

Among the popular fiction genres, detective fiction is still one of the most widely read today. It seems that from the first biblical "thriller" of Cain and Abel, to the elaborate whodunits of Poe, Doyle, Christie, and Sayers, to the cool hard-boiled works of Hammett, Chase, and Gardner, to the dark psychological novels of numerous contemporary masters such as Patterson, Child, Nesbø, and Rendell, we can admire the techniques and the voices of many a gifted writer. Some people read for the enigma, others for the atmosphere, and an even larger group perhaps for the perfect combination of the two. It is a challenge to delve into the shadowy world of crime yet to keep a safe distance as an observer and a judge of character and situation. In other words, "One thing good crime novels give you, along with the puzzle of the crime, is a world" (Carter). Detective fiction offers a world we can vicariously enjoy. Hopefully, it is darker than the one we know, but definitely one that is equally challenging like the world we inhabit.

We might wonder, then, how to choose and where to find the most attractive morsel of detection, but our dilemma does not hold for long. As Dorothy L. Sayers points out, the main task for the reader today is rather simple:

> The reader ought to be able to guess the criminal, if he is sharp enough, and nobody can ask for more than this. It is, after all, the reader's job to keep his wits about him, and, like the perfect detective, to suspect everybody. (98)

Too bad that Sayers does not comment on how to deal with the weirdness that very often confronts the readers of crime fiction, and I do not mean here simply violence or psychological darkness. Rather, I am thinking of those characters who flourish on the quirky and strange, and make the most of these idiosyncrasies in their fictional worlds. Listening to a great master from the golden age of the English crime story discuss the issue would have been enlightening. Such a discussion would have brought to the fore many musings about the adventures and lifestyle of Sherlock Holmes or about the unorthodox attitudes of Hercule Poirot or Miss Marple. Because, after all, besides supreme demonstration of deduction and argumentation, theirs is a world that we would like to step into and learn more about from these geniuses of detection.

In his famous essay "The Simple Art of Murder," Raymond Chandler defines what he calls the "classic detective story" in a rather unflattering way: following abundant examples from the English tradition, he concludes that this model is outdated and the characters are "puppets and cardboard lovers and *papier-mâché* villains and detectives of exquisite and impossible gentility" (230, 232). His conclusions then move in the direction of a new genre that has a typical American ring to it—the genre of noir fiction. In that tradition Chandler, of course, is a master theoretician and artful practitioner. While there are many others whose reputations precede them, I intend to look at what we might consider a transitional literary figure by his own description: a great American detective fiction writer who is on the border of that golden English tradition yet also steps into the noir genre with a literary career that spans forty years. I will read closely the early novels of Rex Stout (1886–1975), one of the grand masters of the classical detective story in American literature, and the creator of an emblematic private eye, Nero Wolfe. It is an exploration worthy of the genre. As John Littlejohn points out, there is charm to Stout's work: "Rex Stout's Nero Wolfe narratives are stylish, readable, and reliable in their basic pattern" (58). By exploring the first five books in the Nero Wolfe series, I will demonstrate how food—an idiosyncratic "character" in Stout's impressive oeuvre—manages to gain a central place in this canonical genre. We read for the detection, no doubt, for the intricate plots too, but most of all we read to get as much as possible—and there is so much left, pun intended—of the gigantic figure of Wolfe and his sidekick, Archie Goodwin.

Wolfe, of course, is described by Stout as an imposing, robust, and formidable figure. In notes typed up in 1949, he is described as 5'11" and more than 270 pounds (Confidential Memo). Yet there is a great symbiosis at work in Stout's novels between the erudite, rotund gourmand Wolfe and the smaller, bouncy, street-smart Archie. Usually, in many of the novels, several things are shared between these two protagonists: one is the desire to enjoy life to its fullest, as one would enjoy a sophisticated dish that needs proper appreciation. Another is the desire to put in some sort of fragile, tentative order a world of crime that needs proper attention. Finally, there is the pleasure of getting paid for the job, too.

In one of his essays, George Grella raises the following argument in relation to the genre of the detective story:

> The central puzzle provides the usual complication, which the detective hero must remove; and its difficulty insures a typically comic engagement of the intellect. The whodunit's plot, full of deception, red herrings, clues real and fabricated, parallels the usually intricate plots of comedy, which often depend upon mistaken motives, confusion, and dissembling; it also supports the familiar romantic subplot. (33)

No doubt Stout provides a real treasure of detection and comedy in the Nero Wolfe narratives and doubles this winning package with a sharp dialogue and mouth-watering descriptions of meals that Epicurus himself would have approved. If we go back to the initial argument about the readers' love of detective fiction, the point that Miranda Carter makes in relation to the use of food in crime fiction is thus succinctly put, "Food also defines, elaborates—and humanizes—character." In this sense, the unforgettable character of Stout's detective is as humanized as it gets: he is almost always eating or talking about food; Wolfe is more of a human than simply "a character," but one very lucky human, of course. He has a genius for deduction, with an outspoken, trusted sidekick, Archie, who keeps him on his toes; a sophisticated personal chef, Fritz Brenner; and a highly skilled personal gardener, Theodore Horstmann. In the novels, in such an elegant male household food is not a decorative element; rather, it becomes a form of daily art and little short of a true necessity. Even more so, the recurrent descriptions of food consumption and drinking in Stout "give a necessary beat, a breath, a lull. They pull back from the blood and chaos. They re-establish the world around the crime. They even create more suspense, as the reader is diverted and waits for the next breakthrough" (Carter).

In both hard-boiled and classical detection, the mystery tends to outshine what is considered a trivial description of food, and readers expect to get involved in solving the case along with the detective in a supreme exercise of rationalization. It is not by chance that, as it turns out, the classic hard-boiled American crime novel is usually food-free. American detectives live off salt, fast food, grease and caffeine; in their world things move too fast for a sit-down dinner. The implication is that fine food is decadent. (Carter)

The puzzle, in other words, "beats" the realism of descriptions of meals; however, in the series, food is impossible to overlook or dismiss. Stout blends features of the classic detective story with elements of the hard-boiled story by creating a street-smart Archie to assist Wolfe, a protagonist larger-than-life, literally. Archie surely seems like an updated Watson figure, a sidekick with investigative skills of his own, but Wolfe looms in all works as a man of both gigantic appetite and intellect, a "gargantuan" figure as he prefers to call himself in front of people who get the literary reference to the comic sixteenth-century character created by the French writer François Rabelais.

Fer-de-Lance

Beginning with the first novel in which the detective is introduced, *Fer-de-Lance* (1934), Stout spins highly entertaining tales of adventure and detection in which knowledge is achieved in a fun, unexpected way. At the opulent table of his home, the brownstone on West 35th Street in New York, Wolfe enjoys absurd amounts of delicacies and gourmet dishes, seldom leaving his home and his beloved orchids. In a way, food turns to be a key element, if not a key "mover," in helping us solve the crimes and grasp his character. As one commentator has observed, "Eating rituals may increase dramatic suspense, but they also mark place and cultural identity and contribute to the psychological characterization of the detective hero" (Anderson et al.). Luckily for us, Wolfe is a foreign body of vaguely defined origin, perhaps born in Montenegro, but, in any case, a permanent fixture in a fabulous brownstone in New York, hardly worried about the speed of life outside. Outside of his enclave, which includes a tropical hothouse on the roof, a comfy bedroom, a fascinating office, and, naturally, a sanctified kitchen and a dining room, there is crime and urban chaos; inside, there is order and repose. Life is set around a precise schedule by the strikes of a trusty clock and the voice of Archie, Stout's even more trusty narrator, who accounts for the time between Wolfe's waking up and drinking a cup of chocolate. The day of the detective then continues with metronomic regularity: 9am to 11am tending to the beloved ten thousand orchids with Horstmann at hand; 11am to 1pm he works in the office—that is, if there is any work proper with clients, or otherwise drinking beer, counting beer tops at his desk, and sparingly responding to the frequent monologues of Archie (because there is so much to think about beyond the intrusions of the sidekick); at 1pm sharp Wolfe stops for a perfect lunch created by Fritz, sometimes shared with unexpected guests, but always enjoyed to the maximum by him; time spent enjoying the beautiful orchids again from 4pm to 6pm, and after that, only if life intrudes once again in the shape of a case, working in the office and drinking more beer until late. By chance—no, rather by rule—it happens that in Wolfe's life, "Where there is a crime, there is, often, food." (Michelis 143)

Between 1934 when *Fer-de-Lance* is published and his death in 1975, Stout completes thirty-three novels, thirty-eight novellas, and many short stories about the adventures of the Wolfe-Goodwin tandem, clearly having found a winning ticket in the genre of detective fiction. A significant number of these works have as a serious "character" food in all its glorious embodiments, and especially so in the Nero Wolfe series. Moreover, food implies drink, too, because no respected gourmand will enjoy their food without an appropriate drink. In *Fer-de-Lance*, Wolfe appears as a "mountain on its feet" (269), a man in his late fifties, a brilliant detective with no lack of self-esteem, as on many occasions he bombastically states, "I'm merely a genius, not a god" (225). Little seems to exceed his love of food or his love of orchids. Even money-making seems to be just a means to keep up the expensive orchid hobby, the absolute dedication to excellent food, and the household already mentioned.

In his attitude to food, Archie is not a gourmand but simply loves to eat; however, he knows the difference between excellent food and "grub." The friendly banter between him, Wolfe, and sometimes Fritz Brenner, the Swiss chef, defines the balance in this perfectly regulated male household where intellect, verbal skills, and gastronomical enjoyment are the simple givens for daily harmony. From the advantageous position of a narrator, Archie can often take comic liberties in interpreting Wolfe's state of mind and behavior, but always up to a point: he is clever enough to note in *The Red Box* (1937), for example,

> I know pretty well what my field is. Aside from my primary function as the thorn in the seat of Wolfe's chair to keep him from going to sleep and waking up only for meals, I'm chiefly cut out for two things: to jump and grab something before the other guy can get his paws on it, and to collect pieces of the puzzle for Wolfe to work on. (154)

And Archie is very right about his own function: in the event that Wolfe is given an opportunity, the danger is that he will happily navigate a simple line of eating and drinking, and tending to his orchids, thus he will destroy the domestic balance, which needs intellectual work on his behalf and physical work on behalf of Archie to keep the finances in check.

In *Fer-de-Lance,* the reader encounters for the first time the scope of Wolfe's attitude to food and his amazing detective skills in solving the case of a double murder. Detective Cramer, a recurring frenemy of both Wolfe and Archie, is at a loss dealing with what he thinks to be a murder case and an accidental death. A serious case, of course, calls for a serious food "spread," and Stout first ventures here on description of dishes that will become emblematic in the Nero Wolfe archive. For example, Archie is described at the start of the novel as having a breakfast of kidneys and waffles (28), quite unusual by contemporary standards, perhaps, but something that he rather enjoys. Fritz has learned how to please the inhabitants of the brownstone by now, Archie living on the premises for the past six years, and there is hardly a dish that the personal chef is incapable of creating for the greatest connoisseur of all, Wolfe. The detective, though, will have only crackers and chocolate for breakfast, but the day has just started and there are only so many hours to juggle food, drinks, orchids, and detective work.

Following up on Grella's argument, Wolfe exhibits "the Holmesian conventions of arcane knowledge, personal eccentricity, and idiosyncratic speech" (37). For any reader of the Nero Wolfe series, these characteristics are very clearly pronounced, starting with the first novel that features the great detective. Archie is no match for Wolfe's eclectic knowledge and reading list, both as idiosyncratic as the very food he opts to eat. His personal eccentricity stretches to the enormous quantities of beer that he starts drinking before lunch only to finish before going to bed, yet with no obvious influence on his clarity of mind and articulation, although definitely adding to the inches of his waist. The great detective counts patiently the beer tops in his desk drawer, probably thinking that he has to cut down on the beer at last, yet never actually cutting down. Archie can quip sarcastically about money or about the character of his patron, but Wolfe also loves the verbal sparring and, undoubtedly, is superior to Archie's linguistic skills. Once reminded about certain promises he has made, Wolfe replies rather provocatively, "Some day, Archie, when I decide you are no longer worth tolerating, you will have to marry a woman of very modest mental capacity to get an appropriate audience for your wretched sarcasms" (54).

One "secret" that Archie discloses as a trusted narrator is about Wolfe's "relapses," as he calls them (75): when frustration in the deductive process hits, the great man becomes an obsessive eater who consumes anything and everything he can think of, even the most inappropriate combinations he can imagine. This is how Archie describes the obsessive-compulsive behavior of the genius:

> Sometimes it seemed plain that it was just ordinary discouragement and funk, ... but other times there was no account for it at all. ... It might last anywhere from one afternoon up to a couple of weeks, or it was even possible that he was out for good and wouldn't come back until something new turned up. While it lasted he acted one of two different ways: either he went to bed and stayed there, living on bread and onion soup, refusing to see anyone but me and forbidding me to mention anything I had on my mind; or he sat in the kitchen telling Fritz how to cook things and then eating them on my little table. He ate a whole half a sheep that way in two days once, different parts of it cooked in twenty different ways. (76)

The gourmand Wolfe turns into an anxiety-ridden neurotic, sometimes literally harassing Fritz to prepare unbelievable kinds—and quantities—of outlandish dishes that he likes to "compose." The detective easily swings into a simple binge-eating parade, the start of which Archie has learned to recognize and, in some cases, knows how to prevent by simply diverting Wolfe's attention with another intellectual challenge. In *Fer-de-Lance*, the growing frustration is detected in the little argument between Fritz and Wolfe about the amount of chives necessary in tomato tarts (75). It will quickly escalate to the point where the detective will sit down in the kitchen and refuse to move, except to give outrageous directions for the preparation of more and more food, which veils his frustration from the lack of progress in the investigation. Once clarity strikes after a successful deduction, the menu quickly changes to a simple roasted lamb leg with garlic courtesy of the kitchen wizard Fritz, and the daily routine goes back to normal (82). Food, therefore, mirrors moods and compulsions too, in addition to the appreciation of haute cuisine.

"I know I am hungry, Archie. It is pleasant to have an appetite again. I've had none for weeks," Wolfe says honestly (97), and it seems he is speaking both literally and metaphorically: literally because he cannot simply put up with a light meal due to his body type and metaphorically because he is hungry for a solution in the case, a clearing that will take him on the path to solve the crime. Archie, on the other hand, does not fall back on a tough day: his breakfast consists of figs, a fat omelet care of Fritz, three cups of coffee, and three pieces of toast. While Archie's breakfast is by no means comparable to a "relapse," it is interesting to observe how the food in this case symbolizes two different things for the two protagonists. In the case of Archie, it is healthy, much-needed nourishment, while in the case of Wolfe's relapses, overeating is a frustrated desire to possess the elusive object—the "solution" to the crime—which escapes the mind of the detective and is restructured, therefore, as a series of dishes he may anticipate.

To get the testimonials of a group of caddies in this novel, Wolfe hosts one of his impromptu lunches and dinners in which, knowingly and unknowingly, witnesses often disclose important details that move the investigation forward. The caddies in this case are a group of young boys with very healthy appetites, and, under the instructions of Wolfe, Fritz serves them a lovely meal of "two enormous chicken pies and four melons" (170). Nothing is wasted in this situation because, between the servings of food, important "servings" of crime-related details come to the surface as well, which ultimately will lead the private detective to the disclosure of truth. A fed witness, it seems, is twice as cooperative as a hungry one, as Wolfe proves on many occasions.

Surveilling, on the other hand, is an equally important element of the detective's work, as is interrogation. It is Archie and often a trusted small group of collaborators who do the surveillance by either following the suspect by car, on foot, or just sitting and waiting in various establishments. One of these, maybe a surprise for contemporary readers, is the drugstore, which usually had a food corner in those days. The drugstore lunch counter provides some form of subsistence, though a far cry from the homemade masterpieces of Fritz. A greasy sandwich in hand while waiting, Archie often thinks about the stuff he is missing on that particular day or night, because the household menu is usually discussed as a matter of fact, and both Wolfe and Fritz inform Archie what to expect or what he has missed on various occasions. Sometimes instead of a flounder with cheese sauce and lettuce and tomato (134), Archie draws the short stick of luck and is forced to eat a simple dish of liver and bacon at the shopwindow of a snack joint (208). Wolfe, however, rarely has to wait—there is a strict daily schedule to follow, after all—and it is a minor disaster if the meals are delayed by an unexpected visitor or a client.

The days otherwise are marked by the enormous quantities of beer and milk consumed, beer for Wolfe and milk for Archie. Wolfe resembles a black hole in which beer easily disappears by the gallon so that on one occasion, probably reevaluating his portly constitution, he contemplates, "I am going to cut down to five quarts a day. Twelve bottles. A bottle doesn't hold a pint" (165). Beer before, during, and after a meal does not stop him from exercising his mind—but, alas, not his body—and the quantities, if calculated per novel, are really astonishing. There is the occasional whisky for Wolfe, too; port and wine are offered to the guests, but there is hardly any other novel or, more precisely, series of novels, where so much beer is consumed by a single character. Archie, on the other hand, can have milk at any time of the day, sometimes drawing the curious looks of characters who expect a tough guy like him to request an alcoholic drink in the spirit of the occasion. Coffee will pour throughout the novels as a third best choice at breakfast and after many meals, and especially during long stakeouts. The closing of *Fer-de-Lance*, however, is left for the reader to enjoy as if Wolfe addresses the readers too in his quip at Archie, "I understand your contention: that a point arrives when finesse must retire and leave the *coup de grâce* for naked force. I understand it, and I deny it vehemently" (270).

In the novels of the series to follow, intellectual work will go on, just as daily orchid hybridization will succeed and delicious food will manifest itself with the prompt regularity that Wolfe demands from the master Fritz—the rest is going to be only "naked force."

The League of Frightened Men

In the second novel, *The League of Frightened Men* (1935), Stout pursues his winning combination of an intricate plot, a fast-paced dialogue, and a gallery of memorable characters. It will soon become obvious that he is one of the most quotable crime writers of all time, whether we stick to the quips and exuberant tirades of Archie or the elaborate speeches of Wolfe. In any case, there are further reasons to place Stout in the group of transitional writers between the golden age of the English detective story and American noir—among them the use of humor and the delightfully detailed descriptions, and overflowing abundance, of food in his novels. If we follow Angelica Michelis, who argues that

> Elements of hard-boiled crime fiction are, however, employed in a more complex manner. Traditionally, texts of this sub-genre offer a first-person narrative from the perspective of an explicitly masculine detective who is unable (and often unwilling) to maintain a reflective distance from the crime investigation. (146)

While the narrative point of view that Archie offers is undoubtedly masculine, the sense of humor and, probably, the coexistence with Wolfe make the novel an example of Stout's transitional approach in entwining fast-paced plot, sometimes rough humor, and unforgettable characters. The second novel in the series is also Stout's attempt—tongue-in-cheek as always—to engage Freudian theory a bit further, not simply with regard to Wolfe's relapses with food, but in relation to the unconventional social dynamics between a group of men that form the so-called "league." The antagonist, Paul Chapin, is clearly defined in the very beginning—a fiction writer, no less—and the moments of deduction in this case are related to the prediction of the players' next moves, just like in chess, rather than the figuring out of an elusive criminal. With this minor change in the plotline, Stout remains true to his interest in developing both Wolfe's and Archie's characters through language, action, and food.

In her discussion of the many uses of food in fiction, Kerri Majors makes the following apt observation, which is quite relevant to the reading of Stout's series in general: "When food is spice in a novel, an accent rather than the primary ingredient, it can be overlooked or savored depending on a reader's tastes" (73). I believe that the reader is given plenty of opportunities to "savor" various foods in *The League of Frightened Men;* overlooking food in Stout is impossible, and this novel makes it especially clear. On a cold morning in November, Wolfe is drinking beer while deeply absorbed by pictures of snowflakes (1), while Archie is trying to involve him in a conversation, first by making a joke about the snowflakes, and after that, since there is no reply, by dropping a white lie about missing orchid bulbs in a recent shipment. When even this does not produce any effect, Archie offers an elaborate lie that "the turkey they sent is too old to broil and will be tough unless it is roasted two hours, which according to you will attenuate the flavor" (2). Wolfe is so absorbed by the pictures that even this important food-related comment is left hanging in the air, maybe because he has confidence in Fritz, who will always take care of such "disasters." Only a further push in relation to a recent obscenity trial brings the detective back in the conversation.

Stirring the mind of the great man, of course, comes at a certain high price: full provision of beer, eclectic dishes, lots of verbal sparring with Archie, a select group of visitors, and a paying client. Humbly, as always, Wolfe admits, "I have no talents. I have genius or nothing" (15). A genius like him needs the stimulation of a challenging case just as much as he needs nourishment, so here comes a dish curated by the hands of the other resident "genius," Fritz. Archie, in his second outing by now, knows too well how to entice further Nero's attention in the potential case:

> Two of the folds in Wolfe's cheeks opened out a little, so I knew he thought he was smiling. I said, "But you may just be pleased because you know it's corn fritters with anchovy sauce for lunch and it's only ten minutes to the bell." (19)

The folds that open a little, the lips that make a slight smacking sound when everything—food and detection—is going well, draw a portrait of Wolfe, the gourmand connoisseur, not the man in addictive relapse. Here is a personal harmony that Archie can read and understand after living with Wolfe for seven years; he even appreciates its glorious dimensions, which inevitably lead to a solved case and a (very well) paying client. Wolfe's personal harmony, as far as food is concerned, is easily procured by Fritz:

> By dinner time Monday we were all set, so we enjoyed the meal in leisure. Fritz was aways happy and put on a little extra effort when he knew things were moving in the office. That night I passed him a wink when I saw how full the soup was of mushrooms, and when I tasted the tarragon in the salad dressing I threw him a kiss. He blushed. Wolfe frequently had compliments for his dishes and expressed them appropriately, and Fritz always blushed. . . . I often wondered if Wolfe noticed it. His attention to food was so alert and comprehensive that I would have said off hand he didn't, but in making any kind of a guess about Wolfe off hand wasn't good enough. (45)

Offhand, as readers, we might have to trust the narrator and suspend any form of prejudice when it comes to Wolfe. Sipping his morning chocolate under an enormous black cover (98), he is the epitome of a human enigma as much as he is solving crime enigmas at any given moment. Fritz's talent to perform daily small miracles in the kitchen is needed in order to preserve the harmony that defines the household and fuels its most sensitive patron.

People unconnected to the household, however, like suspects, criminals, or even the police, might occasionally underestimate Wolfe's attention span and skills; they might be straightforwardly rude to him, as in the case of the suspect's wife, Dora, who verbally attacks the detective by calling him "a fat fool," to which Wolfe simply replies, "Fat visibly, though I prefer Gargantuan. A fool only in the broader sense, as a common characteristic of the race" (120).

We can very easily agree with Wolfe's aphoristic answer about both his Gargantuan statue and his alleged foolishness when we encounter another potential uncontrollable binging on the horizon. The frustration of the temporary dead-end investigation at that point, and the slow process of untangling a knot of human passions, means, and motivations, lead to an ominous situation only too recognizable by Archie as he tells us:

> Sometimes I thought it was a wonder Wolfe and I got on together at all. The differences between us, some of them, showed up plainer at the table than anywhere else. He was a taster and I was a swallower. Not that I didn't know good from bad; after years of education from Fritz's cooking I could even tell, usually, superlative from excellent. But the fact remained that what chiefly attracted Wolfe about food in his pharynx was the affair it was having with his taste buds, whereas with me the important point was that it was bound for my belly. (123)

The inevitable obsessive-compulsive relapse threatens the established balance in the household on one very important level: the vicarious consumption that Wolfe practices on such occasions has to do with the frustration of the mind and the seemingly endless capacity of his body to chew, rather than to enjoy, as is the case in normal circumstances. Archie acknowledges this and points out, "I have seen him, during relapse, dispose completely of a ten-pound goose between eight o'clock and midnight, while I was in a corner with ham sandwiches and milk hoping he will choke. At those times he always ate in the kitchen" (123). Such a capacity for gobbling food is clearly juxtaposed to the eclectic "love affair" between taste buds and ingredients routinely displayed when things are going well. Yet his relapses are not of the bulimic type, but rather stand for a temporary glossing over of frustrations of the intellectual kind.

Archie, with his more pragmatic attitude to food, is interested in being fed in order to fuel his body for the daily running of errands and for the more demanding legwork of following suspects and, sometimes, getting in trouble with criminals. As it happens once, in the middle of the night, he comes home and readily clears the leftovers from the sumptuous dinner. "Fritz had kept some squirrel stew hot for me, and it had long since been put away, with a couple of rye highballs because the black sauce Fritz used for squirrel made milk taste like stale olive juice" (234). We are led to believe we can trust a protagonist like Archie, who can deal equally well with a stew like this or with a greasy sandwich from a shady establishment, if need be. The matter-of-fact descriptions refer to utility and practicality in his attitude, and sometime to his inevitable gullibility where food is concerned. Thus, when food and coffee laced with an undefined sleeping potion are offered by Chapin's wife, Dora, to the unsuspecting Archie, he has only this to say before passing out: "I was hungry and the chicken looked good, I admit that, but the psychology of it was that it looked like I ought to join in. Not to mention the salad, which had green peppers in it" (248). Luckily for Archie, most meals are the delicacies prepared by Fritz rather than the dangerous concoctions mixed by ill-willed criminals. Hence, as a rule, he enjoys the good life just as his patron, Wolfe, does. Waking up on a particular Sunday morning, for example, he is happy to note:

> I knew what had happened when I had called down to Fritz that I was out of the bathtub: he had lined a casserole with butter, put in it six tablespoons of cream, three fresh eggs, four Lambert sausages, salt, pepper, paprika and chives, and conveyed it to the oven. (238)

Of course, to the meat-eaters untroubled by calorie-counting, this sounds like a blissful warm breakfast suitable for a cold November day, which can be improved, possibly, only by a few cups of coffee. Being the hungry type, Archie is quite capable of consuming such dishes first thing in the morning, and the day might then proceed satisfactorily in any way.

The Rubber Band

In the third novel of the series, *The Rubber Band* (1936), Stout makes a small adjustment to the plotline by pitting Wolfe and Archie more seriously against the police. This change becomes a key element in the encounters between the two groups and sharpens, to an even greater extent, the dialogue. The issue, naturally, is not simply a matter of reputation and prestige, but a matter of who will first solve the murders and, in the case of Wolfe, whether he will get paid for it. Needless to point out, he is going to rise to the occasion easily—metaphorically speaking, as far as his body after eating is involved, no doubt. Archie will happily quip that Wolfe is too "house-ridden" to even consider going out (98). An example of a perfect introduction, the comic aspect of the narrative is pointedly emphasized here too, as Archie introduces the new exercise program of the detective:

> He had recently got the impression that he weighed too much—which was about the same as if the Atlantic Ocean formed the opinion that it was too

wet—and so had added a new item to his daily routine. Since he only went outdoors for things like earthquakes and holocausts, he was rarely guilty of movement. (5)

Probably the brownstone household can take only so much of a change in the routine of its famous inhabitant, so the "exercise" here happens in fifteen minutes precisely, and it comprises nothing more nor less than a lovely set of darts, which Wolfe indignantly calls "javelins" (6). Such an "extreme" exercise, however, goes hand in hand with an increased consumption of beer. Hence, the expected comic effect on the weight loss of the detective. Exercise or not, he must always eat well, and here is the point when an unexpected group of clients and a group of nosy policemen barge into his peaceful life, thereby postponing his well-established daily schedule:

> "Fritz."
> "Yes, sir."
> "A calamity. We cannot possibly dine at eight as usual. Not dine, that is. We can eat, and I suppose we shall have to. You have filets of beef with sauce Abano."
> "Yes, sir."
> Wolfe signed again. "You will have to serve it in morsels, for five persons. By adding some of the fresh stock you can have plenty of soup. Open Hungarian *petits poissons*. You have plenty of fruit? Fill in as you can. It is distressing, but there's no hep for it."
> "The sauce is a great success, sir. I could give the others canned chicken and mushrooms—"
> "Confound it, no! If there are to be hardships, I must share them. That's all. Bring me some beer." (43)

The "hardships" are cleverly handled by Fritz under the detective's direction, for one thing is sure: nobody leaves his home poorly fed, not unless they are master criminals or, alas, corpses. In other words, "Wolfe will dig in his heels and stop the world if any guest has not eaten" (McBride 101). Feeding people well, as we have seen previously, has tangible benefits to his reputation as a perfect host, but it also has some intangible ones when it comes to collecting details from the unaware guests.

In *The Rubber Band*, a case of murders because of greed is being investigated, and we are introduced to a female character, Clara Fox, who manages to draw Wolfe's attention for a bit, as if bringing out his best qualities as a host. When it comes to hospitality, any rejection of food, or suggestion of a rejection, is taken very seriously by Wolfe, despite time constraints or lack of preparation in the kitchen. Thus, to Clara's innocent proposal for skipping a meal, Wolfe has only this colorful response, "Great hounds and Cerberus!" He was about as close to a tantrum as he ever got. "Don't need to eat! In heaven's name, are you camels, or bears in for the winter?" (49).

Clara soon will get the point of how important food is to Wolfe, for she is also permitted to spend a few days in the male household—a pleasant exception that he makes after quickly considering all possible routes to evade the police and the killer at the same time.

Throughout the series, Wolfe has an alarming number of unflattering observations about the role of women in society and their characteristic features, probably based on his "poor" experience in the past as the victim of a wife who has tried to poison him. In this novel, though, we can observe him temporally softening to the presence of Clara: reciting poetry in Hungarian at dinnertime and sipping coffee with her, he is quite the gallant, but one who remains alert throughout the case. Wolfe cannot help himself, however, to advise her regarding the set schedule in his home, because "eating from a tray is an atrocious insult both to the food and the feeder, and in that case, luncheon is punctually at one and dinner at eight" (69).

After a stakeout in the town and the errands he needed to take care of, Archie returns home and observes this homey picture. His point of view, quite appreciative of Clara's charms, is pragmatic as he finally sits down to have dinner after a long day: "The yellow dressing-gown wasn't bad on her, at that, but I was hungry. I waded through a plate of minced lamb kidneys with green peppers, and a dish of endive" (115) He follows this with a "hunk of pie," and his own personal peace is restored.

Clara, on the other hand, after enjoying the simple order on which the household is established, notes humorously something that must have crossed the minds of readers too. She says, "No woman in it from top to bottom, but the routine is faultless, the food is perfect, and the sweeping and dusting are impeccable. . . . This place needs some upsetting" (115). Clara's joke, of course, foreshadows the complications and the deductive prowess that Wolfe must demonstrate in solving this complicated criminal case, which has started some thirty years earlier. He will beat the police to the finish line and will get paid for his deductive might by ever-so-thankful clients, but in the meantime only a beautiful dinner of guinea chicken *braziliera* can tickle the taste buds of the culinary maestro. Archie, of course, approves of all these, too: a sterling reputation, a pile of money, and excellent food are all welcome ingredients for a happy household.

The Red Box

Stout's fourth novel, *The Red Box* (1937), represents "a shining example of Wolfe and Archie at their most entertaining and intriguing" (Hart). If we read a few of the novels featuring the emblematic detective and his sidekick, we might entertain the question of whether the author and his protagonist correspond on any level with one another. We may conclude that "the quality that accounts for the greatest charm of the Nero Wolfe series is a love for language. Stout used language with great precision and with great pleasure. Wolfe was surely his alter ego in this glorious pursuit" (Hart).

In *The Red Box*, Wolfe is gently coerced to leave his home for an hour to investigate the murder of a beautiful model, just as he does in *The League of Frightened Men*. It takes, however, an elaborate lie concerning orchids—the other favorite hobby of the detective besides food—which Archie advises the client to use in order to get Wolfe out of the house. In these rare "dynamic" moments, but definitely in the dialogues at home, we have the best of the tandem that makes the series so popular among generations of readers. The narrative always centers on the crime and its solution, but then again it is fleshed out in a fascinating language while the protagonists are fueled by numerous gourmet dishes and an endless supply of beer. Here is Archie's astute observation about his patron, after living under the same roof with Nero Wolfe, now for nine years:

> . . . there were a few points I wasn't skeptical about any more. For instance: That he was the best private detective north of the South Pole. That he was convinced that outdoor air was apt to clog the lungs. That it short-circuited his nervous system to be jiggled and jostled. That he would starve to death if anything had happened to Fritz Brenner, on account of his firm belief that no one's cooking but Fritz's was fit to eat. (2)

Food, again, and comfortable peace of mind build up the harmonious existence, which only criminal activities, active investigation, and earning high fees can shake. The accidental client, Mr. Frost, who entertains the idea of getting Wolfe out of his cozy lair, is evidently wrong when the detective responds to his offer, "You humored me! You speak of my build-up! And you undertake to stampede me into a frantic dash through the maelstrom of the city's traffic—in a taxicab!" (2). It is clear that something more serious than the murder of a beautiful girl needs to happen in order to get Wolfe out of his home, and it concerns the precious ten thousand orchids he so lovingly grows on his roof. A fake letter from a famous "orchid grower" does the job; otherwise, as he says, "You observe my bulk. I am not immovable, but my flesh has a constitutional reluctance to sudden, violent or sustained displacement" (3). It is most amazing that Wolfe speaks of himself not derisively but very seriously, the body being no hindrance, just an appropriate vessel containing his intellectual might.

Out of his brownstone, "braving the elements—the chief element for that day being bright warm March sunshine" (9), Wolfe reaches his destination: a fashion house just a few blocks away from his own house. On its premises he quickly gulps down several bottles of beer either because of the exhausting exercise or simply because he has to confront the petty details of a murder case, as it seems on the surface. The interesting thing in the murder is that it is a case involving poisoned candy and the lack of perceivable motive behind the murder of a young woman working for the fashion house. Naturally, in the posh world that *The Red Box* portrays, the blame points at its main players, and this leads to a series of outbursts: for example, the original client, Mr. Frost, calls Wolfe a "damn fat imbecile" (29), and the detective takes it upon himself to prove him wrong, at least about the "imbecile" part. The investigation continues with a series of experiments and a tasting session of candy that Archie has to perform among "goddesses," as he calls the pretty models, and staff members. Wolfe, surprisingly maybe, is quite impervious to sweets of this kind, for he prefers the sophisticated desserts that Fritz prepares in the home kitchen, hence he quickly retreats back to the brownstone. There is only so much time in a day and so much gourmet food and beer top counting to be done at home!

In her discussion of the role of food in crime fiction, Michelis raises an important point with regard to the complex relation between order and crime, which is relevant here:

> Social order is inaugurated by an act of crime and furthermore, defined by the paradoxical nature underlying this relationship: on the one hand, social order will always have to fear the potential threat of crime but, on the other hand, it is the very presence of crime that constitutes social order. (144)

In the world that Stout creates, "social order" can be interpreted in a couple of ways: one is the social order outside of Wolfe's home where the police, the criminals, and people in general strive to achieve something, each with their motivation and simple goals; the second way is to see the social order within the famous brownstone, with the set schedule, the tasty offerings of its kitchen, the impressive tropical room on the roof, and the comic quips of Archie. In this second kind of social order, Wolfe does not care so much about achievement, but when the two orders collide, he is quick to use his brain and restore the desired peace and the separation between the inside and the outside.

Archie casually enjoys a perfect start to a work day. "Wolfe and I were doing the right thing by some sausage with ten kinds of herbs in it, which he got several times every spring from a Swiss up near Chappaqua who prepared it himself from home-made pigs" (31). The intrusion of the rude client, Mr. Frost, is the possible clash with the social order outside, yet Wolfe enters his office "peaceful and benign but ready to resent any attempt at turbulence, as he always was after a proper and unhurried meal" (31). Easier said than done, preserving the balance between the inside and the outside order! Wolfe stumbles briefly in the detection, and the inevitable relapse is about to disrupt the inside harmony of the household when Archie enters the kitchen to find him at the table giving hectic directions to Fritz:

> "A peafowl's breast flesh will not be sweet and tender and properly developed unless it is well protected from all alarms, especially from the air to prevent nervousness, and Long Island is full of airplanes. The goose for this evening, with the stuffing as arranged, will be quite satisfactory. The kid will be idea for tomorrow. . . . Friday is a problem. If we try the peafowl we shall merely be inviting catastrophe. . . . Let us try a new tack entirely. Do you know shish kabab? I have had it in Turkey. Marinate thin slices of tender lamb for several hours in red wine and spices. Here, I'll put it down: thyme, mace, peppercorn, garlic—"
>
> I stood and took it in. It looked hopeless. There was no question but that it was the beginning of a major relapse. (66)

Archie realizes the monologue about food goes beyond the usual culinary technicalities in which Wolfe likes to engage sometimes. Fritz's competence in the running of the kitchen is beyond doubt, and his culinary skills have been acknowledged time and again. The obsessive-compulsive relapses, however, have a deep personal origin rather than a plain dissatisfaction with the food served. The frustration of a dead-end street in the investigation—temporary as always—threatens the deductive strength of the great man, and he quickly finds respite in talking and/or consuming most outrageous quantities of food in combinations that have little to offer to his gourmand palate. Miraculously, Archie manages to interrupt this uncontrollable outburst by introducing some new evidence in the case, a moment that probably coincides with a deductive clearing in Wolfe's own mind. The result is another female guest being welcomed at the table to enjoy Fritz's cooking under much saner directions. "The fricandeau should be ample. Add lettuce to the salad if the endive is short, and of course increase the oil. Chill a bottle of the '28 Marcobrunner" (138).

On another occasion, Wolfe is having "rice fritters with black currant jam and endive with tarragon, for lunch" (72), while Archie is trying to coax a valuable witness to accompany him back to the brownstone for an urgent interview. The witness is as stubborn as she is beautiful, so they end up stopping for lunch in a restaurant near the fashion house. We can clearly detect the concern in Archie's narrative voice when he contemplates the choice: "Moreland's was one of those dumps where they slice roast beef as thin as paper and specialize in vegetable plates" (75). For the fashion model, perhaps, these dishes are desirable, but for the hard-working sidekick there are clear drawbacks to such a restaurant, especially with the thought of what Wolfe is enjoying at home. The order does not surprise us when Archie notes, "She ordered some kind of goo, and hot tea, and I favored the pork and beans, with a glass of milk" (75).

At the end of *The Red Box*, when the criminal minds are about to get exposed and the murders cracked, Archie describes one of those peaceful, cozy breakfast routines that the male household cherishes,

> As usual, Fritz took a tray of orange juice, crackers, and chocolate to Wolfe's room at the appointed moment. . . . I was seated at the little table in the kitchen, doing the right thing by a pile of toast and four eggs cooked in black butter and sherry under a cover on a slow fire. (223)

There is hardly anything to be done but for Wolfe to invite all involved to his home, criminals and police together, in order to tell the elaborate story that explains motives and methods of murder, therefore to expose the mastermind behind the poisoning. On such an occasion Wolfe is at his rhetorical best, contained, majestic, still sipping his favorite beer. Those who don't know him too well might mistake this calm, relaxed detective for a gullible, overweight joker, but people like Archie and Inspector Cramer know that Wolfe is about to produce a formidable strike in between hearty draughts of beer. In the spirit of their frenemy relationship, Inspector Cramer cannot help but say to Archie, "He ought to start a brewery. Some great men, when they die, leave their brains to a scientific laboratory. Wolfe ought to leave his stomach" (205).

Too Many Cooks

In terms of Stout's use of food in writing, the fifth novel of the Nero Wolfe series, *Too Many Cooks* (1938), offers the reader a gastronomic fête, courtesy of the so-called "Les Quinze Maîtres," or the fifteen masters, at the center of a very convoluted murder case. Wolfe leaves his home in New York to participate in a culinary celebration of haute cuisine in the remote Kanawha Spa resort in West Virginia, yet he gets involved in the investigation of a murder that almost costs him his own life, too. Comic and entertaining, this novel has, literally, all the best ingredients used in the series so far: unexpected events, sharp dialogues between the protagonists, a gallery of unforgettable characters, plus an array of mouth-watering descriptions of dishes from world cuisine that we might find to be slightly out of our reach today. A new element here, in comparison with the previous novels, is an unexpected look at racial discrimination, which is quite unusual for a detective novel of the late 1930s. Without spooning out the portions of equality and justice too generously, Stout masterfully ladles a new ingredient into the well-established series.

The novel opens with a brief foreword by Archie in which he apologetically explains, "I used as few French and miscellaneous fancy words as possible in writing up this stunt of Nero Wolfe's but I couldn't keep them out altogether, on account of the kind of people involved." The people involved are renowned chefs comprising the select group of Les Quinze Maîtres who share the top spots in a worldwide competition for prestige and who speak the international language of culinary success— French. Archie, because of his already established lack of sophisticated verbal dexterity, experiences frequent difficulties with the lingo. Wolfe's place in this select group, however, comes naturally since he is the ultimate gourmand and a genius besides. The group itself is as diverse as it comes in terms of ethnicities and origin: there is one Serbian, one Russian, four French, a couple of Italian, and a couple of English chefs. There is much competition and bad blood displayed between some of the them from the very beginning, and Wolfe will soon turn from a special guest into a murder investigator.

There are two reasons for Wolfe to leave the comforts of his home as the novel opens: one is to make a speech (by invitation, of course) on the last night of the culinary "Olympics" on a very specific topic, as he shares with one of the eminent French chefs traveling on the same train to the event:

> "Mr. Servan has invited me to speak on—as he stated the subject: *Contributions Américaines à la Haute Cuisine.*"
>
> "Bah!" Berin snorted. "There are none."
>
> Wolfe raised his brows. "None, sir?"
>
> "None. I am told there is good family cooking in America; I haven't sampled it. I have heard of the New England boiled dinner and corn pone and clam chowder and milk gravy. This is for the multitude and certainly not to be scorned if good. But it is not for masters." He snorted again. "These things are to la haute cuisine what sentimental love songs are to Beethoven and Wagner." (7)

Wolfe easily accepts such a challenge. He has plenty to say on this occasion and is eager to defend his opinion even more eloquently later at the official dinner in Kanawha Spa. Chef Berin is one of the likable chefs in the group, but the detective cannot spare him and bombards him with a tirade about the dishes that make American cooking competitive on grand scale:

> "Indeed." Wolfe wiggled a finger at him. "Have you eaten terrapin stewed with butter and chicken broth and sherry?"
>
> "No."
>
> "Have you eaten a planked porterhouse steak, two inches thick, surrendering hot red juice under the knife, garnished with American parsley and slices of fresh limes, encompassed with mashed potatoes which melt on the tongue, and escorted by thick slices of fresh mushrooms faintly underdone?" (7)

The list goes on for a while, and Berin will be wondering, probably, how he got himself cornered in such a debate on a train with an extremely well-informed and practiced gourmand. Archie and the rest of the passengers are listening to this outpouring with fascination, while Wolfe continues: "Or the Creole Tripe of New Orleans? Or Missouri Boone Country ham, baked with vinegar, molasses, Worcestershire, sweet cider and herbs? Or Chicken Marengo? Or chicken in curdled egg sauce, with raisins, onions, almonds, sherry and Mexican sausage?" (7). The list of dishes is so long and detailed that it reminds us of a metaphorical "culinary duel" between two proud representatives of French and American cuisines. The fascinating aspect of this conversation is that it is set out in a detective novel like *Too Many Cooks*, which "explicitly intertwines crime narrative with issues of national and cultural identity" (Michelis 150). What is particularly interesting, though, is that Wolfe, not American by birth, has come to appreciate the host country for the best it has to offer in terms of culinary delights. Berin, on the other hand, quips appreciatively, "You live in the wrong country." And Wolfe answers, "Yes? Wait till you taste terrapin Maryland. Or even, if I may say so, oyster pie à la Nero Wolfe, prepared by Fritz Brenner. In comparison with American oysters, those of Europe are mere blobs of coppery protoplasm" (12).

The second reason for Wolfe to leave his home on such a challenging "expedition" is actually even more personal than defending American cuisine: he is in in search of the holy grail of haute cuisine—at least in his books—a specific sausage recipe that left an indelible mark in his mind back when he was young, in "Spain on a confidential mission for the Austrian government" (9). Through an almost poetic description of his casual stroll to a little inn, an encounter with the proprietor who serves him a dish of sausages prepared by her son, it becomes obvious that Wolfe falls in love with it. The story about the sausage sounds comic at the same time, but it clearly portrays his decades-long appreciation and infatuation with that recipe. Would we be surprised to find out that the master of that legendary creation is none other than Berin himself and the name of the sausage, *saucisse minuit*? Wolfe is desperate to get the recipe at any cost, for as he says very seriously, "I recognized that sausage as high art. . . . I did not have to wait for fame to perceive greatness" (10). Berin, like so many chefs, is unwilling even to think about sharing or selling his renowned recipe, despite the sincere admiration of the detective.

> I confess again: I agreed to this outrageous journey, not only because of the honor of the invitation. Chiefly my purpose was to meet you. I have only so long to live—so many books to read, so many ironies to contemplate, so many meals to eat. . . . Five thousand dollars. I detest haggling. (12)

No secret recipe will come out of Berin's mouth on the train, and Wolfe will have to take no for an answer this time, but the plotline will thicken soon enough, and he will have another opportunity to obtain the legendary formula.

From the point of view of Archie, just listening to such a culinary conversation and the mentioning of the outrageous price for a sausage recipe are enough to make him desperate to get off the train. Soon, as they reach Kanawha Spa, he will tell us sincerely,

There was lots of junk to look at if you happened to be interested in it—big clusters of pink flowers everywhere on bushes . . . and a brook zipping along with little bridges across it here and there, and some kind of wild trees in bloom, and birds and evergreens and so on . . . but I must admit it's a poor place to look for excitement. (26)

For Archie who is well versed in the language of the urban jungle, "the junk" of this peaceful resort does not say much, yet real excitement will ensue soon enough. It is inspired by sour exchanges between some of the chefs, the odd mix of accompanying wives and girlfriends, and one very recognizable femme fatale, the "swamp-woman" (33), chef Laszio's wife, Dina.

There is food and more food, and lots of preparations in the reunion of Les Quinze Maîtres or, as Archie calls it, "the gastronomical World's Series" (38). Soon there is a minor event that introduces possible complications ahead: someone tries to poison Chef Laszio while he is preparing Meadowbrook dressing for a salad. As his wife testifies, "They all know that he mixes the sugar and lemon juice and sour cream an hour ahead of time" (34)—a mixing of the sugar and arsenic will make the dressing fatal—but Laszio gets away unhurt this time. Wolfe seems more fascinated by the psychological profile of the "swamp-woman" than by the chef's close call with death.

Archie will try, in his own words, to describe the dinner and the tasting competition planned later that evening. We can only wonder at the extent, fictional as it is, of the quality and volume described, when we have several of Les Quinze Maîtres preparing a dish each. With regard to food, we agree that this novel is not an exception but that the narrative "utilizes food as an ambiguous signifier whose meaning is contingent on context and specific situations" (Michelis 152). In *Too Many Cooks*, the specific situation utilizes as many food signifiers as necessary via Archie's description to baffle the noninitiated among readers in the same way he feels baffled:

The dinner at Pocahontas Pavilion that evening was elegant as to provender, but a little confused in other respects. The soup, by Louis Servan, looked like any consommé, but it wasn't just any. . . . The fish, by Leon Blanc, was little six-inch trout, four to a customer, with a light brown sauce with capers in it, and a tang that didn't seem to come from lemon or any vinegar I had ever heard of. . . . The entrée, by Pierre Mondor, was of such nature that I imitated some of the others and had two helpings . . . and the main ingredients were beef marrow, cracker crumbs, white wine and chicken breast. . . . The roast was young duck à la Mr. Richards, by Marko Vukcic. (37–38)

Readers will try to keep up with the catalog of gourmet dishes and the slightly comic atmosphere of this epicurean dinner that Archie tries to draw for us. As Adam Gopnik has argued about the point of using food in fiction,

> There are four kinds of food in books: food that is served by an author to characters who are not expected to taste it; food that is served by an author to characters in order to show who they are; food that an author cooks for characters in order to eat it with them; and, last (and most recent), food that an author cooks for characters but actually serves to the reader.

In this sense, as readers of the novel, we are easily transformed into observers, alas not participants, of a dinner of epic proportions that will soon have an epic outcome, too. If we agree with Gopnik's classification, we would acknowledge that Stout, ahead of contemporary authors' interest in using food in their works, has successfully mixed, in fact, the second and fourth kinds of food use in fiction: the reader learns a lot about the characters from their choices of food, but, at the same time, we are aware of the extra privilege, as it seems, of sitting down at the same table with the characters, metaphorically speaking.

After the elaborate dinner, which Archie recounts, comes the tasting competition, as Wolfe tells him:

> After the digestion of dinner there is to be a test. The cook will roast squabs, and Mr. Laszio, who volunteered for the function, will make a quantity of Sauce Printemps. That sauce contains nine seasonings, besides salt: cayenne, celery, shallots, chives, chervil, tarragon, peppercorn, thyme and parsley. Nine dishes of it will be prepared, and each will lack one of the seasonings, a different one. . . . The gathering will be in the parlor, and each will go to the dining room, singly to prevent discussion, taste the sauce on bits of squab, and record which dish lacks chives, which peppercorn, and so on. . . . You will not be included. Only the members of Les Quinze Maîtres and myself. (36–37)

At that particular moment, after an elaborate and really long dinner, we might guess that Archie will be only too happy that he is not invited to take the test. Wolfe, like a true gourmand, is more than ready to participate in this competition of top chefs, plus he is only too aware of the abilities of his sidekick in this area. As Archie notes, "There are various kinds of experiments that Wolfe might try with me as the subject, but none of them would be gastronomical" (45).

Ten top chefs present—too many, if we refer to the title of the novel—and Stout is ready to stir a proper murder case with the demise of one. The great detective is somewhat unwilling to investigate the murder; in fact, he has his own deadline to leave Kanawha Spa for New York, but the unfortunate attempt on his own life prompts him to speed up the deductive process before he retreats to his peaceful brownstone, and Chef Berin gets arrested, wrongly, for the murder. In the meantime, Wolfe has a few more eclectic meals to enjoy, if it's possible to do so with a minor wound on his face, plus to deliver the closing speech.

Despite the crime that throws the gathering in an obvious turmoil, food has to be eaten and spoken about, so Chef Servan is preparing his own speech entitled "Les Mysterès du Goût" (the mysteries of taste) "on the preparation of which he had spent two years" (75). Archie, as always, enjoys an excellent meal of rabbit stew, a *civet de lapin* that is "in fact a perfection, except for a slight excess of bouquet garni" (90), if we trust Chef Blanc's opinion. He is even ready to enjoy his cognac and listen to Chef Servan's speech up to the point when it opens in French. As Archie simply says about that experience, "I guess it was a good talk" (91).

The closing dinner does justice to a meeting of Les Quinze Maîtres, which happens only once every five years. The exquisite menu is dedicated to the contributions of American cooking to haute cuisine, as the topic of Wolfe's speech has prompted. It consists of a fascinating array of dishes cooked by Chef Servan: "oysters baked in the shell, terrapin Maryland, beaten biscuits, pan broiled young turkey, rice croquettes with quince jelly, lima beans in cream, Sally Lunn [bread rolls], avocado todhunter, pineapple sherbet, sponge cake, Wisconsin dairy cheese, black coffee" (157). Archie, like the rest of the lucky diners, tucks into the food, but there is a physical limit to how much he can consume in comparison with the rest. He quickly notes, "Those guys eating were like a woman packing a trunk—it's not a question of capacity but of how much she has to put in. . . . Unquestionably it was first class fodder" (158–59).

After this gastronomic spread, there is not much left for Wolfe but to put into words, in the way he knows best, the whole dining experience and to praise American cuisine—all that, plus expose the murderer and his accomplice. Archie is listening attentively, admiring the persuasive rhetorical strength of his patron, and he knows that the deductive power will impress as well. The detective closes his brilliant speech by simply saying to his audience, "I have finished my remarks on cooking.

Now I am going to talk to you about murder" (161), and an equally elegant exposure of the murderer follows. Justice is served in the end, and the owner of the "sacred" recipe for *saucisse minuit* gifts it to a genius detective as a symbol of his deepest gratitude.

Stout's achievement in the first five Nero Wolfe novels does not disappoint when it comes to getting exciting depictions and references to food. We are reminded that "Great masters are not meant to offer small plates" (Gopnik), so it will not be surprising to find out that, in addition to the Nero Wolfe novels, Stout compiled three cookbooks with recipes drawn from the series. In the end, it seems that Majors has a valid point when she argues that "food is also a replicable art. We make our favorite dishes again and again; we buy cookbooks and magazines to discover new ways of treating the same ingredients. . . . In these ways, food is an art that is with us more than any other, every time we grocery shop or sauté onions in butter" (80).

The arguably "replicable art" that Stout offers can be found in his *Recipes from the Fifteenth Annual Meeting of Les Quinze Maîtres* (1938) once appearing as an appendix to *Too Many Cooks,* and *The Nero Wolfe Cookbook* (1973), as well as in a separate box of recipes that was sold a few months before the actual publication of *Too Many Cooks* in 1938. The idea behind these cookbooks, successful as they proved to be, was to offer readers Wolfe's "recipes for dishes as hearty and robust as the crimes which he undertakes to solve; and rules for delicacies as ephemeral as the orchids he tends with such meticulous care," as the introduction to *Recipes from the Fifteenth Annual Meeting* states (qtd. in Davies 474). For those willing to replicate a number of such art forms like "terrapin stewed in butter" or "squirrel stew" or the more manageable "Nero Wolfe's soufflé of sweet potato with rum" and "Nero Wolfe's cream soup Vichyssoise," the cookbooks still remain essential reading and guides.

Choosing a detective novel to read today is easier than ever. The reader's fascination with the process of detection, with investigation of crimes and criminal behavior, has many ways to get channeled in the work of innovative masters of the genre. Stout is not an exception in this sense: his amazing inventiveness is neatly mirrored in complex plotlines and characters that we will remember well. In the long run, encountering the Nero Wolfe series reminds us that

> The act of reading is always a matter of a task begun as much as of a message understood, something that begins on a flat surface, counter or page, and then gets stirred and chopped and blended until what we make, in the end, is a dish, or story, all our own. (Gopnik)

Stout's literary skills in portraying the Wolfe-Goodwin tandem in some forty novels is on par with his creating a world as tangible as the food they eat and talk about with such regularity. Making *their* story ours is a pleasure that can easily be repeated beyond the first five novels in the series. Finally, as the great detective concludes, "It is delightful to talk about food, but infinitely more delightful to eat it; and we have eaten" (*Too Many Cooks* 159).

WORKS CITED

Anderson, M. Jean, Barbara Pezzotti, and Carolina Miranda. "The Meaning of Food in Crime Fiction." *The Conversation*, August 23, 2018, https://theconversation.com /friday-essay-the-meaning-of-food-in-crime-fiction-98005.

Carter, Miranda. "Dining with Death: Crime Fiction's Long Affair with Food." *The Guardian*, November 5, 2016, www.theguardian.com/books/2016/nov/05/dining -death-crime-fiction-miranda-carter.

Chandler, Raymond. "The Simple Act of Murder." *The Art of the Mystery Story: A Collection of Critical Stories*, edited by Howard Haycraft, Simon & Schuster, 1946, pp. 222–37.

Confidential Memo. Appendix to *Fer-de-Lance | The League of Frightened Men*, by Rex Stout, Bantam Books, 2008.

Davies, Ross E. "Another Nero Wolfe Cookbook." George Mason Law & Economics Research Paper No. 12-06, *Green Bag Almanac and Reader*, 2012, pp. 473–514.

Gopnik, Adam. "What's the Point of Food in Fiction?" *New Yorker*, April 2, 2007, www .newyorker.com/magazine/2007/04/09/cooked-books.

Grella, George. "Murder and Manners: The Formal Detective Novel." *NOVEL: A Forum on Fiction*, vol. 4, no. 1, 1970, pp. 30–48.

Hart, Carolyn G. Introduction to *The Red Box*, by Rex Stout. *The Rubber Band | The Red Box*, Bantam, 2009.

Littlejohn, John. "Rex Stout: Fortune and Formula." *Clues*, vol. 29, no. 2, 2011, pp. 58–65.

Majors, Kerri. "Out of the Frying Pan: Food in Fiction." *Midwest Quarterly*, vol. 54, no. 1, 2012, pp. 67–81.

McBride, O. E. *Stout Fellow: A Guide through Nero Wolfe's World*. iUniverse, 2003.

Michelis, Angelica. "Food and Crime: What's Eating the Crime Novel?" *European Journal of English Studies*, vol. 14, no. 2, 2010, pp. 143–57.

Sayers, Dorothy L. Introduction to *The Omnibus of Crime*. *The Art of the Mystery Story: A Collection of Critical Stories*, edited by Howard Haycraft, Simon & Schuster, 1946, pp. 71–109.

Stout, Rex. *Fer-de-Lance | The League of Frightened Men*. Bantam, 2008.

———. *The Rubber Band | The Red Box*. Bantam, 2009.

———. *Too Many Cooks | Champagne for One*. Bantam, 2009.

"I can't work up an appetite just because you want me to"

(Not) Eating One's Identity in
J. D. Salinger's Short Stories

SERENA DEMICHELIS

While J. D. Salinger's "Franny" (1955) has been explored from several perspectives, both as a single work and as part of the so-called Glass family saga, very little attention has been paid to the significance of its setting. The story takes place in a restaurant, a place that, as we shall see, has a strong relation to the identities of its two principal characters. In the short story, the female protagonist, Franny, arrives at the train station of a university town (by exclusion, we understand it is Princeton) to meet her boyfriend, Lane Coutell. Their carefully planned schedule begins with lunch at an "appropriate" restaurant, a normatively controlled situation:

> About an hour later, the two were sitting at a comparatively isolated table in a restaurant called Sickler's, downtown, a highly favored place among, chiefly, the intellectual fringe of students at the college—the same students, more or less, who, had they been Yale or Harvard men, might rather too casually have steered their dates away from Mory's or Cronin's. Sickler's, it might be said, was the only restaurant in town where the steaks weren't "that thick"—thumb and index finger held an inch apart. Sickler's was Snails. Sickler's was where a student and his date either both ordered salad or, usually, neither of them did, because of the garlic seasoning. (9)

"Food," Roland Barthes argues, is "charged with signifying the situation in which it is used" (25). In Salinger, food and consumption choices throughout the short story serve the purpose of signifying a situation of rejection, led by concerns regarding gender and culture. Moreover, similar food habits and situations in other stories by Salinger reinforce the pervasiveness of such a theme.

Not Eating and Sexual Rejection

The connection between food and sensuality is age-old. The preparation of food, indeed, entails a dimension of caring that can evolve into seduction and affirmation of femininity, while at the same time granting agency to the subjects involved in such endeavor (Landrigan 2014). Salinger's awareness of the potential formative power of "food situations" shows from the very first lines set in the restaurant. At Sickler's, students and their dates "either both ordered salad or, usually, neither of them did, because of the garlic seasoning" (9), which would, one suspects, represent an obstacle to intimacy. Lane Coutell, Franny's date, breaks the tacit rule by ordering salad on his own and admitting that he is "going to reek of garlic" (26).

In the cab from the station, Franny realizes that she has not missed Lane at all since they last met. While the slow mounting of her discomfort is often attributed to a generalized spiritual dissatisfaction with herself and the world,[1] the cause for her distress might be something more specific. Spending the weekend, and possibly the night, with Lane entails a perspective of intimacy, openly unveiled only in the final paragraph of the story, that she seems to find unbearable, if not repulsive. Defeating expectations that her presence at Princeton has contributed to building, Franny is perhaps psychologically attempting to find a way out of a situation she *thinks* she is supposed to find desirable—yet she feels, instead, all the guilt and confusion that such a clash of feelings can entail. At the same time, the whole process helps Franny develop a stronger identity, one that cannot (and does not wish to) comply with her supposed role as or on the "ideal college date."

The first step in her heading in this direction manifests as a refusal to participate in the canonical expectations implied in having lunch at Sickler's: Franny will not have the house's specials, and while she drinks martinis (an "appropriate" drink), she will only have a chicken sandwich and a glass of milk for lunch. Her choices outrage Lane, who instead gorges himself on frogs' legs, snails, and salad. Franny's choice of a meal is anti-elitist, ascetic, and reminiscent of childhood. This warning flag is grossly misunderstood by Lane, who is annoyed at Franny and acts as if she were making a show of being "different": "'This is going to be a real little doll of a weekend,' he said. 'A chicken sandwich, for God's sake'" (18). Anything distracting Franny's attention from Lane's personal exhibition of "brilliantness" and the drift of his own conversation is clearly unwelcome. This includes her criticism of departmental academic staff, to which he ultimately replies, "You think *you're* a genius?" (22), as well as her tale about *The Way of a Pilgrim*, which Lane consistently ignores. His comment, offered over the start of their meal, overtly breaches conversational rules and brings the dialogue back to *his* term paper:

> Lane nodded. He cut into his salad with his fork. "I hope to God we get time over the weekend so that you can take a quick look at this goddam paper I told you about," he said. "I don't know. I may not do a damn thing with it—I mean try to publish it or what have you—but I'd like you to sort of glance through it while you're here." (27)

Lane, unlike Franny, eats consistently throughout the conversation and is closely observed while doing so.[2] He is characterized by his relationship to his food as much as Franny is by hers, often in terms that underline his peculiar care for his meal ("attending," "shifted his attention," "swallowed") but that are, at the same time, aggressive ("dismembering," "cut into his salad," "cut into his last pair of frogs' legs," "disjoint a pair of frogs' legs").

By contrast, Franny's near "not eating" becomes a sort of performance and a reaffirmation of independence, a way of regaining control and resisting assimilation into Lane's world. When, at the end of the story, the young man suggests he could sneak into Franny's rented room, she does not reply: self-starvation and her subsequent passing out give her a way out of Lane's unwanted attention. By sending him away to look for water, she interposes distance and highlights her weakness in face of his energetic, myopic physicality.

"Franny" and the "Pregnancy Plot"

The history of "Franny" criticism is characterized by the same kind of uncomprehending behavior that Salinger has Lane play out so masterfully. One of the first major works of criticism about Salinger's fiction described Franny's attitude as "childish" (while Lane is described as "self-consciously diffident" [French 141]). *Franny and Zooey*, in its entirety, was dismissed by fellow writers and critics, who labeled it "*Positive Thinking* for the upper middle classes, . . . *Double Your Energy and*

Live Without Fatigue for Sarah Lawrence girls" (Didion, qtd. in Grunwald 79).

In rather early days, the story has been read as a subliminal narrative of homoerotic desire, made mostly explicit by Franny's attempts to virtually "castrate" her date. Daniel Seitzman went as far as to state that Franny's rejection of men was the ultimate cause of what he calls "her problem": "Franny's hostility, her intense rivalry, and her scarcely concealed wish to emasculate all men are the root of her problem" (59). In the early 1990s, John Paul Wenke acknowledged Franny's wish not to comply with "the role of supportive, adoring female" (70). This line of analysis eventually fell into the trap of the "pregnancy plot" reading of "Franny" suggested by many (Laird 47; Fiedler, "War" 14; Wenke 74–75). Pregnancy has, in fact, been advanced as an explanation for Franny's behavior, but while there are no possible indications as to this being a fact in later works,[3] much has been built upon a few textual "clues."

Indeed, Salinger seems to wink at the possibility of Franny being pregnant—but the person who is feeding readers' suspicions is, more than the protagonist herself, the old waiter: "The waiter, who was not a young man, seemed to look for an instant at her pallor and damp brow, then bowed and left" (23). The words that prompted the "pregnancy plot" are ultimately Lane's, but they remain unconfirmed by the real protagonist: "'You know how long it's been?' Lane said. 'When was that Friday night? Way the hell early last month, wasn't it?' He shook his head. 'That's no good. Too goddam long between drinks. To put it crassly'" (32). In the micro-universe built in the story's pages, the world of men looks at the only girl in the "cast" with a mixture of misunderstanding and pretentious marvel. As much as Lane cannot conceive of Franny's behavior as a form of rejection, the old waiter can only speculate as to her possible state of pregnancy.

However, Franny's self-starvation is rather a way of sabotaging the date without being possibly held responsible for it. Franny reclaims agency in a situation of previous powerlessness; moreover, starvation allows her to distance herself from Lane, who instead keeps on eating relentlessly, uninterested to the point of even talking to his food ("'Hold still,' Lane said to a pair of frogs' legs" [26]). "Franny" is not the gospel of Frances Glass but the analysis of a situation of perceived exceptionality, one that can concern female subjects in a male-oriented world. Indeed, in "Franny," Salinger seems to be using a "mass culture–reminiscent narrator to reveal and review the clichés that assemble postwar femininity and womanhood" (Rodrigues 120), and Franny's resistance to being assimilated into a set of clichés—a not always successful effort—is reflected in her food habits.

In the final part of the dialogue, Lane shifts topics once again, abruptly dismissing Franny's interest for the *Way of a Pilgrim* and turning to his superficial love for her: "Anyway. Just in case I forgot to mention it. I love you. Did I get around to mentioning that?" Deliberately flaunting the Gricean maxim of relation, Franny answers: "Lane, would you excuse me again for just a second?" (30–31). Her closing speech act in the main dialogue thus stresses her rejection of social expectations. This choice is mirrored in her final performance of prayer, in direct contrast to Lane's very last words:

> "O.K., I'll be right back. Don't move." He left the room.
>
> Alone, Franny lay quite still, looking at the ceiling.
>
> Her lips began to move, forming soundless words, and they continued to move. (33)

Lane's intimation for immobilism in the closing lines of the text is opposed by Franny, whose lips "continue to move": this wish for stasis, far from simply defining Lane as a flat character, places him in a dimension of conservativism, one that causes Franny to feel like an estranged (and unwanted) subject, even beyond the immediate context of the date.

Elitism and the Danger of Contamination

By rejecting the house specials, Franny has resisted being assimilated into the guise of the ideal college girl, and she has found an indirect way to express all the strength of her feelings of rejection. However, the food incorporated or not incorporated by the two protagonists gains significance also on another level, which flows from the specific context of a purportedly romantic lunch before evolving into a display of their contemporary sociodemographic reality. Sickler's is a restaurant, but, as Salinger's text makes clear, it is not just *any* restaurant: "Sickler's was Snails" (8; capitalized in the original). The place is a "favored" one among the "intellectual fringe" of Princeton students, supposedly a little less "traditional" than Mory's at Yale and Cronin's at Harvard (8). However, Franny soon realizes how Lane's attitude is an expression of a distinct type of establishment, one symbolic of a particular class and way of life.

As of 1955, Princeton was still the more conservative and less diverse among the "Big Three," with a history of exclusion that was being challenged but had not yet been overcome. In his extensive study on the processes of selection in Ivy League colleges, Jerome Karabel addresses the issue: in 1932 when a new president, who remained in charge until 1957, was taking up his role, Princeton "had many of the qualities of an exclusive, self-perpetuating private club" (228). The comparison is not Karabel's: Princeton presidents and students were the first to admit that the college was more of a country club than a university known for academic excellence. At many times in the college's long history, it merely looked like academic merit was one of the requirements, but absolutely not the most important one, for admission.

The "club" could basically only be accessed by socially desirable individuals, a label that functioned as an umbrella term for fertile grounds of discrimination and prejudice. Moreover, alumni sons (the college was not yet coeducational) were favored in the process of admission, so much so that

> [a]s late as 1958, in a brochure distributed to the alumni, Princeton described its policy bluntly: "Actually, the Princeton son does not have to compete against non-Princeton sons. *No matter how many other boys apply, the Princeton son is judged on this one question: can he be expected to graduate?* If so, he's admitted." (240; emphasis in the original)

The ideal Princeton man was a white, Protestant, economically privileged male, possibly "generationally Princetonian" and coming out of some private boarding school. Black people, Jews, other southern or eastern European immigrants, Irish, ethnically non-Caucasians, and economically disadvantaged youths were either openly or covertly prohibited admission. Discrimination was enacted on levels that ranged from entry regulations and quotas to exclusion from the university's popular eating clubs. The latter institutions held a significant place in enforcing discriminating practices, which made social life at the university unbearable for "unclubbable" students (Karabel 229), among whom Jews suffered marginalization in significant proportions.

Formally independent from the university but nonetheless acknowledged as crucial for students' social life, eating clubs have a history dating back to the end of the nineteenth century, when the lack of dining facilities brought to the institution the first clubs; nowadays, of the eleven eating clubs among which students can choose, six still enact a process of selection known as "bicker." To be deemed "undesirable" by an eating club translated (and, up to a certain point, still translates) into being "relegated to the margins of student life" and thus belonging to "a painfully visible second-class status" (Karabel 229, 243). Even as recently as

2019, students at Princeton pointed out how "the eating club system *de facto* segregates, . . . and this country has a long dark history of using dining as a social sorting system" (Miller, page number unavailable).

While not explicitly prohibited access (as with Black people [Karabel 232]), a Jewish presence was most unwelcome. Famously, Princeton was considered as "the traditionally most inhospitable if not outright anti-Semitic of Ivy League colleges" (Sanua 391), and eating clubs were the ideal place to express such views against Jewish students, who "would end up being cut from the clubs on the pretext of being 'socially unacceptable,' which meant a virtual end to one's Princeton career" (399). Students rejected by popular eating clubs, or those who did not even apply because of their blatant discriminatory policies, joined Prospect, a club "at the bottom of the hierarchy" (Karabel 301), which, in 1958, was "by far the most Jewish of the clubs." The infamous Dirty Bicker of the same year was perhaps the most obvious example of how unwritten discriminatory rules were common practice within the college and its eating clubs, and it exposed the anti-Semitic views of the Princetonian elite to the eyes of the national public and press.[4]

Concomitant to the religious issue, moreover, women were still out of the student body altogether: the college became coeducational in the 1960s, once again not due to a particular desire for inclusion as much as to the fear of losing male candidates to universities that had already opened to female enrollment (as at Harvard and Yale). In this respect, Princeton once again enacted exclusion on the level of eating clubs, and it was not until 1992 that *all* clubs (following a lawsuit filed with the New Jersey Division of Civil Rights) started admitting women.

In this context, Franny's "social identity" is a mark of her times: she is a young half-Jewish (and half–Irish Catholic: another minority)[5] woman of middle-class background,[6] belonging to a generation young enough to be able to attend boarding schools ("Exeter or someplace" [7]) but too old to envision a Princeton that both she and her date could attend. She is not described as a social pariah, and she surely tries to show some interest in the social activities typically offered to university students. However, marginalization in general and anti-Semitism in particular do not belong to the past, no matter how many steps forward society seems to be taking. And while Lane is oblivious, if not fully integrated into the "Princeton spirit,"[7] Franny is profoundly aware of the abyss separating them. Once again, food choices play a significant role in articulating this difference.

Sickler's specials are clearly designed for a clientele that fully conforms to the Princetonian ideal—a WASP one, in short. Lane gorges himself on a vast selection of dishes, while Franny "looked down at the menu on her plate, and consulted it without picking it up. 'All I want's a chicken sandwich. And maybe a glass of milk. . . . You order what you want and all, though. I mean, take snails and octopuses and things. Octopi. I'm really not that hungry'" (18).[8] Snails, octopus, frogs' legs: none of these foods are kosher. Truth be said, chicken and milk *together* are also not kosher, which Franny seems to indicate by not consuming both of the foods together: "'I think I'll just finish my milk. But you have some,' Franny said. The waiter had just taken away her plate with the untouched chicken sandwich" (30).

James Bryan points out how, unlike Franny, Lane is "lustily" devouring "unclean things" (228). The uncleanliness of the "swarming animals" of Leviticus,[9] as opposed to cleaner chicken and plain milk, is not perceived as such by the young elitist, who makes a point about not caring nor believing in anything spiritual. Once Franny is done telling him the story of *The Way of a Pilgrim*, he first challenges her by asking, "You actually believe that stuff, or what?" (29), then he diminishes the argument by accusing it of being less than "elementary": "All that stuff . . . I don't think you leave any margin for the most elementary *psychology*. I mean I think all those religious experiences have a very obvious psychological background—you know what I mean" (30). After this exchange, significantly, Franny passes out one more time.

Salinger's relation to Judaism is a debated one. There is no way, however, he could have ignored micro- to macro-scale events and demonstrations of anti-Semitism surrounding virtually any aspect of his public life. In his first twenty-five years, Jerome David Salinger (a name that, in his daughter Margaret's words, was enough to make more than a few paths unwalkable to him [39]) attended courses at an Ivy League university (Columbia) and enrolled in the army: both places were filled with anti-Semitic sentiment. The fact that he chose to set "Franny" in an environment as "charged" as the Yale game weekend at Princeton, and at a restaurant that is a "favorite" of the university students, is thus all the more significant if we want to look at how food habits and consumption shape individuals in their story-world.

Conclusion

Salinger's popular short story "Franny" places the food choices and habits of the two main characters in a significant critical position. Insofar as eating habits can help define identities, Franny Glass's behavior in these terms has contributed to her placement within a particular identity category, one that informs and prompts her actions and, consequently, the architecture of the story's plot. My view is both critical of previous interpretations of the text and purposeful in terms of a reevaluation of Salinger's oeuvre within the tradition of Jewish American writers. Ellyn Lem adopted the lens of food and eating habits to tackle the issue of Jewishness in Anzia Yezierska and Alice B. Toklas, both of whom had their "religious affiliation" similarly questioned. Indeed, "food has been instrumental in maintaining ethnic distinctions among immigrants to the United States and their descendants, especially in the face of assimilative pressures" (Kraut; qtd. in Lem 410), and, as Lem also notes, "[n]o ethnic group has more ritual foodways and taboos than the Jews" (416). For a writer like Salinger, in whose works a notable few yet precise types of actions tend to occur repeatedly, the very insistence on food habits demands attention and stimulates reflection. "Franny," in particular, is a text where eating/not eating; the nature of the food; and the nature of the place, establishment, and era in which the food is eaten are all crucial for a fuller understanding of the story.

NOTES

1. Franny's discomfort acquires more sense in light of what happens in "Zooey," the companion short story published in 1957. See Gehlawat on how *Franny and Zooey,* the 1961 volume containing both stories, "anticipates the conditions of a cultural crisis we now recognize as postmodernism" (59).

2. "'How's the play?' Lane asked, attending to his snails." (21)
"Lane waited till he had chewed and swallowed, then said, 'Why, for God's sake? I thought the goddam theatre was your passion.'" (21)
"Lane had finished his snails. He sat looking deliberately expressionless." (22)
"Lane had started in on his frogs' legs."(24)
"'The little book in my bag?' Franny said. She watched him disjoint a pair of frogs' legs." (25)
"She watched Lane eat for a moment." (25)
"Lane had just shifted his attention from the frogs' legs to the salad." (25)
"Franny seemed intensely interested in the way Lane was dismembering his frogs' legs. Her eyes remained fixed on the plate as she spoke." (25)
"She watched him butter another piece of bread." (27)

3. No mention of a baby is made, for instance, in "Seymour: An Introduction," which nonetheless gives out a few details about the family as of 1959—including the number of Boo Boo's children. Wenke makes a similar observation, while still maintaining that the choice of suggesting a pregnancy was meant to remind readers that Franny is a flesh-and-blood person.

4. The process of "Bicker" leads selection into the most exclusive clubs at Princeton. In 1958, when attempts on the part of the community to enhance inclusiveness were resisted and thwarted, the discriminatory nature of the process was exposed (Sanua).

5. At the beginning of the century, "[a]t Princeton, whose country club reputation was not without justification, Catholics and Jews together made up only 5 percent of the freshmen" (Karabel 23). Indeed, "anti-Catholic and anti-Semitic sentiments found their way into a variety of mechanisms that were created in response to the undesirable social changes" (Coe and Davidson 236), though Catholics in general were perceived as "more assimilable than Jews" (240). This discrimination against Jews and the exclusion of women was already in the process of changing, though slowly, by 1955.

6. We learn from a subsequent comment by Buddy that it is thanks to the money earned from *It's a Wise Child* that the Glass children were able to go to college (J. D. Salinger, *Raise* 7).

7. At the beginning of the meal, Lane speaks of Flaubert as *lacking* "testicularity": this insistence on manliness is reminiscent of the arbitrary concept of "character," which had been included among the parameters to be evaluated upon admission into Ivy League colleges in the early twentieth century, and which was to influence the imagery of the ideal candidate for decades to come. The "Protestant *ethos*" ruling over the Big Three was such that even a candidate like Franklin Delano Roosevelt, independent of his desirable background, was considered as "somewhat lacking in those 'manly' qualities then so highly valued" (Karabel 16).

8. This is also not the first time a chicken sandwich makes a singularly remarkable appearance in Salinger's stories: in "Just Before the War with the Eskimos," Selena Graff's clumsy older brother Franklin offers half a chicken sandwich to Ginnie Maddox, the story's protagonist. The girl's unwillingness to dispose of the sandwich (as she was incapable of doing with a dead Easter chick) has been read in Christian terms, but, coming from the tradition of a New York "delicatessen," can easily be traced back to a markedly Jewish background. The same goes for the chicken broth a worried Bessie serves a prostrate Franny in the half-Jewish household portrayed in "Zooey": "cup of chicken soup" is an uncommonly appropriate choice. Besides being a "consecrated cup" (note that Salinger explains his symbol), it is sufficiently akin to the symbolic chicken sandwiches and Easter chicks. Finally, chicken soup is, according to Harry Golden's *For Two Cents Plain*, a standard panacea in Jewish households. (The Glasses are half-Jewish.) (Bryan 228)

9. "Every swarming thing that swarms upon the Earth is an abomination" (Lev. 11.41); though not swarming, frogs, like all amphibians and reptiles, are also forbidden food.

WORKS CITED

Barthes, Roland. "Towards a Psychosociology of Contemporary Food Consumption." In *Food and Culture: A Reader*, edited by Carole Counihan and Penny Van Esterik, 2nd ed., Routledge, 2018, pp. 25–32.

Bryan, James E. "J. D. Salinger: The Fat Lady and the Chicken Sandwich." *College English*, vol. 23, no. 3, 1961, pp. 226–29.

Coe, Deborah, and James D. Davidson. "The Origins of Legacy Admissions: A Sociological Explanation." *Review of Religious Research*, vol. 52, no. 3, 2011, pp. 233–47.

"Coeducation: History of Women at Princeton University." Princeton University Library, https://libguides.princeton.edu/c.php?g=84581&p=543232.

Fiedler, Leslie. *Fiedler on the Roof: Essays on Literature and Jewish Identity*. David Godine, 1991.

——— . "The War against the Academy." *Wisconsin Studies in Contemporary Literature*, vol. 5, no. 1, 1964, pp. 5–17.

Fischler, Claude. "Food, Self and Identity." *Social Science Information*, vol. 27, 1988, pp. 275–93.

French, Warren. *J. D. Salinger: Revisited*. Twayne, 1982.

Gardaphé, Fred L., and Wenying Xu. "Food in Multi-Ethnic Literatures." *MELUS*, vol. 32, no. 4, 2007, pp. 5–10.

Gehlawat, Monika. "Desperately Seeking Singularity in *Franny and Zooey.*" *Literature Interpretation Theory*, vol. 22, no. 1, 2011, pp. 59–77.

Grunwald, Henry Anatole. *Salinger: A Critical and Personal Portrait.* Harper Colophon, 1963.

Karabel, Jerome. *The Chosen: The Hidden History of Admission and Exclusion at Harvard, Yale and Princeton.* Mariner Books, 2005.

Kraut, Alan M. "Ethnic Foodways: The Significance of Food in the Designation of Cultural Boundaries between Immigrant Groups in the U.S., 1840–1921." *Journal of American Culture*, vol. 2, no. 3, 1979, pp. 409–20.

Laird, Martin. *Into the Silent Land: A Guide to the Christian Practice of Contemplation.* Oxford University Press, 2006.

Landrigan, Marissa. "'The Bread Rises Like a Voice': The Intersection of Food, Gender, and Place in the Writing of Sheryl St. Germain." *Interdisciplinary Studies in Literature and Environment*, vol. 21, no. 2, 2014, pp. 298–314.

Lem, Ellyn. "You say 'Canapé,' and I say 'Kreplach': Reading the Cultural Culinary Conflicts in Jewish American Writers." *Studies in American Jewish Literature*, vol. 21, 2002, pp. 94–107.

Miller, Jennifer. "Takeover at Princeton Quadrangle. First-generation, Low-income Students Are Commandeering One of the College's Historically Elitist Eating Clubs." *New York Times*, December 12, 2019, www.nytimes.com/2019/12/12/style/FLI-princeton-quadrangle.html.

Rodrigues, Laurie A. "The 'Right-Looking Girl' in the Raccoon Coat: How to Read a Cliché, Like Franny Glass." *Journal of Narrative Theory*, vol. 50, no. 1, 2020, pp. 120–51.

Salinger, J. D. *For Esmé—With Love and Squalor, and Other Stories [Nine Stories].* 1953. Penguin Random House, 2010.

——. *Franny and Zooey.* 1961. Penguin Random House, 2019.

——. *Raise High the Roofbeam, Carpenters and Seymour: An Introduction.* 1963. Little, Brown, 2014.

Salinger, Margaret A. *Dream Catcher: A Memoir.* Simon & Schuster, 2000.

Sanua, Marianne. "Stages in the Development of Jewish Life at Princeton." *American Jewish History*, vol. 76, no. 4, 1987, pp. 391–415.

Seitzman, Daniel. "Salinger's 'Franny': Homoerotic Imagery." *American Imago*, vol. 22, nos. 1/2, 1965, pp. 57–76.

Wenke, John Paul. *J. D. Salinger: A Study of the Short Fiction.* Twayne, 1991.

Notes on the Editors

Jeff Birkenstein, PhD, is a professor of English at Saint Martin's University, Lacey, Washington. His major interests lie in the short story (American, world, and the short story sequence) as well as food and cultural criticism. He has published seven co-edited collection of essays to date: *Reframing 9/11: Film, Popular Culture and the "War on Terror"* (Continuum, 2010) and *The Cinema of Terry Gilliam: It's a Mad World* (Columbia University Press/Wallflower, 2013), with Anna Froula and Karen Randell; *American Writers in Exile* and *Social Justice and American Literature* (both with Salem Press/Grey House, 2015 and 2017, respectively); and *European Writers in Exile* and *Connections and Influence in the Russian and American Short Story* (both with Lexington Press, 2018 and 2021, respectively), all with Robert C. Hauhart, as well as *Classroom on the Road: Designing, Teaching, and Theorizing Out-of-the-Box Faculty-Led Student Travel* (Lexington Books, 2020) with Irina Gendelman. Due in 2024 is *Teaching Food and Literature*, a collection scheduled to be published in the Modern Language Association's (MLA) Options for Teaching series. He received his PhD from the University of Kentucky in 2003; he has a second MA in teaching English as a second/other language. He is a Fulbright Scholar (Petrozavodsk State University, Russia, 2013, and Bar-Ilan University, Israel, 2024). He has eaten scorpions in Beijing but could not bring himself to eat the tarantulas fried in garlic in Cambodia, though he sort of regrets it.

Robert C. Hauhart, PhD, JD, is a professor in the Department of Society and Social Justice at Saint Martin's University, Lacey, Washington. He is the author or co-editor of ten books and numerous published papers in sociology, law, literature, and education journals. In sociology, Dr. Hauhart is a recognized scholar of "the American Dream." His most recent books include the two-volume *Routledge Handbook on the American Dream*, co-edited with Mitja Sardoč (2021, 2022); *The Lonely Quest: Constructing the Self in the Twenty-First-Century United States* (Routledge, 2018) and *Seeking the American Dream: A Sociological Inquiry* (Palgrave Macmillan, 2016), nominated for the Pacific Sociological Association's Distinguished Scholarship Award in 2017. In 2019 Hauhart was the recipient of a Fulbright Scholar Award to teach and research the American Dream at the Slovenian Academy of Sciences and Arts in Ljubljana. In literature, Hauhart is a student of twentieth-century American literature and, in particular, American

Dream themes in American literature. He is the co-editor, with Jeff Birkenstein, of five volumes: *American Writers in Exile* (Salem Press, 2015); *Social Justice in American Literature* (Salem Press, 2017); *European Writers in Exile* (Lexington Books, 2018); *Connections and Influences between the Russian and American Short Story* (Lexington Books, 2021); and the present volume, *Significant Food: Critical Readings to Nourish American Literature* (University of Georgia Press). In education, Hauhart is the co-author, with Jon Grahe, of *Designing and Teaching the Undergraduate Capstone Course* (Jossey-Bass/Wiley, 2015).

Contributor Biographies

Ericka Birkenstein is an adjunct professor of photography in Communication Studies at Saint Martin's University. Her research interests center on dystopia and the grotesque; she has most recently co-authored, with Jeff Birkenstein, "Margaret Atwood and Women's Dystopic Fiction." In addition to teaching, she is the COO and creative director of ImageArts Productions, a commercial production company based in Seattle, Washington.

Edward A. Chamberlain is an associate professor of cultural studies at the University of Washington. His research interests include the study of food, ethnicity, sexual identity, and migration across the Americas. His recent monograph *Imagining LatinX Intimacies: Connecting Queer Stories, Spaces, and Sexualities* was published by Rowman and Littlefield in 2020. He has published research articles in such journals as *Pacific Coast Philology, English Language Notes, Lateral, Prose Studies,* and *The CEA Critic,* among others. He is conducting research for a new monograph that examines the sociopolitical connections of food experience, intersectionality, and consumption practices in several LGBTQ+ contexts.

Mary-Lynn Chambers received her PhD in technical and professional communication from East Carolina University with a focus in digital discourse. She also has a certificate in transnational and multi-cultural literature. This literature focus has taken her around the world and into varied cultures through Asian, African, British, Jewish, and Native American literature studies. She has taught English in Virginia and North Carolina. Her instructional foci are composition, technical writing, and literature, with a research focus in online education and minority literatures. Her book, *Pedagogy and Practice: A Multi-Modal Approach for a Multi-Ethnic Online Classroom,* focuses on online education, while her many articles and presentations highlight her interest in multicultural literature.

Sanghamitra Dalal is a senior lecturer at the College of Creative Arts, Universiti Teknologi MARA (UiTM), Selangor, Malaysia. She completed a PhD in postcolonial diasporic literature at Monash University, Melbourne, Australia, and has taught previously at Goethe University, Frankfurt, Germany, and in different secondary and tertiary academic institutions in India. Dr. Dalal's research interests include postcolonial migration and diasporic literatures, with special interest in South and Southeast Asian literatures in English; transnational and transcultural literatures and cultures; life writing and food writing. She has published articles in indexed journals and book chapters with Routledge and Palgrave Macmillan.

Serena Demichelis holds a PhD in foreign literatures and languages from the University of Verona. Her publications include papers on Herman Melville, contemporary author Rachel Kushner, negative empathy in Holocaust literature, and J. D. Salinger's short prose, which was also the focus of her doctoral thesis. She is part of the editorial staff at *Iperstoria: Journal of American and English Studies* and occasionally helps copyedit *Skenè: Journal of Theatre and Drama Studies*. Among her research interests are the short story in English, the study of characters in fiction, stylistics, literary theory, and comparative literature.

Rachel Fernandes is a doctoral candidate in the Department of English at Queen's University in Kingston, Ontario, where her research is supported by a Social Science and Humanities Research Council grant. Her work is primarily focused on the experiences of mixed-race people in contemporary North American literature. Her dissertation explores expressions of mixed-race identity in different literary forms such as memoir, poetry, and the novel. She is a visiting scholar at the Center for Black Digital Research at Penn State, where she has helped promote and celebrate the life and works of nineteenth-century Black women organizers. Her most recent publication is an article in *Resonance: The Journal of Sound and Culture* entitled "Listening to Loving: Mildred Loving and the Case for Quiet Activism."

Gregory Hartley serves as an associate professor of writing at the University of Alaska Anchorage. Originally raised in the Deep South, his journey west brought with it the eye-opening epiphany of how Indigenous peoples—particularly those in Alaska—have experienced systemic abuse under the American political system. Now a student of Alaska Native culture and practice, he works to heal harms and offer reparations for past grievances.

Shelley Ingram is an associate professor of English and folklore at the University of Louisiana at Lafayette. Her research focuses primarily on the relationship between folklore and literature, including its connections to ethnography and race, folk narrative, food, and place. She has written on the literature of Shirley Jackson, Ishmael Reed, James Hannaham, and Tana French, among others, with essays appearing in edited collections and in journals such as *Food and Foodways* and *African American Review*. Her co-written book, *Implied Nowhere: Absence in Folklore Studies*, was published 2019. She is currently at work on a project about gas station food in the U.S. South.

Méliné Kasparian-Le Fèvre is a doctoral student at Université Bordeaux Montaigne. Her dissertation focuses on the writing of food in the works of contemporary Chicana writers Ana Castillo, Pat Mora, and Sandra Cisneros. She has published a chapter in the edited collection *Consumption and the Literary Cookbook*, edited by Roxanne Harde and Janet Wesselius, as well as in the proceedings for the *Oxford Symposium of Food and Cookery on Food and the Imagi-*

nation (2021). Most recently, she published an article entitled "Feeding the Other, Feeding the Self: Pat Mora and Ana Castillo's Feminist Narratives of Food" in *WiN: The EAAS Women's Network Journal* (2022). Her main research interests are food in literature, food and gender, and women's writing.

Katy Lewis is an independent scholar. She received her doctoral degree from Illinois State University, where she studied children's and young adult literature and taught general education composition and literature courses. Her dissertation work examined the ties between food and diversity in literature for young audiences, and her master's thesis focused on rape culture and young adult literature. Besides food and rape culture, Lewis studies feminist care ethics approaches to relational identity. Her work more broadly theorizes the unintended consequences of literature for children and young adults by examining the power dynamics displayed in these texts as well as exploring how embodiment and identity affect people's experiences.

Molly Mann Lotz is currently director of Research Training Initiatives at SUNY Stony Brook University. She was formerly director of the Center for Advancement of Faculty Excellence (CAFÉ) at St. Francis College in Brooklyn, New York. She holds a PhD in English and master of library science degree from St. John's University. Her research interests include domestic fiction in the long nineteenth century, American modernism, women's labor and its literary representations, food studies, and gender and race in the digital humanities. Her background in libraries and higher education administration often finds her working at the intersection of archival studies, digital scholarship, and literary studies. Mann teaches undergraduate literature and writing courses at St. Francis College and has taught previously at St. John's University and SUNY Farmingdale State College.

Heidi Oberholtzer Lee earned her PhD in English from the University of Notre Dame and currently teaches writing at Eastern University in St. Davids, Pennsylvania. She specializes in early American literatures (Anglo and Ibero), food studies, religion and literature, and travel writing. Her work has appeared in publications such as *Food and Faith in Christian Culture, American Literary Scholarship, The Literary Encyclopedia, Christian Scholar's Review, Journal of Narrative Theory, Early American Studies,* and *Religion and Literature.* Her essay "Tasting: A Hermeneutic of Appetite in Early American Travel Writing" recently appeared in *The Routledge Research Companion to Travel Writing.*

Anton L. Smith is an associate professor of humanities at the Massachusetts Maritime Academy, where he teaches courses in African American and American literature and first-year writing. He is the author of "Sampling Rage: The Acoustics of African American Righteous Discontent from the Harlem Renaissance to the Age of Obama" (*International Journal of Humanities, Art and Social Studies,* March 2022), which explores the phenomenon of Black rage. From Claude McKay to Lauryn Hill, his essay explores how Black writers and artists use rage as a tool for cultural expression and resistance. Currently, he is preparing a book manuscript, "In the Pursuit of Faith: Profiles in African American Literature, Religion, and Spirituality, 1935–1965" that examines how religiosity is negotiated, constructed, and contested through various symbolic resources including soul food, the blues, and nature.

Rossitsa Terzieva-Artemis is professor of literature in the Department of Languages and Literature at the University of Nicosia, Cyprus, and works in the fields of modern English and Anglophone literatures, Continental philosophy, and cultural studies. She holds an MA in English language and literature from the University of Veliko Turnovo, Bulgaria (1993); an MPhil in gender studies from the Central European University, Hungary (1998); an MPhil and a PhD in the human sciences from George Washington University (2005). She is the author of the book *Stories of the Unconscious: Sub-Versions in Freud, Lacan, and Kristeva* as well as editor of a volume of essays on Ford Madox Ford's novel *The Good Soldier* and two special issues of the journal *Studies in the Literary Imagination* on Julia Kristeva and Iris Murdoch. Currently, she is working on the postmodern novel as a genre and the intersections between literature and philosophy.

Carrie Helms Tippen is associate professor of English and assistant dean of the School of Arts, Science, and Business at Chatham University in Pittsburgh, Pennsylvania. She is author of *Inventing Authenticity: How Cookbook Writers Redefine Southern Identity* (University of Arkansas Press, 2018) and *Pain and Pleasure in Southern Cookbooks*, forthcoming from University Press of Mississippi. She is series editor of the Ingrid G. Houck Series on Food and Foodways at University Press of Mississippi. Her academic work has been published in *Gastronomica, Food and Foodways, Southern Quarterly*, and *Food, Culture, and Society*.

Index

Printed in the USA
CPSIA information can be obtained
at www.ICGtesting.com
CBHW030100220624
10487CB00002B/40